Let Right Be Done

Law and Society Series
W. Wesley Pue, General Editor

The Law and Society Series explores law as a socially embedded phenomenon. It is premised on the understanding that the conventional division of law from society creates false dichotomies in thinking, scholarship, educational practice, and social life. Books in the series treat law and society as mutually constitutive and seek to bridge scholarship emerging from interdisciplinary engagement of law with disciplines such as politics, social theory, history, political economy, and gender studies.

Edited by Hamar Foster, Heather Raven,
and Jeremy Webber

Let Right Be Done: Aboriginal Title, the *Calder* Case, and the Future of Indigenous Rights

UBCPress · Vancouver · Toronto

16 15 14 13 12 11 10 09 08 07   5 4 3 2 1

Printed in Canada on ancient-forest-free paper (100% post-consumer recycled)
that is processed chlorine- and acid-free, with vegetable-based inks.

Library and Archives Canada Cataloguing in Publication

Let right be done : Aboriginal title, the Calder case, and the future of Indigenous
rights / edited by Hamar Foster, Heather Raven and Jeremy Webber.

Includes bibliographical references and index.
ISBN 978-0-7748-1403-4 (bound); ISBN 978-0-7748-1404-1 (pbk.)

1. Aboriginal title – Canada. 2. Calder, Frank – Trials, litigation, etc. 3. Aboriginal
title – Canada – Cases. 4. Native peoples – Legal status, laws, etc. – Canada.
5. Indigenous peoples – Land tenure. 6. Canada. Supreme Court. I. Foster, Hamar,
1948- II. Raven, Heather, 1948- III. Webber, Jeremy H. A., 1958-

E78.C2L48 2007   346.7104'3208997   C2007-904281-3

Canadä

UBC Press gratefully acknowledges the financial support for our publishing
program of the Government of Canada through the Book Publishing Industry
Development Program (BPIDP), and of the Canada Council for the Arts, and
the British Columbia Arts Council.

This book has been published with the help of a grant from the Canadian
Federation for the Humanities and Social Sciences, through the Aid to Scholarly
Publications Programme, using funds provided by the Social Sciences and
Humanities Research Council of Canada.

UBC Press
The University of British Columbia
2029 West Mall
Vancouver, BC V6T 1Z2
604-822-5959 / Fax: 604-822-6083
www.ubcpress.ca

This book is dedicated to the generations of Nisga'a people and their supporters who struggled to have Nisga'a title recognized and protected by the Canadian constitution and, in particular, to the plaintiffs in the landmark *Calder et al. v. Attorney-General of British Columbia* decision handed down by the Supreme Court of Canada on 31 January 1973.

As listed in the statement of claim, they were:

Frank Calder, James Gosnell, Nelson Azak, William McKay, Anthony Robinson, Robert Stevens, Hubert Doolan, and Henry McKay, suing on their own behalf and on behalf of all other members of the Nishga Tribal Council;

Roderick Robinson, Cecil Mercer, Jacob Davis, Richard Guno, Chris Clayton, Peter Clayton, and Cecil Morven, suing on their own behalf and on behalf of all other members of the Gitlakdamix Indian Band;

Chester Moore, Henry Azak, and Percy Azak, suing on their own behalf and on behalf of all other members of the Canyon City Indian Band;

W.C. McKay, Henry McKay, Louis McKay, Kelly Stevens, Alvin McKay, and Allan Moore, suing on their own behalf and on behalf of all other members of the Greenville Indian Band; and

Solomon Doolan, Moses Aksidan, Nathan Barton, Nelson Clayton, William Lincoln, Graham Moore, Anthony Robinson, and Hubert Stevens, suing on their own behalf and on behalf of all other members of the Kincolith Indian Band.

Contents

Acknowledgments

A project of this magnitude requires a great deal of help. We were not short of hands in this endeavour. We are very grateful for the assistance of Gary Fiegehen, Hadley Friedland, Rosemary Garton, Kate Gower, Stephanie Hanna, Jamie Kerr, Holly Pattison, Sarah-Dawn Schenk, Pat Skidmore, Elizabeth Wheaton, and Lloy Wylie at many points, including the transcription of the Calder/Berger conversation and the closing comments, the preparation of the bibliography, and the assembling of the manuscript. We thank the anonymous reviewers at UBC Press for their comments on the manuscript, and Stacy Belden for her careful copyediting of the volume. We are most grateful to Tamaki Calder, Kim Recalma-Clutesi, and Peter Baird for their help in securing photographs.

This collection was inspired by a conference held at the Faculty of Law, University of Victoria, on 13-15 November 2003, to commemorate the thirtieth anniversary of the decision in *Calder et al. v. Attorney-General of British Columbia*. Many individuals were involved in organizing that conference. Our thanks to all and especially to John Borrows, Bill White, Stu Whitley, and Corinne Zimmerman, who, in addition to the editors of this volume, were members of the organizing committee. Our special thanks to the Department of Justice of the Government of Canada, the Social Sciences and Humanities Research Council, the Nisga'a Lisims Government, the University of Victoria, the Canada Research Chair in Law and Society, and the Law Foundation of British Columbia, for their financial support for the conference. Several individual contributions to this volume, notably those of Kent McNeil and Jeremy Webber, have benefited from research support from the Social Sciences and Humanities Research Council.

Let Right Be Done

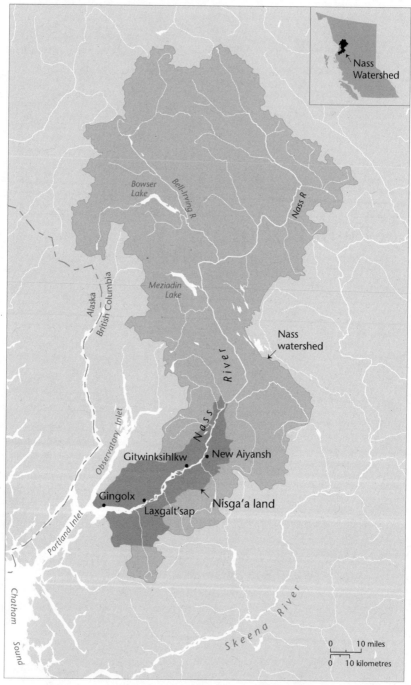

Map of the Nass and Skeena regions of coastal British Columbia, showing the Nisga'a treaty settlement lands. *Cartographer: Eric Leinberger*

1

The *Calder* Decision, Aboriginal Title, Treaties, and the Nisga'a

Christina Godlewska and Jeremy Webber

The Nisga'a Go to Ottawa

There is a photograph, taken in November 1971, of fourteen men and two women in the entrance hall of the Supreme Court of Canada. They are plaintiffs and supporters in the court case that came to be known as *Calder et al. v. Attorney-General of British Columbia*[1] – chiefs of the Nisga'a nation, members of the Nishga Tribal Council, who had come to Ottawa to secure recognition of their title to their ancestral lands.[2] The names of the plaintiffs can be found on the dedication page of this book. Their lands are located in the Nass Valley of what is now northern British Columbia, on the neighbouring coast, and in the adjoining valleys (see Map).

The event recorded in the photograph represented one of several defining moments in a struggle that had lasted ninety years – ever since the Nisga'a had protested against the first incursions of settlers and surveyors onto Nisga'a lands (see Appendix A).[3] For the Nisga'a, *Calder* was not about a land "claim." It was another step in the continued assertion of their right to the lands they had never ceased to occupy and defend. In an interview published in this book, Frank Calder (president of the Nishga Tribal Council at the time of *Calder* and lead plaintiff in the action that bears his name) recounts the story of his people's resistance to the first surveying party in the Nass Valley in the 1880s. From the early years of the twentieth century until about 1927, the Nisga'a campaigned vigorously, in cooperation with other BC First Nations, for the recognition of their rights under Canadian law. Their efforts were frustrated at that time by the refusal of three levels of government – provincial, federal, and imperial – to refer the matter to the courts. In 1927, the Canadian Parliament prohibited the raising of funds for the making of land claims, forcing the Nisga'a's struggle into a twenty-five-year hiatus.

Hamar Foster gives a stimulating account of this early campaign in his contribution to this book, describing the personalities, recounting the initiatives, and explaining the legal and political obstacles that ultimately

The Nisga'a delegation at the Supreme Court of Canada in 1971. *From left to right:* John Clifton, Maurice Nyce, Clarence Joe, James Gosnell, Buddy Recalma, Rod Robinson, Diane Recalma, Frank Calder, William McKay, Alan Moore, Hubert Doolan, Henry McKay, Eli Gosnell, Guy Williams, Anthony Robinson, Mercy Robinson. *Courtesy of Kim Recalma-Clutesi*

frustrated the effort – obstacles that also had an impact on the *Calder* decision itself, as we will see. There were other campaigns for the recognition of Aboriginal title on the Pacific coast. The leaders of other BC First Nations worked to defend their lands, sometimes on their own, sometimes in collaboration. Some of the collaborations are discussed in Foster's account. Paul Tennant and Robert Galois have also published extensively on the history of indigenous advocacy in British Columbia.[4] And Alaskan Aboriginal leaders, just over the border from the Nass Valley, pursued similar initiatives. Stephen Haycox describes those fascinating parallel developments in his contribution to this book.[5]

Despite the frustration of their early campaign, the Nisga'a launched a renewed effort for the legal recognition of their rights in the 1950s, once the prohibition on fundraising had been repealed. It was this second campaign that ultimately led to the event memorialized in the photograph: the hearing of what was to be Canada's most important case on the law of Aboriginal title, which established once and for all that Aboriginal title was a right recognized by contemporary Canadian law. The Supreme Court of Canada delivered this momentous decision on 31 January 1973. While the judgment was immensely significant for the future of Aboriginal title, it was technically a defeat for the plaintiffs. But it was a defeat that established the foundation for important victories. In 1976, three years after the decision in *Calder*, the Canadian government initiated negotiations with the Nisga'a, although the province of British Columbia then refused to participate. The province did join the talks in 1990. In 1996, the parties concluded an agreement-in-principle, in 1998 a final agreement was concluded, and in 2000 this agreement was ratified.[6] The Nisga'a treaty became the first modern-day treaty signed in British Columbia and the first treaty of any kind in British Columbia since the conclusion of Treaty 8 in 1899.

The Decision in *Calder*

The *Calder* decision was of immense significance for the Nisga'a. It was even more important for the development of the law of Aboriginal title in Canada generally.

It is difficult for Canadians today to remember the state of this law prior to *Calder*, given the host of court decisions and negotiations that have dealt with Aboriginal title over the past thirty years, but, in the early 1970s, many questioned whether there was any surviving Aboriginal title in Canada. Just four years prior to *Calder*, the Canadian prime minister, Pierre Elliot Trudeau, had categorically rejected the notion that Aboriginal peoples had rights different from those accorded to other Canadian citizens.[7] The government did not recognize Aboriginal title and, as a result, saw no need to enter into further treaties with Aboriginal peoples. This policy found official expression in the 1969 White Paper on Indian Policy, which reaffirmed the rights of Aboriginal people as individual citizens but repudiated their rights as peoples, asserting that "aboriginal claims to land ... are so general and undefined that it is not realistic to think of them as specific claims capable of remedy except through a policy and program that will end injustice to the Indians as members of the Canadian community."[8] Gérard La Forest was a senior civil servant in the federal Department of Justice and a leading scholar of natural resources law at the time of *Calder* (he ultimately became a justice of the Supreme Court of Canada and participated in several of the most important post-*Calder* decisions).[9] In his chapter in this book, La Forest describes the state of knowledge of Aboriginal land rights within government at the time of the judgment and the revolution in this understanding that was accomplished by the case. Something of the flavour of those times can also be gleaned from the recollections of Thomas Berger, the principal lawyer for the Nisga'a in *Calder*, in the interview with Berger and Frank Calder that is published here.[10]

The decision in *Calder* had its antecedents. There was an extensive pattern of recognition of Aboriginal title in North America up until the early years of the twentieth century, including judicial decisions, the Royal

Proclamation of 1763, and the practice of treaty making in the Maritime provinces, Ontario, and the prairies (all of which we discuss later in this chapter). Even following the long hiatus of the mid-twentieth century, a few cases decided by lower courts in the 1960s had suggested that a distinctive set of Aboriginal rights may have survived.[11] Moreover, on the political front, the federal white paper of 1969 had provoked a vehement reaction from Aboriginal leaders, who strenuously asserted what they certainly considered to be rights. In that same year, what has been described as the "most representative gathering of Aboriginal peoples ever assembled in Ottawa"[12] met to protest the white paper. In the following year, the Indian Chiefs of Alberta presented their "red paper" to the Trudeau cabinet, "opposing the entire concept of termination and arguing for greater recognition of treaty rights, Aboriginal claims, and rights to self-government."[13]

Calder consolidated and extended these developments, firmly establishing the legal foundation of Aboriginal title. The Nisga'a sued for a declaration that their Aboriginal or "Indian" title "has never been lawfully extinguished."[14] In the judgment, this question broke down into three issues: (1) whether Aboriginal title existed in the first place; (2) whether, in the case of the Nisga'a, this title had been lawfully extinguished; and (3) a procedural issue as to whether the Court had jurisdiction to grant such a declaration despite the fact that the Nisga'a had not secured permission to sue the Crown, which at that time was still required in British Columbia. The major victory of *Calder* lies in the fact that of the seven judges, six responded to the first issue by affirming the existence of Aboriginal title at common law. However, they split three to three on the legal foundations of this title and on the question of extinguishment, and the case was ultimately decided on the procedural question.

The first group of three judges, whose reasons were delivered by Justice Wilfred Judson, affirmed the Nisga'a's Aboriginal title based on the simple fact of prior occupation. Although they held that the Nisga'a could not rely on the Royal Proclamation of 1763 to ground their claim (because, in their view, the proclamation did not extend to British Columbia), this decision in no way affected the fact that "when the settlers came, the Indians were there, organized in societies and occupying the land as their forefathers had done for centuries." They concluded that "this is what Indian title means."[15] The second group of three judges, in reasons drafted by Justice Emmett Hall, undertook a thorough review of legal precedent and the relationship of anthropological and historical evidence to common-law concepts such as possession. The review led this group to base Aboriginal title on two foundations that we now see as mutually inconsistent: on the one hand, the common law of possession and, on the other, a recognition that the title held by Aboriginal people prior to British sovereignty continues to persist in contemporary common law. They also took a different stand from

Justice Judson on the application of the Royal Proclamation of 1763, holding that it did extend to the Nisga'a's territory. Yet, although they came to their conclusions by different routes, both Justices Hall and Judson, speaking for six members of the Court, concurred on the fact that the Nisga'a had at least originally held Aboriginal title.

However, Justices Judson and Hall disagreed on the question of extinguishment. Justice Judson, again joined by two other judges, reviewed transactions concerning public lands in British Columbia both before and after British Columbia entered Confederation and concluded that they were "inconsistent with the recognition and continued existence of Indian title."[16] In his view, these transactions demonstrated that Aboriginal title had been extinguished. The three judges led by Justice Hall, on the other hand, concluded that it was "beyond question that the onus of proving that the Sovereign intended to extinguish the Indian title lies on the [government] and that intention must be 'clear and plain.'" Justice Hall found "no such proof in the case at bar; no legislation to that effect."[17] The Nisga'a title therefore remained in effect. Justice Hall also found that proclamations and ordinances issued by Governor James Douglas, on which Justice Judson had relied to find extinguishment, were beyond the power conferred on the governor, if these acts had been intended to extinguish Aboriginal title without compensation.

Thus, on the question of extinguishment, the Court was equally divided with three judges holding that the title had been extinguished long in the past and three holding that it remained in effect. The final decision fell to the seventh judge, Justice Louis-Philippe Pigeon. He avoided all issues of title and extinguishment and, instead, decided the question on a matter of procedure – the requirement, which was still in effect in British Columbia at the time, that a litigant obtain the consent of the attorney general before bringing an action against the province. He rejected arguments that this case fell within the exceptions to this rule. In his view, the plaintiffs in *Calder* required permission. They had not obtained it. Their action therefore failed. At the time, the permission of the attorney general was commonly called a "*fiat*" after the Latin phrase that attorneys general used to signify their assent to the action: *fiat justicia* or, in English, "let right be done." This book takes its title from this phrase.

· The *Calder* case itself, then, was ultimately decided on purely procedural grounds. Yet its primary importance lay in what it said about Aboriginal title. Six of the seven judges had decided that Aboriginal title existed as a right within the common law, regardless of whether it had been recognized by the government or acknowledged in any treaty. Moreover, they decided that Aboriginal title existed not just in territories under European influence at the time of the Royal Proclamation – that is, in eastern Canada and the prairies, where it had already been largely addressed through treaties – but also across the entire continent, including British Columbia. They divided three to three on the important question of how Aboriginal title could be extinguished and especially on whether general provisions for land grants were sufficient to erase the title. However, this issue was not resolved. It was left for future determination – *Calder* itself being decided merely on the procedural requirement that a fiat be obtained before a claim could be brought against the provincial Crown (a requirement that was itself abolished in the year following *Calder*).[18]

As with many leading decisions, *Calder's* implications were difficult to predict at the time. It was entirely possible that a future court would agree with the reasons of Justice Judson and his two colleagues and hold that the colony of British Columbia had extinguished Aboriginal title wholesale (as indeed Chief Justice Allan McEachern did at trial in *Delgamuukw v. British Columbia* eighteen years later).[19] If so, then the First Nations' victory would have been pyrrhic indeed. Furthermore, the Court's reasoning contained the openness and range of possibilities that often mark path-breaking judgments. Even if Aboriginal title had not been extinguished, which of the rationales would have prevailed – those cited by Justice Hall, that expressed by Justice Judson, or some new formulation? What was required to prove the existence of Aboriginal title? What was its scope? What powers of regulation, what powers of governance, were implicit in the title? What constraints did it impose on the provincial administration of public lands? Over the next thirty years – and still today – these issues would be worked out through judicial decisions and treaty negotiations. In this book, the chapters by Michael Asch, Brian Slattery, and Kent McNeil explore many of these developments.

However, *Calder's* general affirmation of Aboriginal title has had a tremendous impact. Not only did it set the terms for the long chain of judicial decisions on Aboriginal title that followed but it also had a sudden and lasting effect on federal policy. Immediately following the decision, both the Progressive Conservative and New Democratic parties took positions that "supported Aboriginal groups in pressing for the resolution of claims."[20] Prime Minister Trudeau "warmly embraced" the proposal by the Yukon Native Brotherhood for the negotiation of land claims in the Yukon, which was presented just two weeks after *Calder*.[21] Finally, on 8 August 1973, less than seven months after *Calder* was handed down, a new federal policy for the settlement of "comprehensive claims" – claims founded on Aboriginal title – was announced by then minister of Indian Affairs and Northern Development, Jean Chrétien.[22] As expressed in a booklet later prepared by the Department of Indian Affairs and Northern Development, "Canada would now negotiate settlements with Aboriginal groups where rights of traditional use and occupancy had been neither extinguished by treaty nor 'superseded by law.'"[23] Thus, the federal government began the long process of negotiating comprehensive settlements of Aboriginal title, eventually concluding modern-day treaties in northern Québec, the Yukon, the former Northwest Territories (including Nunavut), and, ultimately, with the Nisga'a nation itself.[24] Indeed, the process of negotiating claims continues, particularly in British Columbia, the Yukon, and the Northwest Territories.

Moreover, the decision had an important impact on the law of Aboriginal title internationally, especially in Australia and New Zealand. One of the authors of this introduction once asked Ron Castan, QC and lead counsel for the plaintiffs in *Mabo v. Queensland (No. 2)*[25] – the judgment that in 1992 recognized, for the first time, the existence of Aboriginal title in Australia – to what extent he had drawn upon Australian experience with statutory land rights in making his arguments. He replied: "Not at all. I just laid *Calder* before them and said, 'It's all there, your Honours. That is what you have to decide.'" Castan was exaggerating, of course, his response doubtless shaped by courtesy to a Canadian visitor. But it is true that *Mabo* drew very heavily on the precedent in *Calder*, and, indeed, for many years Canadian and Australian courts have relied on each other's Aboriginal-rights decisions in making their own. Garth Nettheim provides a fine assessment of this fruitful exchange in his contribution to this book, also giving a valuable introduction to the law of Native title in Australia. David Williams does the same for New Zealand in his chapter.

The Purpose of This Book

This book takes stock of the doctrine of Aboriginal title thirty years after *Calder*. It places this decision in context, describing the long process of advocacy by the Nisga'a and other peoples of the northwest coast, beginning in the nineteenth century (notably through the contributions of Foster and Haycox). It reminds the reader of the state of Canadian law on Aboriginal title at the time of *Calder* (La Forest) and includes first-hand reflections by two distinguished individuals, Frank Calder and Thomas Berger, who were instrumental in bringing the action.

It then reviews what has happened to Aboriginal title since *Calder*, not by providing a case-by-case account of the many decisions of recent years – there are many such accounts in journals and in textbooks[26] – but by standing back and reflecting upon the possibilities inherent in *Calder*, considering the ways in which some of these possibilities were pursued and others neglected, and suggesting how the law of Aboriginal title might be conceived today. Thus, Michael Asch considers the general ideas of the Aboriginal/non-Aboriginal relationship presented in *Calder* itself, Brian Slattery looks at the structure of Aboriginal rights within Canadian law, and Kent McNeil addresses the governmental dimension inherent in Aboriginal title. These articles are critical and synthetic, with leading scholars providing their best assessment of where we stand. Their conclusions speak to crucial debates in the area.

The book then explores the broader significance of *Calder*, both internationally – in the experience of two closely related settler dominions, Australia (Garth Nettheim) and Aotearoa New Zealand (David Williams) – and for Aboriginal/non-Aboriginal relations within Canada (John Borrows and the distinguished authors who provide the "closing thoughts"). It explores these developments always against the backdrop of the Nisga'a campaign for recognition. One of the reasons for this focus is commemorative. These articles emerged out of a conference held to mark the thirtieth anniversary of *Calder* – a conference that also celebrated the personal contributions of Frank Calder, who simultaneously received an honorary doctorate from the University of Victoria.[27] The conference was both stirring and enlightening. This book attempts to recapture those qualities and convey them to a broader audience. It is easy to forget that *Calder* was the product of a decades-long struggle for legal recognition. The steadfastness, resilience, consistency, seriousness of purpose, and sustained hard work of the Nisga'a were remarkable. Even if one begins one's account of the campaign with the founding of the Nishga Tribal Council in 1955 and ignores the first campaign, the Nisga'a spent eighteen years preparing for the decision in *Calder* and a further twenty-seven years preparing for the resumption of a portion of their lands and the recognition of rights of self-government and resource management under the Final Agreement. Moreover, the Nisga'a nation was very active during those years, holding annual conferences of the Nishga Tribal Council and numerous community meetings, hammering out positions, developing consensus, and deciding what demands were essential and what could be compromised. This foundation of discussion and deliberation allowed the Nisga'a to retain a remarkable degree of unity throughout a long and difficult struggle. It was responsible, in no small measure, for the success they achieved.

However, the focus on the Nisga'a also has a strong analytical purpose. We often forget that these decisions affected real individuals, communities, and peoples. We reduce them to abstract propositions of law, losing sight of their connections to particular people's histories, struggles, and aspirations. No one can read the comments of Frank Calder or Joseph Gosnell – or those of the lieutenant-governor, who speaks of her first education in Aboriginal title as a child among the piers of a salmon cannery on the Skeena River – without seeing what this struggle has meant to the people of the Nass. Placing the issues back in context can also reveal complexities and forgotten dimensions that we have neglected with time. A community's debates are always more contentious, richer, and more vulnerable to uncertainty and adversity than the thumbnail sketches of communities' positions on which we often rely. Reminding ourselves of how these debates appeared at the time can reveal lessons that deserve our concerted attention.

To take one example, it is striking to note the Alaskan Aboriginal leaders' emphasis on the acculturation of Alaskan indigenous people in their early campaigns, which is described by Stephen Haycox. The Nisga'a often took a similar stance. They were virtually alone in supporting the federal government's 1969 white paper; they argued strongly for full legal equality in a manner that drew heavily on the idea that the same laws should apply to all; and Joseph Gosnell recalls how, when the Nisga'a Final Agreement was ratified by the Canadian Parliament, the Nisga'a representatives in the public gallery stood to sing "O Canada." How do we square these facts with the Nisga'a's resolute struggle for the recognition of their Aboriginal title and the restoration of a substantial degree of self-government? We tend to treat the issues now as a simple contrast: either Aboriginal land rights or the same rights; Aboriginal self-government or allegiance to Canada. The strong advocacy of both by the Nisga'a should give us pause, leading us to ask whether the common dichotomies are too simple and whether they may ultimately be reconciled. We do not mean, in this introduction, to suggest facile solutions. We know that different Aboriginal people may well have opposing positions on these issues. Yet the Nisga'a's vigorous advocacy of both should at least prompt us to inquire more deeply in order to understand how they might be combined.[28]

We hope, then, that for readers who already have an extensive background in the law of Aboriginal title, this book will foster a more profound understanding of *Calder*'s context and stimulate reflection on the chief characteristics of the law today, especially how the various elements of this law might be incorporated in a new synthesis. For people without this background, we hope that this book will provide a comprehensive, accessible, and insightful overview of the modern development of this law.

An Overview of Aboriginal Title

We are aware that for many readers this book may be their first encounter with Aboriginal title. In the remainder of this chapter, we provide a brief introduction to the law. We want this to serve as an entrée to the extensive literature on the subject. We have therefore developed the notes so that they serve a bibliographical role, guiding the reader into this literature. They do not cover everything of value. The work on Aboriginal rights in Canada is voluminous. But the notes do provide useful starting points for further reading. One particularly rich source of information and recommendations to which readers are advised to refer is the various reports of the Royal Commission on Aboriginal Peoples, which conducted hearings, sponsored studies, held conferences, and formulated proposals during the period from 1991 to 1996.[29]

Historical Foundations

The foundation of Aboriginal title is intertwined with the history of Aboriginal/ non-Aboriginal encounters in North America. It draws on the common law and international law principles regarding the acquisition of territory; but, as many would strongly argue, its primary elements were formed in the crucible of interaction between colonists and indigenous peoples.[30] Colonists arrived in North America with little sense of the peoples they would meet or the principles on which their relations should be founded. There was considerable variation among the separate British colonies (let alone among the British, French, and Spanish colonies) as they came into contact with First Nations. Violent conflict did occur, sometimes with devastating consequences. For example, the indigenous people of Newfoundland, the Beothuk, ceased to exist (at least as an independent entity) by the early nineteenth century as a result of a combination of factors, including disease, displacement from the coast, disruption of access to resources, and brutal hostility between themselves and the settlers – the Beothuk being especially vulnerable because of their small numbers.[31] However, in general, the interaction of colonists and Aboriginal people was tempered by attempts at peace. Although some colonists thought that they could rely on their land grants and on their own presumed superiority with no concessions to the land's inhabitants, they soon found that this approach was dangerous in the extreme. They began to negotiate with their indigenous neighbours and, in the process, developed a set of expectations and procedures for intercultural interaction.[32]

In the first years of British settlement, these expectations could vary from colony to colony. They were often set aside because of settlers' hunger for land (as colonists pushed into territories not yet opened for settlement) or were vulnerable to the vagaries of colonial politics (as colonial governments calculated, from time to time, that a policy of aggression would bring them greater benefits than one of conciliation). Yet gradually these policies were standardized. The imperial authorities withdrew responsibility for Aboriginal relations from the individual colonies and vested it in officials appointed from London precisely in order to avoid outbreaks of war, obtain (in the northern colonies) the benefits of the fur trade, and secure indigenous allies in Britain's competition with New France. A crucial landmark in this process was the Royal Proclamation of 1763, which was issued in the wake of the British conquest of New France and which provided the first constitution for British colonial government in the former French colonies and – most importantly for our purposes – codified the rules regarding colonial/Aboriginal interaction with respect to land.[33] (The relevant provisions of the Royal Proclamation are quoted in the 1913 Nisga'a petition reproduced in Appendix B of this volume.) It is important to realize that this was a codification, not the enactment of entirely new policies. And it is also important to note that this law was common to all parts of North America then claimed by Britain. The law of Aboriginal title in Canada and the United States shares the same origins,[34] although the subsequent treatment of Aboriginal peoples has differed in these two countries. Indeed, a set of judgments by the United States Supreme Court in the early nineteenth century – the "Marshall judgments,"[35] named after the first chief justice of that court – serves as the foundation of the common law of Aboriginal title in both countries.[36]

The principles enshrined in the Royal Proclamation of 1763 provide a useful summary of this law. First, it prohibited the settlement, or even the surveying, of lands that had not yet been ceded by First Nations to the imperial authorities, and, indeed, it directed settlers already in possession of such lands to vacate them (though to very limited effect). Second, it prohibited entirely private purchases of Aboriginal lands. Third, it established an exclusive process for the acquisition of Aboriginal lands. These were to be purchased by the Crown, through the governors and commanders-in-chief of the various colonies (through officers, that is, who were appointed under imperial authority, not under the authority of the individual colonies themselves), "at some public Meeting or Assembly of the said Indians, to be held for that Purpose."[37] It purported to establish, in other words, a system for the protection of Aboriginal lands until those lands were purchased by public treaty between the principal representatives of the Crown on the one hand and the relevant First Nation (acting collectively) on the other.

Note the nature of this law. It did not determine the internal law – the internal structure of landholding – within each First Nation. It was very much a law of the interface, which recognized First Nations' entitlement to their lands and established an orderly means for those lands' acquisition. It was confined to relations between peoples, not purporting to regulate Aboriginal patterns of landholding. This task was left to each First Nation.

The essential nature of the common law of Aboriginal title has remained very much the same throughout its development. This law is not about the internal regulation of Aboriginal lands. Although Canadian courts have sometimes spoken as though Aboriginal title involved the absorption or translation of Aboriginal property interests into the common law, so that those interests would then be interpreted and enforced by the common law courts,[38] the courts' practice has generally been quite different.[39] They have confined their role to declaring the existence of Aboriginal title, describing its broad outlines, and urging the parties to negotiate the details. Although the courts have over time incrementally extended their description of the title, they have done so reluctantly, in the absence of effective negotiations. And even when the courts have described the contours of Aboriginal title, they have done so very much from the outside, describing its outer boundaries. They have had virtually nothing to say about the apportionment of rights within the laws of the different First Nations. The courts have left this role, at least implicitly, to the First Nation concerned (although, as we will see, First Nations' authority was significantly eroded and, indeed, remains constrained by the *Indian Act*).[40] This reluctance to define and enforce the detail of Aboriginal proprietary rights has been wise. Non-Aboriginal judges are, of course, poorly placed to interpret Aboriginal law, and it would be a matter of some irony if the recognition of Aboriginal title led to its amateurish interpretation by well-meaning, but ill-informed, judges.[41] Rather, the common law of Aboriginal title has focused on respect for First Nations' entitlement to their lands, understood as the First Nation's collective control over these lands, unless and until this authority is extinguished by valid government action. Some have argued that it is more akin to the international law concept of a nation's "territory" than a private law notion of "property" (although the courts continue to use and, to some extent, conceive of Aboriginal title in the latter terms).[42]

Treaty Negotiations and the Imposition of the *Indian Act*

The restrictions imposed by the Royal Proclamation and the common law were often breached. This was especially true in the newly independent United States, where the constraints codified in the Royal Proclamation were soon overthrown. Very substantial erosion occurred in Canada as well (as we will see). However, the recognition of Aboriginal title in imperial policy, the Royal Proclamation, and the common law of Aboriginal title nevertheless provided the foundation for the practice of negotiating treaties in the territory that was to become Canada. This experience divides roughly into four periods: (1) the era of unsystematic treaty making; (2) the era of the "numbered treaties"; (3) an era of paternalistic administration, during which the practice of negotiating treaties was discontinued and many treaty rights were eroded; and (4) the modern treaty era.[43]

The first period lasted from the earliest years of contact until about the middle of the nineteenth century. During this time, treaties tended to be unsystematic, with limited geographical scope and highly variable content. There was no attempt to regulate, in comprehensive fashion, the Aboriginal/non-Aboriginal relationship. Those treaties that dealt simply with the maintenance of good relations are often called "peace and friendship" treaties, although this term is sometimes applied to all of the unsystematic treaties. They are found in eastern Canada, especially the Maritime provinces, southern Ontario, and the area around Montreal, although around fourteen such treaties were also concluded on Vancouver Island in the early 1850s – the so-called "Douglas Treaties" (named after James Douglas, then governor of the colony of Vancouver Island).[44]

Nisga'a Chief Israel Sgat'iin, an early land claims advocate and opponent of reserves, c. 1890. *Courtesy of British Columbia Archives, E-07668.*

These treaties were long considered to be of uncertain status, many entirely forgotten by non-Aboriginal governments. Those same governments often took the view that these treaties created no legal obligations and that they were merely treaties of friendship. But in a series of recent decisions, the courts have affirmed that they did create binding legal rights.[45] One of the most important precursors to the *Calder* decision, the decision in *R. v. White and Bob,* dealt with a Douglas treaty concluded by the Snuneymuxw First Nation of the Nanaimo region.[46] Thomas Berger, lead counsel in *Calder,* had also served as counsel in this case.

The second period of treaty making – the period of the "numbered treaties" – began in the mid-nineteenth century and lasted until 1923. These treaties represented a systematic attempt to deal with Aboriginal title prior to non-Aboriginal settlement or resource extraction in northern Ontario, the Prairie provinces, and a substantial area of the Northwest Territories. They tended to have a standard structure and often very similar terms. They purported to extinguish Aboriginal title over the entirety of the area covered. It is probably best to consider that the numbered treaty era began with the Robinson-Huron and Robinson-Superior treaties of 1850.[47]

The Robinson treaties were prompted by the incursion of miners into Anishinabe territory to the north of the Great Lakes. The Anishinabe hired a lawyer, cited the obligations imposed by the Royal Proclamation of 1763, and demanded a treaty. They were successful. The Robinson treaties were followed by a series of eleven treaties, each identified by number, commencing with Treaty 1 in southern Manitoba (1871) and ending with Treaty 11 in the Northwest Territories (1921).[48] Together, these treaties cover virtually the entirety of western Canada east of the Rockies and south of the tundra (including the watershed of the Peace River in British Columbia). The Williams treaties, which were concluded in 1923, dealt with Ontario First Nations that had been overlooked in previous treaty processes.[49]

The numbered treaties have long been of crucial importance to Aboriginal/non-Aboriginal relations on the prairies, in northern Ontario, and in parts of the Northwest Territories. They have been criticized because of the parties' unequal bargaining power and the impact of this inequality on the treaties' terms, the vulnerability of these terms to erosion over time, the federal government's sometimes rough-and-ready approach to Aboriginal consent, and the fact that the written terms did not always conform to the First Nations' understanding of the agreement. However, it would be a great mistake to discount the treaties altogether. They are deeply valued by treaty nations, who consider them both a matter of fundamental obligation and a cherished expression of a nation-to-nation relationship, even when non-Aboriginal governments have failed to fulfil their terms. This book will not deal in detail with concerns particular to the numbered treaties, but it is worth noting that these treaties have generated many disputes and much litigation over who should be considered parties to the treaties; over the interpretation of their terms (including the rectification of their terms when the text departs from the parties' actual agreement); over the enforcement of their terms (including situations in which promised reserves were never designated or were later reduced); and over the impact of the natural resources transfer agreements (constitutional arrangements that not only transferred the ownership of public lands from the federal government to the Prairie provinces but also provided qualified protection for treaty rights). [50] Indeed, the federal government has set up processes for dealing with "specific claims," a category that includes, among other things, disputes under treaties.[51]

The last of these treaties was concluded in 1923, but, by this date, the nature of federal policy was already changing. In place of a policy founded upon Aboriginal autonomy, negotiations, and treaty making, the federal government was increasingly pursuing a paternalistic approach in which Aboriginal people were treated as wards of the state: their lands and their lives were controlled by government agents, their children were sent to residential schools, their language and customs were suppressed, and reserves were allocated, or reduced, by administrative fiat rather than by treaty. This is the third period that was identified earlier – the era of paternalistic administration. Its centrepiece was the *Indian Act*, originally adopted in 1876.[52] The third period was especially dominant in British Columbia where, west of the Rockies, the only treaties concluded were the Douglas Treaties, and where the provincial government set its face against the recognition of Aboriginal land rights.

The Aboriginal/non-Aboriginal relationship had long been an unequal one, deeply eroded by the decimation of the Aboriginal population by disease, then by the diminishing importance of the fur trade and the rapid increase in European settlement. By the late nineteenth century, First Nations were no longer seen as partners but rather as holdovers from another period – obstacles to non-Aboriginal economic expansion. Increasingly, the relationship was marked by stark conflicts over resources, including land, water rights, and fisheries. First Nations were confined to reserves covering a small portion of their traditional territories and were prohibited from acquiring resources by means available to the settlers. They were unable to homestead land; their right to hunt and fish was restricted; and they were denied water rights, so that streams on which they depended for growing their own crops were diverted to water non-Aboriginal farms.[53] This third period led directly to the social problems of the late twentieth century: economic degradation; alcoholism; family violence; and sometimes a loss of individual and collective self-respect. Many contemporary policies address these and similar issues, although this book can only concentrate on land and related questions.[54]

It was against this background of neglect, paternalism, and hardship that *Calder* was decided. By 1973, the treaty process had been discontinued for half a century. Aboriginal people had been prevented from pursuing their interests before the courts by the need to secure the consent of the Crown to sue and by the *Indian Act*'s 1927 prohibition on fundraising for the pursuit of land rights without the superintendent-general's consent. The last important judgment on the question had occurred in 1888.[55] For many Canadians, then, Aboriginal title was a long-surpassed doctrine of questionable legal effect. Even to many Canadians sympathetic to Aboriginal concerns the essential problem seemed to be one of racial prejudice. The solutions lay, they believed, in targeted social programs and better welfare provision, not in the resurrection of what many considered to be archaic and racially defined rights. This spirit was amply reflected in the federal government's white paper of 1969.[56] Of course, this neglected the fact that First Nations had long campaigned for respect for their lands and that the adjudication of these rights had been consciously excluded from the courts. It also neglected the fact that in many cases dispossession had not occurred long in the past – unless, that is, one adopted a highly abstract concept of dispossession. On the contrary, First Nations like the Nisga'a were still living on their lands and still using them. Dispossession was occurring very much in the present, as hydroelectric dams flooded their territories, hillsides were logged, and governments made further grants.[57]

The Supreme Court of Canada's decision in *Calder* undermined the attempt to ignore Aboriginal title. It made clear that Aboriginal title was a genuine legal right that, if not extinguished, continued to exist. This decision, together with First Nations' fierce criticism of the government's white paper, prompted a dramatic change in government policy, leading to the fourth period in Canadian Aboriginal relations – the era of modern treaties. The first of this new generation of treaties was the *James Bay and Northern Quebec Agreement (JBNQA)*.[58] It covers two-thirds of the province of Québec, an area roughly equal to the entire province of Ontario. It was concluded with the Cree and the Inuit after these peoples objected to the proposed development of an extensive hydroelectric scheme on several rivers flowing into James and Hudson Bays, which was going to flood territory on which they lived, hunted, fished, and trapped. Construction had commenced without any settlement of Aboriginal title. The Cree and Inuit had then obtained an injunction stopping construction on 15 November 1973 in a decision in which the Supreme Court of Canada's decision in *Calder*, rendered a little over nine months previously, played a significant role. The Québec Court of Appeal, pending full hearing of the appeal, quickly suspended this injunction.[59] But the risk of an adverse decision forced the Québec government to the bargaining table. The result was the first modern treaty, signed on 11 November 1975.

The *JBNQA* was followed in 1978 by the *Northeastern Quebec Agreement,*[60] which essentially extended the *JBNQA*'s terms to include the Naskapi First Nation. A series of "complementary agreements" since that time has amended or extended both of these agreements. In addition, in separate negotiations, often lasting many years, final agreements have been concluded with:

- the Inuvialuit in the Northwest Territories (1984)
- the Gwich'in First Nation on the Northwest Territories/Yukon border (1992)
- the Inuit of the eastern Arctic (1993; this agreement led to the division of the Northwest Territories and the creation of the new territory of Nunavut)
- the Council of Yukon Indians (1993; this was an umbrella agreement establishing terms for agreements with individual Yukon First Nations)
- the Sahtu Dene First Nation and associated Métis in the Northwest Territories (1994)
- the Nisga'a First Nation (1998)
- the Tlicho First Nation in the Northwest Territories (2003)
- the Inuit in Labrador (2005)
- the Kwanlin Dun First Nation (2005).[61]

Negotiations continue towards other modern treaties, especially under the British Columbia treaty process, facilitated by the British Columbia Treaty Commission, which was established by the provincial and federal governments and the First Nations Summit in the early 1990s. On 29 October 2006, Canada, British Columbia, and the Lheidli T'enneh First Nation initialled the first draft final agreement under the BC treaty process, although the nation's members ultimately rejected the agreement at a ratification vote. By spring 2007, two further final agreements were initialled.[62]

The modern treaties have a number of common elements:

- They set aside a portion of the territory for the Aboriginal people's exclusive use, effectively (if not actually) in full ownership. In the Nisga'a treaty, these settlement lands amounted to about 8 percent of the area that had been claimed.
- The Aboriginal people are guaranteed more restricted rights to harvest resources in the rest of the lands. The Nisga'a treaty, for example, sets out various rules for determining allocations of fish from the Nass River and also directs the Nisga'a to enter into a harvest agreement with the province. It provides that the Nisga'a can hunt for domestic purposes over the Nass wildlife area (defined in the treaty). Both hunting and fishing rights are subject to measures necessary for conservation and legislation for public health and safety and, in the case of designated species (such as grizzlies), subject to an allocation set out as a percentage of the total allowable harvest set by the province.

- Certain land-use decisions in the broader territory are subjected to co-management – to regulatory bodies made up of representatives of both the Aboriginal people and the non-Aboriginal government. Sometimes this also involves some sharing in resource revenues. For example, the Nisga'a treaty continues the practice of managing the Nisga'a Memorial Lava Bed Park under a joint management committee, delegates the implementation of fishing provisions to a Joint Fisheries Management Committee, and allocates decisions regarding species designation and hunting allocations to a (joint) Wildlife Committee.
- The treaties provide for a degree of Aboriginal self-government, establishing (or recognizing) Aboriginal governmental institutions and specifying their jurisdiction over such things as the administration of justice, schools, and health care. The Nisga'a agreement affirms the Nisga'a's right to self-government in accordance with the terms of their treaty, which includes a framework to establish a Nisga'a constitution and guidelines for relations with residents who are not Nisga'a citizens, and it also grants the Nisga'a government power to make laws with respect to a wide variety of subjects, including Nisga'a public works, incorporations, solemnization of marriages, elections, the definition of citizenship, and the protection of cultural property.
- Financial compensation is provided for the surrender of all other rights or for the crystallization of Aboriginal rights so that their enforcement is limited to those specified in the treaty. In the Nisga'a case, the compensation amounted to approximately $253 million or $46,000 for each of the approximately 5,500 members of the Nisga'a First Nation.[63] However, the entire sum was not available for distribution, since normally, the costs that the First Nation incurs in negotiating the settlement (including lawyers' fees) are subtracted from the compensation. The Nisga'a, for example, were to repay the $50.3 million that the government had advanced to support the negotiating process.

Most of the modern treaties to date have occurred in the Yukon and Northwest Territories. There, it is easier to achieve agreements because Ottawa has complete constitutional authority, extensive tracts of Crown land are available for settlement lands, and First Nations form a much larger proportion of the population. Negotiations are more difficult in southern Canada. There, the potential for conflict over land is substantially increased. Indeed, much of the usable land is often already in private hands. And although only Ottawa has the constitutional authority to alter Aboriginal title, the provinces own public lands and control resource exploitation. Aboriginal title tends to interfere then with provincial resource policies, and, if Aboriginal title is removed, the benefit accrues to the province. Moreover, First Nations inevitably seek some continued role in controlling land use in the territory – some form of co-management. In practice, this means that the First Nation and the province have to find ways to work together for the long term. In the south, then, negotiations necessarily involve both the provincial and federal governments and are often lengthy and contentious.

Aboriginal Title in the Courts and in the Constitution

At the same time as the modern treaty negotiations – indeed, often as an impetus to talks – Aboriginal title has been fought out in the courts. *Calder* was followed by a long series of cases that attempted to define what was necessary to prove Aboriginal title, how Aboriginal title might have been extinguished, the general content of this title, the relationship between rights to hunt and fish and title, whether Aboriginal rights to hunt and fish took precedence over non-Aboriginal activities, whether they extended to commercial hunting and fishing, and whether and how Aboriginal rights could be limited.[64] A great many such issues remain unresolved today, especially the extent of Aboriginal rights to marine and subsurface resources, Aboriginal self-government rights, and the extent to which products harvested under Aboriginal rights can be sold commercially. Indeed, recognizing the magnitude of the task, the courts have often encouraged the parties to deal with these issues themselves, through negotiations.[65]

We will not discuss all of these questions in this introduction. Many are addressed in the chapters by Asch, Slattery, and McNeil, and there is an enormous periodical literature. In this chapter, we will first provide a very brief outline of the common law of Aboriginal title as it has emerged from the recent cases and then focus on two additional developments that have greatly shaped its interpretation: the idea that the Crown owes a fiduciary obligation to Aboriginal people and the recognition of Aboriginal rights in the Canadian constitution.

The Current Structure of the Common Law of Aboriginal Title

Recent cases have drawn a distinction between "Aboriginal title" and "Aboriginal rights."[66] This was especially true of the landmark decision of the Supreme Court of Canada in *Delgamuukw* (1997), which concerned the Gitxsan and Wet'suwet'en peoples (the Nisga'a's neighbours in northern British Columbia).[67] Aboriginal title refers to the right to exclusive use and occupation of land, which is understood as the rough equivalent of full ownership, although the courts have also made clear that Aboriginal title is *sui generis* – that is, not directly comparable to any other interest in the law. Aboriginal title involves the right to the land itself (including subsurface minerals). The land can be used for a wide variety of purposes, including ones that are not based in Aboriginal tradition. The only inherent limitation is that the land "cannot be used in a manner that is irreconcilable with the nature of the claimants' attachment to those lands."[68] Its use must be compatible, for example, with the continued employment of the land into the future.

The Supreme Court of Canada has consistently held that Aboriginal title is communal and that it can only be sold to the Crown, not to any private party. However, it is important to realize that this does not preclude the Aboriginal people from allocating and transferring rights internally according to indigenous law, and, indeed, Aboriginal peoples do recognize that individuals, families, or other groups have rights to different tracts of land within the traditional territory. Once again, the common law of Aboriginal title is best seen as a law of the interface, requiring above all that non-Aboriginal governments respect the Aboriginal people's presence on the land. It is not concerned with enforcing the law of the Aboriginal people (although the courts sometimes speak as though this were the case). From the courts' external perspective, Aboriginal title does appear to be communal, in the sense that it concerns the entire people's right to the territory, not the people's internal attribution of rights.[69]

A people holds Aboriginal title to a particular territory if it had exclusive occupation of this territory at the time that the colonial power asserted its sovereignty over the area. What counts as "occupation" depends on the nature of the Aboriginal community and the types of uses appropriate to the land. The courts have also said that they will take into account the Aboriginal perspective when deciding whether the land had been sufficiently "occupied." Regular use of the area for hunting, fishing, and other activities will generally be sufficient. By "exclusive," the courts mean the ability to exclude non-rights-holders. It is possible, for example, for more than one people to share a particular area. There is no need for the people claiming Aboriginal title to have maintained continuous use of the lands, as long as they have maintained "substantial connection" to them.

Even when an Aboriginal people has not "occupied" the land sufficiently to obtain Aboriginal title, it may possess particular rights over the land – rights to hunt and fish, for example. The Supreme Court of Canada has applied a quite different test to these more limited "Aboriginal rights." In *R. v. Van der Peet* (1996), the Court held that they have to satisfy a cultural test: they must be "an element of a practice, custom or tradition integral to the distinctive culture of the aboriginal group claiming the right";[70] they must constitute a "defining feature"[71] of the Aboriginal culture. The culture is determined against an historical reference point: the protected rights must "have continuity with the practices, customs and traditions that existed prior to contact [with European society]."[72]

This test has been strongly criticized.[73] Commentators have argued that in emphasizing the protection of cultural distinctiveness, the courts may deny protection to interests that have long been important to the economic well-being of indigenous societies but that do not have a distinctly cultural character. It tends to "culturalize" indigenous societies so that they are defined entirely by their cultural specificity, not by, for example, their character as self-determining political communities. Above all, commentators have argued that by using a historical reference point, this test implicitly treats Aboriginal peoples as frozen in time, with their distinctive culture crystallized at the point of contact. The Court in *Van der Peet* anticipated this objection and made clear that the rights only had to be *continuous* with pre-contact practices and that they could be an "exercise in modern form" of a pre-contact practice.[74] Yet many commentators have been concerned that this still ties Aboriginal rights entirely to pre-contact practices and fails to recognize practices that had emerged more recently, taking insufficient account of any culture's potential for change, and perhaps even preventing change, if the change would extend beyond the bounds of the traditional practice. To take one specific and very important example, those practices that emerged in relation to the fur trade – during the very first period of contact – would appear to fall outside the test.

To some extent, *Delgamuukw* represented a corrective to *Van der Peet*, responding to the criticisms and modifying the tests. *Van der Peet* had described Aboriginal title as a particular form of Aboriginal right. As a result, commentators wondered whether Aboriginal title would be subject to the same cultural test and constrained to traditional uses. *Delgamuukw* made clear that it would not. Aboriginal title was defined as a right to the land itself, which could then be used for a wide range of purposes, including uses that had nothing to do with pre-contact practices. The time for determining the existence of Aboriginal title was different from that established for Aboriginal rights in *Van der Peet:* the assertion of sovereignty, not first contact. Henceforth, there would be two types of indigenous right: Aboriginal title (established by the *Delgamuukw* tests) and Aboriginal rights (established by the *Van der Peet* tests). Still, the relationship between these two categories remains ambiguous. One of the purposes of Brian Slattery's contribution to this book is to suggest how we should understand this relationship.

This outline describes in abbreviated form the current state of the law with respect to the nature and proof of Aboriginal title. But it is not sufficient to prove that Aboriginal title existed. One also has to establish that it continues to exist, that it has not been "extinguished." Here, the law has been clarified since *Calder*. Justice Hall's test has been accepted: Aboriginal title could have been extinguished by non-Aboriginal legislative authority (at least prior to constitutional entrenchment in 1982) but that action had to manifest a "clear and plain intention."[75] The simple fact that a legislature may have acted without considering Aboriginal title – the simple fact, for example, that it established a system for granting public lands to settlers without first addressing the Aboriginal interest – was insufficient to establish a clear and plain intention. Aboriginal title in British Columbia was not, then, extinguished wholesale by BC governments' policy with respect to public lands.[76] The courts have also drawn a distinction between extinguishment (which obliterates Aboriginal title) and regulation of this title (where the use of the title may be constrained for a period but where the underlying right persists). This means that Aboriginal title is extinguished only where there is an intention to remove the title altogether. It is not extinguished piecemeal by regulations that restrict its exercise.[77] Finally, Aboriginal title can be extinguished only by a level of government that has constitutional authority to do so. After British Columbia entered confederation, only Ottawa had power to extinguish Aboriginal title.[78]

The aspects of Aboriginal title just discussed develop themes that were already apparent in the Supreme Court of Canada's decision in *Calder*. Since this decision, two further developments have substantially shaped the law.

The Fiduciary Obligations of the Crown

First, the courts have held that Canadian governments owe special duties to Aboriginal peoples, especially a set of "fiduciary obligations."[79]

Fiduciary obligations are like the obligations a trustee owes to the beneficiary of a trust: the trustee should act entirely in the interest of the beneficiary, treating the beneficiary's interests as though they were the trustee's own. Fiduciary obligations are commonly imposed in situations of dependence, often where one person administers another person's property and where the beneficiary must therefore rely entirely on the fiduciary's good faith. In 1984, in *Guerin v. The Queen*, the Supreme Court of Canada held that the Crown owed such a duty to Aboriginal people.[80] *Guerin* itself concerned the federal government's administration of Indian reserve lands. At the time, there was some question whether the duty would be limited to similar situations, where the government was administering Aboriginal assets. Later cases have made clear that the duty is broader, though not unlimited. A distinctly fiduciary duty will apply whenever the Crown has assumed "discretionary control in relation [to particular obligations or interests of Aboriginal people, including Aboriginal rights protected under section 35 of the *Constitution Act, 1982*] sufficient to ground a fiduciary obligation."[81] The courts have begun to differentiate these strictly fiduciary duties from a broader obligation that the Crown also owes to Aboriginal people to engage in fair dealing, to uphold "the honour of the Crown."[82] Both of these special obligations – the fiduciary duties and those flowing from the need to maintain "the honour of the Crown" – bind the federal and the provincial governments.[83]

The "honour of the Crown," together with the more demanding fiduciary duties, builds upon the special relationship between the Crown and Aboriginal peoples reflected in the Royal Proclamation of 1763, the language of the historic treaties, and the control exercised over reserve lands.

The two concepts have been used by the courts to support a demanding test for the extinguishment of Aboriginal title, to establish a relatively lenient standard for the regulation of Aboriginal and treaty rights by non-Aboriginal governments, and to require those governments to respect Aboriginal title even before this title has been established in court.[84] They have served, then, as a crucial influence in the development of the law of Aboriginal title. One wonders, however, how long they will continue to play such an important role. The fiduciary obligation, in particular, tends to have a paternalistic tone, founded as it is on a relationship of dependence. As Aboriginal peoples gain control of their own resources and assume their own government, one suspects that distinctly fiduciary duties will fall away, replaced by the more general "honour of the Crown." Indeed, this appears to be happening in the most recent cases.[85]

Constitutional Protection of Aboriginal Title

The second development is the constitutional protection of Aboriginal rights, including Aboriginal title.[86]

In 1982, following a long period of negotiation and with the approval of the federal and all provincial governments except Québec, the Canadian constitution was "patriated." Essentially, this meant that an amending formula was enacted that would allow the constitution to be changed by Canadian legislatures acting alone (before 1982, most constitutional amendments had to be adopted by the British Parliament, although, in recent years, the British Parliament had acted only on the request of Canadian authorities). At the same time, a number of additional amendments were made, including the adoption of the *Canadian Charter of Rights and Freedoms*.[87] During the discussions that led to patriation, Aboriginal representatives campaigned strongly for the recognition of Aboriginal and treaty rights in the new constitutional order, arguing that otherwise their rights might be prejudiced by the elimination of British authority and by the emphasis on individual rights in the *Charter*.[88] Their efforts resulted in section 35 of the *Constitution Act, 1982*, which stated that "[t]he existing aboriginal and treaty rights of the aboriginal peoples of Canada are hereby recognized and affirmed" and which defined "aboriginal peoples" as including the Indian, Inuit, and Métis peoples. For many Aboriginal representatives, this was not enough. They argued that section 35 failed to define the rights and that the rights should have been "guaranteed," not merely "recognized and affirmed." In response, section 37 was added to the *Constitution Act, 1982*, stating that a constitutional conference would be held within one year of the new provisions entering into force. At this conference, governments would seek to define Aboriginal rights (with Aboriginal participation). Some Aboriginal leaders continued to oppose the new constitution. Nevertheless, the new provisions, including sections 35 and 37, came into effect on 17 April 1982.

The promised constitutional conference was convened in March 1983, and three further conferences were held between then and 1987.[89] They did have some success. The phrase "treaty rights" was defined to include present and future land claims agreements, a clause was added to guarantee gender equality in Aboriginal and treaty rights, and the constitution was amended to require a constitutional conference, with Aboriginal participation, before the Aboriginal provisions of the constitution could be amended. But the conferences failed to achieve what soon became the Aboriginal representatives' primary objective: the constitutional recognition of Aboriginal self-government. By the end of the conferences, the federal government and five provinces supported this objective (although they did not agree with Aboriginal representatives on the form it should take). The governments of British Columbia, Alberta, Saskatchewan, and Newfoundland opposed it, however, and Québec refused to take a position because of its continuing objections to the patriation of the constitution. There was another attempt to write Aboriginal self-government into the constitution in the "Charlottetown Accord" of 1992 – a package of proposed constitutional amendments that covered a wide range of issues, from the recognition of Québec's distinct society to reform of the Senate (including many Aboriginal concerns in addition to self-government).[90] This time, all Canadian governments supported the accord, but the governments had also undertaken to put the package to a national referendum. This occurred on 26 October 1992. The accord was conclusively defeated. Thus, after nearly a decade of constitutional discussions, the principal provision protecting Aboriginal rights (section 35) remained virtually the same, subject only to the modest amendments adopted in 1983.

But what did section 35 mean? The first thing to note is that it protected only "existing" rights. It did not revive rights that had been extinguished prior to adoption of the new constitutional provisions in 1982. Could Aboriginal and treaty rights be limited or extinguished after 1982? The critical issue was the meaning of the phrase "recognized and affirmed." The Supreme Court of Canada soon decided that this did provide a measure of constitutional protection, although the protection was not absolute. Ottawa could still regulate those rights, but, to do so, it had to meet a standard of justification established by the Court. This standard requires, first, that the legislation's objective be "compelling and substantial" and, second, that the action be taken in a manner that is consistent with the honour of the Crown, including the Crown's fiduciary obligations.[91] With respect to the first requirement, conservation, resource management, and safety requirements count as compelling and substantial objectives, as do economic development and "the settlement of foreign populations to support those aims."[92] With respect to the second, the fiduciary obligation requires at least that the Aboriginal people be consulted (in some circumstances, it may require more than that, perhaps even the Aboriginal people's consent) and may also require financial compensation, Aboriginal priority in using certain resources, and an attempt to minimize any impact on Aboriginal interests.[93] Section 35 does, then, offer some protection against legislative action, but the extent of this protection is qualified, depending on the nature of the right, the extent of the infringement, the reason for the infringement, and any offers of compensation.

In addition to protecting Aboriginal rights, section 35 may also have influenced their interpretation. This is more speculative because, ostensibly, section 35 merely protects Aboriginal rights and does not create them. In at least one respect, however, it does appear to have shaped the courts' definition of the rights. In *Van der Peet*, the Supreme Court of Canada emphasized the need to define Aboriginal rights in a manner that reflected their essential purpose. But the purpose on which the Court tended to focus was not that of the underlying rights – not the purpose of Aboriginal title or of hunting and fishing rights under the Royal Proclamation and the common law. Rather, the Court concentrated on section 35's purpose, found it to be the protection of cultural distinctiveness, and then used that as the basis for the cultural test it applied to Aboriginal rights. There is a strong argument that the Court should have been examining the purpose of the rights themselves, not the purpose of section 35, which merely purported to protect rights already in existence.[94]

There are other ways in which section 35 may have shaped the interpretation of the rights. It is likely that constitutionalization, together with the lengthy negotiations over Aboriginal self-government, has advanced the definition of Aboriginal rights. On the other hand, some have worried that constitutionalization might have prompted more limited interpretations of Aboriginal rights because these rights are now much more difficult to change. These arguments remain open. What is undeniable is that the interpretation of Aboriginal rights is no longer simply a matter of the common law. It occurs within a distinctly constitutional framework.

Current Challenges in the Law of Aboriginal Title

In this concluding section, we identify a number of challenges facing the development of Aboriginal rights and the negotiation of treaties. We can do little more than raise these issues. Some are addressed in greater detail in later chapters. As always, we provide references to further discussions in the notes.

The Continuing Challenge of Negotiating Treaties

A number of issues bedevil modern treaty negotiations.[95] The main one is simply a contest over resources. Parties on all sides now accept that a final settlement must involve some sharing of territory. But what shares, organized in what way? The parties are often far apart in their expectations. Second, non-Aboriginal governments have sought a high degree of "certainty" so that the indigenous interest is clarified once and for all. They have tried to achieve this by having treaties "extinguish" Aboriginal rights, replacing those rights with specifically agreed provisions. Aboriginal peoples have deeply resented the language of extinguishment. Those individuals seeking to advance negotiations have tried to find other, more acceptable terms, perhaps structuring the agreements so that they "recognize" Aboriginal rights and render them precise rather than extinguishing them.[96] Third, there has often been deep disagreement over the extent of self-government and co-management. Some provincial governments continue to resist significant Aboriginal powers and have argued that Aboriginal governments should be seen as, in effect, specialized municipalities. First Nations generally argue for much more extensive powers.[97] Fourth, status Indians have long benefited from an exemption from taxation for property on reserve. Modern treaty negotiations inevitably raise the question of whether and, if so, how this exemption should be discontinued.[98]

Behind these issues of substance lie questions of process. How should negotiations be structured so that they lead to lasting agreements? The Royal Commission on Aboriginal Peoples made many recommendations in this regard, arguing especially that a new "royal proclamation" should be adopted to establish the symbolic framework within which comprehensive negotiations could occur. It also recommended that Indian bands, recognized under the *Indian Act*, undergo a process of consolidation to create nations that would be better able to undertake a wide range of responsibilities.[99] Neither of these recommendations was accepted. There is also a growing and highly stimulating theoretical literature on cross-cultural negotiations, some of which tries to combine indigenous and non-indigenous forms.[100] These studies have been complemented by a number of practical initiatives. Important recent examples include the BC treaty process and the process used to settle claims in the Yukon Territory (which involved the negotiation of an umbrella agreement at the territorial level; the subsequent negotiation of specific agreements with each First Nation; the creation of internal constitutions for those nations; and the development of self-government provisions under which the First Nations could periodically draw down powers, tailoring their responsibilities to their capacities).[101]

The development of productive treaty processes has been difficult. It involves balancing demands from the First Nations, the provinces, and the federal government. It often requires that one conciliate profoundly different conceptions about the nature and scope of negotiations. And it also requires processes within each party for working through disagreements, developing a consistent negotiating position, and maintaining popular accountability. This is as true for the non-Aboriginal as it is for the Aboriginal parties. The BC treaty process, for example, has been disrupted by questions of authority and accountability on both the non-Aboriginal and Aboriginal sides; by frustrations over the mandates under which government negotiators operate (mandates that take time to develop and approve, that can shift with the election of a new government, and that are then generally kept confidential from the Aboriginal party); by a new BC government's holding of a province-wide referendum in order to test non-Aboriginal support for a number of features of the process; as well as by disagreements within Aboriginal communities.[102]

One of the most promising steps in recent years has been the gradual acceptance that, prior to the full determination of Aboriginal title, interim measures should be put into place to safeguard the Aboriginal interest and provide some of the benefits of Aboriginal title. This had been one of the recommendations of the Royal Commission on Aboriginal Peoples.[103] Without interim measures, Aboriginal peoples have had to watch as lands over which they claimed Aboriginal title were logged, flooded for hydroelectric projects, mined, hunted upon, subjected to road building, or granted to third parties, generally with no consultation with the Aboriginal people. Often, the only way they could derive any benefit from their title was to engage in long and immensely costly litigation or attempt to force the issue through direct action, such as blockades and the like. Moreover, interim measures have another great benefit: they can provide the skeleton of an eventual agreement. Two reasons why modern-day treaties have been so hard to negotiate are (1) the broad scope of matters up for negotiation – how to come to a single set of terms given the great distance between the parties on so many issues – and (2) the finality of the treaty negotiations – the tendency to approach treaties as though they were once-and-for-all agreements, covering all aspects of Aboriginal rights for all time. Interim measures help to overcome each of these hurdles. They allow the parties to put into place provisional solutions without the pressure of finality, allowing the parties to experiment with different institutional structures and to live with provisional settlements, in the hope that these may one day ripen into full-fledged treaties.

The employment of interim measures was given impetus by the Supreme Court of Canada's 2004 judgment in *Haida Nation v. British Columbia (Minister of Forests),* in which the Court decided that the honour of the Crown required that federal and provincial governments respect, and not simply ignore, the probable existence of Aboriginal title, even before it had been proven in court.[104] At the very least, governments had to consult with First Nations before taking actions that might prejudice the Nations' title and, in appropriate circumstances, enter interim agreements to accommodate that Nation's concerns. In 2005, the BC government announced a "new relationship" with Aboriginal people in which consultation prior to proof of title and other interim measures figured prominently.[105]

Self-Government

A central feature of treaty negotiations is self-government. But the issue extends well beyond treaties. There is a strong argument that governmental autonomy has always been the principal concern of Aboriginal peoples – a concern that was pursued predominantly through the framework of land claims both because of the importance of resources to any true autonomy and because framing the rights in proprietary terms stood a greater chance of acceptance.[106] Kent McNeil's contribution to this book explores the deep connections that exist between the recognition of Aboriginal title and self-government.

Issues of political autonomy remain important to indigenous peoples. In recent years, First Nations have sought to transform band administrations established under the *Indian Act* by rejecting the paternalistic oversight of government officials, reforming their internal processes so that they better reflect First Nations' traditions and experimenting with various ways of blending the traditional authority of Elders with band-level government. First Nations have also taken responsibility for specific governmental services such as schools, child-welfare agencies, and procedures for handling crime in the community. These tend to be community-based experiments, conceived and pursued differently by different bands. They have had varied success. But over time, a number of influential and often highly successful models have emerged. These have, in turn, served as prototypes for self-government provisions in treaties.[107]

With the expansion in the role of First Nations governments, concerns have been raised in some cases over the transparency of decision making, financial management, political accountability, and impartiality in administration. Aboriginal people themselves have often worked to improve governmental performance and accountability and have criticized maladministration. In addition, in 2002, the federal government sought to revise the *Indian Act* regime in order to impose additional controls across all communities. This federal initiative was strongly resisted by First Nations on the grounds that any changes should involve full Aboriginal participation – that they should, in other words, be negotiated. Ottawa ultimately abandoned its bill.[108]

Issues of governance have occasionally been addressed by the courts, either as an extension of the rights associated with Aboriginal title or as a free-standing right under section 35 of the *Constitution Act, 1982*.[109] First Nations have also argued for political autonomy on the basis of the international right of self-determination, especially in international forums.[110] To this point, however, the courts have generally shied away from strong judicial recognition of a right of self-government, leaving it to political negotiations.

The emphasis on the language of rights in arguments for Aboriginal governmental autonomy is understandable and perhaps even necessary, especially given the long history of denial. Yet it also has its limitations –

limitations that are evident in the difficulty First Nations have had establishing governmental authority through the courts. The language of rights stresses entitlement but provides little guidance on how responsibilities should be divided between Aboriginal and non-Aboriginal governments. It speaks in broad and abstract generalities, leading some non-Aboriginal observers to think of Aboriginal self-government either as a complete rejection of co-existence with non-Aboriginal Canadians, as complete governmental separation, or, if independence is not on the cards, as a special right claimed by Aboriginal people on the basis of culture or race – an outcome difficult to reconcile with ideas of the equality of citizens.[111] All of these implications are misleading. A few indigenous people do argue for complete Aboriginal sovereignty, at least as the notional starting point for negotiations. But, more often, the aim is fundamentally federal in nature. They seek spheres of autonomy in which, for certain issues, rules can be framed on the basis of their traditions – as the outcome of debates that occur within their communities – just as British Columbians, Québecers, or Newfoundlanders are able to do within areas of provincial jurisdiction. The authority of First Nations would no doubt be tailored to areas in which they have a particular interest. These areas may well differ from the spheres of provincial authority. But most Aboriginal peoples nevertheless seek only a relative autonomy – one that is potentially consistent with equal participation, as Canadian citizens, on other matters.[112]

Thinking of self-government as a form of federalism may help direct our minds to the central issues (the appropriate division of authority, the relationship between the different orders of government) and suggest ways of reconciling principles of equality and governmental autonomy. It may also help us to understand the apparent paradox noted earlier, namely that the Nisga'a and other First Nations have often embraced an unrelenting commitment to the vindication of Aboriginal title and, at the same time, to legal equality and Canadian citizenship.

Urban Aboriginal People, Métis, and Non-Status Indians

Thus far in this chapter, we have tended to focus on issues principally of interest to the First Nations and the Inuit – and, even then, to members of those peoples resident on their ancestral lands – principally because they are the people to whom the doctrine of Aboriginal title most directly relates. But they are far from the only Aboriginal people. Many people of First Nations ancestry have lost status as "Indians" under the *Indian Act* by the way in which the act defines who is an Indian and who is not, especially as a result of marriages outside the community. These "non-status Indians" lack the right to share in the lands and resources administered by band governments and cannot participate in the political institutions of bands, which are the institutions generally considered to be the contemporary representatives of the First Nations. Even among First Nations people who retain Indian status, a great many – probably at least half – live off-reserve. Many of these individuals retain strong links to their home communities, but many do not. Moreover, there is one constitutionally recognized Aboriginal people – the Métis – that has generally not been treated as a holder of Aboriginal title.[113]

What do concepts such as Aboriginal title and self-government mean to these people? How should Aboriginal identity be accommodated in urban settings, where individuals of different Aboriginal origins often collect together in communities that cross traditional boundaries? Are there ways in which these people can reconnect with their ancestral communities? Should they be encouraged to do so? Are there distinctive forms of self-government that make sense for the Métis, for urban Aboriginal people, or for rural off-reserve non-status Indians, which also fit with their relationship with the broader Canadian community?[114] All of these questions are profoundly important and immensely difficult – questions that are only now receiving the attention they deserve. They are likely to present one of the critical challenges for Aboriginal peoples and non-Aboriginal Canadians alike in the coming decades.

Aboriginal Definitions of Aboriginal Rights
Discussions of Aboriginal rights generally take colonial experience, the treaty process, and the decisions of courts as their point of departure. However, there is another way of approaching these issues. One can start with indigenous traditions, think through what it means to be Cree, Inuvialuit, Coast Salish, Anishinabe, Nisga'a, Miq'maq, or Métis, and then work from there to understand one's relations to the land, responsibility to one's neighbours, political obligations, and institutions. This approach does not deny the fact of colonialism. It may well recognize that, at a later stage, one must think about how distinctively Aboriginal commitments might be reconciled with the need to live together with non-Aboriginal Canadians. But it does insist that Aboriginal traditions are worth understanding on their own terms, in a manner that is not from the very beginning crimped and contorted by a colonial frame.

This resolutely Aboriginal perspective has produced some of the most exciting scholarship in recent years, led by a new generation of indigenous scholars who draw on their community's traditions and use them to address contemporary issues of indigenous rights and governmental reform. John Borrows, the author of the concluding chapter in this book, is one of those scholars, and there are a good many others, some of whose publications you will find cited in the notes.[115]

A variant of this approach is also found in practical action. At several points, especially since the resurgence of Aboriginal advocacy in the 1970s,

Aboriginal peoples have looked to their own resources to rebuild institutions, reforge relationships to the land, and restore their communities. This, indeed, was one of the principal tasks undertaken by the Nisga'a during the long years in which they built the Nishga Tribal Council and prepared and pressed their claims for a treaty. Sometimes this strategy involves direct action: Aboriginal people taking steps to control their own destinies, even before a fully negotiated solution. In the words of Philip Awashish of the Eeyou of Mistissini (one of the nations of the James Bay Cree), some First Nations have recognized that "self-determination is the power of choice in action" and have adopted a "just do it" approach.[116] So, for example, in the early 1980s, the Waglisla First Nation (Bella Bella) created its own school, initially in opposition to provincial authority but ultimately securing provincial funding and recognition. Many other Aboriginal peoples have taken similar action, sometimes peaceably but, at other times, through confrontations that have, on occasion, turned violent.[117] Our intention is not to romanticize these efforts or to suggest that they have all been equally successful, constructive, or worthwhile. Our point is simply to note that issues of Aboriginal title and governmental autonomy have never been exclusively a matter of judicial decision and constitutional text. They have always been driven by commitments and political struggles that find their source within indigenous communities themselves.

This kind of direct initiative from outside the settled confines of the legal order is hardly unprecedented in Canada. It is imprinted in the democratic character of the Canadian constitution, which was achieved not by the free grant of the sovereign but by insistent demands by those excluded from the political process – demands that resulted in the creation of representative assemblies, responsible government, and then the progressive extension of the franchise. Indeed, the very idea of democratic government makes government responsive to unruly popular action, rendering (in Albert Venn Dicey's terms) the legal sovereign answerable to the political sovereign.[118] Moreover, the Canadian constitution has long responded to the special demands of French Canada and of Canada's regional societies, incorporating them through its federal structure, although such institutional accommodations, while essential, have never completely harnessed the political implications of these societies.

Aboriginal peoples have similar potential to shape the Canadian constitutional order from outside. During certain periods of our history, they have had much more than potential. Aboriginal rights, title, treaties, self-government, section 35, and the fiduciary obligation all represent ways of accommodating indigenous societies within the Canadian legal order. But these ways are always first approximations. They never exhaust the creative resources resulting from the continuing encounter between indigenous and non-indigenous societies. The new scholarship on indigenous law and government, developed by indigenous scholars, is only the most recent manifestation of these resources.

Final Comments

The conference on which this book is based ended with a gala event at the University of Victoria to celebrate the contributions of the Nisga'a, particularly those of Frank Calder. One of the authors of this introduction had responsibility for marshalling the platform party for its entry onto the stage. This party consisted of the Honourable Frank Calder in his full regalia; his Nisga'a contemporaries Rod Robinson (who bore the high-ranking name Sim'oogit Minee'eskw and had been a founding member of the revitalized Nisga'a Land Committee in the 1950s) and Hubert Doolan (another leader of the Nisga'a and one of the plaintiffs in *Calder*); Dr. Samuel Sam of the Tsartlip people with his son and assistant, Greg Sam; Chief Joseph Gosnell, then President of the Nisga'a Lisims government; the Honourable Lance Finch, Chief Justice of British Columbia; Professor David Turpin, President of the University of Victoria; and, last but not least, the Honourable Iona Campagnolo, Lieutenant-Governor of British Columbia, assisted by her aide-de-camp. The Nisga'a Ts'amiks Dancers were on stage in force – between forty-five and fifty dancers – to dance in honour of Frank Calder.

The author had been given detailed instructions on the order of precedence for the platform party from the protocol officers at Government House and, like the well-brought-up boy he was, he sought dutifully to obey them. Yet it soon became clear that there was another protocol at work. Gently, firmly, Sim'oogit Minee'eskw was reordering the party, so that they would dance in procession in the manner required by the Ts'amiks Dancers' songs, which were a song of welcome and a song to summon the dignitaries into the Big House. The author stepped back, taking comfort in the fact that this would certainly have been the preference of this lieutenant-governor, raised as she was on the estuary of the Skeena.

Those of us who were there will never forget that evening. The speeches were remarkable (there are excerpts towards the end of this book). But, more than the speeches, the image that will remain in our minds will be that of Sim'oogit Minee'eskw leading the procession, dancing with great dignity to the exuberant singing and dancing of the Ts'amiks Dancers, the other dignitaries dancing in single file behind, some, like Frank Calder, Hubert Doolan, and Joseph Gosnell, secure in their tradition, and others, like the non-Aboriginal participants, following along as best they could, dancing and joining in the spirit of the event.

The evening was a remarkable meeting of cultures and encounter between protocols. The multitude of Ts'amiks Dancers – of all genders and ages, from toddlers to Elders – leaped and turned and sang, led in the dance by their director with cedar-bark hat, button blanket, and talking stick. Their joy and pride was infectious. They and the dignitaries listened respectfully to the songs and prayers of our hosts for the conference, Dr. Samuel Sam and his assistants of the Straits Salish people, as Dr. Sam formally closed the conference, thanked the delegates, and wished them well on their way. Then the two groups joined together, the Salish and the Nisga'a, in the singing of other songs. The platform party once again formed in procession and danced their way around the stage, led by Sim'oogit Minee'eskw, before leaving to the wings. But the singing and the dancing continued long after their departure, generously exceeding the time that the organizers had allotted for the event. As we write, three years later, their songs continue to sound in our minds, voicing a promise of the benefits, indeed the privilege, of encounter.

Part 1
Reflections of the *Calder* Participants

2
Frank Calder and Thomas Berger:
A Conversation

The following interview with the two chief protagonists in *Calder et al. v. Attorney-General of British Columbia*[1] was recorded at a conference to mark the thirtieth anniversary of the Supreme Court of Canada's decision. The conference opened with a prayer and remarks from Dr. Samuel Sam, a Coast and Straits Salish Elder from the local Tsartlip community. Dean Andrew Petter, of the Faculty of Law at the University of Victoria, and Barbara Burns, the Senior Regional Director of the British Columbia Region of the Department of Justice, also made opening remarks. The interview was with Dr. Frank Calder, President Emeritus of the Nishga Tribal Council, who was president of the council at the time the Nisga'a decided to challenge the idea that there was no Aboriginal title in British Columbia, and Thomas Berger, Q.C., barrister and solicitor and former justice of the Supreme Court of British Columbia, who was the Nisga'a's lawyer. Professor Jeremy Webber, Canada Research Chair in Law and Society in the Faculty of Law at the University of Victoria, posed a series of questions to Calder and Berger. Audience members were invited to ask questions and provide comments at the conclusion of the interview.[2]

Jeremy Webber: Frank Calder was born at Nass Harbour on 3 August 1915 and became the adoptive son of the great Nisga'a Chief Arthur Calder. He was active during the 1940s with the Native Brotherhood of British Columbia and became secretary of the Native Brotherhood in 1949. One of the causes of the Native Brotherhood during those years was the extension of the franchise, the extension of the right to vote, to status Indians but also to Canadians of Asian heritage. The right to vote was achieved in 1949 and in that very year Dr. Calder was the first status Indian to be elected to a Canadian legislature. He served as an MLA in the British Columbia legislature for twenty-six years, initially with the CCF [Co-operative Commonwealth Federation], then with the NDP [New Democratic Party] and ultimately with the Social Credit Party. Dr.

The Nishga Tribal Council's delegation in Victoria in 1961. *Courtesy of Tamaki Calder, photographer unknown*

Calder was also the first status Indian to be appointed a minister of the Crown in the British Columbia government. He is best known for his attempt to have Aboriginal title recognized in Canadian law. He was, with Hubert Doolan and Rod Robinson, very active in the founding and early development of the Nishga Tribal Council. He became its first president and held this position until 1974. It was in that capacity that in 1965 he approached Tom Berger in order to pursue the Nisga'a land question before the Canadian courts.

Now, Tom Berger at that time was a young lawyer practising in Vancouver. He had been the lawyer for a number of the members of the Snuneymuxw First Nation in *R. v. White and Bob*,[3] which had begun in 1963 and culminated in the decision of the Supreme Court of Canada in 1965. That case was a very important precursor to the decision in *Calder* because it did two things. It recognized that the Douglas Treaties, the fourteen treaties that exist in this very territory on Vancouver Island, were true treaties that deserved recognition as treaties within Canadian law. The second thing that it did, especially in the reasons of Justice Norris in the Court of Appeal, was to open up the possibility of Aboriginal title being recognized as a legal interest in modern Canadian law.

In the 1960s, Mr. Berger was both an MP and an MLA, and he served for a time as the leader of the provincial NDP. Shortly after the decision in *Calder* he was named to the Supreme Court of British Columbia where he served as a judge for twelve years before returning to the practice of law. And, indeed, in that most recent period of practice, he represented the Nisga'a again, defending the self-government provisions in the Nisga'a treaty.[4] So there is a very long association between Mr. Berger and the issues that we are discussing in this conference.

Now, this is an opportunity for us to discuss with Dr. Calder and with Mr. Berger those events. There will be an opportunity for you, too, to ask questions towards the end of the session. But, I thought I would begin, Dr. Calder, by asking, how did the most important case in the Canadian law of Aboriginal title come to bear your name?

Frank Calder: First of all I would like to thank the Coast Salish representatives here for permission to say a few words. Before I answer your question, you referred to me as being a first MLA, which perhaps is true, but I recall the day that I had to go back to the Nass River and my tribe wanted to know, well what is an MLA? What does this stand for? So I quickly said, "momma's little angel." I thought that would wake you up! In reply to your question, it brings to mind the earlier days. And people have asked me the same question about what prompted you people to start this thing, especially on the twentieth anniversary of the *Calder* decision in Saskatoon, which is the focus up here today. They asked me the same question and so I am going to give you the same answer I gave them during that celebration of the twentieth anniversary.

My grandfather was quite young and he was a member of Old Aiyansh in those days. This was around the very early 1880s, and he was the one that told me this story that really prompted me to start thinking about the British Columbia land question and the Nisga'a land question. He told me that one sunny late afternoon when people were assembled on the grass in front of the river at Old Aiyansh, they were watching the fish jump, the arrival of canoes loaded with our people, some going out, when all of a sudden they saw five people appear on the opposite bank. And they watched these people camp, put up a tent. There were five of them, while the other two were busy setting up a little tripod of something and putting a little instrument on top of it and looking through it. Oh, they were very interesting. So they sat there and watched; there were hundreds of them on the beach watching. So they decided to send a canoe loaded with several of our Nisga'a braves to inquire what they were doing across there. So these people load the canoe. There were no oars so they poled across, went up to the bank, confronted these five people and said, "What are you doing?" Of course, they didn't speak perfect English and maybe they were using the Hudson Bay lingo: "What are you doing?" Well, they said, "We are surveyors. You see this little instrument here, well we're looking through [it] to set a boundary line to go south on the east bank of the river. Then we want to cross the river and we're going to go back to your community with this instrument and cross the river over here and when we're finished we'll come to you and we're going to tell you that The Queen is going to give you this land." Well, the chiefs had already told these people in the canoe not to argue, just come back and tell us what those people said. So, they came back and told the chiefs what they had heard. The next morning at eight o'clock every canoe was loaded with Nisga'a braves, every one of them carrying a Hudson's Bay musket. At eight o'clock those people started to cook; they were just getting ready to go to work. All these braves went up there, confronted them and pointed the gun, and just uttered these words, "Get off my land." Well, God, when you're facing hundreds of Hudson's Bay muskets, what are you going to do? They would have to dismantle the tent and get off. Now to your question: "What was the impact of that order to get off my land?" Number one: a refusal to have any form of an Indian reservation. It was the number one thing. We don't want no reserves. This is our land. We don't have to go and thank The Queen for giving us this land. This is our land. That's the number one thing. Refusal to have an Indian reservation. Number two: it was the first of what we now know as the British Columbia land question. I hope that answers your question. That's the beginning of what we started and it worked right up to the day that we heard of this gentleman [Thomas Berger], who was absolutely brilliant during the course of the court case. I've never said this before, but I say it now Tom.

I was staying in Vancouver and there was an old friend of mine. He was a big guy, they called him Big Chief and I'm the little guy, they called me Little Chief. But Guy Williams told me there was a young fellow working with Tom Hurley who apparently was one of the top criminal lawyers in the land and he was in that office. Also in that office was Mrs. Armitage Moore who was a secretary to Thomas Hurley. You can go wrong [by] hiring any lawyer on this question. It's got to be someone that knows the Indian question, and I was told by Mr. Guy Williams that there was a bright young student in that office. Go and get him. So, I recall the day in the mid-sixties when I walked up the stairway of the Standard Building, knocked on the door. Have you got a young chap here by the name of Tom Berger? Yes. To make a long story short, when the case came up, Tom was brilliant. Thank you.

JW: At the time the Nisga'a brought the action in *Calder*, there was considerable discussion within British Columbia about whether the land question should be pursued through political mechanisms, and there was some discussion of there being a comprehensive land claim made for all First Nations in British Columbia through political discussions rather than through the courts. Could you tell us why the Nisga'a decided to go to court to pursue the question?

FC: Well, our people – don't forget we're isolated in the Nass River. There were no roads or anything, and you could only go in by boat. There was no plane scheduled in those days. But we did hear about the courts and, of course, we didn't know too much about what was written in the constitution. You see, in those days, there was a great dispersement of our people because they were the only ones that anybody can hire to build canneries, to build roads into the mining areas, to assist in cutting down the trees, and this is the young blood that was taking part. But the Elders were thinking a little different: My God, look what they are doing to our land. So they were very serious about what was happening all around them. I call it dispersement because people were living in the camps and going away from their villages. And today we call it urbanization, but they were dispersing into these different areas, and, naturally, the communities lost contact with a lot of their leaders. But then the question arose: if we were to meet this question head on, where do we go? So in this way, through our inquiries and through our missionaries and their teachers, we were told where to go. But then when it stopped right there in 1927[5] after we met defeat in 1927. Of course, I was only twelve years old then. Not too long afterwards, we were told that no lawyers were supposed to take up any more of this question. Tom and his colleagues would be crucified if they were to take up this question. But in 1960, as you pointed out, Rod and I defied that law and appeared before the Joint Parliamentary Committee and there was no reply to that so we just went right on. They didn't tell us to stop.

So we decided that we were going to have to go into court. Then as we were studying the books, those of us that were sort of educated, we found that Ottawa has no say on natural resources. I don't know how dumb the other guy was to let the provinces do the talking in natural resources. That's why we are not united today, really, because we've got ten provinces dealing with each other's natural resources and poor Ottawa sitting there dumb as hell. So, anyway, we decided to go and sue the BC government. Oh jeepers, W.A.C. Bennett, he wasn't just amused, he was speechless! He says: "What are you doing here? You guys belong to the Indian reservations; you should be dealing with Ottawa. And besides that, our lawyers say that you've got to ask permission for a fiat." Well there are times when you have to play dumb. Who the hell knows what a fiat is, eh? So we played dumb. I don't know what fiat means, Mr. Premier. All I know is that you people control the natural resources that are ours. That woke him up. So this is the road we took. Once we were quite sure where we were going, then my tribe ordered me, the president, and said: "You'd better go and look for a good lawyer." So we landed Tom. The man was studying the Indian question, and I think he had a court case before – the *White and Bob* case – and I hope this answers your question as to why we went to the province. As far as we're concerned it was his job.

JW: Mr. Berger, you'd been the counsel of *White and Bob*. And you had the reasons from Justice Norris that were quite promising. Were you on the lookout for a case that would put the question of Aboriginal title squarely before the courts?

Thomas Berger: Well, I had just started my own law practice and I really didn't have any clients, so I was on the lookout for any case. I can tell you that when I argued the *White and Bob* case in Nanaimo, which claimed that the old Douglas Treaties, which guaranteed Indian hunting rights, entitled them to hunt in or out of season, that's the case that went to the Supreme Court of Canada where they upheld the treaties. When I argued that case, Guy Williams, who Frank mentioned, was actually mother-henning that whole case along with the First Nations people at Nanaimo. We had two strings to our bow. I went to Nanaimo and talked to some of the Elders and they talked about this treaty, which, by the way, nobody had ever seen, and they also talked about Aboriginal title. So we worked out the argument, well, we've got a treaty. But if you say we don't have a treaty, well then our Aboriginal title still survives. It's never been extinguished. All of the judges all the way up to the Supreme Court of Canada dealt with it on the basis – did we have a treaty or not – and decided that we did. Justice Norris of the Court of Appeal decided we had a treaty, but then he wrote an extensive judgment about the history of Aboriginal title in English common law and that gave us a foothold, if you will, a purchase, to go on to the next step with a suitable case. Of course, there could not have been a more suitable First Nations group to bring the lawsuit than the Nisga'a because they had such a long tradition of insisting upon the fact that their rights to the land had never been extinguished. I should say that when the Nisga'a brought this lawsuit in the late sixties, my recollection is that all of the other First Nations in British Columbia said: "Don't do it. You'll lose and then we'll be dead. We won't have anything to talk about." I recall being at some meetings with Nisga'a leaders and other First Nations people in British Columbia where we were very much driven to the wall and people said: "Don't do this. You'll lose and then the federal government will say forget about it, we're through." Well the Nisga'a said: "That's pretty much the position anyway, so there can't be very much to lose." I was impressed at the time by the way by the Nisga'a leadership, because they always had statesmanlike leadership, and they said, no, this is our decision and we're going through with it.

JW: Did the provincial government take the claim seriously?

TB: Well, I don't think they did at first. You know, I went to law school in the mid-fifties. I was a little more than an articled student when Frank and I first met at Tom Hurley's office. But when I went to law school in the mid-fifties we never discussed, and the law teachers never discussed, Aboriginal rights and Aboriginal title. We never discussed Indians. It is remarkable today, many of you are students here, you have courses where they answer the question that must be present in your minds when you walk through the door, well, who did we get this province from? You know, who owned it before we came? Do they have any rights today? Those questions were never asked in law school in those days – not in any law school in the country. So, when I took this case on, as I said, I didn't have many clients, so I spent two or three months in the law library looking up the famous cases of Chief Justice John Marshall of the United States, even more recent cases in other parts of the Commonwealth, and I realized there was a body of law we could draw upon and that there was a sound argument, I believed, that Aboriginal title in British Columbia had never been extinguished. The senior counsel for the government of British Columbia was Douglas McKay Brown, who was the leading civil litigator in the province at that time. He stood at the head of the profession and his junior, if you will, was a veteran lawyer in the A.G.'s [attorney general's] ministry, Bill Hobbs. I spent a lot of time with both of them, and I can remember that we had a meeting to talk about how we were going to put all of this together. Doug Brown didn't take it altogether seriously, and I'm not blaming him for that. Nobody in the profession did. But Bill Hobbs did. And he said: "We realize there is an argument here and we've got to meet it, and we were going through the pleadings, that is, formal allegations made by the Nisga'a Tribal Council about the history of the Nass Valley." And we said: "The Nisga'a have lived there since time immemorial. They've used, developed and occupied the land. That is something of course you have to establish to argue Aboriginal title." I can still remember Doug Brown saying to Bill Hobbs: "Well is there any dispute about this?" And Bill Hobbs said: "Well, they've been there since time immemorial. They've used and occupied the land and they are still there." Doug Brown said: "Well, we'll admit that." In Aboriginal land claims cases today, that's two or three years of anthropological evidence and Elders and oral history, but they did the right thing. That's what the attorney general, representing Her Majesty, is supposed to do. If something ought to be admitted, it should be admitted, and Mr.

Brown's stature was such that he could say: "Right, we'll admit that." Some folks from the Department of Justice are here – they'll forgive me for saying this, but now it would have to go through a whole lot of committees and so forth and so on. The answer might well come back: "We can't take a chance on this, so let's have two or three years of testimony." That's why the *Calder* case took a week. Frank testified and the four chiefs from each of the villages in the Nass Valley testified. Of course, once we got to trial I think the trial judge took it seriously. He held against us, but he said, this case really must be considered on appeal. On appeal, it was dismissed again, but they began to take it more seriously and, of course, in the Supreme Court of Canada it was apparent that the judges regarded it as a case of historic importance. We spent five days at trial, five days in the Court of Appeal, and five days in the Supreme Court of Canada. I should say that it was apparent that Justice Hall was very interested. So were Justice Laskin, as he then was, and Justice Spence and Justice Judson. Of course Justice Hall and Justice Judson wrote the main judgments.

JW: Five days of testimony at trial in comparison to months of testimony in current Aboriginal title cases. Dr. Calder, what was it like testifying at trial, appearing in court, along with other leaders of the Nisga'a First Nation and speaking to the title?

FC: There is only one word that I could think of. With all of the years that our people, when they started this question way back, not too long after Canadian Confederation and right up to the time that they were ready to move, there is only one word that permeated in our whole Nisga'a nation and that was "confidence." Someone this morning showed me a picture of my back walking up to the Supreme Court of Canada. He says: "Gee, that's a beautiful picture of your back. What were you thinking about?" Well, that's the question you're asking me. Well, I was thinking, my God this is it. After all of these years, our people have struggled along. How could we feel so bad about this thing? We just had to have that word on behalf of all the people, some of them up in the happy hunting grounds. We've got to go in there with confidence that we're going to win it. And that was in my mind then. I had every confidence.

JW: That confidence must have been tested, because at the first levels the case was convincingly rejected. I was wondering whether the confidence ever wavered and whether there ever were concerns about the wisdom of bringing a case at this time?

FC: Well, we knew we were in a preliminary stage with the Supreme Court of British Columbia and at the appeal. We lost both but there was still the Big One and we had to go into that. Well, for God's sake! There was another picture of me, this time I'm walking down the stairs facing the

Frank Calder going up the steps of the Supreme Court of
Canada on 31 January 1973. *Courtesy of Tamaki Calder,
photographer unknown*

camera and I had a grin on my face – three to three. Of course, one guy
chickened out, you know.

JW: And the three to three – you didn't take that as a defeat?

FC: He refused to pass judgment. He was still yakking about this fiat business. So forget about that. But then the three-to-three decision that the
papers and everybody else, including some of Tom's colleagues, would
say: "Well, its three to three and you lost." We DID NOT lose. I didn't
want to win, I didn't tell Tom this, I didn't want to win, I didn't want to
lose. Well, forget about it! No ... but three to three, that was a major
victory. That's terrific! You see, we didn't establish the Indian reservations. Those guys that we faced in court, they did it. His colleagues set
up the reservations. To confine people inside that boundary, you have
to be on top of them. You're both in the gutter. Right? If somebody's
holding down that First Nation inside that reservation, somebody's got
to be on his back and that guy on his back is controlling the law books.
So the three-to-three decision meant that he had to get off my back and
we'd turn around and face each other and talk. That was the birth of
the negotiations, which in my book is the major number one victory of
the *Calder* case. Because that was the case that brought in negotiations
all over the world. That's a major victory – that three-to-three decision.

JW: Mr. Berger, your sense as the case progresses. Did you have the same confidence?

TB: Those were the Trudeau years. Prime Minister Trudeau towered over the political scene. He was a man of great intellect, and he had studied this question. He came to Vancouver in 1969, about the time we were in the Court of Appeal, and he was asked about it and he said: "As far as we're concerned Aboriginal rights is an historical 'might have been.' We have to do justice in our time. This meant we cannot recognize Aboriginal rights. It's an anomaly." When I argued the case in the Court of Appeal, I had the distinct feeling I was not succeeding because I can remember the judges saying: "Well, what is Aboriginal title?" They were raised in a legal culture where you had to have a document signed by a notary with seals on it and go to the Land Titles Office and there it is. And, of course, all of us hold title to our homes and businesses on that footing. I remember them saying: "Well what is Aboriginal title? Can you describe it?" I said: "Well it's held communally; it's alienable only to the Crown," and I had two other characteristics, I wish I could remember what they were, but I was doing my level best, and I said: "You don't have to determine all the features of Aboriginal title at this stage, but if I demonstrate that it's a concept known to the common law and

Senator Len Marchand, Frank Calder, Prime Minister Pierre Elliott Trudeau, and Eli Gosnell in Ottawa in 1973. *Courtesy of Tamaki Calder, photographer unknown*

that it was never extinguished in our province, that's the declaration the Nisga'a are seeking." If you've read the judgment of the Court of Appeal, you know we got nowhere. They thought this was, I shouldn't say fantasyland, but they just couldn't take it on board. In the Supreme Court of Canada, I remember Don Rosenbloom came with me as junior counsel, Don is here today, and I remember we were struck after the first day at how seriously the Supreme Court of Canada was taking the case. We thought, my gosh, they're listening to us. They want to sort this thing out. When the three-to-three judgment came down, as far as Prime Minister Trudeau was concerned, it obliged him to set up negotiations with the Nisga'a and begin comprehensive claims negotiations for non-treaty First Nations all over the country, because, of course, the way he read them was this: "Well, three of them, in a powerful judgment by Justice Emmett Hall, say that Aboriginal title has not been extinguished. Well, if that's right we have to sit down and negotiate with these folks." And then he said: "But if Justice Judson who wrote for the other three is right, he says, well, they had Aboriginal title. It was a concept well known to the law and we extinguished it without compensation. So, if he's right we have to sit down and negotiate." So, in a way, Frank's thesis about three to three [was correct], and I am not absolutely certain he knew it would turn out that way. It worked out well, and it was marvelous at the time to realize that this idea had taken root, finally. The judgment of Justice Emmett Hall is an historic piece of work. I should tell you that when Frank and I were at the University of Saskatchewan Law School in Saskatoon, for the twentieth-year anniversary [in 1993], Justice Emmett Hall, who was retired and living in Saskatoon, was also there. We're missing him today, but he was a great figure in Canadian law.

JW: Shortly after the judgment, you had a meeting with the prime minister, with Prime Minister Trudeau, and with the person who is now prime minister, Jean Chrétien, and we've got a lovely picture in the brochure of that meeting between you and Trudeau and Chrétien. What was the content of that meeting?

FC: I think Trudeau had to appear on television and this is where he made the commitment. He told us what he would be saying, that after talking to Tom and all the rest of our delegation that he decided that the government was going to open the door for negotiations. Like I say, that was part of the major victory of the decision. And that was the content of that meeting. And, of course, the picture shows us laughing, the three of us, well I was telling a joke. But anyway, seriously, we knew what he would be talking about, and we were very happy that day, that he committed himself, the government, and the people of Canada and that they were going to proceed with negotiations.

Frank Calder, Minister of Indian Affairs and Northern Development Jean Chrétien, and Prime Minister Pierre Elliot Trudeau in Ottawa in 1973, following the delivery of the Supreme Court of Canada decision. *Courtesy of Indian and Northern Affairs Canada, photographer unknown*

JW: You both mentioned that the judgment was three to three, with Justice Pigeon deciding against the Nisga'a on the grounds that a fiat had not been obtained. My last question is why wasn't the fiat obtained? Was it requested?

TB: No, it wasn't requested. The policy of the government, some legal historians here may have a fresher recollection of this than I do, but I know I was very much concerned about our standing to sue. The policy of the government, though, was that where you were suing the estate of the Crown – that is, you wanted Crown land or Crown resources – they would not issue a fiat. They would in tort cases but not in contract and not in cases where you were trying to, the expression I think is, "impeach the estate of the Crown." My argument was: "We're not impeaching the estate of the Crown. All we want is a declaration. We're not asking for damages. We're not asking for an order that you deliver the Nass Valley to us by five o'clock on Thursday. We just want a declaration that our Aboriginal title has never been extinguished, so we aren't caught by this fiat rule." But Justice Pigeon was off and running with this and decided that we were impeaching the estate of the Crown and, therefore, we should have obtained a fiat. The policy of the government was not to issue a fiat in those circumstances. That's my recollection. I know I spent a lot of time figuring out how to answer the question: "Are we impeaching the estate of the Crown?" I thought I had the answer and it turns out I didn't, but it didn't matter anyway.

JW: Fiat is the short form for the reference to the terms in which the attorney general would endorse the writ in order to permit the suit to proceed. The Latin expression is *fiat justitia* and, in fact, the motto of this conference, "Let Right Be Done," is a translation of the terms that would have been inscribed upon the writ had a fiat been issued. Now it's the audience's opportunity to ask questions. Any questions?

Question from the floor: I just wondered if either lawyer or client have any speculation, or, better yet, knowledge, which you can share as to why the Supreme Court of Canada split as it did?

TB: It became apparent, I think, when we were arguing the case that Justices Hall, Spence, and Laskin were very sympathetic because Justice Hall, as was his wont, would question the lawyers from British Columbia: "What is your answer for this; what is your answer for that?" It was hard to read some of the other members of the Court, but, in the end, I think that we came out of it as well as we could have. I should tell you that when we were flying down to Ottawa from Vancouver, Don Rosenbloom and John Baigent, who were with me, were flying economy and Doug Brown and Bill Hobbs were flying first class, and they came back to say hi to us and to join us in a delightful snack of crackers and cheese. There were nine judges on the Court, and Chief Justice Fauteux – there had been a death in his family – so he wasn't going to sit. So Doug Brown, who knew about all of these things that we, in economy, didn't, said to me: "Justice Hall isn't sitting and they're going to drop Justice Bora Laskin, the newest appointment, because he's the junior judge."[6] And I hope we didn't betray our alarm at this. He said, "Justice Hall isn't sitting because he's going to retire and he doesn't want to sit on a case where there might be reserved judgment for a period of time." And then he said: "So they're going to drop the junior judge which is Justice Laskin." So, we would have lost Emmett Hall and Bora Laskin, who were two of the judges that, in the end, decided in our favour. And we went to the home of the late Ken Lysyk, who was then teaching in Toronto, on our way to Ottawa for me to present the case to Ken and some law professors because they were all fairly interested. And we said: "We just had some terrible news. Hall is retiring and Laskin is going to be dropped because he's the junior judge." And one of the law professors said: "Well one of my students is the clerk to Emmett Hall. I'll phone him." And he came back and he said: "Well, the clerk says that Emmett Hall has postponed his retirement." So when we arrived in Ottawa, it turned out that Chief Justice Fauteux and Justice Abbott were not sitting, and anyone familiar with their judgments knows that was deliverance for us, because they were the least likely to have decided in our favour. I'm sure they would have gone off on this fiat.

Comment from the floor by Don Rosenbloom: If I can just fill in a few little gaps. The first point I want to make is to those of you who haven't had the opportunity to read the judgments from the Court. It is a fascinating and rich history of the pursuit of this issue by the Nishga Tribal Council, and when I joined Tom's firm as an articling student I had one of the more fascinating experiences in terms of articling. Where most of my colleagues were over at the Land Registry filing documents, I was doing anthropological work in support of establishing the principle of time immemorial occupation – that the Nisga'a had, in fact, occupied the Nass Valley since time immemorial. As Tom appropriately reports to you, the end of my work, leading towards the Court house steps, was when the Crown decided to concede that issue and acknowledge that there had been time immemorial occupation. So all of my research over my year of articling went poof, like that, but we celebrated for reasons that have already been made clear to you. However, I invite you all to read the judgments if you haven't had the opportunity, because in the judgments of Justice Hall and the other side, they give excerpts of transcripts of testimony given by the Nisga'a chiefs at the Royal Commission inquiries both in 1887, if my memory's right, and in 1913, where the Nisga'a asserted their ownership and testified and there were translators brought into the Nass Valley to have the testimony put into transcript form, where they asserted title and gave the history of why they took the position that they continue to own the land. Another brief point to make with you is that it has always fascinated me and hasn't been mentioned at this point that the Nisga'a retained a legal firm in 1912, and Frank will correct me, [it was] a firm in London, England, known as Fox and Preece, Fifteen Dean's Yard, Westminster Southwest. And this firm was retained by the Nisga'a, who were living in total isolation up in the Nass Valley at that point, to prepare a document that became known as the Nisga'a Petition of 1913 and was filed with royalty in England at that time.[7] It is a beautiful document in terms of those of you that enjoy legalese, where it basically establishes the Nisga'a's claim to the Nass Valley and seeks the intervention of the British Crown against the Canadian government to pursue the justice of the claim in kind. So those of you who haven't read the judgment, you may be very, very interested in a lot of the historical information. As Tom said early on, the Nisga'a were a very appropriate First Nation to take this lead case because they had been living in total isolation. There was very little third party alienation within the Nass Valley, so if the Court of Appeal and the Supreme Court of British Columbia were in fear of the consequences of this case, at least we had an easier time of it with the Nisga'a case as opposed to certain other First Nations, for example, more urban communities such as the Musqueam or Squamish, because we had so little third party alienation in that area. It was fascinating that a community so isolated would retain a law firm and have the progressive initiative to seek a petition and have it served on the British Crown, and it's called the Nisga'a Petition and was cited by Tom and by legal counsel during the case as it went through the Court of Appeal and the Supreme Court of Canada.

JW: This is, of course, Don Rosenbloom who was junior counsel to Tom Berger throughout the *Calder* litigation. Do you have anything to add about the case and about the traditions within the Nisga'a nation of asserting the title and of not letting the title rest?

FC: Yes, I would like to bring up something. I don't know if it is in the minds of the people. Meeting after meeting in all these years, it never did come up. But I'll bring it up. Where did the money come from? Well, I'm going to tell you. When the Nass River people started this movement way back even before the reservation stuff, when they decided that they were going to make a move towards this case, our people started to dig into their pockets. I just want to leave word with you that we never accepted any money from anybody, especially from the governments. It was the Nisga'a's own pocket money that took us almost eighty years to go into court. Don't ever ask me what we paid – I was president – what we paid Tom Berger. We paid him a pittance. He practically did it for nothing compared to what we pay lawyers today. But we footed that bill ourselves and I want to point that out because in all of the meetings all these years ever since I was young – and, today, I am eighty-eight – nobody has ever asked me the question, who paid the bill? We did. Every cent of it. We did receive, only once, a donation from the Anglican Church. I was not only president but I handled the money end of it, so we didn't use that particular money for this case. It was the Nass River people's very own money right from the start to the end. We didn't accept any donation from anybody. It was from our pockets and that's a story in itself. When you look at it today, you've got to go and beg for money from somebody else to fight your case. We did not and this I wanted to leave with the people here.

TB: Could I add a footnote to what Don said? The trial only took a week. Of course, Frank and the four chiefs of the villages testified, and we put in the historical evidence. After Frank's forbearers chased off the surveyors with muskets in the 1880s, there was the Royal Commission sent up to the Nass Valley and the Nisga'a people testified and that is preserved, and we read much of that into the record and, as Don said, the judges of the Supreme Court of Canada were very impressed and included excerpts in their judgments. There was another Royal Commission that went to the Nass Valley around 1913, and there was further testimony that shows the continuity of the assertion of Aboriginal title. I should just mention one other thing, that an anthropologist named Wilson Duff testified in the *White and Bob* case in Nanaimo and then he testified in the *Calder* case. His evidence was very, very helpful. I think he was the first anthropologist to use his expertise in aid of the assertion of Aboriginal rights in this province or anywhere else in the country and his contribution shouldn't be overlooked.

Question from the floor: I was very struck by the fact that the Nisga'a were suing the provincial government and opened negotiations with the federal government and was wondering what the province's reaction was in the aftermath of the case, knowing that they didn't admit that they needed to sit at the table until 1990. But in the immediate aftermath of the case, the party that the Nisga'a were suing, how did they respond to the decision?

TB: The suit was brought against the province because Aboriginal title, not to put too fine a point on it, is a burden on the underlying title of the Crown, which was held by the province. So it was appropriate to sue the province. But, of course, the responsibility for settling land claims lies with the federal government. I think it is fair to say that all of the governments in British Columbia until 1990, Liberal, Conservative, Social Credit, and NDP had refused to recognize Aboriginal title and had refused to negotiate. Now the Nisga'a negotiated with the federal government until 1990 and sorted out issues such as the fisheries, but it wasn't until 1990 that the province said, yes, we'll come to the table because, of course, if you are going to have land for the Nisga'a included in the settlement you have to have the landlord – the province – at the table, and they came in 1990.

JW: In fact, Dr. Calder, you were in the legislature at the time, so were in daily contact with the provincial government. What is your sense of how the province received the *Calder* decision?

FC: With your question and the gentleman's question, I'll have to bring up this, just where the province comes into the picture. Mind you, like I said earlier that the province controls the natural resources and that our number one interest is the land. The land and everything else is in the hands of the province. The reason why, sir, that things are very slow in moving today is because of the provincial government. They have the first and last say on natural resources, and they don't really want to sit on the tri-party negotiation and I'll tell you why. It is the province that said that private property shall not be on the table of negotiations and that statement still stands today. And what are those private properties? The mining areas, the forest areas, tree farm licenses, and whatnot: the big forest reserves all over the province; the mining reserves all over the province; the fishing reserves all over the province, the railway right-of-ways all over the country, the road right-of-ways, and the animal life areas. These are considered by the province to be private property, and they said, in no uncertain terms, that private property shall not be on the table in the negotiations. And now you know why it's almost endless, what they are negotiating on. Because the invader said it's his territory. Just to continue, we call it the Indian land claims. Let me tell you, Mr. Chairman, that there is no such thing as the First Nations land claims. There is no such thing as an Indian land claims. He's got nothing to claim, we own the territory. It should have been called "White land claims."

JW: That brings us to the end of this illuminating discussion with two people at the very centre of the struggle to establish, before the Canadian courts, the existence of Aboriginal title in contemporary Canadian law. I ask you to thank Dr. Frank Calder and Mr. Thomas Berger.

Applause.

3
Reminiscences of Aboriginal Rights at the Time of the *Calder* Case and Its Aftermath
Honourable Gérard V. La Forest

When I was approached to give this talk, I suggested that it should be in the nature of reminiscences rather than what the French refer to as a scientific study. My reasons for this decision were as follows. We are celebrating at this conference one of the landmark cases in Canadian constitutional law, specifically the most important case governing Canada's relationship with its Aboriginal people. And it occurred to me that it would help you to fully understand how momentous a change the case effected if you were able to see it through the eyes of a then young scholar who a few years later would become a senior public servant with the federal government and play a central role in devising government policy following the decision in *Calder et al. v. Attorney-General of British Columbia*.[1]

Things were very different before this case. There was not even a passing reference to Aboriginal title when I attended law school in the late 1940s – a far cry from the situation today where every law school in Canada gives considerable attention to the subject. I first became familiar with the concept in 1962 when I was a law professor at the University of New Brunswick. I had been invited to give a course at the doctoral level at the newly established Institut de recherche en droit public at the Université de Montréal (which is now the Centre de recherche en droit public). The course could be on any constitutional law subject of my choosing, so I decided on natural resources and public property under the Canadian constitution, a subject that, though a major pillar of Canadian federalism, had largely been neglected by academics. It was when slogging away at these lectures during the summer of 1962 that I first became familiar with the concept of Aboriginal rights. Should you think my education had been neglected at the University of New Brunswick, I would point out that to find anything useful of a scholarly nature on this question I had to go nearly fifty years back to Clement's book on the constitution, the last edition of which was published in 1916.[2]

Nor was there much judicial authority in more recent years. The defining cases, for example, *St. Catherine's Milling & Lumber Co. v. R.*,[3] for the most part dated from the latter part of the nineteenth century. Interestingly, while these cases considered the legal character of Aboriginal title, the litigation really involved the rights and obligations of the federal government and the provinces or their grantees. They did establish, however, that Aboriginal rights were protected from provincial intrusion as a "trust" under section 109 of the *Constitution Act, 1867*.[4] As to the federal government, it could, absent legislation, dispose of Aboriginal lands only if the Aboriginals surrendered them. Compensation was paid on surrender, but whether this arose out of a legal, as opposed to a political, duty was an open question.

These early cases related solely to lands directly set aside for the Indians under the Royal Proclamation of 1763. Probably as a result of this, I assumed that some specific grant must have been made to create Indian title. Of course, the proclamation covered an extensive territory extending beyond Ontario to parts of the Prairie provinces. And, as I saw it, provisions in several other constitutional documents, such as the transfer of Rupert's Land and the Hudson's Bay territory, as well as boundary extension provisions and provincial Terms of Union,[5] made it clear that Indian title also extended to other areas, including northern Québec and Ontario, parts of the Prairie provinces, and probably British Columbia. As a result of the widely different treaty and statutory background in the Atlantic provinces, the situation was by no means clear there.

Those of you who are not immersed in the subject may be wondering why, in all of the time since the early cases I have mentioned, there had been no case, at least of any significance, where Aboriginals were directly involved. One might speculate that there was no need to do so in earlier times and that it took some time for Aboriginals to become accustomed to the newcomers' governmental and legal processes. But there was far more to it than that. The absence of claims was not owing to a lack of interest or complacency by the Aboriginals or the groups that supported them. There were serious roadblocks at the judicial, administrative, and legislative levels. There was judicial support for the view that the Aboriginals were wards of the Crown and that, consequently, only the Crown could bring action on their behalf. That, on the administrative level, was the position taken by the Department of Indian Affairs. As a practical matter, the Aboriginals could not easily initiate legal proceedings because there was a provision in the *Indian Act* prohibiting Indians from raising funds to prosecute claims.[6]

Still, between the time I gave my lectures in 1962 and 1969 when they were published,[7] a number of cases, such as *R. v. Sikyea* and *R. v. White and Bob*,[8] indicated that Aboriginal land claims were far from dead. This fact, however, appears to have been lost on the federal government. The low point was reached when, as a result of a general review of Aboriginal policy in 1968-69, the government issued a white paper proposing the phasing out of all legal distinctions between Aboriginals and other Canadians.[9] In particular, it described Aboriginal rights as being so general and undefined that it was not realistic to think of them as capable of remedy except through a policy or program that would end in justice to them.

This was, then, in broad terms, the situation when *Calder* was decided.[10] As you know, the Supreme Court of Canada, by a four-to-three margin, dismissed the Aboriginals' case on procedural grounds. But it was the kind of situation where one loses the battle but wins the war. Six of the judges recognized the validity of land claims until their extinguishment (and this in the absence of any grant from the Crown) – Justice Wilfred Judson, for three of the justices, on the simple ground that when the Europeans came to this country, the Aboriginals were already settled here, living in societies, and Justice Emmett Hall, for three others, on the basis of *Campbell v. Hall*,[11] which held that when the Crown takes possession of another country, the laws and property of the inhabitants remain until extinguished. Justice Hall added that the Royal Proclamation followed the flag.

The substantial difference between Justices Judson and Hall was that the former was of the view that the extent to which the land had been regulated before Confederation constituted an extinguishment of the right, while the latter held that any extinguishment had to be "clear and plain" and that compensation was legally required on surrender.[12] Though I have some reservations about Justice Hall's ground regarding the Royal Proclamation of 1763, except as a way of saying that other claims are similar, I think he was manifestly right on the ground that Aboriginal land rights (which are in their nature proprietary) require clear terms for their extinguishment. As an aside, I should say that in 1983 I adopted Justice Hall's view for the New Brunswick Court of Appeal in *Canadian Pacific Ltd. v. Paul*, but other cases disagreed, and the Supreme Court of Canada left the issue open until *R. v. Sparrow* in 1990 when it, too, adopted it.[13]

Shortly after *Calder* was decided, the federal government began to reconsider its options. I was then serving my second stint at the Department of Justice in Ottawa. I had returned in late 1970 but had not until then been engaged in Aboriginal land claims. My involvement came about in this way. Shortly after the judgment was released on 31 January 1973, I and several of the senior departmental officers were in then minister Otto Lang's office, discussing a variety of issues of concern to him. At some stage, the issue of *Calder* came up, and, in the course of the discussion, I volunteered the view that we should recognize the claim. I was soon to find that I was probably the only one of the officials in that room to be of that opinion. I later learned that that was not the opinion of the department, and I heard nothing further about the matter for approximately two months. On 31 March, however, a new deputy minister of Justice, Donald Thorson, was appointed, and, almost immediately afterwards, I was given the file on the matter and asked to devise policy regarding the stance the government should take on the issues. I was given no other instructions.

Since I was already fully immersed in the subject, I was within days able to produce, on the basis of the legal implications of the decision, a draft position recommending an overall policy of acceptance of Aboriginal title throughout the country wherever it could be established. Other policy options might well have been pursued by the government. It could, for example, have ignored Justice Hall's reasons on the basis that Justice Judson's view was consistent with previous authorities. But this posed important difficulties. The Aboriginal claims relating to the James Bay project in Québec were then before the courts, and these were buttressed by constitutional documents. The case might therefore well have gone in favour of the Aboriginals, as, in fact, it ultimately did. I have been told that notes by my students at the Montreal lectures had proved helpful in framing the Aboriginals' case.[14] A little later, Justice William Morrow also recognized Aboriginal title in the Northwest Territories.[15] Another factor was that ignoring the Hall judgment would have been bitterly resented by the Aboriginals – the unrest that was already present being underlined not long afterwards when a number of Aboriginals took over the headquarters of the Department of Indian Affairs. By then, I had prepared a Cabinet document on the basis of the views I had expressed.

Not surprisingly, in light of the virtually unanimous contrary views of my colleagues, I had some passing concerns about the advice I was giving the government. However, I need not have worried. Unknown to me at the time, and, indeed, until quite recently, Prime Minister Pierre Trudeau had begun to modify his views after reading Justice Hall's minority reasons and on 7 February had advised Frank Calder of this change and promised to enter negotiations. It is not beside the point to add that the government was then in a minority position, and the opposition parties were both in favour of negotiations.

Aboriginal policy was, of course, primarily within the jurisdiction of the Department of Indian Affairs, which also favoured the settlement of all Aboriginal claims, not only comprehensive claims like *Calder* but specific claims as well. There followed extensive consultations between both departments at all levels as well as with the minister, and I found myself effectively in the position of being the principal advisor to both departments on the matter. I remember, for example, that it was at my suggestion that a special structure was established to deal with specific claims. I was then asked to prepare a Cabinet document expressing the combined views of the two departments.

On 8 August 1973, the minister of Indian Affairs and Northern Development, Jean Chrétien, issued a statement signifying the government's recognition and acceptance of the continuing constitutional responsibility of the government for Indians and lands reserved for the Indians and stating that, whatever differences there might be about judicial interpretation, an historic evolution dating back to the Royal Proclamation of 1763 stood as a basic declaration of the Indian people's interest in land in this country.[16] The statement went on for the first time to express the government's willingness to negotiate regarding claims of Aboriginal title wherever it could be established. In particular, it indicated the government's willingness to negotiate claims of Aboriginal title specifically in northern Québec, the Northwest Territories, and British Columbia. It had already agreed to negotiate in the Yukon, an activity in which I was one of the original members of the federal negotiating team. The situations in Québec and the Atlantic provinces were looked upon as being of a different character, and the government was providing money to enable the Aboriginals to undertake the necessary research. So far as specific claims were concerned, the government undertook to fulfil its lawful obligations without regard to such defences as statutes of limitations.

The policy was essentially the genesis of the specific and comprehensive land claims policy, which largely continues to this day. It was the *Calder* case that acted as the catalyst for these momentous changes in government attitude. It soon bore fruit for Aboriginals in other parts of Canada. In 1974, the Québec government entered into an agreement with the Cree regarding the James Bay development – the first modern settlement of Aboriginal claims.[17] I take considerable satisfaction in the behind-the-scene role I played in the development of the new attitude towards Aboriginals rights in this country.

Part 2
Historical Background

4

We Are Not O'Meara's Children: Law, Lawyers, and the First Campaign for Aboriginal Title in British Columbia, 1908–28

Hamar Foster

> "We feel ... that we have treated you rather unfairly. It seems history is to blame."
>
> – James Joyce, *Ulysses*

Since the decision of the Supreme Court of Canada in *Calder et al. v. Attorney-General of British Columbia* more than thirty years ago, a decision whose thirtieth anniversary we are commemorating with this volume, Aboriginal title has become an issue of increasing importance.[1] Today, for example, most Canadians are aware that the courts have played a continuing and critical role in confirming that such title is a legal right, which, once established by litigation or treaty, is protected by the constitution.[2] Many are also aware that the title issue is especially acute in British Columbia, where – apart from a few treaties on Vancouver Island during the colonial period – most of the land has never been surrendered to the Crown as originally contemplated by the Royal Proclamation of 1763.[3]

What is less well known is that, fully a century ago, Aboriginal people in British Columbia translated their long-standing demand for recognition of their rights into a twenty-year campaign to have the "land question" referred to the courts. They did so because the provincial government consistently refused to acknowledge even the possibility of Aboriginal title and was adamant that its position not be tested in the courts. Since the dominion – notwithstanding its trust-like obligations to Canada's Aboriginal peoples – was ultimately unwilling to force the issue, this campaign failed, and the province won the day. Until, of course, the matter was resurrected decades later.[4]

This chapter is an account of some of the moves and counter-moves in the campaign for Aboriginal title that ended in 1928, which I have chosen to call the first legal campaign. The second legal campaign may be regarded as beginning in the 1950s, after some of the obstacles to litigating Aboriginal title had been removed and the Nishga Tribal Council was established.[5] It really got rolling in the 1960s, when lawyers discovered the Douglas Treaties and when the petition in the *Calder* case was filed. Thomas Berger, QC, played a central role. He was defence counsel in *R. v. White and Bob*, which established the importance of the Douglas Treaties, and counsel for the plaintiffs in *Calder*.[6] According to his client, Frank Calder, who was the lead plaintiff in the case that bears his name, the strategy they adopted in this second campaign was very much a revival of the one employed by his own father in the first. It was an appeal, guided by lawyers but directed by the Aboriginal clients, to what used to be called "British justice." And this appeal, not unlike the one that ended in 1928, was made necessary by the refusal of the provincial and, eventually, the federal government to settle the land question. This article is therefore also about those who, in the first legal campaign during the first quarter of the twentieth century, led the way.

I am being careful to refer to these campaigns as *legal* campaigns because, of course, the Aboriginal peoples of British Columbia did not suddenly decide they had title to their traditional territories in 1909.[7] In the nineteenth century, various First Nations, including the Nisga'a, objected to the local government's land policies, sending delegations to Victoria and even to Ottawa to protest what was happening to their lands and to their traditional way of life. To take but one example, the Cowichan of southern Vancouver Island have pressed their claims since at least 1862, when in all probability Governor James Douglas made a treaty with them that was subsequently broken.[8] However, the nineteenth-century tribal protesters, although they may have invoked the idea of justice and even occasionally divine or natural law, did not base their claims specifically on British law, nor did they seek redress in the courts. Theirs were instead simple pleas for fair treatment, sometimes – but not always – put into writing and presented to the authorities by local missionaries.[9]

Notwithstanding their lack of knowledge of the common law, what some of the early advocates of land rights had to say was legally accurate and quite compatible with British law. Listen, for example, to Nisga'a Charles Russ, speaking to a royal commission sent to the northwest coast to inquire into disturbances there in 1887. On this occasion, the commissioners, who had been instructed by the government "to discountenance, should it arise, any claim of Indian title," had rather patronizingly explained that the Queen owned all of the land.[10] The reaction of the chiefs was, at first, laughter. However, this changed quickly to astonishment and then to anger once it became clear that these fellows were actually serious. "We took the Queen's flag and laws to honour them," said Russ. "We never thought when we did that that she was taking the land away from us."[11]

What a wonderful thing to say. And it is of course a more accurate statement of the legal situation than anything that fell from the commissioners or the politicians who appointed them.[12] Even in 1887, British imperial law had long distinguished between sovereignty over territory, which the courts have said that Great Britain obtained over British Columbia by virtue of the Treaty of Washington in 1846, and ownership of land within that territory.[13] But whether the treaty established British sovereignty or not – and in the twenty-first century this conclusion is unlikely to be successfully challenged – Russ was correct. Even if the Nisga'a had acknowledged the sovereignty of Britain by accepting the Queen's flag and laws, it did not mean that the Queen had taken their land.[14] And if the Nisga'a and the Crown both claimed ownership of a particular piece of ground, it was a dispute that, as Prime Minister Wilfrid Laurier would say in 1911, should have been for the courts to settle.

By 1887, however, Aboriginal people had become a minority in British Columbia, separated internally by a host of different languages and cultures. They were, moreover, a politically and legally disadvantaged minority. They could not vote, stand for elected office, or pre-empt land as non-Aboriginal people could, and none of this would change until the mid-twentieth century. The reason for this disqualification was explained in an editorial in 1866. If Indians could vote, some "ten thousand whites would have to contend at the polls with fifty thousand painted, whisky-drinking 'red skin' voters ... peradventure to sit in a Legislature in which the savage element largely predominated."[15] Nor did Aboriginal people in nineteenth-century British Columbia have the means or the education to make a court challenge possible. Even if they had, such a challenge was hardly a realistic option. The Supreme Court of British Columbia was staffed by judges who were unsympathetic to the notion that Indians had land rights outside their reserves and unwilling to look deeply enough into the law to discover that their position was, at the very least, debatable.[16]

An equally formidable obstacle was the doctrine of sovereign immunity, which stipulated that the Crown could not be sued without permission. As a result, the issue of Indian title tended to arise only collaterally, either as a defence to a criminal charge or in a dispute where the issue was the validity of a purported sale of land by indigenous people to settlers. It was raised in this fashion only once in the courts of British Columbia before the *Calder* case, when Aboriginal title was put forward as a defence in a case involving trespass at Metlakatla in 1886.[17] The defence was quickly dismissed, and, of course, no appeal to the distant and impossibly expensive Judicial Committee of the Privy Council in London was taken. As a consequence, the 1887 commissioners' view of the law, which reflected that of the provincial government and of the vast majority of the settler population, prevailed.[18]

In what follows, I provide a very brief narrative of the two decades of activity comprising the early twentieth-century campaign, from the first petitions – and the earliest was probably sent in 1901 – to the hearing before the joint parliamentary committee that investigated the claims of the Allied Indian Tribes of British Columbia in 1927. I then discuss four strategies for getting this campaign into court, the obstacles that were in the way of these strategies, and the reasons why in each case the obstacles prevailed. Finally, I conclude with some remarks about how the lawyer who represented both the Nisga'a and the Allied Indian Tribes of British Columbia in those years has been treated by posterity.

Books, Barristers, and Boom Times

For at least three reasons, conditions more favourable to effective political and legal action developed once the twentieth century got under way. First of all, the future leaders of the campaign for title began to attend residential school, where they not only improved their English but also made contacts and became more aware of what non-Aboriginal society was all about. Some took their education even further. Haida chief Peter Kelly, for example, went on to theological college, and Squamish leader Andy Paull apprenticed to a lawyer (although he was not called to the bar because, as an Indian, he could not vote).[19] Both men were soon focusing their newly acquired skills on learning about Aboriginal land rights under British law, and, by 1916, Kelly would be chairman and Paull would be secretary of the Allied Indian Tribes of British Columbia. Second, by 1903 a decade-long economic boom was beginning, which conveyed a very explicit message to Aboriginal people. This message was that, while some of them would benefit from the economic activity engendered by the boom, many would not and that without clearly articulated land rights much of their traditional territories would be expropriated or despoiled.[20] Third, the intensifying protests by Aboriginal people against these incursions into their lands attracted, for the first time, the attention of a very small number of sympathetic lawyers. Indeed, by June 1910, a newspaper was describing the Nisga'a, who had retained "eminent" counsel, as "defending their claim with white man's law and logic in a manner that would do credit to a Philadelphia lawyer."[21]

The photographs taken by a North Vancouver photographer record the changes wrought by increasing economic activity and even, in one instance, the Aboriginal reaction to it. They were collected in 1981 and published as *The Boom Years: G.G. Nye's Photographs of North Vancouver, 1905-1909.*[22] In the middle of this book, amid all the pictures of new construction and cleared land, is a photograph taken around 1906 of a middle-aged man in a fur hat and fringed coat. The man is Chief Joe Capilano, and, as the accompanying text notes, by the time he died in 1910 "many of his people's traditional lifestyles had been altered" by development and the land around their

Chief Joe Capilano, c. 1906. Superintendent F.S. Hussey of the BC Provincial Police regarded him as a "dangerous man" and wanted him arrested for his land claims activities. *Photograph by G.G. Nye, courtesy of the North Shore Museum and Archives, NVMA 2849*

villages "was rapidly being settled." Nye chose his subject wisely because Chief Capilano was a central figure in the "agitation" that began shortly after the turn of the century. By 1908, the authorities were even considering arresting him.[23] Certainly, it would have been an easy thing to do. At the time, the *Criminal Code* provided that it was an offence to incite or "stir up" Indians to riotous or disorderly behaviour. Indeed, it was even an offence to incite them "to make any request or demand of government in a disorderly manner."[24]

The Nisga'a Land Committee, c. 1913. Original caption: "British Subjects Seeking British Justice." *Courtesy of Tamaki Calder, photographer unknown*

Capilano, like Andy Paull, was Squamish, which is a division of the Coast Salish peoples, who with other Interior and Coast Salish First Nations were very active in sending delegations to the pope in 1903, to King Edward VII in 1906, and to Ottawa in 1908.[25] At about the same time, the Nisga'a, notably men such as Frank Barton and Arthur Calder, were moving towards setting up the Nisga'a Land Committee, an organization that would be re-established as the Nishga Tribal Council fifty years later. This activity – or "agitation," as the government tended to call it – was prompted by economic development, not just in the south but also in the remoter regions to the north and especially in the valleys of the Nass, Skeena, and Bulkley Rivers. Indeed, so determined was the Aboriginal opposition to the land grants on the Skeena that violence ensued. Aboriginal people were forcibly dispossessed, and, on occasion, they forcibly responded. These incidents, coupled with an abortive attempt in 1908 by the BC government to have the provincial courts affirm its view of its proprietary rights in Indian reserves, prompted two very different but equally significant initiatives.[26]

The Cowichan Petition and Its Aftermath

The first of these was the filing of the Cowichan Petition in 1909.[27] This remarkable document was the first legally sophisticated articulation of the doctrine of Aboriginal title on behalf of Aboriginal people in British Columbia, by which I mean that it based the Cowichan claim squarely on British law. Although the initiative was Cowichan, two of the main movers were Charles M. Tate, a Protestant missionary then living among them, and Arthur Eugene O'Meara, who was in the process of relocating from the Yukon to

British Columbia.[28] O'Meara's father was an Anglican clergymen – his father had, in fact, been a prominent missionary to the Ojibwa – and so were all of his brothers. But O'Meara took to the law, practising in Ontario for twenty years before the lure of the "family business" became too great. Ordained a deacon in 1906, he left his practice behind and moved his family to the Yukon, where he became a missionary to the miners. This experience, it seemed, caused him to take an interest in the situation of the Aboriginal population. He was his father's son, after all. And when he discovered that the tribes in British Columbia were organizing to protect their rights in a more effective way than was the case in the Yukon, O'Meara moved south.[29]

The main source of legal expertise for the petition, however, was probably John Murray McShane Clark, KC, of Toronto, who was one of the most prominent barristers in the nation.[30] He was an expert in Aboriginal law who was to play an important role in the campaign, and he appears to have brought O'Meara up to speed.[31] In any event, these three, and particularly Clark and O'Meara, produced a document that Clark signed and that O'Meara conveyed to England and lodged with the Colonial Office. Then, in 1910, Clark drafted and submitted his "Statement of Facts and Claims on Behalf of the Indians of British Columbia."[32] This statement, together with the Cowichan Petition, set the terms of a legal debate that was not resolved until the Supreme Court of Canada handed down its decision in *Delgamuukw v. British Columbia* eighty-seven years later.[33] Yet neither the statement nor the Cowichan Petition is well known today. Nor are they mentioned in *Delgamuukw*, a decision that, for all its importance, can give one the very mistaken impression that Aboriginal title is a recent legal development.[34]

The second initiative was related to the first. In the spring of 1909, when O'Meara was in England with the Cowichan Petition, the dominion government retained lawyer T.R.E. (Tom) McInnes to provide a legal opinion on whether land claims had any substance. McInnes reported in August and did not mince words. He was sharply critical of BC government policy since the 1860s and said that, in his view, there was clearly land in British Columbia outside the recognized reserves that was subject to unextinguished Aboriginal title. He also advised the dominion government that, as trustee for the Indians of the province, it was under an obligation to put forward the legal case on their behalf.[35] This one-hundred-page opinion is also virtually unknown today, but McInnes's advice was taken seriously. When Prime Minister Laurier met with a delegation composed of the Friends of the Indians of British Columbia and the Moral and Social Reform Council of Canada in April 1911, he made this clear. The provincial government, he said, might be "right or wrong in their assertion that the Indians have no claim whatsoever. Courts of law are just for that purpose – where a man asserts a claim and it is denied by another." He added that the dominion was unsure whether it could force British Columbia into court, but, at the time, it was an understandable concern.[36] The provinces were challenging Ottawa's authority to refer questions affecting provincial jurisdiction to the Supreme Court of Canada, and, although this Court had dismissed their challenge, the provinces' appeal to the Judicial Committee of the Privy Council was not scheduled to be heard until December (and, indeed, the decision was not handed down until May 1912).[37] Although the legal situation was therefore unclear, Laurier assured the delegation that "[i]f we can find a way I may say we shall surely do so."[38]

In making this statement, Laurier appears to have been sincere because after an attempt in 1910 to refer the claim to the Supreme Court of Canada failed due to the provincial government's refusal to cooperate, the dominion enacted legislation designed to force British Columbia into court.[39] Laurier also had some support in the media. The *Prince Rupert News*, for example, was a paper in the heart of the northwest coast land claims area, and it described Conservative premier Richard McBride's refusal to allow the Indians to go to court as "a policy worthy only of a set of claim jumpers." The editors – Liberals, no doubt – also speculated that McBride's position may have been influenced by the fact that Indians could not vote.[40] Before anything further could be done, however, Laurier called an election, and, by September 1911, there was a new, Conservative government in Ottawa and a new prime minister, Robert Borden. Although it seemed at first that the new administration, like Laurier's, might be willing to seek a judicial solution, these hopes were quickly dispelled. Borden, who tried to persuade McBride to leave provincial politics and join the new dominion government, was unwilling to offend British Columbia even though his solicitation of McBride was unsuccessful. Accordingly, less than a year after the election the two Conservative administrations reached a compromise on Indian lands – the McKenna-McBride Agreement of 1912 – that was designed to avoid litigation. Instead, the Aboriginal title question would be set aside, and a joint dominion-provincial commission would be established whose mandate, rather like that of the commission in 1887, was confined to adjusting the size of Indian reserves.[41]

One result of this change in circumstance was the Nisga'a Petition of 1913 (see Appendix B herein), a document very like the earlier Cowichan Petition.[42] Three years later, a number of organizations coalesced into the Allied Indian Tribes of British Columbia, primarily to protest the mandate of the McKenna-McBride Commission, which was established pursuant to the 1912 agreement. However, the historical moment had passed. Although years of "agitation" ensued, the Aboriginal title question would not get to the courts until the *Calder* litigation in the 1960s. It is true that in 1914, 1918, and on a couple of occasions in the 1920s a resolution of what, since the 1870s, had been known as the British Columbia Indian land question appeared to be, if not exactly imminent, at least within reach. But once the two governments had agreed, more or less, on how the McKenna-McBride Commission's report would be implemented, Ottawa's commitment to resolving the matter of Aboriginal title on its own quickly flagged.

By 1927, the dominion government had had enough. As it had done in 1875 when it agreed to establish the very first Indian reserve commission and, again in 1912, when it signed the McKenna-McBride Agreement,

PRIVY COUNCIL OFFICE
REG: 21 MAY 1913
N. 111098

IN THE MATTER OF THE TERRITORY OF THE NISHGA NATION OR TRIBE OF INDIANS.

TO THE KING'S MOST EXCELLENT MAJESTY IN COUNCIL.

The HUMBLE PETITION of The Nishga Nation or Tribe of Indians

SHEWETH AS FOLLOWS :—

1. From time immemorial the said Nation or Tribe of Indians exclusively possessed, occupied and used and exercised sovereignty over that portion of the territory now forming the Province of British Columbia which is included within the following limits, that is to say :—Commencing at a stone situate on the south shore of Kinnamox or Quinamass Bay and marking the boundary line between the territory of the said Nishga Nation or Tribe and that of the Tsimpshean Nation or Tribe of Indians, running thence easterly along said boundary line to the height of land lying between the Naas River and the Skeena River, thence in a line following the height of land surround-
10 ing the valley of the Naas River and its tributaries to and including the height of land surrounding the north-west end of Mitseah or Meziadan Lake, thence in a straight line to the northerly end of Portland Canal, thence southerly along the international boundary to the centre line of the passage between Pearse Island and Wales Island, thence south-easterly along said centre line to the centre line of Portland Inlet, thence north-easterly along said centre line to the point at which the same is intersected by the centre line of Kinnamox or Quinamass Bay, thence in a straight line to the point of commencement.

2. Your Petitioners believe the fact to be that, when sovereignty
20 over the territory included within the aforesaid limits (hereinafter referred to as " the said territory ") was assumed by Great Britain, such sovereignty was accepted by the said Nation or Tribe, and the right of the said Nation or Tribe to possess, occupy and use the said territory was recognised by Great Britain.
18   V. & S., Ltd.—36591.   ▲

Page 1 of the Nisga'a Petition, 1913. (The full text is reproduced in Appendix B.)
Courtesy of the Public Record Office, Kew, England

Ottawa took Aboriginal title off the table. It did this, first, by amending the *Indian Act* to provide, in section 141, that it was an offence for anyone to raise money from any Indian or Indians for the purpose of prosecuting any claim against government unless the minister's permission had first been obtained.[43] And, shortly thereafter, a parliamentary joint committee – not a court of law, but a committee – decided that there was no unextinguished Aboriginal title in British Columbia. Judging by what many Aboriginal Elders remember section 141 prohibiting, it is clear that some Indian agents and missionaries gave it an extremely wide interpretation. Yet, misinterpreted or not, section 141 and the findings of the 1927 joint committee put an end to the first campaign for title. Land claims talk therefore went "underground" in the late 1920s and more or less stayed there until the prohibition on hiring lawyers for such claims was dropped from the revised *Indian Act* in 1951.[44]

Four Strategies for Getting into Court
Between 1910 and 1927, the Interior Tribes, the Indian Rights Association, the Allied Indian Tribes of British Columbia, the Friends of the Indians of British Columbia, and the Nisga'a all worked – not always in harmony – to resolve the BC Indian land question.[45] However, given the intransigence of the province and the inconstancy of the dominion, it soon became clear that only the courts could resolve the matter – or at least move it forward. The problem was getting into court, and it was no small problem. There were, at most, four possible courses of action, none of which was straightforward.

An Aboriginal Lawsuit
The first was an Aboriginal lawsuit against the Crown in right of the province, which, in legal theory, held the "underlying" title to all land in British Columbia and was therefore the appropriate defendant. There were at least two serious problems with this strategy, however. The first was resources. Title to most of British Columbia, then as now, was a matter that, if unresolved through negotiations, would have to be decided by the highest tribunal – in other words, the Judicial Committee of the Privy Council in England. If the Nisga'a or the Allied Indian Tribes of British Columbia were to go it alone, they would have to raise a great deal of money in order to argue their case through three and probably four levels of court.[46] Money was raised – dollar by dollar, from individuals and tribes who had little if any to spare – but not enough to finance a case such as this. Even if sufficient funds could be raised, there was another, even more formidable, obstacle: the Crown's sovereign immunity from suit. No one, whether Aboriginal or not, could sue the Crown without first obtaining the Crown's permission to do so.

People today no doubt find this surprising. It is perhaps even more surprising that this was the law in British Columbia until 1974, too late for the *Calder* litigation.[47] However, the Crown usually granted persons who wished to sue permission to do so if there was some merit to the claim. The procedure was to file a "petition of right" that, if the attorney general approved, would be endorsed with the words: "Let right be done." This written permission to sue gave the courts jurisdiction to hear the case and was referred to as a "fiat" because in Latin the equivalent words were *fiat justicia*. However, the granting of a fiat was a matter of grace, not of right.[48] Just how gracious the government of British Columbia was prepared to be where questions of Aboriginal title were concerned is aptly summarized in a draft letter from Premier Richard McBride to Prime Minister Laurier in November 1910. A court decision in favour of the Indians, wrote McBride,

> would affect the title to all the land on the mainland ... and more than half of the land ... on Vancouver Island, and would have a most disastrous effect on our financial standing and would jeopardize the very large sums of money already invested in this province by English and other investors. I think you will agree with me that this is too serious a matter to be submitted to the determination of any court, *however competent from a legal point of view.* In other words, the considerations involved in this are *political considerations and not legal questions* ... The Government of British Columbia therefore cannot agree to submit to a determination even by the Privy Council [of] a question of policy of such importance.[49]

In other words, Indian claims should be regarded as a matter of policy and politics, not legal right, and under no circumstances would the provincial government be prepared to risk a court saying otherwise.

Given that the Judicial Committee of the Privy Council had said something important about Indian title in *St. Catherine's Milling & Lumber Co. v. R.* more than twenty years earlier, McBride's position was debatable, to say the least. In that case, the Judicial Committee had confirmed that Aboriginal title is "an interest other than that of the province" in the lands of the province, and Lord Watson had explained that the province's beneficial interest in such lands was available to it "as a source of revenue *whenever the estate of the crown is disencumbered of the Indian title.*"[50] Presumably, then, such title had to be extinguished, and the underlying provincial title thereby "disencumbered," before resource extraction and other forms of development could legally proceed. This process, of course, had not happened in most of British Columbia.

It is true that in 1925, towards the end of the campaign, the dominion minister responsible for Indian affairs told the House of Commons that he was willing to issue a fiat.[51] He may even have been sincere. But this seems doubtful. Although Ottawa was supposed to be the Indians' trustee, its offer did not include financial assistance, and neither the Nisga'a nor the Allied Indian Tribes of British Columbia could afford to engage in such expensive litigation on their own. More importantly, whether the land at issue was subject to unextinguished title or not, the underlying title was not in the Crown in right of Canada but in the Crown in right of British Columbia. A dominion fiat was therefore irrelevant.[52] Indeed, fifty years later, the Nisga'a technically lost the *Calder* case – to which Ottawa was not even a party – because they did not have a fiat from British Columbia authorizing the suit. The Supreme Court of Canada ruled in *Calder* that, even though counsel for the Nisga'a had asked for no remedy other than a declaration as to whether their title to their traditional lands still existed, a fiat was required because such a declaration would directly affect the land rights of the Crown in that province.[53] As Justice Louis-Philippe Pigeon put it, the courts had no jurisdiction to make the declaration requested without a provincial fiat. He added:

> I am deeply conscious of the hardship involved in holding that the access to the Court for the determination of the plaintiffs' claim is barred by sovereign immunity from suit without a fiat. However, I would point out that in the United States, claims in respect of the taking of lands outside of reserves and not covered by any treaty were not held justiciable until legislative provisions had removed the obstacle created by the doctrine of immunity. In Canada, immunity from suit has been removed by legislation at the federal level and in most provinces. However, this has not yet been done in British Columbia.[54]

So if the strategy of suing the provincial Crown directly was a non-starter in 1973, it was hardly an option sixty years earlier.

A Reference to the Supreme Court of Canada

The second strategy was to persuade Canada to refer the title question to the Supreme Court of Canada, thus avoiding the province's veto respecting private lawsuits. The problem here was that the provinces maintained that Ottawa could not refer a matter that affected provincial interests to the Supreme Court of Canada without provincial consent, and the Laurier administration was reluctant to test this by proceeding unilaterally. So when McInnes advised in 1909 that there was a legitimate issue for the courts to adjudicate upon, the dominion tried to obtain BC's consent. Surprisingly, this procedure almost worked. The deputy minister of Justice and BC's deputy attorney general met in 1910 and with their staff hammered out ten questions that they agreed were appropriate for submission to the Court[55] – legally appropriate, that is. Politics was another matter, and, although most of the questions concerned BC's reversionary rights in Indian reserves, the first three dealt with Aboriginal title. When Premier McBride reflected on the implications of this proposal, he refused to cooperate, and by the time the Judicial Committee of the Privy Council ruled in 1912 that provincial consent was not required it was too late.[56] By then Robert Borden's Conservatives were in power, and, as we have seen, they decided that the title question would be dropped.

A Dominion Action in Ejectment

The third strategy, which I shall call the "McInnes gambit," was the most audacious. When Tom McInnes provided his legal opinion to Ottawa in 1909, he predicted – accurately, as it turned out – that Premier McBride would never consent to a reference. He therefore recommended a different strategy. The dominion, he said, should commence a common law action of ejectment against homesteaders on the Skeena River, where most of the agitation and even violence was occurring that year. The action would be brought by Ottawa as the trustee for the Indians and would allege that the homesteaders were wrongfully in possession of Indian land. They would in turn rely upon their Crown grants from the government of British Columbia as proof of their title (the feudal term was that they would "vouch the province to warranty"), which would then oblige British Columbia to defend its right to make the homestead grants in the first place. The burden would thus be on the province to prove its title rather than on the Indians to prove theirs.[57]

Once it became clear that Premier McBride would never consent to a reference, the Laurier administration decided to give this strategy a try – but cautiously. The Judicial Committee had yet to pronounce on the reference issue and there was a lingering uncertainty about whether the Crown, which was theoretically a unity, could "sue itself." The course of action recommended by McInnes appeared to be a way around this difficulty, so procedural amendments were introduced to the *Indian Act* in 1910 and again in 1911 to facilitate such a lawsuit in the Exchequer Court of Canada.[58] A month after Prime Minister Laurier had made his assurances to the delegation that had come to see him in April 1911, a dominion order-in-council was passed setting out the strategy that Ottawa proposed to pursue. Significantly, the schedule to this order-in-council was a lengthy document prepared by O'Meara on behalf of the Conference of Friends of the Indians of British Columbia, which described the legal basis for the claim and the relevant events of the previous three years. The order-in-council described O'Meara's account as "substantially correct."[59]

However, once again, timing was all. The province's challenge to Ottawa's reference power was still before the Judicial Committee of the Privy Council, and, if the provinces lost, Prime Minister Laurier could unilaterally refer the BC Indian land question to the Supreme Court of Canada, thus avoiding the nastiness of a lawsuit against settlers on the Skeena. So it was in Ottawa's interest to delay. In the event, however, this delay brought the defeat of the Laurier Liberals and the installation of the Borden Conservatives, who were reluctant to refer the BC Indian land question to the Supreme Court of Canada and who would never resort to the "McInnes gambit."

A Petition to the Judicial Committee of the Privy Council
The fourth and last strategy was perhaps the most interesting of all – a direct appeal to the Judicial Committee of the Privy Council in London. O'Meara, who tried for years to get the Privy Council to refer the Nisga'a Petition to the Judicial Committee, has been severely criticized for doing so, both at the time and since. The chairman of the McKenna-McBride Commission, for example, dismissed the possibility of a direct appeal to the Judicial Committee when it was raised during the commission's 1913 visit to Skidegate in the Queen Charlotte Islands.[60] And years later, both Alan Morley, Peter Kelly's biographer, and anthropologist Philip Drucker poured scorn on O'Meara's abilities generally and, more specifically, upon what they saw as his delusional belief that he could bypass the Canadian courts in this way. To Morley, writing in 1966, O'Meara was a "professional Indian-lover" who fastened his "meager [sic] mind" on the Aboriginal title claim, which was in reality "a frivolous and stupid contention." Drucker, who wrote at about the same time, agreed, but his language is a little more restrained.[61]

The reason for this derision is that O'Meara's critics believed, as probably many lawyers still believe, that there was only one way to get a case from a colony or a dominion to the Judicial Committee of the Privy Council. You had to file suit in the local courts and then, if you lost in the highest of these, appeal to the Judicial Committee. This was, it is true, the usual procedure. In fact, it was the procedure in the majority of cases. Nonetheless, there was another way, and this way is set out quite clearly in the 1833 statute that regularized the procedure of the Judicial Committee, *An Act for the Better Administration of Justice in His Majesty's Privy Council*.[62] Section 4 of this act provides that, in addition to appeals from colonial courts, it is lawful "for His Majesty to refer to the ... Judicial Committee for Hearing or Consideration any such other Matters whatsoever as His Majesty shall think fit, and such Committee shall thereupon hear or consider the same, and shall advise His Majesty thereon." So if the Privy Council advised the government to refer a matter to the Judicial Committee, there was no need to go through the Canadian courts first. This was the section upon which O'Meara, eventually, staked everything. He would no doubt have preferred negotiations or a more conventional legal strategy, but, in the end, he had little choice.

More importantly, O'Meara was not the only lawyer who thought that if Canada and British Columbia would not cooperate section 4 of the 1833 statute was a viable avenue of redress. In 1913, when J.M. Clark, KC, was still counsel for the Indian Rights Association, he advised F.C. Wade, KC, of the Friends of the Indians that he was "more confident than ever" that the Judicial Committee would hear the case.[63] And Clark was one of the most prominent lawyers in the country. He had, for example, been counsel for Ontario in *Ontario Mining Company v. Seybold*, a decision that is well known to practitioners of Canadian Aboriginal law even today.[64] It therefore seems clear to me that, although Clark ceased to represent BC's Indians in 1916, he was the original architect of the strategy of going directly to London. Nor was O'Meara, though admittedly a lesser figure at the bar, a novice. He had practised for twenty years in Ontario, where for a short time he was associated with Sir John A. Macdonald's law firm in Toronto, and he had appeared in a case in the Judicial Committee of the Privy Council that is still cited in Canadian constitutional law textbooks.[65]

Why, then, would two experienced lawyers opt for such a discretionary long shot? The reason, by now, should be clear. British Columbia would consent neither to a lawsuit nor to a reference to the Supreme Court of Canada, and Canada would not act unilaterally. After 1912, the "McInnes gambit" was a dead letter and so was a reference by Ottawa to the Supreme Court of Canada. Finally, the McKenna-McBride Agreement had closed off any possibility, as provided for in the Terms of Union, of an appeal to the imperial secretary of state for the colonies. Such an appeal could occur only if there were a disagreement between the two governments. Since the Nisga'a and the Allied Indian Tribes of British Columbia had been pressing Ottawa to launch such an appeal, a good case can therefore be made that one of the purposes of the McKenna-McBride Agreement was the neutralization of this avenue of redress by securing an end to the dispute between the two governments over Indian reserves.[66] So section 4 of the 1833 *Act for the Better Administration of Justice in His Majesty's Privy Council* was really the only option.

Nor did the Privy Council dismiss this possibility out of hand. The fascinating details of the fifteen-year struggle to have the case heard in London are beyond the scope of the present essay, but it remains true that in 1913 and again in 1918 the officials in the Privy Council seriously considered whether the Nisga'a Petition should be referred directly to the Judicial Committee. It is also fair to say that the decision not to do so in 1913 was based partly upon misinformation supplied by Ottawa, although this is an allegation that I shall have to justify elsewhere.[67] Five years later, when the Privy Council was asked to reconsider, it was politics of a different sort that scotched the reference. The British government may have been willing to pull rank in 1867 or 1909 or perhaps even in 1913. Yet by 1918, thousands of Canadians had sacrificed their lives for the British Empire in the trenches of France and Belgium, and most of those who survived felt that Canada had more than paid for its right to self-determination with the blood of its young manhood. The fact that the dominion government was opposed to having the Nisga'a case referred to the Judicial Committee meant that an already politically difficult issue was now coloured by Canada's desire to assert and defend its hard-won national independence.

It is not surprising, therefore, that a month after the armistice in November 1918 the British government advised O'Meara that if the nature of the Nisga'a claim were legal, they had to sue in the Canadian courts first and then appeal to the Judicial Committee if they lost. On the other hand, if it were simply a political complaint the Nisga'a could go directly to the Privy Council – *if* Canada consented.[68] This was, in my view, a debatable interpretation of the legal situation, particularly when one considers that only six years earlier the Judicial Committee had described the jurisdiction to refer matters directly under section 4 of the 1833 act very widely.[69] It also sat most uneasily with assurances that O'Meara had received in 1916 from the Duke of Connaught, the governor-general of Canada, that if the Nisga'a did not agree with the report of the McKenna-McBride Commission they could appeal to the Privy Council in England, "where their case [would] have every consideration."[70] The governor-general, it is true, did not have the authority to decide what would be referred to the Judicial Committee – that was a matter for the British Privy Council. But he was the king's representative in Canada, and it is therefore not difficult to see why the Nisga'a and the Allied Indian Tribes of British Columbia felt they had been misled.

In any event, the game was up.[71] The Nisga'a could not sue in the British Columbia courts because the provincial government would not grant a fiat, and they could not go directly to the Privy Council because Canada would not consent. Nor would Ottawa refer the case directly to the Supreme Court of Canada or pursue what I have called the "McInnes gambit." The province's intransigence, plus all of those dead soldiers, had effectively doomed the Nisga'a cause. However, because the Privy Council had not regarded its decision in 1913 against referring the matter to the Judicial Committee as final, and had been willing to reconsider it in 1918, O'Meara and his clients carried on. There was, after all, a slim possibility that the Privy Council might reconsider again, and this possibility enabled O'Meara to advise his clients that the Nisga'a Petition was still "before" the Privy Council, albeit not the Judicial Committee.

By the end of 1918, when the Nisga'a Petition was rejected for the second time, O'Meara had been legally on his own for more than two years. The Aboriginal leadership had decided that they preferred his advice to the increasingly cautious (and more expensive) variety that Clark was dispensing, and Clark's role in the campaign for title had therefore come to an end in 1916.[72] So if it was a stretch to rely upon the distinction between having a petition lodged with the Privy Council and having it actually referred by that body to the Judicial Committee of the Privy Council, the responsibility is his. Certainly, it is not a distinction that many clients would have appreciated, and, as the years passed, it became increasingly unrealistic to think that there would ever be a reference. Yet what O'Meara told his clients was technically accurate, and, given the attitude of the governments involved, there seemed to be no alternative to pressing on.[73] It is therefore a tribute to O'Meara's perseverance, and to his faith that justice would eventually be done, that the file in the Privy Council was active right up until 1927.

In trying to assess the validity of the reasons given for the Privy Council's refusal to refer O'Meara's petition to the Judicial Committee, it is helpful to compare the Nisga'a claim with *In re Southern Rhodesia*, which the Judicial Committee decided at about the same time.[74] Like the Nisga'a case, it alleged the violation of legal, not political, rights. Like the Nisga'a case, it involved the question of Native title, although not directly. And, like the Nisga'a case, it had not been litigated in the colonial courts. Yet the Privy Council referred it to the Judicial Committee under section 4 of the 1833 *Act for the Better Administration of Justice in His Majesty's Privy Council*. Seeing this, the London solicitors for the Nisga'a wrote to the secretary of the Privy Council, drawing his attention to the "close relation" between the *Southern Rhodesia* case and theirs. They also said that because the issues had a "most important bearing" on the Nisga'a claim, their case might be seriously prejudiced if it were not given a hearing first.[75]

However, this entreaty made no difference. Not only were the "Natives" of Rhodesia not a party in the African case, but the main issue there was whether the British South Africa Company or the Crown held title to unalienated lands in that colony.[76] This was clearly a matter of vital interest to the British Crown, and what ultimately turned out to be at stake was an award of £4,400,000 to the company – an immense sum at that time.[77] Clearly, corporate rights in an African colony were one thing, and Aboriginal title in a self-governing dominion were quite another.

In rendering the Judicial Committee's opinion in the case, Lord Sumner rather condescendingly described the African Natives as "incapable of urging, and perhaps unconscious of possessing, any case at all." He accordingly went on to commend the "disinterested liberality" of the English barristers who came forward to argue the case for Native title when it appeared that something should be said on the subject.[78] Lord Sumner also remarked that the dispute between the company and the Crown should have been dealt with years before, because it had "given rise to conflicting opinions in Southern Rhodesia" for many years. Moreover, uncertainty about land titles was an issue that must "sooner or later come home to roost."[79] Indeed.

The irony is painful because, of course, Lord Sumner might well have been describing British Columbia and the uncertainty associated with the British Columbia Indian land question. Equally obvious was the fact that in British Columbia the Indians did not require the intervention of altruistic British barristers. They and their lawyers were well aware of the case for Aboriginal title and had, in fact, been begging for an opportunity to have the matter decided by the courts since 1909. The only "disinterested liberality" they needed was the government's permission, and the funds, to make their case. Nonetheless, the South African company got its £4,400,000, and the Nisga'a were told to sue in Canada.

Once the McKenna-McBride Commission's report was approved by both the federal and provincial governments in the 1920s, British Columbia took the position that it had discharged any and all responsibilities it may have had under the Terms of Union respecting the BC Indian land question – even though implementation was delayed until 1938. This, of course, is one of the main reasons why the Nisga'a and the Allied Indian Tribes of British Columbia had opposed the establishment of the commission. They knew that, despite the protestations to the contrary by the Department of Indian Affairs, Ottawa would lose interest in Aboriginal title once the McKenna-McBride Agreement, which addressed both governments' concerns about Indian reserves and little else, had been finalized. And, in fact, the commitment of dominion politicians and officials to resolving the Aboriginal title question, which had been in decline since 1912, completely evaporated in the late 1920s.

These politicians and officials, most of whom appear to have thought that social dysfunction and assimilation would make the "Indian problem" ultimately go away on its own, defended their reluctance to act on several grounds. They pointed out that the Indians were not united in their views; that the Allied Indian Tribes of British Columbia never came up with a clear set of questions for the courts to answer; that a significant judgment in favour of Aboriginal title in British Columbia would incite the envy of the tribes in the rest of the country, who had settled decades and even centuries earlier for much less; and, rather inconsistently, that even if the Indians won in court, all they would get was a judgment entitling them to compensation on the same scale as the nineteenth-century prairie treaties, unadjusted for inflation. Assessing the legitimacy of this outlook, and the extent to which dominion officials misled the Allied Indian Tribes of British Columbia with respect to the effect of the McKenna-McBride Commission's report, would take several more articles as long as this one – so I shall desist.[80] Suffice it to say that there will always be disunity; that the material produced by Clark, O'Meara, and MacInnes, the dominion's own lawyer, was more than adequate to support the sort of limited judicial determination that, ultimately, came to pass in *Calder*; that in 1910 even British Columbia's deputy attorney general had agreed to ten questions that were suitable for a judicial reference; and, finally, that, as Laurier had said in 1911, deciding contrary claims is what courts are for.[81]

We Are Not O'Meara's Children

In June 1913, O'Meara wrote to his friend and ally, F.C. Wade, KC, that he had succeeded "in placing the case of the Indians before the Privy Council, the petition of the Nishga having been lodged last month." He meant of course that the Privy Council had accepted it and that its officials would now have to decide whether they would recommend that it be referred directly to the Judicial Committee. O'Meara went on to say that the "severe strain under which I have been living for many months threatens to prove itself too much for me. I have therefore been constrained by medical advice to take a short rest."[82] The strain to which O'Meara was referring was not only that which was occasioned by his journey to England in 1913. The real cause was the two years of effort that preceded it. He and various Aboriginal organizations and non-Aboriginal support groups had lobbied vigorously, in Canada and in England, to persuade the Borden administration to continue Laurier's policy and get British Columbia to soften its stance. This attempt was to no avail. Ottawa and London waffled and prevaricated, and British Columbia simply repeated its firm and unequivocal refusal. As Premier McBride told the British secretary of state for the colonies when he visited London in 1912, "[h]ands off British Columbia."[83] It is true that Ottawa made a proposal in 1914 that would have resulted in a reference to the courts and that Clark appears to have recommended acceptance. However, the Aboriginal organizations, on O'Meara's advice, rejected it because they regarded the terms of the order-in-council containing the proposal as being unreasonable. One of these terms made any court reference conditional upon the Indians agreeing, in advance, that if the courts upheld their title it would be extinguished "in accordance with past usage." Other conditions were that they would accept the findings of the McKenna-McBride Commission (which had not yet written its report) and that only counsel appointed by the dominion could represent them. The proposal also stipulated that, once British Columbia had implemented the McKenna-McBride recommendations, it "shall be held to have satisfied all the claims of the Indians against the Province."[84] As the Friends of the Indians and the Social Services Committee of Canada observed, "what the Government proposes to the Indians is – If you will first surrender all your rights we will submit to the Courts the question of whether you ever had any rights."[85] It would therefore appear that, if O'Meara had contributed nothing else to the campaign for title, his advice on this issue alone would have justified his modest retainer.[86]

I suspect that, even when he recommended against accepting the terms put forward by Ottawa in 1914, O'Meara understood that his best opportunity to achieve his goals had come and gone three years earlier, in 1911. Yet he and his clients soldiered on, largely because they shared a firm faith that, eventually, right would be done. As Haida Chief Peter Kelly had put it in an address to the provincial government when a large delegation of chiefs descended on Victoria in March 1911,

> [w]hy are we here, dragging our weary bodies such long distances? It is because of our great faith in British justice, and our confidence that, wherever the Union Jack floats, there reigns Justice of the highest order, unmolested, not only to white men, but unto every British subject, which we lay claim to be in the fullest sense.[87]

Romantic rhetoric? Perhaps. But Kelly meant every word and clearly took the ideology of British constitutionalism more seriously than the premier of British Columbia did. Half a century later, Frank Calder would say much the same thing at the annual meeting of the Nishga Tribal Council that approved the lawsuit that became the *Calder* case.

Of course, no one who was involved in the first legal campaign for Aboriginal title in British Columbia lived to see their vindication in the Supreme Court of Canada's decision in *Calder*, let alone the developments represented by *Delgamuukw*, the Nisga'a treaty, and the BC treaty process. Instead, they had to put up with being called "O'Meara's children" and to endure what appeared at the time to be the permanent defeat of their cause after the parliamentary committee hearings in 1927.[88] Aboriginal people were the chief, but not the only, victims of the failure of this campaign. O'Meara was subjected to constant criticism while he was alive, and to the extent that anyone remembers him now, those few have generally joined in what can only be called a chorus of derision.[89] A typical example was his treatment by the parliamentary joint committee in 1927. By then, O'Meara was in his late sixties, and, undoubtedly, his skills had declined, but although he was courteous he was repeatedly cut short and insulted. An exchange that occurred when he was discussing the *St. Catherine's Milling* case makes the point. O'Meara told the committee that the case was authority for the proposition that, until extinguished, Aboriginal title formed a burden on the underlying title of a province in its ungranted lands. However, because the language of the decision spoke of "lands reserved for the Indians," some of the committee members insisted that the case dealt only with *Indian Act* reserves and was therefore irrelevant to the matter of Aboriginal title:

Hon. Mr. Stevens: the language which you have read refers entirely to Reserves ... There is no use in kidding ourselves about this; we have to face the facts. You cannot hypnotize yourself or your clients ...

Mr. O'Meara: The *St. Catherine's Milling Case* has reference to the territory of a tribe and not to a reserve. We have the text of it here. Undoubtedly that case deals with the general question of Indian title.

O'Meara went on to quote from the case and explain, but the committee members were having none of it:

Hon. Mr. Stevens: No one can be surprised that your clients have been misled by your advice.

Mr. O'Meara: On what point, Mr. Stevens.

Hon. Mr. Stevens: On all points.

Mr. O'Meara: Well, if my advice is as sound on other points as on this, I think it is all right; because everyone who has studied this case knows absolutely that what was dealt with was the large territory that has been occupied by the tribes.

Hon. Mr. Stevens: They know nothing of the kind.

Hon. Mr. Murphy: The report of that decision speaks for itself. Let us get on.[90]

Peter Kelly tried to explain to the committee that they were confusing *Indian Act* reserves with tribal territories, but he had an equal lack of success. Yet not only was O'Meara's analysis of the *St. Catherine's Milling* case correct but his basic argument with respect to Aboriginal title was also quite consistent with what the Supreme Court of Canada accepts as orthodox today.

On the other hand, an even-handed assessment of the record compels me to observe that O'Meara was not much of an advocate, particularly as he got older. When he made presentations, he tended to bury his audience in an avalanche of documents and quotations, and, by the time he appeared before the joint committee in 1927, the years of defeat had taken their toll. When he had been a missionary in the Yukon twenty years earlier, he managed to annoy a surprising number of people, and taking up the cause of Aboriginal title enabled him to irritate even more. After a while, this sort of thing adds up. But, for all that, O'Meara was a good lawyer, which is not quite the same thing as being a good advocate. His arguments on Aboriginal title were soundly based on principle and precedent. The fact that the deck was heavily stacked against him and his clients from the outset makes the successes of the period 1909–11 all the more remarkable.

O'Meara was accused not only of incompetence. Equally unsettling was the charge that he was getting rich on the backs of the Indians. In 1920, for example, a member of parliament had charged that O'Meara "annually makes a business of going to the Indians and collecting a few hundred dollars to keep him going."[91] And, in 1927, when Minister Charles Stewart introduced section 141, the amendment to the *Indian Act* restricting access to legal counsel, he explained that the proposed law was necessary to protect Indians from unscrupulous lawyers. After adding that those in the know "would not have to go very far to cite" a BC example of such behaviour, he proceeded to describe, although he did not name, O'Meara.[92] Given that the evil that Stewart said the amendment was designed to end appears to have been contingency fees, some providing for as much as 50 percent of the recovery, the reference to O'Meara was unfair. I have been able to find no evidence that O'Meara had ever done anything remotely like this. Indeed, by 1915, he appears to have spent $2,500 of his own money on the campaign.[93]

Nonetheless, only months after section 141 was enacted the Department of Indian Affairs began compiling a dossier on O'Meara, who had returned to the Nass Valley after the committee hearings to see if there was any stomach to continue what was now not only a hopeless, but also probably an illegal, struggle. Unfortunately for Deputy Superintendent General Duncan Campbell Scott, the evidence gathered by the police and the local Indian agent was disappointing. It amounted to little more than the fact that O'Meara was back in the area and that he had written a letter to the Nisga'a Land Committee requesting that it pay him $30 that he had loaned a Nisga'a delegate for travel expenses, plus a further $50, which was outstanding from one of O'Meara's earlier visits to the Nass. He explained that he needed the money because he had had to borrow $80 from his bank to cover these costs.[94] All in all, such evidence was not much to justify what would be the very first prosecution under section 141. Scott instructed his men in the field to keep gathering evidence anyway.[95]

He need not have bothered. O'Meara put an end to the police investigation – and to his own dogged and quixotic campaign for title – by dying in April 1928. And what did he have to show for his twenty years' work on behalf of the Aboriginal peoples of British Columbia? According to probate records, his estate consisted solely of two life insurance policies for his widow and children, the net value of which was about $1,600.[96] This amount was not much for an unscrupulous lawyer who had, allegedly, been fleecing his Aboriginal clients. Particularly when one compares it to the $30,000 that the BC government had paid lawyer H.D. Helmcken in 1911 for negotiating the removal of the Songhees from their reserve in downtown Victoria. A local newspaper owner who had helped to broker the deal was paid even more.[97] And that same year – the year that O'Meara, Clark, Kelly, and others had believed themselves so close to winning their campaign for title – the Grand Trunk Pacific Railway apparently paid a priest $10,000 to get him "in the proper frame of mind to recommend" to an Indian band in northern

British Columbia that they surrender their reserve.[98] So while there may well have been overpaid or even unscrupulous characters out there, the Reverend O'Meara was not among them.[99]

Worse still, the campaign for title may have resulted in his losing the support, perhaps even the love, of his family. Arthur Eugene O'Meara was a difficult man, full of Christian zeal and cursed by a tendency to get on just about everyone's nerves. Obtaining justice for the Indians of British Columbia was a cause that came to dominate his life, perhaps to the exclusion of almost everything else. What he sacrificed can only be guessed at, but his sole lineal descendant advises that there are almost no family photographs or memorabilia and that her father – O'Meara's only son – never spoke of him.[100]

Losing the twenty-year struggle for title also undermined O'Meara's position with some of his clients. Peter Kelly's biographer alleges that after it was all over Kelly said that the Allied Indian Tribes of British Columbia could have done better without him.[101] If so, these words are a heart-breaking epitaph to a career that, in the last decade of his life, was simply one defeat after another. They also point to what may have been O'Meara's greatest flaw. None of his clients liked it when their opponents in government and the media called them "O'Meara's children." The slogan suggested that their counsel was a kind of legal Wizard of Oz, exploiting for his own ends gullible and unlettered Indians who had been taken in by his confident assurances that the law was on their side. The Aboriginal leadership therefore never missed an opportunity to deny the charges that lurked in this patronizing and infantilizing phrase, notably during the dispute that erupted in the early 1920s over the dominion bill that authorized implementing the McKenna-McBride Commission's report. Peter Kelly was addressing the same charge when he assured the parliamentary joint committee in 1927 that O'Meara was simply a lawyer and that "he agitates just insofar as we allow him to agitate, just as any legal adviser."[102] However, given the lack of adequate funds, the problems involved in travel and communicating over distances in those days, and, of course, O'Meara's own personality, he probably did take charge more than he should have. He was, after all, a non-Aboriginal lawyer and cleric who doubtless thought he knew best. So it is not surprising that those who most resented the suggestion that they were O'Meara's children might have reflected bitterly that, on occasion, O'Meara may have acted as if it were true.[103] And, to make matters worse, he failed.

Obviously there is more – much more – to the story of the first campaign than this chapter can provide. But for now I will close with some words from Peter Kelly to the joint parliamentary committee that investigated the claims of the Allied Indian Tribes of British Columbia in 1927. Kelly had just been asked what the Indians would do if – as turned out to be the case – the committee refused to acknowledge their title. He replied:

Then the position that we would have to take would be this: that we are simply dependent people. Then we would have to accept from you, just as an act of grace, whatever you saw fit to give us. Now that is putting it in plain language. The Indians have no voice in the affairs of the country. They have not a solitary way of bringing anything before the Parliament of this country, except as we have done last year by petition, and it is a mighty hard thing. If we press for that we are called agitators, simply agitators, trouble makers, when we try to get what we consider to be our rights. It is a mighty hard thing, and ... it has taken us between forty and fifty years to get where we are today. And, perhaps, if we are turned down now, if this Committee sees fit to turn down what we are pressing for, it might be another century before a new generation will rise up and begin to press this claim. If this question is not settled, in a proper way and on a sound basis, it will not be settled properly. Now, that is the point we want to stress.[104]

And there it is. He predicted that if their rights were denied, a future of welfare dependence stretched out before the Aboriginal peoples of British Columbia, because their reserves and other resources were not sufficient to make them economically self-sustaining. Nor would it put an end to the land question. If the campaigners who stood before the joint committee in 1927 failed, others would eventually take their place. Kelly was, of course, right on both counts. He was just a little conservative in his estimate as to how long it would take Frank Calder, Rod Robinson, Hubert Doolan, Tom Berger, and the many others who contributed to the *Calder* case to pick up the torch. And here we all are.

5

Then Fight For It: William Lewis Paul and Alaska Native Land Claims

Stephen Haycox

The history of the Nisga'a land claim, and the extraordinary contribution of Frank Calder, prompts interest in land claims elsewhere in British Columbia, in Canada, and, ultimately, perhaps, in the United States. As it happens, at roughly the same time that the Nisga'a claim was being framed in British Columbia, there was a land claim in Alaska, *Tlingit and Haida Indians of Alaska v. U.S.*, which, at first glance, seems to show some remarkable similarities with the Nisga'a's claim.[1] There were also similarities between Frank Calder's unusual work and the career of the Tlingit leader, William Lewis Paul. In 1924, William Paul became the first Native to be elected to the Alaska territorial legislature.[2] He was also, in 1920, the first Alaska Native to be admitted to the Alaska Bar.[3] In the 1920s, he became the principal leader of the regional Alaska Native Brotherhood (ANB). He served both as secretary and legal counsel to the organization. In 1923, he started a monthly newspaper, the *Alaska Fisherman* and, in the same year, won a Native voting rights case in Alaska District Court.[4] In 1929, he won a school desegregation case.[5] In the 1930s, Paul worked two summers in Washington, DC, with officials of the Department of the Interior, the Office of Indian Affairs, and Alaska's delegate to Congress, to craft amendments to allow the landmark *Indian Reorganization Act* of 1934 to be applied in Alaska.[6] He also worked with officials to write the jurisdictional act under which the Tlingit and Haida Indians would ultimately bring their case for ownership of all of the land in the Alexander Archipelago in southeast Alaska to the US Court of Claims.[7] Although it would take a long time, the Indians would eventually win this case.

In the 1950s, Paul would challenge the theory of the *Tlingit and Haida* suit in a case, *Tee-Hit-Ton Indians v. U.S.*, which would ultimately be decided by the US Supreme Court.[8] In *Tee-Hit-Ton*, the court confirmed that the United States was not required to pay compensation for extinguishments of Native title. Far more important, by so ruling, the court confirmed that Aboriginal title did exist in Alaska and that it had not been extinguished.

Subsequently, acting on this finding, the US Congress in 1971 would pass the monumental *Alaska Native Claims Settlement Act* (*ANCSA*), which would extinguish Aboriginal title to all but 12 percent of Alaska's lands and would pay $1 billion in compensation for the title extinguished.[9] This $1 billion would be used to capitalize Alaska's existing thirteen regional economic development corporations and 174 Native village corporations, in one or the other of which the 75,000 Natives living in 1971 became sharehold-ers.[10] Although Paul was not a principal in the work that resulted in the 1971 *ANCSA*, he did informally advise many Native leaders who did partici-pate in fashioning the final product, and a number credited the hours they spent with William Paul with giving them the legal and contextual know-ledge that they needed to do so effectively.[11]

Paul's biography is remarkable, and it helps to contextualize the develop-ment of the Tlingit-Haida land claim, which was first conceived in approxi-mately 1929, filed with the US Court of Federal Claims in 1947, decided by that court in 1959, and finally settled with a compensatory award in 1968. Clearly, William Paul was a man of considerable drive and intelligence as well as remarkable achievement. He was also a complex individual who, despite some significant political success, often alienated others, and ran afoul of the legal ethics of his time through lapses in personal judgment.

William Paul was born in 1885 in Fort Simpson, British Columbia, the nearest hospital to his mother's family home at the time, which was in the small village of Tongass, on the Alaskan island of the same name along the north edge of Dixon Entrance. Paul's mother, widowed just days before his birth, went to work at the Reverend Sheldon Jackson's Presbyterian Sitka (Indian) Industrial Training School. Jackson, the first American organizer to missionize in Alaska after the American purchase in 1867, had established the board-ing school at Sitka in 1879. William and his two brothers, one older and one younger, were raised Christian and "white" in the acculturating envi-ronment of the Sitka school. As they entered their teenage years, Jackson and his mother sent all three boys to General Richard Pratt's Carlisle Indian School in Pennsylvania. William studied there for two and a half years. Pratt believed militantly in acculturation and assimilation as the only vi-able alternative to the extermination of Native Americans, a conviction held by most secular and religious government and private Indian reformers of the period.[12] Leaving Carlisle in 1902, Paul worked in Philadelphia for a while and then attended Dickinson College. After returning home for a year at his mother's request, he enrolled in 1905 at Whitworth College, which was then located in Tacoma, and graduated in 1909. After gradua-tion, he worked as a bank clerk and an insurance company cashier. He re-turned to Alaska in 1920, intending only to make money in commercial fishing for a season before moving to New York City to pursue a singing career. He would remain in Alaska for a generation.[13]

William Paul's younger brother, Louis, had served in the US Army during the First World War, and, after the war, had chafed under the non-citizen status of American Natives at the time. Expanding on ideas he had absorbed at Carlisle, he developed the notion that all American Natives were citizens under the terms of the Fourteenth Amendment, which guarantees equal rights to all persons born in the United States. Americans had considered the applicability of the amendment to Native Americans briefly after the Civil War, but both Congress and the courts had rejected the idea, mostly on the grounds that tribal organization and allegiance appeared contradictory to the notion of national sovereignty and citizenship.[14] Louis interested William in the idea that Indians were in fact citizens, and the two of them used it to energize the fledgling ANB, in which they both became officers soon after William's return to the territory.

The ANB was founded in Juneau in 1912 by a group of Tlingit, Haida, and Tsimshian Indians who had responded to a call from William Beattie, the superintendent of government schools in southeast Alaska, to attend and advise teachers and staff at an education conference in the fall of that year. Most of the founders had attended the Sitka Industrial Training School, which by then had been renamed the Sheldon Jackson School. The leader of the group was Peter Simpson, a Tsimshian from Metlakatla who later lived on the grounds of the Sitka school. Simpson counselled students there to become literate and educated, speak English, wear store-bought clothing, and work for wages. He told them that in doing these things they would confirm their fitness for citizenship. However, while Simpson articulated the long-term goal, he did not have a strategy for achieving it.

Whether the Paul brothers' insistence that Natives were citizens by virtue of the Fourteenth Amendment would have fared well in the courts became moot in 1924 when the US Congress passed the *Indian Citizenship Act*, making citizens of all American Natives who were not already.[15] By then, William Paul had embarked on a political career. Initially, he took advantage of a significant ambiguity regarding the status of Alaska Natives, which was a function of the 1887 *Dawes Act*.[16] This act provided that Indians who formally severed their relationship with their tribe would be allotted 160-acre land parcels. If after twenty years of such severance and allotment they manifested behaviours associated with a civilized life, they might be granted citizenship.[17] None of the tribes in Alaska were federally recognized in the 1920s, but Congress had passed an allotment act specifically for Alaska in 1906 and government officials had informally accepted certain citizen actions by acculturated Natives, including paying the annual territorial school tax and voting in municipal and territorial elections. In 1922, William Paul used the various ANB chapters to organize Indian voters in a number of Tlingit and Haida villages in southeast Alaska for the election for the territorial legislature that year. He was able to deliver enough Indian votes to make the difference in several close contests in southeast Alaska. With this example before him, Paul decided to run for the legislature himself in 1924. He was elected handily in a campaign that featured considerable racist-inspired rhetoric and advertising by his opponents and by the mainstream press. He proved an aggressive and effective legislator and was re-elected in 1926, although he lost his bid for a third term in 1928.

To understand the genesis of Alaska Native land claims and their relationship to British Columbia and other Canadian claims, it is important to recognize the unique status of Alaska Natives. Unlike all American Indians in the contiguous US states, the United States government made no treaties with Alaska Natives. This is because soon after the 1867 Alaska purchase, in 1871, Congress halted all treaty making.[18] From time to time, however, Congress did vote to authorize tribes to take suits to the US Court of Federal Claims for compensation for takings of traditional lands. From 1823, the US Supreme Court had recognized Native title – Aboriginal title – to lands that Natives had utilized and occupied. In Alaska, the 1867 *Treaty Concerning the Cession of the Russian Possessions in North America by His Majesty the Emperor of All the Russias to the United States of America* (*Alaska Purchase Treaty*) provided that Natives were not to be disturbed in occupation of their lands, but no attempt was made to determine what those lands might be.[19] This was still the situation in the 1920s when William Paul served in the Alaska territorial legislature and when he was forcibly retired from this job.

In 1929, the annual convention of the ANB, the Grand Camp, voted on a resolution to pursue a jurisdictional act in the US Congress that would authorize the Tlingit and Haida Indians to bring suit in the claims court for compensation for the US taking of Indian land in the establishment of the Tongass National Forest between 1902 and 1909.[20] This forest would eventually include nearly sixteen million of the eighteen million acres of land in the Alexander Archipelago. In later years, William Paul would assert that in 1925 Peter Simpson had taken him aside and asked him if the land in the archipelago belonged to the Tlingit and Haida people. When Paul responded "yes," Simpson is supposed to have replied: "Then fight for it." Paul later wrote that he went on to spend four years working to persuade the Indians to approve the suit. However, Donald Craig Mitchell, the former general counsel for the Alaska Federation of Natives, has recently completed two major books tracing the history of Alaska Native land claims from the time that Alaska was purchased to the passage of the 1971 *ANCSA*. Mitchell's research is both prodigious and meticulous. Based on his research, Mitchell disputes Paul's version of the genesis of the Tlingit-Haida claim. There is no mention of the conversation between Simpson and Paul in any of Paul's correspondence from the period. Nor is there mention of a conversation about a Tlingit-Haida land claim before November 1929 in the newspaper that Paul published monthly for the ANB from 1923 to 1932.[21]

On the other hand, there is positive evidence to support a different reconstruction of the genesis of the suit, which Mitchell attributes to James Wickersham. Wickersham was Alaska's delegate to Congress from 1908 to 1920, during which time he observed congressional action on a number of Native claim jurisdictional bills in the contiguous states. He was also aware of jurisdictional acts passed in the 1920s for the Muckelshoot, San Juan, Nook-Sack, Suattle, Chinook, Upper Chehalis, Lower Chehalis, and Humptulip tribes and bands of Indians in Washington State. In 1930, Wickersham decided to run again for Alaska territorial delegate to Congress. In his diary, he describes his intention to introduce a Tlingit-Haida jurisdictional act in Congress if he is elected and to partner with William Paul in representing the Indians. At the 1929 ANB convention in Haines, Alaska, Wickersham addressed the Indian delegates on this subject prior to their passing the resolution approving the plan. Wickersham was elected, but even before he took office, the outgoing delegate, Dan Sutherland, introduced the legislation. It did not get out of committee. In 1931, Wickersham persuaded the chair of the Senate Committee on Indian Affairs to shepherd a bill through the Senate, which he did, but Wickersham was unsuccessful in getting it through the House of Representatives. In 1932, Anthony Dimond was elected Alaska's congressional delegate in the Democratic sweep of that year. In 1933, Dimond introduced the bill, but the House of Representatives Committee on Indian Affairs did not act on it. In 1935, Dimond introduced it again. This time, the *Act Authorizing the Tlingit and Haida Indians of Alaska to Bring Suit in the United States Court of Claims, and Conferring Jurisdiction upon Said Court to Hear, Examine, Adjudicate, and Enter Judgment upon Any and All Claims which Said Indians May Have, or Claim to Have, against the United States, and For Other Purposes* (*Tlingit-Haida Jurisdictional Act*) passed both houses of Congress, and President Theodore Roosevelt signed it.[22]

Perhaps the most important provision of the 1935 *Tlingit-Haida Jurisdictional Act* called for the Bureau of Indian Affairs to hold in trust for the economic security and stability of the Indians of southeast Alaska in aggregate any compensatory award the court might approve. The ANB had accepted this provision, preferring a central fund to a per capita distribution, which would have been quickly dissipated. In addition, the bill required a committee elected by all of the Indians of southeast Alaska to select the attorneys to prosecute the suit and required the secretary of the interior and the commissioner of Indian affairs to approve the committee's choices. As work on the suit progressed, William Paul would object to each of these provisions.[23]

Before the 1929 Haines convention, Paul and Wickersham agreed that if Congress authorized the Tlingit-Haida suit, the two would seek approval as the appointed attorneys. They agreed to charge 15 percent of whatever compensation was recovered for their services, which they would split evenly.

In 1937, however, while working as a Bureau of Indian Affairs field agent in Alaska, William Paul was disbarred for unethical practices as an attorney. Among the charges brought against him were embezzlement and misrepresentation of ownership of property.[24] Clearly, Paul was mendacious. Although he was given a year to do so, he did not defend himself against the charges. By then, Wickersham had withdrawn from any interest in the land claims suit.

There is no question that William Paul was sincere in his dedication to the representation of Alaska Native rights. His career through the 1920s demonstrated both his ability and his commitment – a commitment that would last a lifetime. Yet Paul's willingness to bend the truth, perforce, damaged his effectiveness. In addition, he was also haughty and acerbic in manner. Together, these various factors made him a truly tragic figure. Paul's disbarment, however, gave his enemies in the ANB the opportunity to express their displeasure with Paul's character and his methods. Beginning in 1937, strong opposition to William, his brother Louis, and his sons William, Jr., and Fred, challenged the Paul family's seventeen-year leadership of the ANB, and, by 1940, the Peratrovich family of Klawock and others would emerge as the new leaders of the organization. However, remarkably, William Paul did not give up. Rather, he sought to buy time. By then he had two sons in law school at the University of Washington, William Paul, Jr., and Fred Paul. He hoped to persuade the ANB to appoint his sons as the claims attorneys. In the meantime, Paul addressed the question of what body should be designated to administer whatever award the court should assign. He proposed that it should be the ANB. The Bureau of Indian Affairs objected on the grounds that not all Tlingit and Haida Indians were ANB members and that some non-Indians had been accepted into the membership. Instead, the bureau mandated that delegates to a land claims committee be elected from each Tlingit and Haida village and that they meet to select the attorneys. This was acceptable to the ANB, and the election as well as a land claims convention were held in Wrangell in 1940.

William Paul, however, by no means accepted these events as a defeat. He sought to control the claims convention so as to install his two sons as the attorneys for the suit and to use the blessing of the convention by the Bureau of Indian Affairs as a legitimization of their selection. His method was clever. He asked the convention delegates to bar bureau officials from the convention proceedings on the grounds that they were from an Indian organization conducting Indian business and needed to be free of the paternalism and intimidation implied by their presence. He did not prevail in that manoeuvre for the Bureau of Indian Affairs argued successfully that their officers needed to be present to certify the validity of the vote. On the other hand, Paul did succeed with a resolution prohibiting the officials from speaking on the record.

However, at this point, Paul encountered a new obstacle. Since his disbarment, opposition to Paul, which normally was *sotto voce*, hidden and not overt, became more outspoken.[25] This opposition, which focused on the Paul brothers' exclusion of a number of younger men from leadership positions, on William Paul's acerbic personality and his questionable judgment, and on discomfiture at the overt political endorsements and activity of the ANB under the Pauls' leadership, increasingly coalesced around the powerful Peratrovich family from Klawock. Distrusting Paul, and buoyed by the growing visibility of anti-Paul sentiment, the Peratroviches threatened that if the Paul brothers were selected as the attorneys, the Klawock faction would withdraw from the suit and perhaps even the ANB, a move that would sabotage both the process and the organization. Also distrustful of Paul, the Bureau of Indian Affairs supported this threat. Secretary of the Interior Harold Ickes told the Alaska director of the bureau that he would not approve William Paul, Jr., (Fred Paul was still finishing his degree at the University of Washington Law School) as chief attorney for the claims suit. However, Paul, Sr., still commanded considerable loyalty within the ANB, and, in the end, he was able to forge a compromise with both the brotherhood and the government. The claims committee, which would adopt the name Tlingit and Haida Central Council, would appoint the Paul brothers as attorneys, but they would serve as co-counsels with an experienced and recognized Indian claims attorney from Washington, DC, who had been approved by the Indian commissioner and the Interior secretary.[26] These provisions constituted a significant limitation on the Pauls' freedom to pursue the suit in their own way under their own direction. Cementing the Pauls' fall from grace within the ANB, delegates handily elected Roy Peratrovich as grand president over Louis Paul at the ANB convention in November 1940 in Klawock. Roy Peratrovich would serve five successive terms as ANB grand president.

The reality of the compromise was demonstrated in a particularly visible and dramatic fashion. The ANB directed both William Paul, Sr., and Roy Peratrovich, who were by now brothers in enmity, to travel together to Washington, DC, to consult with officials from the Bureau of Indian Affairs and the Department of the Interior in the selection of the experienced attorney who was to guide the Tlingit-Haida suit. It would fall to Felix Cohen, associate solicitor in the Department of the Interior, to meet with the two ANB officials (Paul was a member of the executive committee by virtue of his past grand presidency) and direct the selection of the attorney. After considerable searching, he chose James Curry, who had worked at the Bureau of Indian Affairs in the 1930s and who was the unpaid general counsel of a new Indian advocacy organization, the National Congress of American Indians.[27]

In assembling the Tlingit-Haida suit, Curry almost immediately fell afoul of the US Forest Service. After the Second World War, the Alaska regional forest director aggressively pursued a plan to develop as many as five major pulp mills in the Tongass Forest. Forest Service bureaucrats discounted the notion of Aboriginal title, arguing that the most land in the archipelago that Indians might be entitled to was that which their dwellings occupied. In 1947, Forest Service officials, working with Alaska's congressional delegate and territorial governor, and over the objections of ANB leaders, secured congressional passage of an act authorizing timber lease sales throughout the forest, placing the receipts in escrow until such time as the claims court should have ruled on the Tlingit-Haida land claim.[28] The US Forest Service is in the Department of Agriculture, while the Bureau of Indian Affairs, the National Park Service, and other agencies are in the Department of the Interior. The secretary of the Interior disagreed with the Forest Service and suggested that large tracts within the forest might be subject to Aboriginal title. However, until the courts might rule on Aboriginal title, the congressional action gave the Forest Service the signal it needed to proceed with pulp mill and timber lease development.[29]

When the court test came, it would not be from James Curry but, rather, from William Paul. Curry was preparing to file a single suit on behalf of all of the Tlingit and Haida Indians of Alaska. For whatever reason, Paul had come to the conclusion that neither the Tlingit nor the Haida people constituted a tribe, and he was convinced that because the US courts in all previous land claims cases had dealt with a tribal entity, they would insist on dealing with tribal entities in Alaska. In Alaska, each Tlingit and Haida village was composed of several clans, each of which recognized property rights. Paul argued that each clan needed to file a separate claims suit, using the term "tribe" to mean the particular clan people of a specific village. William Paul was a Tee-Hit-Ton from Wrangell, and he persuaded another Washington, DC, attorney to file a claims suit in the Court of Federal Claims on behalf of this tribe. The court found against the Tee-Hit-Tons, and the attorney took the case to the US Supreme Court, which accepted it. Again, Paul lost, the court finding that Congress had not recognized the Tee-Hit-Tons' Aboriginal title in the actions that it had taken to create the Tongass Forest and to authorize pulp mill and timber leases.[30] But for the Indian attorneys, there was a world of opportunity in the court's language, for when the court said that Congress had not recognized the Tee-Hit-Ton title, it implied that the title had been there either for Congress to recognize or not. It was the first judicial confirmation of Aboriginal title in Alaska, and it would apply to all Native groups across the territory. It was the beginning of the idea of a blanket claim on behalf of all Alaska Natives, and it would be the link between the Tlingit-Haida suit and the later 1971 *ANCSA*.

In the meantime, James Curry proceeded with the Tlingit-Haida suit, formally filing it in 1947. Yet Curry's fate was not a happy one. When he was general counsel of the National Congress of Indians, Curry had solicited Indian claims cases that he did not intend to work on himself. Rather, he had brokered them to other attorneys for a portion of their fees. In addition, he had represented himself as holding contracts before he actually had them, and he had colluded with his client's opponents without telling his clients. In 1952, the commissioner of Indian affairs and the US senator from New Mexico convened congressional hearings intended to expose Curry's unethical practices. When the hearings confirmed all that had been charged, the Indian office cancelled all of Curry's contracts. He was out of business.

The Tlingit-Haida suit was taken over by one of the premier Indian attorneys in the United States, Arthur Lazarus, and his partner, Israel "Lefty" Weissbrodt. They pursued the suit in the US Court of Federal Claims, basing their case on Aboriginal title and the demonstrable property rights of the Tlingit and Haida tribes. The court found that, by virtue of unextinguished Aboriginal title, the Tlingit and Haida Indians of Alaska had owned all of the land in the Alexander Archipelago in 1867. In its finding, which was handed down in 1959, the Court of Federal Claims stated that the use and occupancy title of the Tlingit and Haida Indians "was not extinguished by the Treaty of 1867 [the *Alaska Purchase Treaty*] between the United States and Russia ... nor were any rights held by these Indians arising out of their occupancy and use extinguished by the Treaty."[31] Whatever land the Indians had title to in 1867 prior to the treaty therefore remained following the treaty.[32] The court found further that between 1905 and 1907 the United States had extinguished much of this title, all but 2.6 million acres of nearly eighteen million acres, in the creation of the Tongass National Forest. And although the US Supreme Court in *Tee-Hit-Ton* had ruled that such an act of Congress – that is, one that extinguishes Aboriginal title – is not compensable under the Fifth Amendment, it implied that if it were the compensation would be sizeable. Moreover, compensation pursuant to the jurisdictional act referred to earlier was available in the Court of Federal Claims.

The finding of the existence of Aboriginal title for the Tlingit and Haida Indians had very significant implications for all Alaska Natives, for if the 1867 *Alaska Purchase Treaty* did not extinguish this title for the Tlingit and Haida people, it likely did not extinguish it for other Alaska Natives either. In *Tlingit and Haida Indians of Alaska et al. v. U.S.*, the claims court had also found that the first organic act passed by Congress for Alaska in 1884 also protected Native title in the territory.[33] Section 8 of *An Act Providing a Civil Government for Alaska* provides that "the Indians or other persons of said district shall not be disturbed in their possession or any lands actually in their use or occupation or now claimed by them." Further, the treaty reads "the terms under which such persons may acquire title to such lands is reserved for future legislation by Congress."[34] For a variety of reasons, there had been no further congressional legislation on the matter of Alaska Native claims after 1884. This included treaties with Alaska Natives, for the US Congress had ceased Indian treaty making in 1871. Thus, all of Alaska, save the lands that had not been subject to a formal taking by Congress, was potentially subject to Native land claims on the basis of Aboriginal title and protection by the 1884 *Act Providing a Civil Government for Alaska*. Thus, the *Tlingit and Haida* finding was one of profound magnitude, and, had Alaska's circumstances been different, it likely would have resulted in a broad array of land claims cases brought before the federal courts over succeeding decades.

Following loose ends that existed in the *Tlingit and Haida* case, Congress, in 1965, recognized the Central Council of Tlingit and Haida Indian Tribes of Alaska as an Alaska Indian tribe (though not necessarily the only Tlingit or Haida tribe, as subsequent adjudication would test) and also as the proper body to which a compensatory award in the *Tlingit and Haida* suit might be made. The same legislation authorized the Council to prepare plans for use of the anticipated judgment fund.[35] In 1968, the US Court of Federal Claims found that the Tlingit and Haida Indians of Alaska were entitled to $7.5 million for the 1905 and 1907 taking of their lands in the creation of the Tongass National Forest.[36] The amount of the award, which was far less than the Indians had anticipated, was based on the value of the accessible, commercial timber at the time of the taking in 1905 and 1907. The Tlingit and Haida had considered passing up the opportunity to be included in the general settlement of Alaska Native claims that was then under consideration, but the paltry amount of the award forced them to reconsider this notion and to join with other Alaska Natives in the drive for a comprehensive claims settlement in Alaska.[37]

In the 1930s, the Department of the Interior had addressed the question of land claims and distribution in Alaska, but the challenges of the Great Depression and inter-agency rivalries had prevented concerted action. The question arose again during the debates in the constitutional convention preceding statehood, but delegates failed to act on Native land issues, which seemed daunting and complicated. The Congress voted on Alaska's statehood in the summer of 1958, and the new state was officially created on 3 January 1959. Section 4 of the *Alaska Statehood Act* was a disclaimer of any right or title by the people of Alaska to any lands that might be subject to Native title.[38] On the basis of *Hualapai Indians v. Santa Fe Railroad*, which was confirmed in *Tlingit and Haida*, no one knew just which lands those might be, but they might be all land in Alaska that was not formally withdrawn by Congress – well over 300 million acres.[39] At the same time, section 6 of the *Alaska Statehood Act* authorized state selection for state title of 104 million acres of "unreserved and unoccupied land."

Soon after statehood, the state lands division began to identify areas of the state to request title that would be under the 104-million-acre grant in the *Alaska Statehood Act*.[40] The first selections were lands with economic potential and included the Kenai Peninsula and Cook Inlet oil lands and the area on the north slope between the federal Petroleum Reserve No. 4 and the Arctic National Wildlife Refuge, including, fortuitously, Prudhoe Bay.[41] By the mid-1960s, title to about twelve million acres had been conveyed. At the same time the state was making its selections, however, Natives began to protest some of the choices. The Department of the Interior interpreted section 4 to mean not just lands to which individual Natives might have title by allotment, or by explicit grant or reservation, but all lands subject to Aboriginal title – lands that Natives had at one time utilized and occupied, even if that land had been abandoned subsequently. Native villages and groups in Alaska, spurred to action by the state's selections of its lands, worked with the legal division of the Bureau of Indian Affairs and with a number of Alaska attorneys to begin identifying lands that they considered subject to Native title. Since a number of Native claims overlapped, Native protests to state land selections totalled more than the 375 million acres of land in all of Alaska by 1965. The perceived need to assemble land claims also spurred the development of new regional Native organizations and, in 1965, the first viable statewide confederation of such groups, the Alaska Federation of Natives, was formed. Although some Alaska attorneys worked with a few Native groups on the issue, there was no widespread recognition in the state that Native claims would be a critical issue. However, in 1965, secretary of the interior, Stewart Udall, responding to Native protests and also to changes in the national perception of minority rights, addressed the situation in Alaska in dramatic fashion. He issued a temporary injunction halting any further conveyances of land title to the state until the Native claims problem could be resolved.

The secretary's action took most political and economic leaders in the state by surprise, and they reacted accordingly. Alaskans called the action a "land freeze" and a "lock up."[42] Most non-Native Alaskans seem to have considered the provision of some land around villages and some hunting opportunities as being a sufficient response to Native land claims and the protection of their integrity. In particular, few appreciated the significance of the theory of Aboriginal title, which might require formal extinguishment by the Congress and perhaps some sort of compensatory award. Until the areas actually subject to Native title could be identified, the land freeze implied that in areas under Native protest economic development would be suspended, pending some resolution.

The state protested the land freeze, arguing that it constituted a violation of the provision for state land selection in Article 6 of the *Alaska Statehood Act*. In addition, the state questioned the secretary's authority to take such an action at all. Native leaders in Alaska, however, applauded the action, as did major attorneys for Native Americans and civil rights leaders nationally. The discovery of North America's largest oil deposit at Prudhoe Bay on Alaska's north slope in 1968 exacerbated the necessity of a resolution to the land claims conundrum, for no economic development could take place in the new state until the Native claims were resolved.

This resolution came with congressional action in 1971, namely the *ANCSA*.[43] The Natives, the Department of the Interior, and the state agreed that the Native entitlement would be about forty-four million acres and that Congress would authorize $962.5 million in compensation for the extinguishment of title to all other Native claims and land in the state. The money would capitalize twelve regional Native economic development corporations and as many village corporations as members of the 208 identified villages chose to form. All Natives would be given the opportunity to become stock holders both in a regional and a village corporation, which were organized as profit-generating entities under the corporation laws of the state of Alaska. Regional corporations would own the subsurface estate in the region, while village corporations would own the surface estate in or near their villages. This settlement passed the Congress on 17 December 1971. Being a comprehensive and complete settlement of Alaska Native land claims, the act empowered Alaska Natives, unlike anything heretofore in their modern history, while, at the same time, clearing the way for new economic development in the state.[44]

William Lewis Paul played only a supporting role in the dramatic resolution of Alaska Native land claims. In 1959, Fred Paul had persuaded the Alaska bar in the new state of Alaska to reinstate his father. Recognized in his later years for his dedication to Alaska Native rights and causes, William Paul often lectured at the Mount Edgecumbe Native School in Sitka and spent many hours counselling younger Alaska Native leaders on Aboriginal title, congressional recognition, and Indian law. Many of those leaders played key roles in helping to fashion the 1971 claims settlement. William Paul died in 1977 at age ninety-one. In his history of Alaska Native land claims, Don Mitchell paid him this tribute: "[H]e was the new generation's most important link to their historic past."[45] Indeed he was.

There is one final note to the story of William Paul and Alaska Native land claims. In all of the records pertaining to his life and work, and to the assembling and pursuit of Alaska Native claims, there is no documentary record of contact or correspondence between William Paul and Frank Calder. Calder recalls corresponding with Paul about British Columbia claims in Dixon Entrance, near Prince Rupert, but Paul's surviving papers include no reference to the correspondence. Although British Columbia and Alaska Native land claims proceeded nearly apace in time and in proximity, there was apparently no direct connection between the two. Whether this was a function of cultural barriers and habits, or the absence of a linking legal context, it is impossible to say. It must be sufficient to note for historians and others that proximity does not necessarily equate to relationship.

Part 3
Calder and Its Implications

6

Calder and the Representation of Indigenous Society in Canadian Jurisprudence

Michael Asch

Rarely in the history of a country is a court judgment so momentous that it causes society to reexamine basic premises. Such was the impact in the United States of *Brown v. Board of Education*,[1] of *Mabo v. Queensland (No. 2)*[2] in Australia, and, I predict, of the recent *Alexkor Ltd. v. Richtersveld Community and Others*[3] judgment in South Africa. Among these must be counted the 1973 judgment of the Supreme Court of Canada in *Calder et al. v. Attorney-General of British Columbia*.[4] It mounted a fundamental challenge to the way in which Canada constructs Aboriginal rights and, in so doing, propelled this issue from the periphery to the centre of Canadian political life.

The watershed that was *Calder* is succinctly summed up in two statements. The first, which was made at the time of the trial court judgment by the government of Canada's white paper in 1969 (the same year as the trial judgment in *Calder*), confidently declared that Aboriginal rights "are so general and undefined that it is not realistic to think of them as specific claims capable of remedy."[5] The second, made in 1973 by then Prime Minister Pierre Trudeau immediately following the judgment of the Supreme Court of Canada, conceded that "perhaps you had more legal rights than we thought you had when we did the White Paper."[6] The occasion of the judgment marked the beginning of the journey towards reconciliation of relations between indigenous peoples and Canada on which we are still proceeding.

What is it about *Calder* that it remains, thirty years on, a crucial guide for the present and future? In my view, it lies particularly in the understanding that it conveys about our current relationship with indigenous peoples and the kind of rethinking we need to do to square that relationship with our sense of justice. Given space constraints, I can only sketch what I mean. I will do so by reference to what I consider to be a crucial matter raised in the judgment, namely, the choice between two ways to represent indigenous society at the time of the first European settlement and the implications for creating a political relationship that follow from it.

The Representations of Indigenous Society in *Calder*

The judgment by Chief Justice Herbert William Davey in the British Columbia Court of Appeal depicted indigenous society at the time of European settlement as follows:

> [I]n spite of the commendation of Mr. Duff, a well-known anthropologist, of the native culture of the Indians on the mainland of British Columbia, they were undoubtedly at the time of settlement a very primitive people with few of the institutions of civilized society, and none at all of our notions of private property.

Thus, he continued:

> I see no evidence to justify a conclusion that the aboriginal rights claimed by the successors of these primitive people are of a kind that it should be assumed the Crown recognized them when it acquired the mainland of British Columbia by occupation. [7]

In other words, in Chief Justice Davey's representation, indigenous peoples were very different from the settlers for they were at a "very primitive" stage of society. Hence, it could not be presumed that their society, such as it might be, was sufficiently organized to presume that they had any rights of a kind that required Crown recognition at the time of European settlement. As will be discussed briefly in this chapter, this representation was not of Chief Justice Davey's invention but was derived through reference to English law of the colonial period, of which *In re Southern Rhodesia* represents a leading authority.[8]

At the Supreme Court of Canada, Justice Emmett Hall weighed this perspective with another. The comparison was expressed in the following salient passage from his judgment:

> The assessment and interpretation of the historical documents and enactments tendered in evidence must be approached in the light of present-day research and knowledge disregarding ancient concepts formulated when understanding of the customs and culture of our original people was rudimentary and incomplete and when they were thought to be wholly without cohesion, laws or culture, in effect a subhuman species.[9]

Using this measure, Justice Hall went on to rebuke the representation of indigenous society advanced at the Court of Appeal in the following cogent extract:

Chief Justice Davey in the judgment under appeal with all the historical research and material available since 1823 and notwithstanding the evidence in the record which Gould J. found was given "with total integrity," said of the Indians of the mainland of British Columbia that "... they were undoubtedly at the time of the settlement a very primitive people with few of the institutions of civilized society, and none at all of our notions of private property."

In so saying this in 1970, he was assessing the Indian culture of 1858 by the same standards that the Europeans applied to the Indians of North America two or more centuries before.[10]

The Hall judgment also laid out an alternative representation. It is, to paraphrase Justice Hall's language, that, if we are to rely on contemporary Western standards, judgments must be based on the presumption that indigenous societies were, at the time of settlement, wholly cohesive, with law and culture, in effect human societies like any other.[11] It follows from this premise that there can be no hierarchy of societies, as posited by Chief Justice Davey, for, unlike the situation in the mid-nineteenth century that Justice Hall describes earlier and given contemporary standards, all societies must be presumed to be fully organized in every respect and have equivalent standing with respect to each other.[12] Therefore, as Justice Hall's judgment indicates, it follows that, because indigenous peoples at the time of European settlement lived in societies that were equal in standing to that of the settlers, their members had rights that required recognition by the settlers and their sovereign.

Applying this perspective to the case at hand, Justice Hall concludes that, at the time of European settlement,

> [w]hat emerges from the ... evidence is that the Nishgas [common spelling at the time] in fact are and were from time immemorial a distinctive cultural entity with concepts of ownership indigenous to their culture and capable of articulation under the common law.[13]

Justice Hall's understanding is fully supported in the other substantive judgment in *Calder*, which was penned by Justice Wilfred Judson. He states his comprehensive view of indigenous society and his specific finding with regard to the Nisga'a clearly and succinctly in the following passage:

> The fact is that when the settlers came the Indians were there, organized in societies and occupying the land as their forefathers had done for centuries. That is what Indian title means. What they are asserting in this action is

that they had a right to continue to live on their lands as their forefathers had lived and that this right has never been lawfully extinguished.[14]

Thus, notwithstanding the division that occurred respecting whether indigenous rights could survive general legislation respecting them, both substantive judgments agreed with respect to how indigenous societies at the time of European settlement should be conceptualized. Therefore, it is fair to conclude that it represents the perspective shared by the six justices who participated in the substantive judgment and can be appropriately described as the representation favoured in *Calder*.

The Post-*Calder* Representation of Indigenous Society in Jurisprudence

Notwithstanding the clarity with which the *Calder* court spoke, its way of representing indigenous society has not been favoured in post-*Calder* jurisprudence. Rather, with certain exceptions, this jurisprudence has adopted the representation espoused by Chief Justice Davey and rejected by Justice Hall. First, let me briefly discuss the exceptions. There are aspects of Aboriginal rights where the courts and the state no longer question that indigenous peoples lived in societies that are equal in standing to all others. These aspects relate largely to "the subsistence sector of the 'traditional' economy and other Indigenous cultural practices."[15] It is here that, beginning with *Calder*, "Aboriginal rights discourse has produced a range of beneficial ... rights that could not have been imagined in 1973."[16]

At the same time, there are many other areas of rights discourse where success cannot be readily demonstrated. These include commercial rights for fishing and other traditional activities, Aboriginal title, sub-surface rights, and, of course, political rights. Although I cannot elaborate on this division more fully in this chapter, I think it will become apparent that it arises from the perspective that dominates current jurisprudence, which is that indigenous society was "primitive" and only incompletely organized when compared with that of the European settlers they first encountered. I will illustrate this point by referring to two matters I have previously addressed more fully elsewhere.[17] These are the test derived from *Hamlet of Baker Lake v. Minister of Indian Affairs and Northern Development* and the presumption, made explicit in *R. v. Sparrow*,[18] that Crown sovereignty extended to what is now Canada from the moment of European settlement.

Baker Lake

Baker Lake was a 1978 judgment in the Federal Court of Canada.[19] It concerned a request to grant an order, based on Aboriginal title, restraining the government of Canada from issuing, among other things, land use permits on the traditional lands of the Inuit of Baker Lake. In the course of making his findings of fact, Justice Patrick Mahoney laid out four criteria that the Inuit needed to meet in order "to establish aboriginal title cognizable at common law."[20] This is what has become known as the "*Baker Lake* test," and it has been applied, either directly or indirectly,[21] in much recent litigation regarding both Aboriginal title and Aboriginal rights.

It is to the first criterion in the test that I wish to draw attention. It states that the indigenous party must establish "that they and their ancestors were members of an organized society" at the time (to quote from the fourth criterion) "sovereignty was asserted by England."[22] To a layman, this question appears to enquire into whether the indigenous party is, in fact, a random group of individuals or a collectivity of some kind. However, the courts have not seen it in this way. Rather, beginning with *Baker Lake*, jurisprudence seeks to determine two matters about an indigenous society at the time of European settlement as a pre-condition for assessing whether the right it seeks to have enforced exists in the law. The first is to establish, on the basis of evidence, *if* the indigenous collectivity was living in an organized society or *if* it should be considered, in law, as existing at a level that one might define as "pre-organized" or "not organized." And, second, when the courts accept that the collectivity did exist as an organized society, it must then establish, again on the basis of evidence led by the indigenous party, whether this society was *sufficiently* organized to gain recognition of the right in question.

To arrive at this interpretation of the phrase "they and their ancestors were members of an organized society," Justice Mahoney relied explicitly on representations of indigenous society found in English law precedents from the later colonial period. The paramount authority, which Justice Mahoney cited at length, is *Southern Rhodesia*, a 1919 judgment of the Judicial Committee of the Privy Council of Great Britain. In advancing this viewpoint, Justice Mahoney turns specifically to a lengthy passage in this judgment, which contains a key segment:

> The estimation of the rights of aboriginal tribes is always inherently difficult. Some tribes are so low in the scale of social organization that their usages and conceptions of rights and duties are not to be reconciled with the institutions or legal ideas of civilized society. Such a gulf cannot be bridged.[23]

Justice Mahoney relies on this authority uncritically in developing a way to test the phrase "they and their ancestors were living in an organized society." That is, he concludes that precedent requires that "the existence of an organized society is a prerequisite to the existence of aboriginal title" and that

[t]he thrust of all the authorities is not that the common law necessarily deprives aborigines of their enjoyment of the land in any particular but, rather, that it can give effect only to those incidents of that enjoyment that were, themselves, given effect by the regime that prevailed before.[24]

He then applies this reasoning to the Inuit of Baker Lake and concludes:

[T]he aboriginal Inuit had an organized society. It was not a society with very elaborate institutions but it was a society organized to exploit the resources available on the barrens and essential to sustain human life there. That was about all they could do: hunt and fish and survive.[25]

Thus, according to the terms of the *Baker Lake* test, the Inuit were determined to have been living in an organized society. However, their form of society was organized only to the extent that it could "sustain human life there." Given that the right in question related to hunting and fishing, Justice Mahoney agreed that they had a valid claim for an injunction on at least part of their traditional territory. However, his words invite the conclusion that, were the Inuit to ask for legal relief concerning an aspect of an organized society that was considered "very elaborate," the Inuit would not pass that test and, hence, would lose.

It is transparent that the passage from *Southern Rhodesia* (and, indeed, from the judgment itself) is racist and ethnocentric in its portrayal of indigenous society. It is a passage that, I expect, all would consider offensive in light of the present-day understandings. It depicts the way of understanding that was dominant in the colonial era, which the *Calder* court completely rejected. And, as can be seen from the conclusions drawn by Justice Mahoney regarding the Baker Lake Inuit, because of its presuppositions, it is fated to represent indigenous society (or, indeed, any society one might wish) as being incommensurate with and, in fundamental ways, inferior to our own. Yet, as I will outline in this chapter with reference to two important post-*Calder* cases, it remains the line of reasoning that dominates recent jurisprudence, both directly and indirectly.

My first example is the trial judgment in *Delgamuukw v. British Columbia*, the case in which the question of Aboriginal title was raised for the first time after the entrenchment of Aboriginal rights in the constitution.[26] Following the precedent laid out in *Baker Lake*, the Gitxsan and Wet'suwet'en led extensive evidence concerning the laws, customs, institutions, and values they had in relation to land title in order to establish that they and their ancestors were an organized society of sufficient standing at the time of European settlement to succeed in this action. Based on this information, Chief Justice Allan McEachern applied the rationale of the *Baker Lake* test in rendering his judgment. With regard to the necessity to demonstrate "the existence of an organized society" as a "prerequisite" to finding "aboriginal title," the trial judgment agreed that the Gitxsan and Wet'suwet'en existed as "organized societies" at the time of European settlement. However, he determined that this existence was at such a primitive level that it was based not on reason but, rather, on instinct[27] or, as is attested to in the following quotation, living in the state of nature as it was imagined in *The Leviathan*:

> It would not be accurate to assume that even pre-contact existence in the territory was in the least idyllic. The plaintiffs' ancestors had no written language, no horses or wheeled vehicles, slavery and starvation were not uncommon, wars with neighbouring peoples were common, and there is no doubt, to quote Hobbs [sic], that aboriginal life in the territory was, at best, "nasty, brutish and short."[28]

Based on this finding of fact, Chief Justice McEachern concluded that "in the legal and jurisdictional vacuum ... [that] existed prior to British sovereignty the organization of these people was the only form of ownership and jurisdiction which existed."[29] However, he limited the scope of ownership and jurisdiction to the areas of the villages, for, as he went on, he "would not make the same finding with respect to the rest of the territory, even to areas over which, I believe, their ancestors roamed for sustenance purposes."[30] Hence, he concluded that "the interest of the plaintiffs' ancestors ... w[as] nothing more than the right to use the land"[31] and, thus, that, "as of the date of British sovereignty," the Gitxsan and Wet'suwet'en had established in law recognition only of their "continued residence in the villages, and for non-exclusive aboriginal sustenance rights within [certain] portions of the territory. These aboriginal rights do not include commercial practices."[32] And, hence, "the interest of the plaintiffs' ancestors ... w[as] nothing more than the right to use the land."[33] Happily, the Supreme Court of Canada allowed the appeal and called for a retrial based on the clarifications it had made. At the same time, the Court did not address the idea found in the *Baker Lake* test that requires First Nations to establish that they had existed as organized societies as a "prerequisite" for establishing a right nor the ethnocentric representation of indigenous society that emerged through its application in *Delgamuukw*.

As the second example, *R. v. Van der Peet,* attests, the Supreme Court of Canada did, in fact, embrace this very perspective.[34] *Van der Peet* concerns whether the Stó:lō First Nation has a constitutionally protected right to fish commercially. To determine this right, the Supreme Court of Canada relied explicitly on the notion arising from *Baker Lake* that the protection of an Aboriginal right depends on an assessment of the level of social organization of a First Nation. Specifically, the Court, relying on evidence adduced at trial, determined that the Stó:lō did not have a constitutionally recognized

Aboriginal right to fish commercially because this society was too primitive to establish such a right under the test they established.[35] They determined that such a right could not be established, given the level of organization of a band-level society. Therefore, as the Stó:lō had not been sufficiently organized at the time of European settlement to have practised an activity that could have become a "commercial" fishing right in the period after settlement, constitutional protection for this Aboriginal right was denied.

Sparrow and the Status of Crown Sovereignty at Settlement

As we know, jurisprudence distinguishes between the establishment of Crown sovereignty in colonies established through the settlement of unoccupied lands and those obtained by cession and/or conquest of lands that are already occupied. Furthermore, jurisprudence makes it clear that it is not always necessary for a new territory to be devoid of human inhabitants in order for English law to presume that it was unoccupied or a *terra nullius*. For example, Australian jurisprudence, as per *Mabo*, has made explicit that the Crown assumed, however wrongly, that the indigenous peoples of that continent were too primitive to have a form of political society requiring recognition by the settlers. Therefore, it was legitimate for the Crown to assume Australia was a legal *terra nullius* and, as a consequence, that sovereignty could be legitimately acquired without regard to the fact that indigenous societies were already present on those lands. In Canada, things appear to be more complex, for we have other instruments, such as treaties, that appear to provide legitimacy for the assertion of Crown sovereignty. Nonetheless, there is good cause to conclude that an underlying premise of our political legitimacy is also founded on the presumption, following *terra nullius*, that indigenous society was sufficiently primitive that no means other than settlement by Europeans was *required* to establish our sovereignty. As far as I am aware, this tenet is spelled out explicitly in only one passage in post-*Calder* jurisprudence. In *Sparrow*, it is raised in aid of introducing a rationale for the assumption that Aboriginal rights are ultimately subject to the legislative authority of Parliament. This passage reads:

> It is worth recalling that while British policy towards the native population was based on respect for their right to occupy their traditional lands, a proposition to which the Royal Proclamation of 1763 bears witness, there was from the outset never any doubt that sovereignty and legislative power, and indeed the underlying title, to such lands vested in the Crown.[36]

As Patrick Macklem and I point out,[37] the conclusion that "sovereignty and legislative power, and indeed underlying title to the lands of Indigenous peoples vest in the Crown" "*from the outset*" suggests the application of the doctrine of *terra nullius* to the Canadian context, for if Crown authority arises with the *arrival and settlement* of authorized settlers, then, unlike the situation with conquest and cession, the lands they settle are presumed to have been previously unoccupied. And, given that the judgment admits that there was a Native population that was occupying "their traditional lands" at the time of European settlement, it follows that these "traditional lands" were "occupied" by peoples whose laws, sovereignty, and jurisdiction did not need to be acknowledged by the Crown. In short, this passage indicates that, as far as jurisprudence is concerned, either indigenous peoples did not live in political societies prior to European settlement or, if they did, these societies were of a nature that did not require recognition by settlers from Europe.[38] It is, again, a representation more in keeping with Chief Justice Davey's position than that advocated in the *Calder* judgments at the Supreme Court of Canada.

In sum, as the *Baker Lake* test and *Sparrow* illustrate, post-*Calder* jurisprudence relies on the presumption, which is counter to that espoused by Justices Hall and Judson, that, until they provide proof to the contrary, indigenous peoples are assumed to have been living at the time of European settlement in a form of life that is less than our own. It is thus fair to say that recent jurisprudence still has not escaped the colonialist representation of indigenous peoples already discounted in *Calder* thirty years ago.

Where Do We Go from Here?

Given that the Supreme Court of Canada characterized Chief Justice Davey's representation of indigenous society as contrary to contemporary standards and provided a clear alternative to it, it is hard to understand at first blush why post-*Calder* jurisprudence has not simply rejected this representation in favour of the one that the Supreme Court of Canada unanimously endorsed. There are a number of possible explanations, and I will address one that I believe goes to the heart of the lesson of *Calder*. Explicitly, my proposition states that, were the courts to fully adopt the representation of the Supreme Court of Canada, they would, of necessity, open up a challenge to the political tenets that explain the legitimacy of the Canadian state, which are so sweeping and fundamental that no court would dare to do it on its own. Here is what I mean.

In the final analysis, Canada still rests its foundational political legitimacy on the ideology and legal reasoning of English colonialism. The lynch pin of this ideology and legal regime is the firm conviction that the acquisition of sovereignty, legislative authority, and underlying title by the Crown is unproblematic even without the agreement of the indigenous peoples on whose territories we settled. Were the court to adopt the representation of indigenous society advanced in *Calder*, it would, by necessity, invalidate this assumption, for, under such conditions, the legitimacy of our claim to sovereignty, legislative authority, and underlying title without the express consent of indigenous peoples is called into question. These are dangerous grounds for the judiciary to occupy, both in terms of audacity and of its very capacity as a creature of the state within which it is embedded.

Therefore, I predict that the representation favoured by Chief Justice Davey will remain dominant until Canadians show that we are prepared to face up to the reality that the legitimacy of the Canadian state rests on ethnocentric and racist beliefs that are colonial in origin and that we are prepared to reject it. In this sense, the courts rely on this representation because at this time, to borrow a relevant phrase from the majority in *Van der Peet*, it is *integral* to the political culture of Canadians. Thus, while I believe that much of the odious ethnocentric and biased language that pervades so many post-*Calder* judgments will be eschewed as judges become more conversant with its offensive character, until we change our political culture, the courts, albeit expressed in more subtle terms, will remain faithful to it. One cannot, as the Royal Commission on Aboriginal Peoples has recommended, simply do away with the *terra nullius* doctrine by fiat – too much is at stake. It is a move that can take place only when Canadians are prepared to accept the consequences. However, this position is not new, it is only what the *Calder* judgment already made clear to us in 1973.

Conclusion

Three decades ago, *Calder* laid out a stark choice that Canada must make about building relations with indigenous peoples. It gave us compelling reasons to choose the option consistent with contemporary understandings, which it underscored by making this choice in the judgment. Then, wisely realizing the decentring ramifications that making this choice would bring, the Court suspended its application, but left uncertain whether, in future, it might be adopted within a legal regime where indigenous rights survived general legislation. In so doing, *Calder* instructed governments to take this matter up urgently and beseeched Canadians to face the challenge it represents. It then, quite properly in my view, left it up to us, where it unfortunately still sits, some thirty years on. As I see it, the legacy of *Calder* lies not so much as a precedent in jurisprudence or as an instruction for government, as important as these have been and will continue to be. Rather, its enduring value is as a teaching that urges us to reconsider the inhumane way in which Canada treats indigenous peoples today. It is a teaching that empowers us to believe that forging a relationship faithful to our own sense of justice is within our reach. It is a teaching that is as instructive today as it was on the day it was delivered.

7
A Taxonomy of Aboriginal Rights
Brian Slattery

Section 35(1) of the *Constitution Act, 1982* recognizes and affirms the "existing aboriginal and treaty rights of the aboriginal peoples of Canada."[1] The provision is heavily indebted to the recognition of Aboriginal rights in the landmark case *Calder et al. v. Attorney-General of British Columbia*,[2] which was decided by the Supreme Court of Canada a decade earlier. However, the sparse wording leaves open a number of fundamental questions. What precisely are Aboriginal rights and what is their legal basis? What relationship, if any, do they bear to one another? Do all Aboriginal peoples have the same set of rights or does each group have its own specific set?

These are difficult questions, which do not allow for simple or pat answers. Since 1982, the Supreme Court of Canada has delivered a series of decisions that furnish many important pieces of the puzzle. However, the pieces still lie scattered about in a somewhat disconnected fashion. This chapter attempts to fit them together and fill in the gaps, so as to provide a coherent taxonomy of Aboriginal rights in Canada. The chapter deals first with the important distinction between specific and generic rights, which emerges from the Court's judgments in *R. v. Van der Peet*[3] and *Delgamuukw v. British Columbia*.[4] It then discusses the main types of generic rights and their relationship to specific rights, arguing that generic rights provide the foundation for specific rights and supply the criteria that govern them. Generic rights are not only uniform in character but also universal in distribution. They comprise a set of fundamental rights held by all Aboriginal groups in Canada.

Specific and Generic Rights[5]
In the *Van der Peet* case, the Supreme Court of Canada recognized a class of Aboriginal rights whose nature and scope are determined by the particular circumstances of each specific Aboriginal group.[6] The Court held that in order to constitute an Aboriginal right protected by section 35(1) of the

Constitution Act, 1982, a present-day activity of an Aboriginal group must be based on a practice, custom, or tradition that was integral to the distinctive culture of that specific group in the period prior to European contact.[7] To qualify as being "integral" to a particular culture, a practice has to be a central and significant part of the culture – one of the things that makes the society what it is. Aspects of the society that are only incidental or occasional do not qualify. They must be defining and central features of the society.[8] A practice has to be a characteristic element of the culture; however, it does not need to be unique or different from the practices of other societies. So, for example, fishing for food may constitute an Aboriginal right, even though it is practised by many different societies around the world.[9]

The rights recognized in *Van der Peet* are what we may call *specific rights* – rights whose existence, nature, and scope are determined by factors that are particular to each Aboriginal group. Specific rights differ from group to group and sometimes take quite specialized forms. For example, in *R. v. Gladstone*, the Supreme Court of Canada held that the members of the Heiltsuk people of British Columbia had an Aboriginal right to trade in herring spawn on kelp (a kind of seaweed) and that this trade might be conducted on a commercial basis.[10] The Court's holding was based on historical and anthropological evidence showing that the Heiltsuk had engaged in such a trade as an integral part of their culture prior to contact with Europeans. The right was obviously one that few other Aboriginal groups would be able to claim. It was rooted in the distinctive practices of the Heiltsuk nation and, indeed, was confined to trade in a single, rather exotic, commodity.

In *Van der Peet*, the Supreme Court expressed the view that all Aboriginal rights were specific rights.[11] However, this proved to be a premature generalization. It was quietly discarded by the Court in *Delgamuukw*, which was decided the following year.[12] The hereditary chiefs of the Gitxsan and Wet'suwet'en peoples asserted Aboriginal title to a large tract of land in northern British Columbia, a claim that was contested by the British Columbia government. In argument before the Court, the parties to the case advanced strikingly different conceptions of Aboriginal title, which effectively raised the issue whether Aboriginal title was a specific right, grounded in factors particular to each Aboriginal group, or a right of a more generalized nature. The Aboriginal claimants maintained that Aboriginal title was equivalent to an inalienable fee simple, arguing that it was a right of a fixed and uniform character, similar in this respect to standard estates known to the English law of real property. According to this view, the nature of Aboriginal title did not vary from group to group, depending on their particular culture or customs, but was the same in all cases. As such, Aboriginal title did not constitute a specific right but was a right of a standardized character.

In reply, the governmental parties maintained that Aboriginal title to land was simply a collection of particular Aboriginal rights to engage in specific culture-based activities on the land. In other words, Aboriginal title had no definite character – it was just a bundle of specific Aboriginal rights, each of which had to be proven independently. At best, Aboriginal title gave a group the right to the exclusive use and occupation of the land in order to exercise these specific rights. The group would not be entitled to use the land for any purposes it wanted. It would be limited to exercising the rights in its particular bundle. In effect, in order to engage in a certain activity on the land, a claimant group would have to prove that the particular activity in question satisfied the *Van der Peet* test – that it was an element of a practice, custom, or tradition that was integral to the group's distinctive society at the time of European contact.[13] Thus, according to the governmental argument, the content of Aboriginal title was *variable*. It differed from group to group, depending on the group's particular cultural practices at the time of European contact. By contrast, according to the Aboriginal parties, the content of Aboriginal title was *uniform* and did not depend on the group's historical practices. If a group had Aboriginal title, it could use the land in any way it wanted, subject only to a restriction on transfers to third parties.

In its judgment, the Supreme Court of Canada rejected the governmental argument and adopted a position close to that of the Aboriginal parties. Chief Justice Antonio Lamer stated that Aboriginal title is governed by two principles.[14] Under the *first principle*, a group holding Aboriginal title has the right to the exclusive use and occupation of the land for a broad range of purposes. These purposes do not need to be grounded in the group's ancestral practices, customs, and traditions. So, a group that originally lived mainly by hunting, fishing, and gathering would be free to farm the land, raise cattle on it, exploit its natural resources, or use it for residential, commercial, or industrial purposes. Nevertheless, according to the *second principle*, land held under Aboriginal title is subject to an "inherent limit." This prevents the land from being used in a manner that is irreconcilable with the fundamental nature of the group's attachment to the land, so as to ensure that the land is preserved for use by future generations. In other words, the group may not ruin the land or render it unusable for its original purposes.

The crucial point to note is that the Supreme Court treats Aboriginal title as a *uniform right*, whose basic dimensions do not vary from group to group according to their traditional ways of life. All groups holding Aboriginal title have fundamentally the same kind of right, subject only to minor variations stemming from the inherent limit. In effect, the Court recognizes that Aboriginal title is not a *specific right* of the kind envisaged in *Van der Peet* or even a bundle of specific rights. Aboriginal title is what we may call a *generic right* – a right of a standardized character that is basically identical in all Aboriginal groups where it occurs. The fundamental dimensions of the right are determined by the common law doctrine of Aboriginal rights rather than by the unique circumstances of each group.

In short, in *Van der Peet* and *Delgamuukw,* the Supreme Court of Canada recognized two different kinds of Aboriginal rights – specific rights and generic rights. Specific rights are rights whose nature and scope are defined by factors pertaining to a particular Aboriginal group. As such, they vary in character from group to group. Of course, different Aboriginal groups may have similar specific rights, but this is just happenstance. It does not flow from the nature of the right. By contrast, generic rights are rights of a uniform character whose basic contours are established by the common law of Aboriginal rights. All Aboriginal groups holding a certain generic right have basically the same kind of right. The essential nature of the right does not vary according to factors peculiar to the group.

The distinction between specific and generic rights gives rise to a number of important questions. First, is Aboriginal title the sole instance of a generic right or are there others? Second, what is the precise relationship between generic and specific rights? Are they completely distinct or do they overlap in some fashion? Third, are generic rights not only *uniform* in character but also *universal* in distribution – that is, are they held by all Aboriginal groups or only by certain groups and not others? Fourth, are generic and specific rights both grounded in historical practice? If so, are they open to evolution and change? The remainder of this chapter will be devoted to answering these questions.

The Range and Character of Generic Rights

Is Aboriginal title the only example of a generic right? If we review the *Van der Peet* decision in the light of *Delgamuukw*, we come to a surprising conclusion. Recall that in *Van der Peet* the Court held that Aboriginal groups have the right to engage in activities based on the practices, customs, and traditions that were integral to their distinctive cultures at the time of European contact. To be "integral" to a particular culture, a practice must be a central and significant part of the culture, one of the things that makes the society what it is.[15] When we stand back from this decision, we can see that it has the effect of recognizing another generic right: namely, *the right of Aboriginal peoples to maintain and develop the central and significant elements of their ancestral cultures.*

At the abstract level, this right has a fixed and uniform character. Each and every Aboriginal group has the same general right – to maintain the central and significant aspects of their culture. Of course, what is "central and significant" varies from group to group, in accordance with their particular circumstances, so that at the concrete level the abstract right blossoms into a variety of distinctive specific rights – a matter we will come back to later. However, the point to grasp here is that the abstract right itself is uniform. As such, it constitutes a generic right – what we may call the *right of cultural integrity*.

Are there still other generic Aboriginal rights? A little reflection shows that the answer is yes. A tentative list of generic rights follows, which includes the two rights already identified:

- the right to conclude treaties
- the right to customary law
- the right to honourable treatment by the Crown
- the right to an ancestral territory (Aboriginal title)
- the right of cultural integrity
- the right of self-government

This list is not necessarily complete, and some rights (such as the right of cultural integrity) may need to be subdivided. However, it includes the most important generic rights tacitly recognized in Supreme Court of Canada cases so far. As the jurisprudence evolves, further generic rights may come to light. We will say a few words about each of the rights listed, enough to give a taste of the subject.

The Right to Conclude Treaties

Aboriginal peoples have the right to conclude binding treaties with the Crown and to enforce the Crown's treaty promises in the courts.[16] At Canadian common law, the treaty-making capacity of Aboriginal groups has a fixed and uniform character that does not vary from group to group. The capacity of the Blackfoot is no greater or less than that of the Mi'kmaq or the Innu. All have the same power to negotiate treaties with the Crown, which are protected under section 35(1) of the *Constitution Act, 1982*.[17] As such, the right to conclude treaties constitutes a generic Aboriginal right. The right of Aboriginal peoples to treat with the Crown is matched by the Crown's right to treat with Aboriginal peoples under the royal prerogative. In both cases, the power flows from the inter-societal law of Aboriginal rights, which forms part of the common law of Canada.[18] Since the time of Confederation, the Crown's power in this area has vested primarily in the federal government under section 91(24) of the *Constitution Act, 1867*.[19]

The right to conclude treaties is one of the most important of the generic rights held by Aboriginal peoples, with roots reaching back to the earliest days of European settlement on the continent. It is a highly distinctive right, without exact parallels in other spheres of Canadian constitutional law. Although provincial governments may conclude agreements with the federal government, these agreements have a quite different character and do not hold the constitutional status and protection enjoyed by Aboriginal treaties.[20]

The Right to Customary Law

Aboriginal peoples have the right to maintain and develop their distinctive systems of customary law within an all-embracing federal framework that features multiple and overlapping legal systems and levels of government.[21] The introduction of French and English laws into the colonies founded by the European powers did not have the effect of wiping out the customary laws of Aboriginal groups, which continued to operate within their respective spheres. As Justice Beverley McLachlin observes in *Van der Peet:*

> The history of the interface of Europeans and the common law with aboriginal peoples is a long one. As might be expected of such a long history, the principles by which the interface has been governed have not always been consistently applied. Yet running through this history, from its earliest beginnings to the present time is a golden thread – the recognition by the common law of the ancestral laws and customs [of] the aboriginal peoples who occupied the land prior to European settlement.[22]

The right of Aboriginal peoples to maintain their own laws is a generic right, whose basic scope is determined by the common law doctrine of Aboriginal rights. It does not differ from group to group or from area to area. The Mohawk and Haida peoples are equally entitled to enjoy their respective systems of customary law. Nevertheless, the legal systems protected by the generic right obviously differ in content. Mohawk laws are not the same as Haida laws.

Aboriginal systems of customary law have a status similar to that of provincial legal systems. At Confederation, the *Constitution Act, 1867* provided that the laws in force in the provinces would continue in force, subject to the legislative powers of the federal and provincial governments.[23] Existing bodies of provincial law were carried forward into the new federation, and the power to amend or repeal those laws was distributed between the two main levels of government.

The Right to Honourable Treatment by the Crown

Aboriginal peoples have the right to the fiduciary protection of the Crown and the right to the performance of particular fiduciary duties flowing from that relationship.[24] In *R. v. Sparrow*, the Supreme Court of Canada stated:

> [T]he Government has the responsibility to act in a fiduciary capacity with respect to aboriginal peoples. The relationship between the Government

and aboriginals is trust-like, rather than adversarial, and contemporary recognition and affirmation of aboriginal rights must be defined in light of
this historic relationship.[25]

Although the Court was referring to section 35(1) of the *Constitution Act,
1982*, subsequent Supreme Court of Canada decisions have made it clear
that the Crown's fiduciary responsibility is not confined to this context but
accompanies and controls the discretionary powers that the Crown historically has assumed over the lives of Aboriginal peoples.[26] As Chief Justice
McLachlin noted in *Mitchell v. M.N.R.*,[27] from early days the Crown asserted
sovereignty over Aboriginal lands and underlying title to the soil; from this
assertion "arose an obligation to treat aboriginal peoples fairly and honourably, and to protect them from exploitation."

At the most abstract level, the right to honourable treatment by the Crown
is a generic right, which vests uniformly in Aboriginal peoples across Canada. The point is underlined in *Haida Nation v. British Columbia (Minister of
Forests)*, where Chief Justice McLachlin held that the honour of the Crown
is always at stake in its dealings with Aboriginal peoples.[28] The Crown has
the general duty to determine, recognize, and respect the rights of Aboriginal groups over which it has asserted sovereignty. This, in turn, binds the
Crown to enter into treaty negotiations with Aboriginal peoples for the
purpose of reconciling their rights with the advent of Crown sovereignty
and to achieve a just settlement. Pending the conclusion of treaties determining these rights, the Crown has a duty to consult with Aboriginal peoples
whenever it undertakes actions that may affect their asserted rights and
also to accommodate these rights where necessary. In situations where the
Crown has assumed discretionary control over specific Aboriginal interests,
the honour of the Crown gives rise to a fiduciary duty. This generally requires the Crown to act with reference to the Aboriginal group's best interest in exercising its discretion over the specific Aboriginal interest at stake.

In effect, then, the generic right to honourable treatment gives rise to a
range of more precise rights and duties that attach to specific subject matters in particular contexts. As Justice Ian Binnie explains in *Wewaykum Indian Band v. Canada*,[29] not all obligations existing between the parties to a
fiduciary relationship are themselves fiduciary in nature, and this observation holds true of the relationship between the Crown and Aboriginal
peoples. It is necessary to focus on the particular obligation or interest that
is the subject matter of the dispute and to inquire whether the Crown had
assumed sufficient discretionary control in relation thereto to ground a fiduciary obligation.

In the context of Indian reserves, for example, the nature and intensity
of the Crown's fiduciary duties differ depending on whether the subject

matter relates to the creation of a new reserve or the protection of an existing reserve.[30] When the Crown sets out to create a new reserve in lands where the Indian beneficiaries have no prior treaty or Aboriginal claims, its fiduciary duties are limited to the basic obligations of loyalty and good faith in the discharge of its mandate, providing full appropriate disclosure, and acting in the best interest of the beneficiaries. However, once a reserve has been created, the Crown's fiduciary duties expand to include the protection and preservation of the Indian band's interest from exploitation.

The Right to an Ancestral Territory (Aboriginal Title)
Aboriginal peoples have the right to the exclusive possession and use of lands occupied at the time of sovereignty. Aboriginal title exists as a burden on the Crown's underlying title and may not be transferred to third parties; it may be ceded only to the Crown.[31] As seen earlier, Aboriginal title has a uniform legal character, which does not vary from group to group according to their traditional practices and customs. At the same time, Aboriginal title provides a framework for the internal operation of the distinctive land laws of each Aboriginal group and so allows for quite varied regimes of property rights and interests.[32] Aboriginal title is similar in this respect to the title held by the provinces to lands within their boundaries under section 109 of the *Constitution Act, 1867*. In principle, the provincial title is a uniform one and gives provinces the same range of rights to their lands and resources, subject to any specific constitutional provisions. However, land laws vary from province to province and generate distinctive regimes of property rights and interests. The property system of Québec is very different from that of Manitoba.

The Right of Cultural Integrity
As seen earlier, in *Van der Peet*, the Supreme Court of Canada recognizes that Aboriginal peoples have the right to maintain and develop the central and significant elements of their ancestral cultures. The generic right of cultural integrity gives birth to a host of specific rights that differ from group to group in accordance with their distinctive practices, customs, and traditions, such as the right to hunt in a certain area, the right to fish in certain waters, the right to harvest certain natural resources, the right to practise a certain religion, the right to speak a certain language, and so on. Despite such differences, these specific rights fall into a number of broad classes, which relate to such subjects as livelihood, religion, language, and art. These classes constitute generic cultural rights of intermediate generality.

For example, the right to practise a traditional religion arguably qualifies as an intermediate cultural right because spirituality is normally a central and significant feature of Aboriginal societies. Viewed in the abstract, this right has a uniform scope, which does not vary from one Aboriginal people to another. However, the particular activities protected by the right differ from group to group, depending on the distinctive religious practices and beliefs of the group. In effect, then, the generic right of cultural integrity harbours an intermediate right to practise a traditional religion, which, in turn, shelters a plethora of specific religious rights vested in particular Aboriginal groups.

Consider another example. Aboriginal groups arguably have the constitutional right to use their ancestral languages and to enjoy the educational and cultural institutions needed to maintain and develop them. The language of a group is normally an integral feature of its ancestral culture and an important means by which the culture is manifested, nurtured, and transmitted. So the right to use an Aboriginal language has a strong claim to qualify as a cultural right of intermediate generality. According to this approach, the abstract dimensions of the right are identical in all Aboriginal groups where it occurs; however, it gives rise to specific rights to speak and transmit particular Aboriginal languages.

Perhaps the most important intermediate right is what we may call the right of traditional livelihood. A fundamental principle informing the Crown's acquisition of sovereignty was that an Aboriginal people could continue to gain its living in its accustomed manner. Justice McLachlin identified this right in her dissenting opinion in the *Van der Peet* case.[33] Citing the terms of treaties and the Royal Proclamation of 1763,[34] she observed:

> These arrangements bear testimony to the acceptance by the colonizers of the principle that the aboriginal peoples who occupied what is now Canada were regarded as possessing the aboriginal right to live off their lands and the resources found in their forests and streams to the extent they had traditionally done so. The fundamental understanding – the *Grundnorm* of settlement in Canada – was that the aboriginal people could only be deprived of the sustenance they traditionally drew from the land and adjacent waters by solemn treaty with the Crown, on terms that would ensure to them and to their successors a replacement for the livelihood that their lands, forests and streams had since ancestral times provided them.[35]

This viewpoint later attracted the Supreme Court of Canada's support in *R. v. Marshall*.[36] In the course of interpreting a Mi'kmaq treaty of 1760, Justice Binnie appealed to a fundamental precept of British imperial practice in North America, which held that when an Aboriginal people passed under Crown sovereignty it was entitled to continue to sustain itself in the manner it had done previously. As Justice Binnie noted dryly, this principle was not wholly altruistic:

Peace was bound up with the ability of the Mi'kmaq people to sustain themselves economically. Starvation breeds discontent. The British certainly did not want the Mi'kmaq to become an unnecessary drain on the public purse of the colony of Nova Scotia or of the Imperial purse in London, as the trial judge found. To avoid such a result, it became necessary to protect the traditional Mi'kmaq economy, including hunting, gathering and fishing.[37]

The right of livelihood recently attracted detailed discussion in *R. v. Sappier; R. v. Gray*, where Justice Michel Bastarache held that the weight of authority supports the view that section 35 protects the means by which an Aboriginal society traditionally sustained itself.[38] He went on to explain that the doctrine of Aboriginal rights arises from the simple fact of prior occupation of the lands now forming Canada. So the Court's focus should be on the nature of this prior occupation. This involves an inquiry into the traditional way of life of a particular Aboriginal community, including its means of survival.

In summary, the right of cultural integrity forms a pyramid with three levels. At the top is the abstract right itself, which takes the same general form in all Aboriginal groups. Beneath this level lies a tier of intermediate generic rights that relate to distinct subject matters such as livelihood, religion, language, and the like. At the bottom rests a broad range of specific rights that differ from group to group in accordance with their particular cultural characteristics.

The Right of Self-Government

Aboriginal peoples have the right to govern themselves within a federal constitutional framework characterized by a division of powers among various orders of government.[39] This right finds its source in the British Crown's recognition that it could not secure the amity of the indigenous nations over which it claimed sovereignty without acknowledging their right to manage their own internal affairs. As Justice Lamer noted in *R. v. Sioui*, the Crown treated Indian nations with generosity and respect, out of the fear that the safety and development of British colonies would otherwise be compromised:

> The British Crown recognized that the Indians had certain ownership rights over their land, it sought to establish trade with them which would rise above the level of exploitation and give them a fair return. *It also allowed them autonomy in their internal affairs, intervening in this area as little as possible.*[40]

It is submitted that the right of self-government is a generic right, which recognizes a uniform set of governmental powers held by Aboriginal peoples as a distinct order of government within the Canadian federal system. At the same time, it allows Aboriginal groups to establish and maintain their own constitutions, which take a variety of forms. There are close parallels to the provinces, which not only possess a set of generic governmental powers under section 92 of the *Constitution Act, 1867* but also are entitled to maintain distinctive provincial constitutions.

It could be argued that the Aboriginal right of self-government is not a generic right but a collection of specific rights, each of which has to be proven separately under the *Van der Peet* test.[41] In *R. v. Pamajewon*, the Supreme Court of Canada viewed the question through the lens of *Van der Peet* and held that the right of self-government would have to be proven as an element of specific practices, customs, and traditions integral to the particular Aboriginal society in question.[42] According to this approach, the right of self-government would be a collage of specific rights to govern particular activities rather than a generic right to deal with a range of abstract subject matters. However, the *Pamajewon* case was decided prior to the Court's decision in *Delgamuukw*, which expanded the horizons of Aboriginal rights and recognized the category of generic rights.

In light of *Delgamuukw*, it seems more sensible to treat the right of self-government as a generic Aboriginal right, on the model of Aboriginal title, rather than as a bundle of specific rights. In this view, the right of self-government is governed by uniform principles laid down by Canadian common law. The basic scope of the right does not vary from group to group. However, its application to a particular group differs depending on the circumstances. This is the approach taken in the *Report of the Royal Commission on Aboriginal Peoples*, which the Supreme Court of Canada cites in its brief comments on self-government in the *Delgamuukw* case.[43]

Nevertheless, certain other observations in *Delgamuukw* arguably rule out this approach. In declining to be drawn into an analysis of self-government, the Court reiterates its holding in *Pamajewon* that rights to self-government cannot be framed in "excessively general terms" and notes that the Aboriginal parties to the case had advanced the right to self-government "in very broad terms, and therefore in a manner not cognizable under s. 35(1)."[44] It is submitted that these remarks should be understood simply as a warning against over-ambitious litigation, which attempts to induce the courts to settle very difficult questions in a vacuum, without an appropriate factual or doctrinal context.[45]

The Relationship between Generic and Specific Rights

The link between generic and specific rights should now be clear. Specific rights are concrete instances of generic rights. So, for example, the generic right to honourable treatment by the Crown operates at a high level of abstraction and harbours a range of intermediate generic rights relating to different subject matters, such as the creation of Indian reserves or the protection of existing reserves. These intermediate rights, in turn, engender myriad specific fiduciary rights vesting in particular Aboriginal groups, whose precise scope is determined by the concrete circumstances in which they arise. Similarly, the broad right of cultural integrity fosters a range of intermediate generic rights, which relate to such matters as livelihood, language, and religion. These intermediate rights give birth to specific rights, whose character is shaped by the practices, customs, and traditions of particular Aboriginal groups.

The precise relationship between generic and specific rights varies depending on the generic right in question. Consider, for example, the generic right of self-government. As just seen, this right arguably confers the same set of governmental powers on all Aboriginal peoples in Canada. In this respect, the right of self-government resembles the uniform package of governmental powers vested in the provinces. However, this abstract homogeneity does not mean that Aboriginal peoples possess the same *internal* constitutions and governmental structures or that they exercise their governmental powers up to their full theoretical limits. An important component of the Aboriginal right of self-government is the power of an Aboriginal group to establish and amend its own constitution within the overarching framework of the Canadian constitution. This power parallels the power of a province to amend its own constitution under section 45 of the *Constitution Act, 1982*. So, it appears that the generic right of self-government, in allowing for the creation of a variety of governmental structures, engenders a range of specific governmental powers and rights, as detailed in the particular constitutions of Aboriginal groups.

It might be argued that not all generic rights blossom into specific *rights*; rather, some generic rights give rise to specific *institutions*, which represent a complex mix of rules, rights, and obligations. For example, the generic right to conclude treaties empowers Aboriginal groups to enter into binding agreements with the Crown. As such, the right spawns an array of particular agreements differing in subject-matter and scope. According to this argument, while it is true that each treaty represents the concrete exercise of the generic right, it does not follow that the treaty itself is a "specific right" or that the rights embodied in the treaty are "specific rights." Rather, the generic right to conclude treaties gives rise to a web of reciprocal rights and obligations embodied in a concrete agreement, which is best characterized as an *institution*.

How persuasive is this argument? In some respects, it is correct. A treaty does not, itself, constitute a specific right, nor do its terms necessarily embody specific rights. Indeed, treaties often contain a blend of generic and specific rights. Nevertheless, it remains true that the Aboriginal party to a treaty has a specific right to its performance, and the nature and scope of that right and the remedies to which it gives rise are shaped by the generic right that engenders it.

Similarly, the generic right to customary law harbours a host of distinct legal systems held by particular Aboriginal groups. Although each system is a concrete manifestation of the overarching generic right, it seems clear that the legal system is not itself a specific right. Nevertheless, it is also true that an Aboriginal group has a specific right to *enjoy* its own legal system to the extent determined by the generic right that governs it.

Just as all generic rights give birth to specific rights, so also are all specific rights the offspring of generic rights. In other words, there are no "orphan" specific rights. The reason is that generic rights provide the basic rules governing the existence and scope of specific rights. So an Aboriginal group cannot possess a specific right unless it is rooted in a generic right. By the same token, the scope of a specific right cannot exceed the basic dimensions of the generic right that engenders it.

The Universality of Generic Rights

Generic rights are not only *uniform* in character, they are also *universal* in distribution. They make up a set of fundamental rights presumptively held by all Aboriginal groups in Canada. There is no need to prove in each case that a group has the right to conclude treaties with the Crown, to enjoy a customary legal system, to benefit from the honour of the Crown, to occupy its ancestral territory, to maintain the central attributes of its culture, or to govern itself under the Crown's protection. It is presumed that every Aboriginal group in Canada has these fundamental rights, in the absence of valid legislation or treaty stipulations to the contrary. This situation is hardly surprising, given the uniform application of the doctrine of Aboriginal rights throughout the various territories that make up Canada, regardless of their precise historical origins or previous positions as French or English colonies.[46]

The generic rights held by Aboriginal peoples resemble the set of constitutional rights vested in the provinces under the general provisions of the *Constitution Act, 1867*. Just as every province presumptively enjoys the same array of governmental powers, regardless of its size, population, wealth, resources, or historical circumstances, so also every Aboriginal group, large or small, presumptively enjoys the same range of generic Aboriginal rights. However, this conclusion could be disputed. For example, it could be argued that the generic right of Aboriginal title is not a universal right. According to this viewpoint, some Aboriginal peoples did not have sufficiently stable connections with a definite territory to hold Aboriginal title, although they may have possessed specific rights of hunting, fishing, and gathering. Certain musings of the Supreme Court of Canada seem to entertain this possibility.[47] However, the better view is that every Aboriginal group presumptively holds Aboriginal title to an ancestral territory, unless there is very strong evidence to the contrary.

The Critical Date for Aboriginal Rights

As a matter of Canadian law, Aboriginal rights came into existence when the Crown gained sovereignty over an Aboriginal people – what we will call the "time of sovereignty." Before this time, the relations between an Aboriginal people and the Crown were governed by international law and the terms of any treaties. Although Aboriginal peoples clearly held rights in international law prior to the time of sovereignty (and continue to hold certain international rights today), it was only when the Crown gained sovereignty that Aboriginal rights as such arose in Canadian law.[48] So, it seems natural to think that the critical date for establishing the existence of Aboriginal rights is the time of sovereignty. However, the matter is not so straightforward. We have to distinguish between generic and specific rights.

Generic Rights

As seen earlier, when an Aboriginal people passes under the Crown's sovereignty, it automatically gains a set of generic rights – the right of cultural integrity, the right to honourable treatment by the Crown, and so on. These rights come into existence at the time of sovereignty and possess a uniform character. Nevertheless, some generic rights have concrete aspects that change over time. For example, although the generic right to customary law arises at the time of sovereignty, the particular bodies of customary law protected by the right are not static but continue to evolve and adapt to keep pace with societal changes. It follows that the relevant date for determining the existence of a particular rule of customary law is not the date of sovereignty but the date of the activity or transaction whose legality is in question. So, for instance, the validity of a customary adoption that took place in 1960 would be governed by the customary rules prevailing at that date, rather than the time of sovereignty. Of course, rules must normally be followed for an appreciable period of time before they gain the status of customary law. However, there is no need to show that they existed at the time of sovereignty.

Aboriginal title provides a different example. As seen earlier, when an Aboriginal people passes under Crown sovereignty, it automatically gains title to its ancestral territories in Canadian law. So, *prima facie*, the boundaries of an Aboriginal territory are ascertained by reference to the situation at the time of sovereignty.[49] However, this general rule is subject to two qualifications, which we can discuss only briefly. The first relates to the Royal Proclamation of 1763 and the second to historical migrations. The Royal

Proclamation of 1763 recognizes the rights of all Aboriginal peoples living under the Crown's protection to the lands in their possession.[50] It accepts the pattern of indigenous occupation existing in 1763 as the basis for Aboriginal land rights, regardless of patterns of occupation that prevailed in earlier eras. So the Royal Proclamation seems to provide a common historical baseline for all Aboriginal groups living under British protection in 1763. However, there is reason to think that, at this date, the British Crown claimed sovereignty over the entirety of the territories now making up Canada.[51] So, the year 1763 arguably constitutes a uniform baseline for the entire country, from Newfoundland in the east to British Columbia in the west.

The second qualification relates to historical migrations. In the fluid conditions that prevailed in earlier periods of Canadian history, it was common for Aboriginal groups to migrate to new areas due to conflict, environmental change, resource depletion, economic opportunities, and similar factors. The onset of Crown sovereignty did not bring this process to a sudden halt. Aboriginal groups continued to migrate in response to changes in their circumstances. With the establishment of effective British government and the creation of reserves, Aboriginal mobility was gradually reduced, although in some areas it persisted into relatively recent times. When an Aboriginal group voluntarily migrated to a new area after the date of Crown sovereignty (or after the year 1763, whichever is later), it seems arguable that within a certain period – perhaps twenty to fifty years – it would gain Aboriginal title to the new territory that it occupied while losing title to the territory it left behind.[52]

Specific Rights

As we have seen, specific Aboriginal rights arise under the auspices of their generic counterparts. While generic rights come into existence at the time of sovereignty, specific rights do not necessarily originate at that date. For example, the broad principle of the honour of the Crown takes force at the time of sovereignty, however, specific fiduciary rights normally stem from events occurring well after that time, as when Aboriginal lands are ceded to the Crown or a reserve is created. In such cases, the relevant date for proving a specific fiduciary right is obviously the date of the event that triggered it, not the date of sovereignty.

A more difficult issue is posed by the right of cultural integrity. Like other generic rights, the abstract right comes into existence at the time of sovereignty, and the same holds true of the intermediate generic rights that shelter under its auspices. What, then, of the specific cultural rights that occupy the bottom tier in the pyramid? In principle these specific rights cannot date from a period *earlier* than the time of sovereignty because, as a matter of Canadian law (as distinct from indigenous law or international law), they do not exist prior to that date. So, presumably, they must arise either at the time of sovereignty or at some later period, depending on the precise nature of the right in question.

However, here we must draw a distinction between the date that a specific cultural right *comes into existence* and the date by reference to which *its concrete content is ascertained* – for the two are not necessarily the same. Supposing that a specific cultural right originates at the time of sovereignty, at what date is its concrete content fixed? This question is bedevilled by a puzzling problem. It stems from the fact that Aboriginal cultures (like all cultures) are not static but undergo significant changes over time. After Europeans arrived in North America, Aboriginal societies responded in a dynamic fashion to new opportunities, circumstances, and influences.[53] Just as European cultures quickly adopted many products of American origin, such as tomatoes, corn, and potatoes (to say nothing of tobacco), so also Native American cultures swiftly absorbed many items of European origin, such as horses, metal artefacts, and firearms. Trade in furs, skins, and fish transformed the economies of Aboriginal societies and helped sustain the economies of the settler colonies. Christianity also had a notable impact on many Aboriginal societies, as did Aboriginal conceptions of personal freedom and federalism on European political thought. European diseases such as smallpox decimated many Aboriginal societies and caused important changes in lifestyle, political organization, and outlook, while syphilis (thought to be of American origin) took its toll in Europe.[54] So the question arises, given the dynamic nature of Aboriginal cultures and the fact that they underwent significant changes both before and after sovereignty, by reference to what date should the concrete content of specific cultural rights be ascertained?

The most workable answer is as follows. The doctrine of Aboriginal rights and the honour of the Crown assured an Aboriginal society that it had the right to maintain and develop the central features of its culture as these existed at the time of *effective Crown control*. This approach universalizes the critical date laid down for Métis peoples in *R. v. Powley*, where the Court held that section 35 protects the customs and traditions that were historically important features of Métis communities "prior to the time of effective European control."[55] While the ruling is explicitly limited to Métis groups, we suggest that it should apply to Aboriginal groups across the board. It is hard to see why Indian and Inuit peoples, who often had close social and economic links with their Métis neighbours and descendants, should have their Aboriginal rights determined at a different and earlier date. Such a discrepancy would inevitably produce bizarre and unjust results. Take, for example, two Aboriginal groups, one Indian and the other Métis, that became partners in a commercial trading relationship after European contact but before effective Crown control: the Métis group would gain an Aboriginal right to engage in the trade but the Indian group would not.

Of course, Aboriginal cultures could (and did) change dramatically after the time of effective Crown control. In principle, an Aboriginal society was free to take its cultural and economic life in any direction it saw fit. However, the Crown's honour was pledged to protect only the central aspects of an Aboriginal society as these aspects existed at the time of effective control and as they subsequently adapted to modern conditions.[56] Beyond this point, the members of Aboriginal societies enjoyed the same legal rights and liabilities at common law as other members of the larger society.[57]

The rationale for this approach is not hard to understand. When Aboriginal peoples were confronted with encroaching Crown control, they were apprehensive that their lives would undergo swift and forced change in unwelcome and harmful ways. They required assurance that they could continue in their current modes of life and adapt their societies at the pace and in the ways they considered desirable. The honour of the Crown was committed to providing this assurance, both as a matter of basic justice and also because it was necessary to maintain the friendship of Aboriginal peoples, which was crucial to the peace and security of the colonies. So, in light of this rationale, it is submitted that the critical date for specific cultural rights is the period at which the Crown gained effective control over a particular Aboriginal group.

However, in *Van der Peet*, the Supreme Court of Canada took a different approach.[58] It held that the date for ascertaining the content of specific cultural rights is the time of European contact rather than effective control. The Court reasoned that the right of cultural integrity was designed to preserve the central aspects of an Aboriginal culture as these existed in their "original" form, prior to the impact of Europeans. The Court seems to have thought that there existed ideal types of Aboriginal societies, untouched by outside influences, in the misty period before Europeans arrived. However, this approach loses sight of the underlying rationale for the right of cultural integrity, which, as just seen, is rooted in the honour of the Crown at the time it assumed effective control. The critical date of "contact" also makes little historical sense. For example, when the Indian nations of New France fell under British rule after 1763, it would have been strange for the Crown to promise solemnly to respect not their current customs but rather their long-vanished ways of life as these existed some two centuries previous when the French first sailed up the St. Lawrence River. An approach less apt to win the friendship of the Indian nations can hardly be imagined.

Conclusion

We have seen that Aboriginal rights fall into two basic classes: generic rights and specific rights. Generic rights comprise a range of basic rights presumptively held by all Aboriginal groups under Canadian common law. They include the right to conclude treaties, the right to customary law, the

8
Judicial Approaches to Self-Government since *Calder*: Searching for Doctrinal Coherence
Kent McNeil

When *Calder et al. v. Attorney-General of British Columbia* was commenced in the late 1960s, it was a bold initiative indeed.[1] Despite recognition of Aboriginal rights in the Royal Proclamation of 1763 and other constitutional documents,[2] and a long history of treaty making in most of British North America, by the 1920s the government of Canada was no longer prepared to acknowledge the legal validity of Aboriginal rights to land. Adhesions to existing treaties apart, the Williams treaties in Ontario in 1923 were the last of the historic treaties that Canada negotiated. After this, treaty making entered a period of abeyance, until it was revived in the 1970s by the *James Bay and Northern Quebec Agreement*[3] and the comprehensive land claims process that was prompted in large part by the *Calder* case itself. It was during the 1920s as well that Parliament enacted the shameful amendment to the *Indian Act* that made it an offence for anyone without government consent to solicit money or receive payment from an Indian to pursue any claim on behalf of that Indian's tribe or band, thereby effectively preventing First Nations from hiring legal counsel to assist them with their claims.[4] While repeal of this provision in 1951 removed one impediment to pursuing Aboriginal claims in court, the attitude of the Canadian government remained unreceptive. This was starkly revealed in the 1969 white paper,[5] which distinguished Aboriginal land claims from "lawful obligations," as land claims were said to be "so general and undefined that it is not realistic to think of them as specific claims capable of remedy except through a policy and program that will end injustice to Indians as members of the Canadian community."[6] Significantly, this policy statement (which was later withdrawn, principally as a result of Indian opposition[7]) was placed before the House of Commons by then minister of Indian Affairs, Jean Chrétien, at the very time the *Calder* case was before the trial judge in the British Columbia Supreme Court. Moreover, despite Parliament's exclusive jurisdiction over "Indians, and Lands reserved for the Indians,"[8] the attorney general of Canada declined to intervene in the case.[9]

While I have described Canada's attitude to Aboriginal land claims in the 1960s as unreceptive, the attitude of British Columbia at the time – and, indeed, since before the province joined Confederation in 1871 – can more appropriately be termed hostile.[10] It is well known that the reason why treaties were not negotiated in most of British Columbia is that the province did not acknowledge the existence of Aboriginal land rights.[11] In deciding to challenge the province's denial of Aboriginal title by asking for a judicial declaration that their title had never been lawfully extinguished, the Nisga'a were thus confronting a century of provincial intransigence without federal support. Moreover, their chances of convincing the courts of the validity of their claim were at best uncertain,[12] a reality reflected in the unanimously negative decisions of the British Columbia Supreme Court and Court of Appeal,[13] and the even split in the Supreme Court of Canada on the substantive issue of extinguishment.[14] In these circumstances, it was therefore strategically prudent for the Nisga'a to restrict their claim as they did to a proprietary right to land, in the nature of the Indian title described eighty years earlier by the Privy Council in *St. Catherine's Milling & Lumber Co. v. R.*[15] Whatever the Nisga'a thought at the time of the Crown's unilateral assertion of sovereignty over them and their lands, and the impact of this action on their authority to govern themselves, they would have risked all had they challenged the Crown's jurisdiction, as well as its proprietary rights, by raising the controversial issue of self-government in the *Calder* litigation.[16] While there was a history of recognition of Aboriginal land rights in Canada that the judges could comfortably rely upon in *Calder*, an assertion of a right of self-government by the Nisga'a might have appeared unprecedented and potentially threatening.[17] As a general rule, it is not wise to ask judges to stick their necks out too far by stepping way ahead of the society in which they live.[18]

Although self-government was not an issue in the *Calder* case, I am nonetheless of the view that the judicial seeds of an inherent right of self-government were planted by the Supreme Court of Canada in its decision that Aboriginal title could exist in British Columbia as a legal right apart from the Royal Proclamation of 1763.[19] The action was commenced by Frank Calder and other Nisga'a leaders as representatives of the Nisga'a tribe or nation. They sought judicial acknowledgment, not of individual property interests but rather of a communal Aboriginal title held by the Nisga'a nation as a whole. This was the way the claim was dealt with by the courts, and this was the kind of title the Supreme Court of Canada envisaged, subject to the matter of extinguishment on which the Court split three to three.[20] As we shall see, a communal title necessarily entails authority within the community to make decisions about how the benefits of this title will be distributed within the community and how communal land use will be regulated. This decision-making authority, it will be argued, is governmental in nature. But I am getting ahead of myself, so let me back up and start by considering how recognition of an inherent right of self-government began to emerge after *Calder*.

Emerging Acknowledgment of the Inherent Right of Self-Government

Political acknowledgment of limited rights of self-government preceded judicial recognition in the post-*Calder* period. For example, the 1975 *James Bay and Northern Quebec Agreement* provided for the legislative implementation of Cree local government, especially over lands set aside for exclusive Cree use and benefit.[21] Canada fulfilled this aspect of the agreement by enacting the *Cree-Naskapi (of Quebec) Act* in 1984.[22] More significantly, recognition and affirmation of existing Aboriginal and treaty rights by section 35(1) of the *Constitution Act, 1982*[23] led to prolonged debate over whether self-government is an Aboriginal and treaty right that now enjoys constitutional protection. This issue dominated the agendas of the four constitutional conferences held during the 1980s to try to identify and define section 35(1) rights.[24] Although no resolution of this issue emerged from these conferences, and a further attempt in 1992 to entrench self-government in the constitution explicitly by way of the *Charlottetown Accord* failed,[25] the Canadian government in 1995 accepted that the Aboriginal peoples of Canada have an inherent right of self-government.[26] Modern land claims agreements that include provision for self-government are negotiated on this basis.[27]

Judicial recognition of the inherent right of self-government has been more hesitant. To this point, judges have displayed evident reluctance to face the issue at all, combined with uncertainty over how self-government claims that they have been unable to avoid should be assessed as a matter of law. The leading cases we are about to discuss reveal a remarkable divergence of opinion, with no real consensus on the issue. In my opinion, this judicial uncertainty provides an opportunity for creative legal thinking because judges who have not made up their minds should be open to persuasion.

Self-Regulation of Aboriginal Rights: *R. v. Sparrow*

The Supreme Court of Canada had an opportunity to consider the matter of self-government in *R. v. Sparrow*,[28] which was the very first case involving section 35(1) rights to come before it. Counsel for the Musqueam nation, whose Aboriginal fishing right was in question, had raised the issue by arguing that "the right to regulate is part of the right to use the resource."[29] For this reason, they contended that primary authority to regulate the fishing right vested in the Musqueam nation, with the result that federal authority was limited by section 35(1) to situations where, for example, "[conservation] measures were necessary to prevent serious impairment of the aboriginal rights of present and future generations, where conservation could only be achieved by restricting the right and not by restricting fishing by other users, and where the aboriginal group concerned was unwilling to implement necessary conservation measures."[30] This argument necessarily rested on a claim of a right of self-government in relation to Musqueam fishing – a claim that was explicitly rejected by the British Columbia Court of Appeal:

> The constitutional recognition of the right to fish cannot entail restoring the relationship between Indians and salmon as it existed 150 years ago. The world has changed. The right must now exist in the context of a parliamentary system of government and a federal division of powers. It cannot be defined as if the Musqueam band *had continued to be a self-governing entity*, or as if its members were not citizens of Canada and residents of British Columbia.[31]

Unlike the British Columbia Court of Appeal, the Supreme Court of Canada did not deal directly with the self-government issue. Instead, it addressed the Musqueam's argument that authority to regulate is part of their Aboriginal fishing right in more general terms, starting with the assertion that "there was from the outset never any doubt that sovereignty and legislative power ... vested in the Crown."[32] While acknowledging that section 35(1) does provide some protection against this power, the Court went on to hold that the protection is not absolute:

> Federal legislative powers continue, including, of course, the right to legislate with respect to Indians pursuant to s. 91(24) of the *Constitution Act, 1867*. These powers must, however, now be read together with s. 35(1). In other words, federal power must be reconciled with federal duty and the best way to achieve that reconciliation is to demand the justification of any government regulation that infringes upon or denies aboriginal rights.[33]

The Court then set out the familiar justificatory test for infringement of Aboriginal rights, without saying anything more about whether the Musqueam also have the authority to regulate their fishing. The British Columbia Court of Appeal's denial that the Musqueam "continued to be a self-governing entity" is significantly absent from the Supreme Court of Canada's judgment. The Supreme Court may, therefore, have consciously left the issue of self-regulation open for subsequent consideration, a conclusion supported by decisions to be examined later in this chapter.[34]

Integral to Distinctive Culture: *R. v. Pamajewon*

The matter of self-government could not be so easily avoided in *R. v. Pamajewon*,[35] a decision on two cases involving criminal charges of unlawful gambling brought against members of two Ontario First Nations. The Shawanaga First Nation and the Eagle Lake First Nation had each enacted a lottery law, pursuant to an asserted right of self-government, purporting to authorize and regulate gambling activities on their reserves. Unlike in *Sparrow*, the Supreme Court of Canada was confronted with a direct conflict between a federal statute[36] and the actual exercise of asserted self-government authority by First Nations. Chief Justice Antonio Lamer, in a relatively short judgment concurred in by seven members of the Court,[37] assumed, without deciding, that section 35(1) encompasses self-government claims.[38] He nonetheless characterized the right in question much more narrowly than the First Nations, who claimed in part that their gambling laws and activities were included within "a broad right to manage and use their reserve lands."[39] In response, Chief Justice Lamer stated:

> To so characterize the appellants' claim would be to cast the Court's inquiry at a level of excessive generality. Aboriginal rights, including any asserted right to self-government, must be looked at in light of the specific circumstances of each case and, in particular, in light of the specific history and culture of the aboriginal group claiming the right.[40]

Relying on *R. v. Van der Peet*,[41] handed down by the Court the day before the *R. v. Pamajewon* judgment was released, he then characterized the claim as an asserted right "to participate in, and to regulate, gambling activities on their respective reserve lands."[42]

After characterizing the claim in this way, Chief Justice Lamer proceeded to apply the second branch of the "integral to the distinctive culture" test formulated in *Van der Peet*. This test places the onus on the Aboriginal claimants to prove that the activity in relation to which they assert an Aboriginal right was "an element of a practice, custom or tradition integral to [their] distinctive culture" at the time of contact with Europeans.[43] The chief justice provided a terse explanation for applying this test to self-government claims:

> Assuming s. 35(1) encompasses claims to aboriginal self-government, such claims must be considered in light of the purposes underlying that provision and must, therefore, be considered against the test derived from consideration of those purposes. This is the test laid out in *Van der Peet, supra*. In so far as they can be made under s. 35(1), claims to self-government are no different from other claims to the enjoyment of aboriginal rights and must, as such, be measured against the same standard.[44]

Chief Justice Lamer went on to find, as had the Ontario Court of Appeal, that the "evidence presented at both the Pamajewon and Gardner trials does not demonstrate that gambling, or that the regulation of gambling, was an integral part of the distinctive cultures of the Shawanaga or Eagle Lake First Nations."[45] He also agreed with Justice Coulter Osborne, who wrote the unanimous judgment of the Ontario Court of Appeal, that there was no evidence that gambling was "an aspect of their use of their land."[46] The appeals of the convictions were accordingly dismissed.

In my respectful opinion, there are several problems with the *Pamajewon* decision.[47] The first is the commingling in Chief Justice Lamer's judgment of two distinct bases for the claim of an Aboriginal right of self-government over gambling. In the Ontario Court of Appeal, Justice Osborne dealt with these bases separately under the headings "The Aboriginal Title Issue" and "The Inherent Right to Self-Government Issue."[48] The Aboriginal title approach based the right on assertions that the reserves were part of the Aboriginal title lands of the First Nations concerned (this was not contested by the Crown) and that authorization of gambling was an economic decision made by them as an incident of their broader authority to decide how those lands were to be used.[49] Put another way, the appellants contended that a right of self-government over land use, including gambling, is incidental to Aboriginal title. Justice Osborne did not address this contention directly. Instead, he rejected the appellants' argument on the ground that Aboriginal title is restricted to activity-based and site-specific traditional uses of the land and so does not encompass activities such as high-stakes gambling, which were not part of historic Aboriginal cultures.

In reaching this conclusion, he followed the majority decision of the British Columbia Court of Appeal in *Delgamuukw v. British Columbia*,[50] which restricted Aboriginal title to traditional uses. This is problematic because, a year after it decided *Pamajewon*, the Supreme Court of Canada overruled this aspect of the British Columbia Court of Appeal's decision in *Delgamuukw*, holding instead that "aboriginal title encompasses the right to exclusive use and occupation of the land held pursuant to that title for a variety of purposes, which need not be aspects of those aboriginal practices, customs and traditions which are integral to distinctive aboriginal cultures."[51] In light of this holding, Justice Osborne's reason for rejecting the Aboriginal title basis for the claim in *Pamajewon* is no longer valid. And yet we have seen that Chief Justice Lamer accepted Justice Osborne's conclusion that there was no evidence that gambling was "part of the First Nations' historic cultures and traditions, or an aspect of their use of their land."[52] Why, one might ask, was the second factual finding, in particular, relevant if Justice Osborne was wrong in restricting Aboriginal title to traditional activities and uses?[53]

In the alternative, the appellants in *Pamajewon* argued before the Ontario Court of Appeal that they have an inherent right of self-government that includes jurisdiction over gambling on their reserves. Justice Osborne rejected this contention by relying on the earlier-quoted passage from *Sparrow* that sovereignty and legislative power had vested in the Crown.[54] In his view, this power had been validly exercised by Parliament when it criminalized certain gambling activities, thereby extinguishing any self-government rights First Nations may have had regarding these activities.[55] For good measure, he found as well that there was "no evidence that gambling on the reserve lands generally was ever the subject matter of aboriginal regulation."[56] As we have seen, Chief Justice Lamer also relied on this finding in rejecting the self-government claim.[57] Given that the chief justice decided that a right of self-government had not been established in accordance with the *Van der Peet* test, he was thus able to avoid the extinguishment issue.

Although Chief Justice Lamer agreed with the factual conclusions that Justice Osborne had used to reject both the Aboriginal title and inherent right of self-government approaches, he focused his attention on the inherent right argument. He treated this inherent right claim in the same way that he had treated a claim to a fishing right in *Van der Peet*, as though there is no difference in this context between an Aboriginal right to engage in an activity such as fishing and an Aboriginal right to exercise jurisdiction. This is surprising, given the fundamental and long-standing distinction in the common law between natural resource rights, which are generally proprietary in nature,[58] and jurisdiction, which is governmental in nature.[59] Where private resource rights are concerned, they are invariably subject to governmental authority, the source and nature of which has little in common with the rights themselves.[60] In Canadian constitutional law as well, this distinction between resource rights and jurisdiction was clearly (and, in light of *Pamajewon*, ironically) drawn early on in the context of Aboriginal title to land.[61] So how can it be, as Chief Justice Lamer said, that "claims to self-government are no different from other claims to the enjoyment of Aboriginal rights"?[62]

Nor does Chief Justice Lamer's decision to apply the *Van der Peet* test to self-government claims seem to be justified by his assertion that, because those claims have to be considered in light of section 35(1)'s purposes, they must "be considered against the test derived from consideration of those purposes."[63] The purpose for section 35(1) articulated in *Van der Peet* was "the reconciliation of the pre-existence of aboriginal societies with the sovereignty of the Crown."[64] With respect, it is not apparent to me that this purpose mandates a single test for the identification of Aboriginal rights, especially in light of Chief Justice Lamer's decision soon after in *Delgamuukw*,[65] where he acknowledged that aspects of the *Van der Peet* test are not appropriate for Aboriginal title claims and created a new test for title based on exclusive occupation of land at the time of Crown assertion of sovereignty. If the differences between mainly *quantitative* Aboriginal title and Aboriginal resource rights are sufficient to justify different tests, why are the more significant *qualitative* differences between self-government and resource rights not sufficient?[66]

Although Chief Justice Lamer did not expressly say that a right of self-government over a specific activity such as gambling can only be established if the Aboriginal group in question proves that it regulated the activity prior to contact with Europeans, this is certainly suggested in his judgment.[67] This, however, begs the question of what is meant by regulation in the context of Aboriginal societies with political systems that varied greatly among themselves and differed even more significantly from those of Western Europe.[68] Moreover, what if Aboriginal regulation of an important activity such as coastal fishing was unnecessary prior to the arrival of Europeans, given Aboriginal populations and the abundance of the resource? Should this preclude a right of self-government in relation to this Aboriginal activity today? But even if proof of historic Aboriginal regulation is necessary, it should be a requirement only where the primary right asserted is an inherent right of self-government over the activity. If the primary right is Aboriginal title or another right other than self-government, and authority to regulate this title or right is claimed as an incident of it, then proof that self-regulation actually occurred prior to the assertion of Crown sovereignty (in the case of title) or European contact (in the case of other Aboriginal rights) should not be necessary. This conclusion would seem to be consistent with the way in which Aboriginal title and inherent rights claims were dealt with separately by the Ontario Court of Appeal in *Pamajewon*,[69] and accords with the Supreme Court of Canada's decision in *Delgamuukw* and the British Columbia Supreme Court's decision in *Campbell v. British Columbia (Attorney General)*,[70] which are discussed later in this chapter.

A final criticism of the way the Supreme Court of Canada dealt with the self-government claim in *Pamajewon* is the impracticality of the Court's approach. If every aspect of Aboriginal jurisdiction has to be proven by each Aboriginal group in relation to specific matters such as gambling, establishing Aboriginal self-government rights in the courts will be a very time-consuming and costly process.[71] This effort could drain valuable resources from Aboriginal communities that could more usefully be directed towards pressing social needs such as health, education, housing, and economic development. It could also place extra burdens on overworked courts. Surely there are better ways for dealing with Aboriginal self-government claims judicially, which brings us to *Delgamuukw*, the most important self-government case to reach the Supreme Court of Canada since *Pamajewon*.

Decision-Making Authority over Communal Rights: *Delgamuukw*

Delgamuukw is, of course, best known as the case in which the Supreme Court of Canada defined Aboriginal title and explained how it can be proven. However, the original claim of the Gitxsan and Wet'suwet'en nations included

an assertion of jurisdiction or a right of self-government over their traditional territories in what is now British Columbia.[72] At trial, Chief Justice
Allan McEachern dismissed the self-government claim by holding that, even
if the Gitxsan and Wet'suwet'en had exercised governmental authority prior
to European colonization (which he doubted), establishment of sovereignty
by the Crown and reception of English law excluded the possibility of any
Aboriginal right of self-government thereafter.[73] A majority of the British
Columbia Court of Appeal agreed, holding as well that the distribution of
legislative powers between Parliament and the provincial legislatures by
the *Constitution Act, 1867* "left no room for a third order of government."[74]

The Supreme Court of Canada neither affirmed nor reversed this aspect
of the decisions of the lower courts, preferring to send the self-government
issue back to trial along with the Aboriginal title issue. However, while the
Court gave the trial court extensive guidance on how the title issue should be
dealt with, it provided no explicit advice on the matter of self-government.
After noting that the parties had given much less weight to self-government
arguments on appeal, Chief Justice Lamer said:

> One source of the decreased emphasis on the right to self-government on
> appeal is this Court's judgment *Pamajewon*. There, I held that rights to self-
> government, if they existed, cannot be framed in excessively general terms.
> The appellants did not have the benefit of my judgment at trial.
> Unsurprisingly, as counsel for the Wet'suwet'en specifically concedes, the
> appellants advanced the right to self-government in very broad terms, and
> therefore in a manner not cognizable by s. 35(1).[75]

The chief justice went on to point out that self-government raises difficult
conceptual issues, the complexity of which can be gleaned from the fact
that the Royal Commission on Aboriginal Peoples devoted 277 pages to it
in its report.[76] Without more assistance from counsel, Chief Justice Lamer
said, "it would be imprudent for the Court to step into the breach," and so
"the issue of self-government will fall to be determined at trial."[77]

While the Court's refusal to deal with self-government, or even "to lay
down the legal principles to guide future litigation,"[78] might be taken to
mean that the *Delgamuukw* decision sheds no light on the issue, I think this
is an overly dismissive interpretation. Recall that both the trial judge and a
majority of the British Columbia Court of Appeal held that any rights of
self-government the Gitxsan and Wet'suwet'en may have had did not survive either acquisition of Crown sovereignty or Confederation. As Kerry
Wilkins has pointed out, if the Supreme Court of Canada agreed with this,
the *Delgamuukw* case provided them with a convenient opportunity to say
so.[79] Instead, they left the matter open, inviting the appellants to frame
their self-government claims more narrowly in accordance with the

Pamajewon approach. This suggests that the Court probably did not think self-government rights had been extinguished by Crown sovereignty or Confederation,[80] for if that had happened, why encourage the appellants to go to the trouble and expense of trying to prove the rights in accordance with an approach that depends on their survival?

Even more significantly, Chief Justice Lamer's judgment in *Delgamuukw* also supports the self-regulation approach to Aboriginal rights argued in *Sparrow* and *Pamajewon*. As we have seen, the Supreme Court of Canada avoided confronting this argument directly in both cases.[81] In *Delgamuukw*, the Court separated Aboriginal title from the inherent right of self-government, as though they are distinct issues. As in *Pamajewon*, the Court appears to have expected the inherent right claim to be proven in accordance with the *Van der Peet* "integral to the distinctive culture" test. Aboriginal title, on the other hand, depends on proof of exclusive occupation of land at the time of Crown assertion of sovereignty. Yet, in describing the *sui generis* aspects of Aboriginal title, the chief justice stated:

> A further dimension of aboriginal title is the fact that it is held *communally*. Aboriginal title cannot be held by individual aboriginal persons. It is a collective right to land held by all members of an aboriginal nation. Decisions with respect to that land are also made by that community.[82]

In this vital passage, Chief Justice Lamer appears to have accepted the self-regulation argument the Court had previously avoided. Decision-making authority in relation to Aboriginal title must encompass authority to decide what uses can be made of the land[83] and how those uses are to be regulated.[84] This was the very argument made in *Pamajewon* as an alternative to the inherent right of self-government argument and rejected by the Ontario Court of Appeal because it held that the uses that Aboriginal titleholders can make of their lands are limited to traditional uses and so do not include high-stakes gambling. However, as we have seen, this reason for rejecting the argument now suffers from the fact that the conception of Aboriginal title relied upon by the Ontario Court of Appeal was rejected by Chief Justice Lamer in *Delgamuukw* and replaced by his more inclusive definition.[85] Any use of the land that is encompassed by Aboriginal titleholders' "right to exclusive use and occupation" should therefore be subject to their decision-making authority.[86] This would no doubt include uses of the land involving extraction of natural resources, as was explicitly held in *Delgamuukw*,[87] and other direct uses such as hunting, fishing, ranching, farming, erecting buildings and other structures, and so on. However, not every activity that takes place on land can be classified as a use of land as such.[88] Thus, despite Chief Justice Lamer's broad definition of Aboriginal title, it is questionable whether gambling, for example, would be a use coming within the decision-making authority that he said Aboriginal titleholders have over their land.[89]

This brings us to *Campbell*,[90] which is the most significant decision involving the Nisga'a nation since *Calder*. In it, Justice Paul Williamson of the British Columbia Supreme Court clearly recognized the implications for self-government in Chief Justice Lamer's description of Aboriginal title as a communal right that includes authority to make decisions respecting the land.

The Nisga'a Treaty: *Campbell*

The *Campbell* case arose out of a challenge to the self-government aspects of the Nisga'a treaty,[91] brought by Gordon Campbell (then leader of the opposition in the BC legislature) and a couple of his Liberal colleagues. Among its detailed provisions, the treaty contains a chapter entitled "Nisga'a Government," setting out the self-government powers of the Nisga'a nation and providing for such matters as paramountcy in situations where Nisga'a jurisdiction is concurrent with federal or provincial jurisdiction. The main contention of the plaintiffs in *Campbell* was that these self-government provisions are unconstitutional because they create a third order of government, contrary to Confederation's federal structure dividing legislative authority between Parliament and the provincial legislatures.[92] In effect, this was a rerun of the exhaustive distribution of powers argument that had been accepted by the British Columbia Court of Appeal in *Delgamuukw* and arguably rejected by the Supreme Court of Canada when it sent the matter back to trial.[93] However, the plaintiffs' challenge went further, for in addition to alleging that self-government rights did not survive Confederation they contended that, as a result of this exhaustive distribution of powers, self-government arrangements giving laws made by Aboriginal governments paramountcy over federal or provincial laws are unconstitutional.[94]

Justice Williamson rejected the exhaustive distribution of legislative powers argument, in part by relying on the preamble to the *Constitution Act, 1867*,[95] which the Supreme Court of Canada has held incorporates fundamental, unwritten principles into the Canadian constitution.[96] He pointed out that

> British imperial policy, reflected in the instructions given to colonial authorities in North America prior to Confederation, recognized a continued form, albeit diminished, of Aboriginal self-government after the assertion of sovereignty by the Crown. This Imperial policy, through the preamble to the *Constitution Act, 1867*, assists in filling out "gaps in the express terms of the constitutional scheme."[97]

Justice Williamson also relied on the post-Confederation negotiation of Indian treaties, the continuing authority of courts to develop the common law, the power of the Imperial Parliament to legislate for Canada after 1867, and other judicial decisions to conclude that "a right to self-government akin to a legislative power to make laws, survived as one of the unwritten 'underlying values' of the Constitution outside the powers distributed to Parliament and the legislatures in 1867."[98] Moreover, section 91(24) of the *Constitution Act, 1867* assigning to Parliament exclusive jurisdiction over "Indians, and Lands reserved for the Indians," did not extinguish self-government rights, since this provision transferred responsibility for the Crown's obligations from the British Crown to the Crown in right of Canada without diminishing the rights of the Aboriginal peoples.[99]

After finding additional support for the continuation of self-government rights in American case law cited by the Supreme Court of Canada,[100] and Canadian judgments involving customary marriages and adoptions and the selection of band councils by custom,[101] Justice Williamson turned to section 35(1) of the *Constitution Act, 1982*.[102] Given that the Aboriginal and treaty rights recognized and affirmed by this subsection can still be infringed in justifiable circumstances,[103] he held that Parliament did not, upon entering into the Nisga'a treaty, permanently abdicate legislative authority in relation to the exercise of governmental authority by the Nisga'a nation.[104] More importantly for the purposes of this chapter, however, he also found that the communal Aboriginal title of the Nisga'a nation includes the right "to make decisions about ... occupation and use, matters commonly described as governmental functions. This seems essential when the ownership is communal."[105] He found support for this in *Delgamuukw*, particularly in Chief Justice Lamer's observation that Aboriginal title is communal and decisions respecting the land are made by the community.[106] He concluded as follows:

> Can it be, as the plaintiffs' submission would hold, that a limited right to self-government cannot be protected constitutionally by Section 35(1)? I think not. The above passages from *Delgamuukw* suggesting the right for the community to decide to what uses the land encompassed by their aboriginal title can be put are determinative of the question. The right to aboriginal title "in its full form," including the right for the community to make decisions as to the use of the land and therefore the right to have a political structure for making those decisions, is, I conclude, constitutionally guaranteed by Section 35.
>
> An analysis of the reasoning of the Supreme Court of Canada in *Delgamuukw* can lead to no other result.[107]

Justice Williamson thus recognized clearly that it is the combination of a communal title and decision-making authority that necessitates political structures in Aboriginal communities. As Chief Justice Lamer said in *Delgamuukw*, the communal nature of Aboriginal title is one of the *sui generis* aspects that distinguishes it from other property rights.[108] In the common law, property rights are generally held by individuals, either natural persons or corporations. Property can be held by a number of individuals at the same time, as in a joint tenancy or tenancy in common, but, in those situations, the title is still vested in the individuals, not in the group as such. This is because the common law does not accord the legal personality necessary to hold property to unincorporated collections of individuals.[109] So although joint tenants and tenants in common, like all property holders, have decision-making authority over their property, this authority is vested in them as individuals rather than as collectivities.[110] Their decision-making authority is therefore individualistic and proprietary, not collective and jurisdictional, in nature. The decision-making authority that Aboriginal title-holders have over their lands is qualitatively different because the communal nature of their title places this authority in the Aboriginal community as a collective entity. As Justice Williamson observed, this unique characteristic of Aboriginal title necessitates a political structure because when a community makes decisions about its collective rights it is exercising a function that is governmental.[111] Without such a structure, there would be no mechanism within the community for making collective decisions about how Aboriginal title lands are to be used or how the benefits of them are to be distributed. Self-government authority over those lands is therefore a practical necessity as well as an essential legal incident arising from the *sui generis* nature of Aboriginal title.[112]

However, is the *Campbell* decision consistent with *Pamajewon*? Justice Williamson's only reference to *Pamajewon* in *Campbell* appears in his discussion of *Delgamuukw*, where he observed that Chief Justice Lamer referred to *Pamajewon* "in which the court had found that a claim in that case for the right to self-government was framed 'in excessively general terms' and therefore was not 'cognizable' to the court."[113] Justice Williamson concluded:

> The legislative power set out in the Nisga'a Treaty does not succumb to the failing of being "excessively general." Rather, it is a detailed document setting out precisely what powers and what limitations to those powers reside with each party.[114]

Where governmental powers are set out in detail in an agreement such as the Nisga'a treaty, apparently *Pamajewon* is inapplicable because it was concerned with proof of an inherent Aboriginal right of self-government. Where there is a treaty, courts generally do not go behind it to see whether the rights set out in it existed previously as Aboriginal rights.[115] In *Campbell*, however, the plaintiffs argued that a court does have to go behind a treaty that sets out rights of self-government that enjoy section 35(1) constitutional protection, and Justice Williamson seems to have accepted this argument because he did inquire into the existence of the inherent right. He did not, however, bother with the details of the inherent right of self-government of the Nisga'a, since the mere existence of the right, whatever its content, appears to have been sufficient for him to conclude that it could be validly defined in a modern-day treaty.

We have seen that Justice Williamson, in finding the Nisga'a's inherent right of self-government to exist, relied in part on Chief Justice Lamer's pronouncements in *Delgamuukw* that Aboriginal title to land is communal and that Aboriginal communities have decision-making authority over it.[116] This approach closely resembles one of the arguments that had been made by the plaintiffs in *Pamajewon* and rejected by the Ontario Court of Appeal, although for reasons that are now questionable.[117] Unfortunately, the Supreme Court of Canada in *Pamajewon* commingled the two bases on which the claims to self-government were made in the case (that is, as an inherent right and as an incident to Aboriginal title), thereby blurring the distinction between them.[118] And yet Chief Justice Lamer's acknowledgment of communal decision-making authority over Aboriginal title in *Delgamuukw* does appear, as Justice Williamson observed, to necessitate an acceptance of a right of self-government as an incident of Aboriginal title.

So are *Pamajewon* and *Delgamuukw* consistent on the matter of self-government? One way of attempting to reconcile them is to reject Justice Williamson's interpretation and conclude that the decision-making authority acknowledged in *Delgamuukw* is proprietary rather than jurisdictional in nature, but, as already explained, I think this is wrong.[119] Instead, I think what *Delgamuukw* has done is limit *Pamajewon* to situations where there is a direct claim to an inherent right of self-government, which is why the self-government claim itself was sent back to trial with a direction to the parties to take account of *Pamajewon*.[120] Where self-government is claimed as an incident of Aboriginal title, *Delgamuukw* strongly suggests that the communal nature of this title includes jurisdictional authority. Moreover, there is no reason why this incidental approach to self-government should be limited to situations where Aboriginal title exists, since the Supreme Court of Canada has also described other Aboriginal rights as being communal.[121] The same characterization has been applied to treaty rights as well, particularly in *R. v. Marshall (No. 2)*, where the Court said that "treaty rights do not belong to the individual, but are exercised *by the authority of the local community* to which the accused belongs."[122] As in the case of decision-making authority over Aboriginal title, this authority must be governmental in nature.

One can therefore envisage that the *Pamajewon* approach to self-government will be applied only where a right of self-government is claimed directly as an inherent right. Where a right of self-government is claimed incidentally to other Aboriginal or treaty rights that are communal in nature (as they generally appear to be), there should be no need to meet the *Pamajewon* test for proof of the right of self-government independently. Instead, proof of the Aboriginal or treaty right should suffice to establish the governmental decision-making authority over it that flows from its communal nature. Where Aboriginal title is concerned, this means that exclusive occupation of the land over which that authority is claimed would have to be proven in accordance with the *Delgamukw* test. Where other Aboriginal rights are in question, they would have to be proven in accordance with the *Van der Peet* integral-to-the-distinctive-culture test. Finally, where a treaty right is alleged, it would have to be established on a proper interpretation of the relevant treaty. This incidental approach to self-government is therefore still piecemeal. Its broadest application would no doubt be in regard to Aboriginal title, where the decision-making authority is not limited to traditional uses of the land. But even in this context, it would probably be limited to activities that can properly be classified as uses of the land, rather than as encompassing all activities that might take place on the land.[123]

Is this the full extent to which claims to self-government are likely to succeed in Canadian courts? Possibly, though there are indications that the Supreme Court of Canada may be willing to embrace a broader conception of self-government. These glimmers of a more expansive approach can be found mainly in references by the Court to leading American decisions on self-government and to the *Report of the Royal Commission on Aboriginal Peoples*.[124]

A Broader Conception of Self-Government: Will the Supreme Court of Canada Reconsider?

Since inclusion of section 35 in the constitution in 1982, the Supreme Court of Canada has often relied on American decisions involving Aboriginal and treaty rights, including decisions acknowledging the residual sovereignty of the Indian nations in the United States. Some prominent post-1982 examples include the following.[125] In *R. v. Sioui*,[126] the Supreme Court of Canada considered whether promises made by Brigadier General James Murray to the Hurons of Lorette in 1760 after the surrender of Québec by the French constitute a treaty for the purposes of section 88 of the *Indian Act*.[127] In deciding that the document in question is a treaty and that it provides a defence to charges brought under provincial legislation, Justice Lamer (as he then was), for a unanimous Court, accepted Chief Justice John Marshall's description in *Worcester v. Georgia* of British policy respecting the Indian nations in the mid-eighteenth century:

Such was the policy of Great Britain towards the Indian nations inhabiting the territory from which she excluded all other Europeans; such her claims, and such her practical exposition of the charters she had granted: *she considered them as nations capable of maintaining the relations of peace and war; of governing themselves, under her protection; and she made treaties with them, the obligation of which she acknowledged.*[128]

While this was a description of policy, not a statement of law, it nonetheless reveals that for the British Crown at the time there was apparently no inconsistency between claiming sovereignty against other European powers such as the French and acknowledging the independence and governmental authority of the Indian nations – a reality that Chief Justice Marshall and Justice Lamer both accepted. This is confirmed further in the following passage from Justice Lamer's judgment:

> [W]e can conclude from the historical documents that both Great Britain and France felt that the Indian nations had sufficient independence and played a large enough role in North America for it to be good policy to maintain relations with them very close to those maintained between sovereign nations.
>
> The mother countries did everything in their power to secure the alliance of each Indian nation and to encourage nations allied with the enemy to change sides. When these efforts met with success, they were incorporated in treaties of alliance or neutrality. This clearly indicates that the Indian nations were regarded in their relations with the European nations which occupied North America as independent nations.[129]

In his majority judgment in *Van der Peet*, Chief Justice Lamer commented directly on the relevance of American decisions on Aboriginal law to Canada:

> Although the constitutional structure of the United States is different from that of Canada, and its aboriginal law has developed in unique directions, I agree with Professor Slattery both when he describes the Marshall decisions as providing "structure and coherence to an untidy and diffuse body of customary law based on official practice" and when he asserts that these decisions are "as relevant to Canada as they are to the United States" ... I would add to Professor Slattery's comments only the observation that the fact that aboriginal law in the United States is significantly different from Canadian aboriginal law means that the relevance of these cases arises from their articulation of general principles, rather than their specific legal holdings.[130]

The chief justice's acceptance of Brian Slattery's characterization of Aboriginal law as a "body of customary law based on official practice" reveals that what was described as "policy" in the passages from *Sioui*, quoted earlier, could well form the basis for law. This interpretation is fortified by lengthy quotations in *Van der Peet* from *Johnson v. M'Intosh* and *Worcester v. Georgia*,[131] where Chief Justice Marshall viewed the practices of the British Crown and other European powers in relation to the Indian nations as creating legal norms. In one of the paragraphs from *Johnson v. M'Intosh* quoted by Chief Justice Lamer, Chief Justice Marshall wrote:

> In the establishment of these relations [between the Indian and European nations], the rights of the original inhabitants were, in no instance, entirely disregarded; but were necessarily, to a considerable extent, impaired. They were admitted to be the rightful occupants of the soil, with a legal as well as just claim to retain possession of it, and to use it according to their own discretion; but their rights to complete sovereignty, as independent nations, were necessarily diminished, and their power to dispose of the soil at their own will, to whomsoever they pleased, was denied by the original fundamental principle, that discovery gave exclusive title to those who made it.[132]

In this passage, Chief Justice Marshall acknowledged, and Chief Justice Lamer apparently accepted, that the Indian nations had "complete sovereignty" before European colonization of North America and that the effect of European assertion of sovereignty was to diminish, but not extinguish, their sovereignty.[133]

Chief Justice Lamer then turned to *Worcester v. Georgia*, a case in which, in his words, "the court considered the nature and basis of the Cherokee claims to the land and to governance over that land."[134] He quoted lengthy passages from Chief Justice Marshall's judgment that included the following observations:

> America, separated from Europe by a wide ocean, was inhabited by a distinct people, divided into separate nations, independent of each other and of the rest of the world, having institutions of their own, and governing themselves by their own laws ...
>
> *The Indian nations had always been considered as distinct, independent political communities, retaining their original natural rights, as the undisputed possessors of the soil, from time immemorial, with the single exception of that imposed by irresistible power, which excluded them from intercourse with any other European potentate than the first discoverer of the coast of the particular region claimed.*[135]

In these passages, Chief Justice Marshall was describing two periods of North American history in terms that Chief Justice Lamer apparently accepted: first, the period prior to European arrival, when the Indian nations were completely independent and, second, the period immediately thereafter when this independence was reduced only to the extent that the power of individual European nations prevented the Indian nations from interacting with other European nations. In the latter period, the Indian nations were still independent, except in external relations with other European nations.[136] As in *Johnson*, Chief Justice Marshall's starting point was thus the complete independence and all-encompassing authority of the Indian nations, which was then reduced to the extent – and only to the extent – that the European powers actually diminished it.

It is somewhat surprising that Chief Justice Lamer in *Van der Peet* relied upon and even emphasized passages from Chief Justice Marshall's judgments that acknowledged the complete pre-colonial independence of the Indian nations and their post-colonial residual sovereignty because Chief Justice Marshall's position on these matters is diametrically opposed to Chief Justice Lamer's own approach in *Pamajewon*, written reasons for which were handed down the day after *Van der Peet*. As we have seen, in *Pamajewon*, he limited rights of self-government to matters that had been integral to distinctive Aboriginal cultures and regulated by Aboriginal peoples prior to contact with Europeans.[137] In other words, he started with what has sometimes been called an "empty box" of jurisdictional rights, which Aboriginal peoples have to attempt to fill item by item.[138] By contrast, in acknowledging the complete independence of the Indian nations before contact with Europeans, Chief Justice Marshall started with a "full box" of jurisdictional rights, which could then be shown to have been diminished by the exercise of European and then American power. This has been the situation in the United States ever since the Marshall decisions. Indian sovereignty is residual, encompassing all areas of jurisdiction that have not been taken away either by acquisition of European and then American sovereignty, treaty, or Acts of Congress.[139] Moreover, because there is a presumption in favour of Indian sovereignty, the burden of proof is not on the Indian nations to prove any aspect of their sovereignty but, rather, on the United States to show how their presumptively all-encompassing internal sovereignty has been diminished.[140] The contrast with the *Pamajewon* approach, which is the exact opposite, could not be starker.

An examination of Chief Justice Lamer's tentative treatment of the inherent right of self-government therefore reveals striking inconsistencies. First, there is his apparent acknowledgment in *Sioui* and *Van der Peet*, through reliance on American case law, of the complete pre-colonization sovereignty of the Indian nations and of their continuing residual sovereignty thereafter. Then comes his implicit rejection of this approach in *Pamajewon*, where broad self-government claims were dismissed and an onerous burden was placed on Aboriginal claimants to prove self-government jurisdiction piecemeal through the integral-to-the-distinctive-culture test. Finally, in *Delgamuukw*, he appears to have accepted the self-regulation approach to self-government that was first articulated in argument in *Sparrow* but not given serious consideration in *Pamajewon*.[141] So where can we expect the Supreme Court of Canada to go from here?

The most recent attempt by a Supreme Court of Canada judge to shed some light on the right of self-government was by Justice Ian Binnie in his concurring judgment in *Mitchell v. M.N.R.*[142] As characterized in the principal judgment written by Chief Justice McLachlin, the claim involved an assertion that the Mohawks of Akwesasne (whose territory straddles the international border) had an Aboriginal right to bring goods from the United States across the St. Lawrence River into Canada for trade purposes without paying Canadian customs duties.[143] One argument made by the Crown was that the claimed right, even if proven in accordance with the integral-to-the-distinctive-culture test laid down in *Van der Peet*, could not have been recognized and affirmed by section 35(1) of the *Constitution Act, 1982* because it would be inconsistent with Canadian sovereignty, specifically with control of Canada's borders. Chief Justice McLachlin found it unnecessary to address the "sovereign incompatibility" argument because she decided that the claimed right had not been established on the facts.[144] Justice Binnie, in a judgment concurred in by Justice Major, agreed with the chief justice that the right had not been established, but he went on to deal with the sovereignty argument. He concluded that an Aboriginal right to bring goods into Canada duty-free would entail a mobility right that would be inconsistent with Canada's sovereign authority to control its borders and, thus, could not exist under section 35(1). While this aspect of his judgment has been criticized,[145] I do not find it particularly surprising for a couple of reasons. First, it is consistent with American jurisprudence, which, while endorsing the concept of inherent Indian sovereignty, has maintained that the imposition of European and then American sovereignty diminished Indian sovereignty so that it could only be exercised internally within the United States.[146] Second, as one of the three branches of government deriving authority from Crown sovereignty, Canadian courts are unwilling and perhaps unable to question its existence.[147] This does not mean that European colonization and Crown assertion of sovereignty were legitimate or even legal. Questions can and, indeed, should be posed as to how and when Crown sovereignty was acquired and whether it violated applicable ethical or legal norms.[148] Yet ultimately the exercise of sovereignty is a matter of political and military power that domestic courts regard as beyond their jurisdiction.[149]

More importantly for the purposes of this chapter, Justice Binnie carefully avoided deciding that an Aboriginal right of *internal* self-government would be incompatible with Crown sovereignty. He pointed out that "the sovereign incompatibility principle has not prevented the United States (albeit with its very different constitutional framework) from continuing to recognize forms of *internal* aboriginal self-government which it considers to be expressions of residual aboriginal sovereignty."[150] He went on to observe that the conceptualization of the Indian peoples as "domestic dependent nations" originated in Chief Justice Marshall's judgment in *Cherokee Nation v. Georgia*[151] and has been more recently expressed by the US Supreme Court in *United States v. Wheeler*, where Justice Potter Stewart stated that "[t]he powers of Indian tribes are, in general, '*inherent powers of a limited sovereignty which has never been extinguished.*'"[152] Justice Binnie concluded:

> I refer to the U.S. law only to alleviate any concern that addressing aspects of the sovereignty issue in the context of a claim to an international trading and mobility right would prejudice one way or the other a resolution of the much larger and more complex claim of First Nations in Canada to *internal* self-governing institutions. The United States has lived with internal tribal self-government within the framework of external relations determined wholly by the United States government without doctrinal difficulties since *Johnson v. M'Intosh* was decided almost 170 years ago.[153]

Justice Binnie clearly regarded sovereignty over international affairs and control of borders as having passed to the Canadian government. He said that "assertion of British sovereignty to the Akwesasne area was certainly no later than the Treaty of Paris 1763," whereby France ceded its rights to New France to Britain.[154] By the subsequent Treaty of Paris between Britain and the United States in 1783, the international boundary was drawn through the Mohawk territory. For Justice Binnie, the question was therefore "whether the asserted legal right to the autonomous exercise of international trade and mobility was compatible with the new European (now Canadian) sovereignty and the reciprocal loss (or impairment) of Mohawk sovereignty."[155] In light of the fact that Chief Mitchell claimed this right, not as a citizen of Canada but as a citizen of the Haudenosaunee or Iroquois Confederacy, Justice Binnie found it to be "incompatible with the historical attributes of Canadian sovereignty," which include control of borders.[156] In other words, Mohawk and Haudenosaunee sovereignty in relation to movement of goods and people over what became the international boundary had been lost by the imposition of European and, hence, Canadian sovereignty over the area.[157]

Despite this conclusion, Justice Binnie seems to have approved of the concept of "merged" or "shared" sovereignty that he found expressed in the *Report of the Royal Commission on Aboriginal Peoples*.[158] He said:

> "Merged sovereignty" asserts that First Nations were not wholly subordinated to non-aboriginal sovereignty but over time became merger partners.

The final *Report of the Royal Commission on Aboriginal Peoples*, vol. 2 (*Restructuring the Relationship* (1996)), at p. 214, says that "Aboriginal governments give the constitution [of Canada] its deepest and most resilient roots in Canadian soil." This updated concept of Crown sovereignty is of importance. Whereas historically the Crown may have been portrayed as an entity across the seas with which aboriginal people could scarcely be expected to identify, this was no longer the case in 1982 when the s. 35(1) reconciliation process was established. The Constitution was patriated and all aspects of our sovereignty became firmly located within our borders. If the principle of "merged sovereignty" articulated by the Royal Commission on Aboriginal Peoples is to have any true meaning, it must include at least the idea that aboriginal and non-aboriginal Canadians *together* form a sovereign entity with a measure of common purpose and united effort. It is this new entity, as inheritor of the historical attributes of sovereignty, with which existing aboriginal and treaty rights must be reconciled.[159]

The Royal Commission on Aboriginal Peoples had explained its understanding of how sovereignty is shared in Canada in this way:

The enactment of section 35 of the *Constitution Act, 1982* had far-reaching structural significance. It confirmed the status of Aboriginal peoples as partners in the complex federal arrangements that make up Canada. It provided the basis for recognizing Aboriginal governments as one of three distinct orders of government in Canada: Aboriginal, provincial and federal. The governments making up these three orders share the sovereign powers of Canada as a whole, powers that represent a pooling of existing sovereignties.[160]

The commissioners then went on, in a passage quoted by Justice Binnie, to state:

Shared sovereignty, in our view, is a hallmark of the Canadian federation and a central feature of the three-cornered relations that link Aboriginal governments, provincial governments and the federal government. These governments are sovereign within their respective spheres and hold their powers by virtue of their constitutional status rather than by delegation. Nevertheless, many of their powers are shared in practice and may be exercised by more than one order of government.[161]

Apparently rejecting the out-dated constitutional dogma of the unity of the Crown, the commissioners regarded patriation of the constitution in 1982 as having "confirmed that the Canadian Crown is constitutionally distinct from the British Crown, even if for historical reasons the two offices continue to be occupied by the same person."[162] They then described their understanding of the position of the Canadian Crown:

> The Crown of Canada is, in part, the symbol of the constitutional relationship among various autonomous political communities, each with its distinctive history and internal constitution; it also represents the federal institutions that give concrete expression to this relationship. Contrary to some imperial views, the Canadian Crown is not the notional fountain of all governmental power and jurisdiction; to the contrary, it represents a partial pooling of powers that flow from a variety of sources, Aboriginal and non-Aboriginal alike.
>
> It would be wrong to say that the Crown has sovereignty over Aboriginal peoples, on a quasi-imperial model. Rather, it is the living symbol of a federal arrangement involving a partial merging of sovereignty and the guaranteed retention of certain sovereign powers by the various political units that make up Canada, including Aboriginal peoples.[163]

The Royal Commission on Aboriginal Peoples' conceptions of shared sovereignty and of the position of the Canadian Crown raise complex issues of constitutional theory that cannot be pursued in this chapter.[164] For present purposes, what I regard as important is Justice Binnie's apparent willingness to take these conceptions seriously and envisage the possibility that the Canadian constitution contains space for Aboriginal governments that share sovereignty with the federal and provincial governments.[165] While it is clear from his judgment that Aboriginal sovereignty cannot extend to matters that are essential to Canadian sovereignty internationally,[166] such as the control of borders and the maintenance of armed forces,[167] he also said that the doctrine of sovereign incompatibility must be applied "sparingly" and "with caution."[168] Although he was careful neither to foreclose nor endorse "any position on the compatibility or incompatibility of *internal* self-governing institutions of First Nations with Crown sovereignty,"[169] I think the overall tenor of his judgment, including his reliance on the *Report of Royal Commission on Aboriginal Peoples* and on American law with its long-standing acceptance of "residual aboriginal sovereignty,"[170] envisages an inherent right of self-government that is much more broadly based, theoretically sound, and practical than the narrow approach taken by Chief Justice Lamer in *Pamajewon*.

Conclusion

The Nisga'a nation initiated the modern era of Aboriginal rights litigation in Canada with *Calder*. In this case, they strategically and, in my opinion, wisely limited their claim to Aboriginal title, avoiding the more contentious and politically charged issue of self-government. Since then, they have chosen to seek acknowledgment of their Aboriginal rights, including their right of self-government, through negotiations with the Canadian and British Columbia governments. By this means, they have established another landmark, namely the Nisga'a treaty, which is the first treaty to be entered into in the province in the past hundred years and to explicitly include provisions for self-government. They were also successful in defending the constitutional validity of those self-government provisions in the *Campbell* case, which, at the same time, created what in my view is the strongest precedent to date on self-government as an inherent Aboriginal right.

It is no doubt more appropriate to resolve the issue of self-government through negotiations than through the courts, as long as this can be achieved without Aboriginal peoples having to compromise their rights too drastically and give up too much. However, without court decisions supporting the validity of, and giving substance to, the right of self-government, the bargaining position of the Aboriginal peoples is weak. With a decision such as *Pamajewon* standing as the main Supreme Court of Canada precedent on the content of the right of self-government, negotiators for non-Aboriginal governments can always say: "Fine, if you don't like what we are offering, then you can go to court and try to prove your right of self-government in the piece-meal fashion of *Pamajewon*, but don't expect to have jurisdiction over any matters that were not integral to your distinctive cultures and regulated by you prior to European contact." If the *Pamajewon* approach is a full expression of the litigation alternative, this boxes Aboriginal peoples in and leaves them with little choice other than to negotiate on non-Aboriginal governments' terms.

However, there is now a second line of jurisprudence originating from the assertion in argument in *Sparrow* that Aboriginal peoples have authority to regulate their rights themselves. This argument appears to have been accepted by the Supreme Court of Canada in *Delgamuukw* in relation to Aboriginal title and in *Marshall (No. 2)* in relation to treaty rights.[171] The implications for self-government of this acceptance in *Delgamuukw* were clearly recognized and expressed by Justice Williamson in *Campbell*. As a result, it can now be contended that incidental to every other Aboriginal and treaty right is a right of self-government in relation thereto, making it unnecessary to try to prove rights of self-government independently in accordance with the *Pamajewon* approach. One limitation on this incidental approach is that Aboriginal or treaty rights have to be established first. While the *Delgamuukw* litigation, which at trial alone took 374 days, reveals how complex and costly this can be, at least Aboriginal title, if established, is not limited to traditional uses of the land. Other Aboriginal rights, however, are still subject to the *Van der Peet* test, limiting them to practices, customs, and traditions integral to distinctive Aboriginal cultures prior to contact with Europeans. This could exclude the possibility of self-government authority over any matters arising post-contact that are not related to the use of Aboriginal title lands.

A different approach to self-government has been taken in the United States. Ever since the decisions of Chief Justice Marshall in the 1820s and 1830s, the US Supreme Court has acknowledged the complete independence of the Indian nations prior to European colonization. Post-colonization, their sovereignty has continued to the extent it has not been diminished by the imposition of European and American sovereignty, voluntarily relinquished by treaty, or taken away by Acts of Congress. I find it puzzling that Chief Justice Lamer, in *Sioui* and *Van der Peet*, appears to have accepted the validity of Chief Justice Marshall's analysis of Indian sovereignty yet applied a test for self-government in *Pamajewon* that contradicts that analysis by limiting self-government to pre-contact practices, customs, and traditions that Aboriginal peoples can prove were integral to their distinctive cultures and regulated by them. Since the Marshall decisions, American law has consistently acknowledged that Indian sovereignty is residual; consequently, its existence and extent are presumed. The onus is therefore on the United States government to prove how that sovereignty has been diminished.

As the Supreme Court of Canada has pointed out, the constitutional context for Aboriginal rights and the specifics of Aboriginal law are different in the United States. Nonetheless, the Court has recognized that the same general principles underlie Aboriginal law in both countries. This must be particularly so when the issue is the impact of European colonization upon pre-existing Aboriginal sovereignty, since this issue relates to the period prior to the creation of the United States and the development of American law. One also has to ask which approach is more in keeping with historical reality and common sense – an approach that limits the right of self-government to authority actually exercised by Aboriginal nations over integral aspects of their societies centuries ago or an approach that acknowledges their complete independence at that time and their presumptive authority to exercise broad jurisdiction over their lands and peoples today. For me, the answer is obvious. The starting point in Canada should be no different from what it is in the United States in this respect. The extent to which the Aboriginal right of self-government has been impacted upon by treaties, Canada's constitutional structure, and the exercise of Crown sovereignty would, nonetheless, be unique to Canada. However, as in the United States, we should begin with the presumption that Aboriginal sovereignty continues to the extent that it has not been shown to have been diminished.

Part 4
International Impact

9
Customary Rights and Crown Claims: *Calder* and Aboriginal Title in Aotearoa New Zealand
David V. Williams

Radical Title, Aboriginal Title, and Maori Customary Rights

In February 1840, officials representing the British Crown entered into treaty negotiations with the chiefs of the indigenous Maori tribes of the islands known to Europeans as New Zealand and now generally known in the Maori language as Aotearoa.[1] A treaty, written in Maori and known as the Treaty of Waitangi, was agreed between the Crown and many of those chiefs.[2] It offered the Queen's protection to the Maori and certain guarantees of their rights to land and important treasures. An English translation clearly asserted that the chiefs were ceding their sovereignty to the Crown, but the treaty itself was not clear on this point. Some Maori remain of the view that the treaty affirmed the prior power, prestige, and authority of the Maori and invited the Crown to govern only the European settlers who had already begun to arrive in the territory.[3] Such discrepancies did not bother colonial officials, nor were they concerned by the fact that not all tribes adhered to the treaty. The entire territory of New Zealand was proclaimed to be a British colony, and all Maori people were deemed to be British subjects regardless of whether they belonged to signatory or non-signatory tribes.[4] This point was emphasized later by the *Native Rights Act 1865*.[5]

When the colonial state of New Zealand was established, it was plain as a matter of imperial policy that New Zealand was to be a settlement colony and that European settlers needed land to be made available to them. Land policy and immigration were therefore crucial to the imperial and colonial officials. On the other hand, the cultural and spiritual relationships and interconnections between land and people were central to the precepts of the indigenous systems of customary law, known generally as "tikanga Maori." The notion of sharing resources with incomers, under arrangements that involved an ongoing commitment to mutually beneficial and reciprocal outcomes, was entirely possible under tikanga Maori. In many parts of the country, there had been a number of European sealers, whalers, traders, and missionaries who had lived under customary law regimes in the fifty years of contact prior to 1840. The notion of permanent alienation of land, or even of "ownership" of land as such, was not imaginable, however. Patu Hohepa, former Maori language commissioner, wrote about "whenua" – the Maori word for land – in this way:

> For Maori, whenua has an added meaning, being the human placenta or afterbirth. Through various birth ceremonies the placenta is returned to the land, and that results in each Maori person having personal, spiritual, symbolic and sacred links to the land where their whenua (placenta) is part of the whenua (land). The words "nooku teenei whenua" (This is my land) is given a much stronger meaning because of the above extensions. Having ancestral and birth connections the above is also translated as "I belong to this land, so do my ancestors, and when I die I join them so I too will be totally part of this land."[6]

The paradigms of land tenure written by the Colonial Office in instructions to governors as implemented by the *Land Claims Ordinance 1841* were very different.[7] The ordinance declared that "all unappropriated lands within the said Colony of New Zealand, subject however to the rightful and necessary occupation and use thereof by the aboriginal inhabitants of the said Colony, are and remain Crown or Domain Lands of Her Majesty." This was an assertion of the radical title of the Crown to all land. The question then arose as to whether, in order to provide land for settlers, Maori customary rights had first to be extinguished in respect of *all* land or only in respect of land actually occupied and cultivated at the time (in a fashion that John Locke might understand) by Maori tribes. Earl Grey's 1846 instructions to a new governor, George Grey (not a relative), were avowedly based on the opinions of the historian Thomas Arnold in the Lockean mould:

> [So] much does the right of property go along with labour, that civilized nations have never scrupled to take possession of countries inhabited only by tribes of savages – countries which have been hunted over but never subdued or cultivated.[8]

Earl Grey (then Lord Howick) had been the author of a House of Commons committee report in 1844 arguing for the settlement of waste lands in the colony without undue deference to the "injudicious proceedings" of the Treaty of Waitangi. As secretary of state for the colonies, he strongly dissented from the notion that Aboriginal inhabitants were the proprietors of every part of the soil of any country. For him, civilized (that is, European) men had a right to step in and take possession of vacant territory: "[All] lands not actually occupied in the sense in which alone occupation can give a right of possession ought to have been considered as the property of the Crown." The governor was expressly empowered to depart from the strict application of these principles if it would be impracticable to enforce this policy.[9]

To clarify the land policy for the colony, in view of his predecessor's purported waiver of Crown pre-emption to permit settlers to engage in direct purchasing of land from the Maori, Grey initiated a test case in the Supreme Court.[10] In *Queen v. Symonds* in 1847, the judges of the Supreme Court asserted the paramount importance of the Crown's pre-emptive monopoly right to purchase lands from the Maori.[11] Nevertheless, relying on the US Supreme Court judgments of Chief Justice John Marshall and the commentaries of Chancellor James Kent, they took a more liberal view of the scope of Aboriginal title than Earl Grey had:

> Whatever may be the opinion of jurists as to the strength or weakness of the Native title, whatsoever may have been the past vague notions of the Natives of this country, whatever may be their present clearer and still growing conception of their own dominion over land, it cannot be too solemnly asserted that it is entitled to be respected, that it cannot be extinguished (at least in times of peace) otherwise than by the free consent of the Native occupiers. But for their protection, and for the sake of humanity, the Government is bound to maintain, and the Courts to assert, the Queen's exclusive right to extinguish it.[12]

Customary Rights Rejected

Thirty years later, the settler population had grown larger than the indigenous population and imperial armed might had broken the resistance of those Maori tribes who sought to retain their autonomy, albeit with considerable difficulty during a period of warfare lasting twelve years.[13] The Supreme Court, now composed of judges appointed by the settler government, resiled from its fulsome recognition of Aboriginal title rights in 1847. In *Wi Parata v. Bishop of Wellington,* the court reinterpreted the reasoning of *R. v. Symonds*.[14] The radical title of the Crown to all lands was emphasized, and the court took the view that it had no jurisdiction to go behind a Crown grant and inquire into the extinguishment or otherwise of any prior rights. In the judgment of Chief Justice Sir James Prendergast and Justice C. William Richmond, which was delivered by the chief justice, the 1841 ordinance was said to "express the well-known legal incidents of a settlement planted by a civilised Power in the midst of uncivilised tribes."[15] The Treaty of Waitangi was dismissed "as a simple nullity. No body politic existed capable of making a cession of sovereignty, nor could the thing itself exist. So far as the proprietary rights of the Natives are concerned, the so-called treaty merely affirms the rights and obligations which, *jure gentium*, vested in and devolved upon the Crown."[16] Nor did an explicit provision in the *Native Rights*

Act 1865 make a difference. This act speaks, the judges wrote, "of the 'Ancient Custom and Usage of the Maori people,' as if some such body of customary law did in reality exist. But a phrase in a statute cannot call what is non-existent into being." Rather, "in the case of primitive barbarians, the supreme executive Government must acquit itself, as best it may, of its obligation to respect Native proprietary rights, and of necessity must be the sole arbiter of its own justice."[17]

The *Wi Parata* approach replaced legal obligations to respect indigenous customary rights with an unenforceable and non-justiciable moral obligation on the executive branch of government to deal with those rights as it saw fit. The proclamation of British sovereignty and the concomitant radical title of the Crown to all land were supported by the court in its refusal to permit the impeaching of Crown grants. A number of aspects of the *Wi Parata* judgment attracted criticism from the Privy Council in later cases. In *Nireaha Tamaki v. Baker* and *Wallis v. Solicitor-General*, the Judicial Committee pointed to the incontrovertible statutory recognition of the existence of customary Maori rights and the capacity of Maori tribes to enter into legal transactions.[18] The colonial judges, however, showed little inclination to distance themselves from *Wi Parata* and to respect the admonitions of the final appellate court for the Empire.[19] Nor did they need to since the legislature had no compunction about intervening to reverse inconvenient Privy Council decisions and even to bar further litigation by a successful Maori litigant such as Nireaha Tamaki.[20] On one extraordinary occasion, the judges in Wellington publicly lambasted the Privy Council, not only for insinuating that the colonial judges were beholden to the executive but also for their lordships' palpable ignorance, as the colonial bench viewed it, of laws and practices concerning Native land issues. Consistent with the reasoning of *Wi Parata*, Chief Justice Robert Stout's protest included the assertion that "[a]ll lands of the Colony belonged to the Crown, and it was for the Crown under Letters Patent to grant to the parties to the Treaty such lands as the Crown had agreed to grant."[21]

It was the views of the chief justices, Prendergast and Stout, in preference to the views of the Privy Council, that Parliament codified in the *Native Land Act 1909*.[22] This act was drafted by the famous jurist and long-serving solicitor-general John Salmond. The non-justiciability of any Maori claims asserting that customary title rights had not been properly extinguished was most explicitly dealt with by sections 84 to 87 of the 1909 act.[23] Salmond's private explanation to Apirana Ngata, an eminent Maori member of Parliament, of those clauses in his bill was as follows:

> The intention is that when a dispute arises between Natives and the Crown as to the right to customary land, the dispute shall be settled by Parliament

and not otherwise. The Native race will have nothing to fear from the decision of that tribunal, and to allow the matter to be fought out in the Law Courts would not, I think, be either in the public interest or in the interests of the Natives themselves.[24]

His explanatory memorandum accompanying the bill made it clear that, in his view, customary title existed only at the pleasure of the Crown:

> Customary land, since it has never been Crown-granted, belongs to the Crown. It is in a wide sense of the term Crown land, subject, however, to the right of those Natives who by virtue of Maori custom have a claim to it to obtain a Crown grant (or a certificate of title under the Land Transfer Act in lieu of a grant) on the ascertainment of their customary titles by the Native Land Court. This right of the Natives to their customary lands was recognised by the Treaty of Waitangi in 1840. In its origin it was merely a moral claim, dependent on the good will of the Crown, and not recognisable or enforceable at law.

Salmond went on to argue that whether or not legislative recognition of Maori custom had created a legal right enforceable against the Crown "was left an open question by the Privy Council in *Nireaha Tamaki v. Baker.*" On the other hand, "it is settled" by *Wi Parata* and once a Crown grant has been issued then "the validity of the title so obtained cannot be questioned on the ground that the antecedent Native title to that land had not been lawfully extinguished."[25] Hence, the definition in section 2 of the *Native Land Act 1909* was that "Customary land" means "land (vested in the Crown) held by Natives under the customs and usages of the Maori people."[26]

By 1911, the area of dry land not yet investigated by the Native Land Court, with the consequent extinguishment of customary title, was tiny.[27] Just when the government thought that all customary land issues had been well taken care of, however, Maori customary claims to the land comprised in the beds of inland lakes provided a thorny problem for Crown policy. The Court of Appeal affirmed the right of plaintiffs from the Te Arawa tribes to have the Native Land Court investigate their title to the bed of Lake Rotorua in *Tamihana Korokai v. Solicitor-General.*[28] In arguments to the court and in internal memoranda, Salmond, as solicitor-general, expressed indignation that the judges had failed to understand the nature of the Crown's right to prevent customary title issues becoming justiciable issues. The government then worked hard to ensure that this and other lakebed issues would not come to a hearing before the Native Land Court. In direct negotiations, the government persuaded Maori tribes to accept the Crown's assertion of ownership in return for various forms of compensation, sometimes including a proportion of the fishing licence revenues for fishing in those lakes.[29] For Salmond, "[i]t could never have been the intention of the Legislature to recognise and give legal effect to any Native claim to the exclusive ownership of the great navigable waters of the Dominion."[30]

Aboriginal Title Revives: Fisheries Cases

One might have assumed that the *Wi Parata* doctrine and its statutory codification had led to the total demise of Aboriginal title as a concept relevant to law in New Zealand. The Maori cultural renaissance of the 1970s, however, led to a strong questioning of many of the assumptions of the assimilation and integration policies pursued by successive governments over many decades.[31] Furthermore, within governing circles, hesitant steps were being taken to move away from the colonial settler picture of New Zealand as a "Better Britain" in the south seas and the most loyal of the British dominions to New Zealand as an independent nation in the South Pacific.[32] Some scholars speak of the emergence of "post-colonialism" at this time. Yet constitutional structures derived from the colonial era firmly remained in place – even if, from time to time, some of the British imperial and monarchical trappings have been shed.

From the 1970s, however, there was a renewed political focus on the Treaty of Waitangi as the foundation of the New Zealand nation. Waitangi Day became the country's national day of commemoration (and also the focus of political protests led by Maori nationalists). There was also an emerging awareness of the position of indigenous peoples in other countries who also had become a minority population in their own land. For the peoples of most territories colonized by European powers, acts of self-determination led to political independence in the decades after the Second World War. However, indigenous First Nation peoples in the Americas, the Pacific Rim, Scandinavia, and elsewhere were not given an opportunity to exercise the right of self-determination.

In the 1980s, the focus of action to promote the Maori cultural renaissance moved from protests, petitions, occupations, and marches to litigation. As a result, legal scholars and practitioners began to craft arguments that would advance Maori causes. Most of this effort was directed towards an enhanced status of the guarantees to the Maori contained in the Treaty of Waitangi and the enhanced powers for the Waitangi Tribunal created by the *Treaty of Waitangi Act 1975*.[33] This was consistent with the long history of Maori seeking the ratification of the treaty as an enforceable legal instrument. These efforts over many decades had included court cases, petitions to Parliament, petitions to the British monarch in person, resolutions of autonomous Maori Parliaments, and the rise of independent Maori political movements and churches. I was one of the scholars who argued in the

The late Dame Whina Cooper, leader of the Maori Land March in 1975, as she began her walk down the length of the North Island from Te Hapua to Wellington. This march is viewed by many people as the signal event in the modern political and cultural renaissance of the Maori. *Courtesy of the New Zealand Herald*

1980s that the time had come for an enhanced legal status to be accorded to the Treaty of Waitangi. This was a consensual solemn compact between the Crown and the Maori, whereas the so-called "common law" doctrine of Aboriginal title was a doctrine of imperial law that did not contest the framework of British sovereignty claims. Moreover, this doctrine had always permitted the Crown to extinguish customary title by overriding acts of Parliament, including confiscation and other forms of extinguishment without compensation and without the explicit consent of the indigenous people.[34] On the other hand, those Maori willing to resort to the courts of the state's legal system, not surprisingly, were less concerned than I with ideological purity. They were more concerned with seeking favourable practical outcomes by advancing legal arguments that might persuade the judges to recognize Maori customary entitlements. This is where the decisions of Canadian courts came to play a significant role in the development of a new New Zealand common law.

The Impact of *Calder et al. v. Attorney-General of British Columbia* and Other Canadian Decisions

The landmark judgments in *Calder*, the decision of the Supreme Court of Canada concerning the Nisga'a nation, are the focus of attention in this chapter.[35] They were not a clear-cut victory for the indigenous plaintiffs.[36] Nevertheless, for the Maori litigants and their lawyers, the doctrine of Aboriginal title discussed in *Calder* hinted at the possibility of favourable outcomes for the Maori. With such slim pickings available in New Zealand's own legal history, this possibility was seized upon by the courts and the Waitangi Tribunal in the 1980s. The tribunal's first substantive report was published in 1983, and it concerned potential contamination of a coastal fishing ground of great importance to a Maori tribe. The tribunal, chaired by Chief Judge Edward Taihakurei Durie, wrote:

> Nonetheless the approach of the New Zealand Courts, and of successive Governments, does not compare favourably with that taken by other Courts and Governments in their consideration of indigenous minorities. In North America for example treaties with the original Indian populations have been recognised by the Courts, and in areas not covered by treaties, common law rights are regarded as vesting in Native peoples by virtue of their prior occupation (refer for example, *Calder et al. v. Attorney-General of British Columbia* (1973) 34 D.L.R. 145).
>
> The overseas experience must cause us to re-think our perception of the Treaty of Waitangi and of its significance. In its consideration of a major oil pipeline running the length of Canada for example, and in proposing a moratorium on the continuation of the works, the Royal Commission in the McKenzie Valley Pipeline Inquiry (Justice Thomas R. Berger) considered it necessary that Native Land Claims be first settled, and that "native hunting, trapping and fishing rights ... be guaranteed." We consider that it will be increasingly unrealistic for New Zealanders to assess the Treaty of Waitangi in the context only of their own history.[37]

This paragraph follows after a long list of New Zealand cases that gave the treaty "a dubious status in international and municipal law." The *Calder* case was in fact the only actual case cited for the more favourable legal climate in North America.

The re-thinking foreshadowed by the tribunal was taken a big step further in 1986 when the High Court held, in *Te Weehi v. Regional Fisheries Officer,* that even if customary rights had been extinguished along the adjacent shoreline, customary fishing rights below the high-water mark in a coastal area would remain unextinguished.[38] In the 1914 *Waipapakura* case, John Salmond, as solicitor-general, had argued that tidal waters vested in the Crown by its prerogative were free of any customary rights.[39] Accepting the Crown's position, Chief Justice Robert Stout for the full court denied that the mere saving of "existing Maori fishing rights" in a section of the *Fisheries Act 1908* permitted customary fishing rights to harvest whitebait in tidal waters. Such customary rights were unexercisable unless they had been explicitly recognized in an act of Parliament.[40] This was another example of the *Wi Parata*-type reasoning that prevailed at that time.

In 1986, however, the High Court held that customary rights continued to subsist and continued to have the protection accorded by the Aboriginal title doctrines of the common law outlined in the (now remembered) *Symonds* case. These rights had continued to be available to the Maori unless they had been clearly and plainly extinguished by a statute or other lawful means. Mere assertion of Crown prerogative rights would not suffice, and the onus of proving extinguishment lay on the Crown. Justice Neil Williamson was assisted by the *Calder* decision, four other recent Canadian cases, and the writings of a New Zealand expatriate academic, Paul McHugh, in restrictively distinguishing the earlier decision in *Waipapakura v. Hempton.*[41]

Following *Te Weehi,* the Waitangi Tribunal undertook an extensive inquiry into the nature and extent of Maori customary fishing rights in its *Muriwhenua Fishing Claims Report,* which was published in 1988. Counsel for the claimants submitted a number of overseas cases for the tribunal's consideration, including *Calder* and the other Canadian cases relied on in *Te Weehi.*[42] In its detailed (and controversial) report, the tribunal found as a historical fact that Maori fishing rights were not merely traditional practices for subsistence living but also included commercial opportunities exploited well prior to 1840 by Maori tribes. It also found that a principle of the Treaty of Waitangi was the principle of development, so that the Maori were not restricted to pre-colonial technologies in exercising their ongoing commercial fishing rights.[43]

It should be noted that the tribunal received submissions from the Fishing Industry Council. The industry relied on the doctrine of Aboriginal title not to promote the scope of the Treaty of Waitangi rights, as put forward by the claimants, but, rather, to narrow them. Its submission emphasized the usufructuary nature of Aboriginal title rights as expounded by the Privy Council in cases such as *Amodu Tijani v. Secretary, Southern Nigeria.*[44] It argued that the Maori had no right to participate in modern commercial fisheries

or to obtain the quota rights created by statute to control access to commercial fisheries. The tribunal wrote of the treaty principles of active protection
and of development. It did not delve deeply into the content of Aboriginal
title rights, but it rejected the industry's submissions:

> The doctrine, it was claimed, upheld fishing rights but not exclusive rights,
> recognised fishing grounds but not zones, and was directed to sustaining
> traditional lifestyles, not to the pursuit of Western forms of trade. We were
> given to understand that the Treaty therefore had to mean the same ...
>   We reject the Industry's approach. While the doctrine of aboriginal title
> does form part of the necessary background to Colonial Office opinions as
> held at the time of the Treaty, and there is some concurrence between the
> doctrine and the Treaty principle of protecting Maori interests, the one is
> not determinative of the meaning of the other, and both have an aura of
> their own.[45]

The tribunal took the position that its primary task was to develop treaty
principles with practical applications for the Maori claimants. It was for the
ordinary courts to develop the Aboriginal title doctrine.[46] The opportunity
for the courts to do so arose soon enough.

In *Te Runanga o Muriwhenua v. Attorney-General*, the Court of Appeal had
its first chance to consider the modern relevance of Aboriginal title rights
since the *Te Weehi* case.[47] The actual decisions of the court related to procedural matters and the evidential value of the tribunal's *Muriwhenua Fishing
Claims Report* in the High Court proceedings. Yet President Sir Robin Cooke
(as he was then named; later, he was elevated to the House of Lords as Lord
Cooke of Thorndon) seized the opportunity to offer some wide-ranging
observations on Aboriginal title. His judgment for the court declared the
1914 *Waipapakura* decision on fishing rights, which had been followed in a
number of subsequent cases prior to *Te Weehi*, to be "a dubious authority,
especially in the light of the Privy Council's subsequent exposition in *Amodu
Tijani v. Secretary, Southern Nigeria* of the principle of the preservation of the
Native title after cession of sovereignty."[48] In his lengthy *obiter dicta* on this
topic, the president waxed eloquently upon the virtues of Canadian case
law. He went back to the old Privy Council case *St. Catherine's Milling &
Lumber Co. v. R.* on the survival of fishing rights even though land titles had
been extinguished.[49] He also praised the 1980s decisions of the Supreme
Court of Canada in *Guerin v. The Queen* and *Simon v. R.:*

> More recently in Canada Indian rights have been identified as pre-existing
> legal rights not created by Royal Proclamation, statute or executive order. It
> has been recognised that, in some circumstances at least, the Crown is un-
> der a fiduciary duty to holders of such rights in dealings related to their

extinction ... There are constitutional differences between Canada and New Zealand, but the *Guerin* judgments do not appear to turn on these. Moreover, in interpreting New Zealand parliamentary and common law it must be right for New Zealand Courts to lean against any inference that in this democracy the rights of the Maori people are less respected than the rights of aboriginal peoples are in North America.[50]

The Interface between Court Decisions and Direct Negotiations

There is an interesting interface between court decisions supporting the Aboriginal title rights of indigenous peoples and the process of direct negotiations between the Crown and the Maori interests that often follows such decisions. This is a topic that has been thoughtfully considered by Jeremy Webber. He has argued that Aboriginal title litigation is less about the detailed specification and enforcement of substantive rights and more about the recognition of the fact of separate societies possessing their own bodies of law. Once the courts have recognized this fact, then it becomes a matter of direct negotiation rather than further litigation to work out how the customary rights can be exercised in present-day circumstances.[51] Given the disparity of the bargaining power between governments and indigenous communities, I am not entirely convinced of the merits of this approach. I agree that non-indigenous courts are hardly an appropriate forum to define indigenous customary entitlements and that many Maori leaders, as with indigenous communities elsewhere, have decided to "negotiate" for whatever deals are currently on offer from the government of the day. The alternative – holding out for the enforceability of customary rights defined only in accordance with the authentic norms of tikanga Maori – can be criticized as wishful thinking and political futility. Nevertheless, it is important that distinctive Maori identities and spheres of authority – mana Maori motuhake – and Maori cultural knowledge systems are not totally subsumed within the rights integration trajectory of negotiated contemporary settlements.

In extra-judicial comments published in 2002, Justice Durie acknowledged the central role of the decisions in *Calder* and *Te Weehi* in the litigation/ direct negotiation interface as it has opened up in New Zealand:

> *Te Weehi* was consistent with modern developments of the doctrine of aboriginal title in commonwealth jurisdictions. These were set in motion by the Canadian case of *Calder v. Attorney-General of British Columbia* ... *Calder*, like *Te Weehi*, recognised the continued existence of customary rights and in effect forced negotiation of claims to aboriginal title with indigenous groups.[52]

Direct negotiations have been used to create modern instruments for the partial recognition of the bundle of customary rights claimed by the Maori.

These rights are a complex (and often undifferentiated) amalgam of customary rights under tikanga Maori, along with Treaty of Waitangi rights, Aboriginal title rights, and rights flowing from the principles of the Treaty of Waitangi that have been created by Parliament, the courts, and the tribunal since the *Treaty of Waitangi Act 1975*. Crown policy in an ad hoc way prior to 1992, and in a more systematic manner since then, has sought to persuade the Maori to agree to comprehensive settlement packages intended to achieve "durable, fair and final settlements" of all historical claims. Government ministers and legal advisers were taken by surprise with a number of the decisions of superior courts in the 1980s. In addition to the cases on customary and commercial fishing rights mentioned earlier, the Court of Appeal found against the attorney general three times within two years. Litigation was launched by the Maori to prevent the neo-liberal policies of corporatization and privatization undermining the opportunity to make good their claims for the return of Crown land and assets in partial satisfaction of historic grievances. The court thrice found that the government was in breach of a statutory obligation not to act "in a manner inconsistent with the principles of the Treaty of Waitangi."[53] This obligation was originally meant to be a largely meaningless device to appease the Maori. However, the Court of Appeal insisted that words in a statute have to have a meaning and thus took seriously the opportunity judicially to create a jurisprudence of "principles of the Treaty," which Parliament had left undefined. This legal reasoning then flowed into the analysis of those treaty principles in the Waitangi Tribunal reports.[54]

All of these activities induced successive governments to elaborate a coordinated approach to treaty issues and then to establish a policy on the settlement of historical treaty claims. This began with the formulation of principles for Crown action in 1989, a settlement policy in 1994, and a revised settlement policy in 2000.[55] The possibility of the Maori claimants relying on customary rights and Aboriginal title arguments was specifically addressed by Crown advisers. With respect to the historical claims from 1840 to 1992, all customary entitlements were extinguished as part and parcel of the treaty settlement process that claimants must agree to if they are to receive a Crown apology and the cultural and commercial redress package on offer in the direct negotiations.

The litigation/negotiations interface was highly relevant in the case *Te Runanga o Muriwhenua* referred to earlier in this chapter. Following *Te Weehi*, a number of proceedings were instituted by the Maori plaintiffs that succeeded in obtaining interim injunctions to prevent the government implementing its quota management fisheries policy until the position of Maori fisheries had been clarified.[56] As a first response to the hiatus thus created, the Crown/Maori negotiations led to the *Maori Fisheries Act 1989*,[57] which provided for the progressive transfer to Maori interests of 10 percent of the total allowable catch but did not repeal section 88(2) of the *Maori Fisheries Act 1983*, which still saved "any Maori fishing rights." In addition to the *obiter dicta* quoted earlier on the importance of the Maori receiving as much respect for their rights as Canadian indigenous peoples, the president made some observations that "the task of the Courts in this field may be to interpret and apply the legislation in a way taking into account the realities of life in present-day New Zealand. A balancing and adjusting exercise may be called for." This was essentially a warning to the Maori not to hold out in negotiations for the full extent of their exclusive fishing rights as guaranteed in the Treaty of Waitangi: "The position resulting from 150 years of history cannot be done away with overnight. The Treaty obligations are ongoing. They will evolve from generation to generation as conditions change."[58] In support of this pragmatic position, President Cooke cited the Washington State fisheries litigation, as written up by "Phil Lancaster for the Canadian Bar Association Committee on Native Justice, 1988."[59]

Further litigation and then further negotiations led to a more comprehensive settlement of these commercial fisheries issues in 1992. This time, the Maori negotiators and a national *hui* (meeting) agreed to the extinguishment of all commercial fishing customary rights and the statutory regulation of non-commercial customary fishing rights. In return for this extinguishment and the discontinuance of all litigation, a commercial settlement valued at NZ$170 million – including control of the largest fisheries company Sealord Limited (which fortuitously had been put up for sale at the time) and access to further quota entitlements. This resource was to be made available to the *iwi* (the traditional tribes) for the benefit of the Maori people. This settlement package for the extinguishment of treaty rights came to be known as the "Sealord settlement."[60]

The Sealord settlement was not greeted with universal approval by all Maori. The Court of Appeal was called upon by a significant number of dissenting Maori tribes and organizations to intervene so as to prevent the negotiated memorandum of understanding being translated into statute law. It refused. Again, President Cooke delivered the judgment of the court in *Te Runanga o Wharekauri Rekohu Inc v. Attorney-General*. Again, he praised Canadian contributions, especially *R. v. Sparrow*, as "part of widespread international recognition that the rights of indigenous peoples are entitled to some effective protection and advancement."[61] He then made a comment on the speed of negotiations following court decisions in New Zealand. His judgment was delivered just twelve days after the end of the hearing – rather than the eighteen months the Supreme Court of Canada required in *Sparrow* and the year the High Court of Australia took in *Mabo v. Queensland (No. 2)*:[62] "[I]n New Zealand circumstances this Court has had to move more quickly – possibly at the cost of some public and other understanding of the complexity of the task." This did not deter him from concluding that the settlement proposals were "in accord with the evolving concept spoken of in our *Muriwhenua* judgments" and were "an historic step." "The Sealord opportunity was a tide which had to be taken at the flood."[63]

Aboriginal Title: River Cases

President Cooke's willingness, in *obiter dicta*, to paint a picture of the law's magnanimous treatment of indigenous peoples certainly did not mean that the Maori litigants necessarily achieved the outcomes they sought. This was particularly clear in *Te Runanganui o Te Ika Whenua Inc. v. Attorney-General* in 1994.[64] As part of the ongoing neo-liberal project of successive New Zealand governments, the *Energy Companies Act 1992* had been enacted.[65] Pursuant to this act, certain state-owned hydro-electricity dams were about to be transferred from Crown ownership to newly established energy companies. The plaintiffs were Maori claimants with customary rights over two rivers that had been dammed for electricity generation stations. At their instance, the Waitangi Tribunal issued an interim report recommending that the legal status quo be maintained until ownership and control issues were inquired into thoroughly. In both the *Te Ika Whenua – Energy Assets Report* in 1993 and the *Mohaka River Report* in 1992, the tribunal had found that rivers as "a whole indivisible entity, not separated into bed, banks and waters" were a "taonga" (treasure) explicitly guaranteed by the Treaty of Waitangi.[66] President Cooke cited these reports and went on to express doubt about the authority of a 1963 decision of the Court of Appeal, *In re the Bed of the Wanganui River:*

> Perhaps the approach which counsel for Maori argued for in that line of cases, emphasising the bed and the adjacent land more than the flow of the water, is an example of the tendency against which the Privy Council warned in *Amodu Tijani* (at p. 403) of rendering Native title conceptually in terms which are appropriate only to systems which have grown up under English law.[67]

President Cooke went on to heap further praise on the Canadian courts for developing the principle of fiduciary duty linked with Aboriginal title and cited *Baker Lake, Guerin,* and *Sparrow.*[68] These Canadian cases, *Mabo,* and other New Zealand cases that indicated that "the Treaty of Waitangi has been acquiring some permeating influence in New Zealand law" led the president to conclude: "The legal system is not powerless to provide remedies for racial injustice in appropriate cases, and decisions of the Courts in this field have assisted the parties to achieve voluntary settlements."[69]

It has to be added, though, that the court's actual decision did not assist the negotiating position of the Te Ika Whenua claimants at all – quite the contrary. The judgment insisted that an extinguishment of customary title by less than fair conduct would be "a breach of the fiduciary duty widely and increasingly recognised as falling on the colonising power," referring to earlier Canadian and New Zealand precedents and adding two more recent Canadian Federal Court of Appeal decisions. Yet the crucial conclusion, in the court's baldly stated assessment of customary rights, was that "however liberally Maori customary title and treaty rights may be construed, one cannot think that they were ever conceived as including the right to generate electricity by harnessing water power."[70]

No consideration at all was given by the Court of Appeal to the findings of the Waitangi Tribunal in earlier hearings where a treaty principle of development and mutual benefit had been discussed. In *Muriwhenua Fishing Claims Report*, as noted earlier, the tribunal accepted that the Maori had commercial fishing rights and that these rights included the right to use modern technology in pursuit of fish. In its interim *Radio Frequencies Report* in 1990, the tribunal found, using concepts drawn from the Maori text of the treaty, as follows:

> As we see it the ceding of kawanatanga to the Queen did not involve the acceptance of an unfettered legislative supremacy over resources ... Tribal rangatiratanga gives Maori greater right of access to the newly discovered spectrum. In any scheme of spectrum management it has rights greater than the general public, and especially when it is being used for the protection of taonga of the language and culture.[71]

With respect to radio spectrum and other broadcasting assets issues, litigation was taken all the way to Privy Council hearings in London. Subsequent negotiations led to the establishment in 1995 of the Te Mangai Paho (the Maori Broadcasting Funding Agency). This agency now funds, among other things, twenty-one *iwi* radio stations in many parts of the country.[72] The government was open to negotiation on radio resources, but it remained adamant that Crown ownership over rivers should be maintained. The Court of Appeal's *Te Runanui o Te Ika Whenua* judgment did not help the Maori claimants at all, but it significantly strengthened the Crown's position at the negotiations table.

Ironically, the most recent (and most thorough) discussion of the *Calder* case in the New Zealand legal system arose from the fact that it was put at the forefront of Crown legal submissions to the Waitangi Tribunal's inquiry on the Whanganui River. In its 1999 report, the tribunal considered claims by the tribe Te Atihaunui-a-Paparangi that its tribal customary rights to the waters of the river amounted to the equivalent of ownership of the river. Crown counsel, citing *Calder*, agreed that Aboriginal title recognizes a right to water but argued that this can be no more than a use-right only. Any sort of ownership claim to running water is novel and should be rejected. The tribunal report extensively considered the views expressed in the judgments of Justices Wilfred Judson, Emmett Hall, and Louis-Philippe Pigeon, especially with respect to the expert evidence of Wilson Duff. The report on *Calder* concludes:

> In our view, this case, which was invoked by the Crown, does not support their contention that Te Atihaunui-a-Paparangi had no more than a use right in their river. Rather it supports the view that they did in fact own it. Dr Duff's statement, approved by six of the Supreme Court judges in *Calder* that the Nishga "patterns of ownership and utilization which they imposed upon the lands and waters were different from those recognised by our system of law, but were nonetheless clearly defined and mutually respected" applies equally to the relationship of the Whanganui iwi to their river ... Lord Haldane's warning [in *Amodu Tijani*] against imposing common law notions on those of indigenous peoples with a distinct concept of ownership should be applied to Atihaunui in our view, and to their concept of their relationship with the river.[73]

Aboriginal Title Reappears Again (But Only Briefly)

In June 2003, the Court of Appeal decided that the Maori Land Court had jurisdiction to inquire into customary entitlements to foreshore and seabed lands. The Court of Appeal media release stressed that the court's "decision is a preliminary one about the ability of the iwi to bring their claims. The validity and extent of the customary claims in issue have yet to be decided by the Maori Land Court. The impact of other legislation controlling the management and use of the resources of maritime areas also remains to be considered."[74] The court's decision in *Attorney-General v. Ngati Apa & Others* was a modest procedural victory for seven tribes from the north of the South Island.[75] They had resorted to litigation after years of unresolved difficulties over procedures to obtain permission to engage in commercial aquaculture activities on the foreshore and seabed lands of the Marlborough Sounds. The court decision did not define their customary rights, if any. It merely enabled the plaintiffs to adduce evidence of their rights to the Maori Land Court since statutory assertions of Crown ownership were insufficient to abrogate and extinguish all customary rights. Nevertheless, the court ruling created a storm of controversy. The fierce debates on talkback radio, letters to editors, opposition political party rallies, and the like went on about "public access to beaches" being threatened by Maori claims to exclusive rights. This rhetoric had little or no connection to the narrow findings of the Court of Appeal or to the actual practical claims of the plaintiffs with respect to access to aquaculture licences in the Marlborough Sounds.

The normal means to resolve ambiguities in the law, following the due process that is supposed to be a fundamental feature of the common law heritage, is to allow a court to hear evidence and to make a ruling based on this evidence. The government immediately decided that it could not and would not wait. The received polls-based political wisdom was that the majority of the population was deeply incensed by the "judicial activism" of the Court of Appeal. Therefore, the government would introduce legislation to assert unambiguous Crown ownership over the foreshore/seabed areas.[76] This decision then provoked a howl of anguish from Maori interests, including the government's own Maori members of parliament. Eventually one of those Maori members, Tariana Turia, M.P., left the government and has since been re-elected to Parliament as leader of a newly established and independent Maori Party. Meanwhile, what followed initially was a proposal to create a new concept of "public domain" and to recognize customary rights if, and only if, these rights stopped well short of ownership rights.[77] It was decided that the Maori Land Court must be deprived of its jurisdiction to hear evidence from the tribes of their claims to customary entitlements in accordance with tikanga Maori, and the High Court must be deprived of its jurisdiction to apply the doctrine of Aboriginal title to similar effect. Thus, no court judgment as to the property rights, if any, that might flow from any proven customary rights would be allowed to proceed. The government also flatly rejected the carefully crafted recommendations of the Waitangi Tribunal, following an urgent hearing that called for a "longer conversation" between the Crown and the Maori on these matters.[78]

In order to ensure a parliamentary majority for the Foreshore and Seabed Bill when it was introduced in 2004, even the "public domain" concept was dropped and "full legal and beneficial ownership of the Crown" over the contested lands, with existing customary entitlements extinguished, was re-asserted. As eventually enacted in the *Foreshore and Seabed Act 2004*, after fierce debates (and in spite of mammoth Maori protest actions), customary entitlements were replaced by a complex regime of court proceedings that purport to permit recognition of the customary rights of Maori in relation to specific foreshore and seabed lands.[79] However, these rights are now defined only in terms of the statute's parameters and preconditions and are without reference to the actual indicia of tikanga Maori entitlements. If the Maori litigants might otherwise have been entitled to a property right equivalent to a freehold title based on common law Aboriginal title, then they must now negotiate with the government for such "redress" as the government thinks fit to offer to them.[80]

The *Ngati Apa* Case Considered

It is apparent that the government was unprepared for the unanimous decision of the five-judge bench of the Court of Appeal in the *Ngati Apa* case. Crown advisers had assumed the indisputable correctness of the 1963 Court of Appeal decision in *In Re the Ninety-Mile Beach*.[81] In fact, however, *In Re the Ninety-Mile Beach* had long been the subject of sustained academic criticism.[82] This decision was based on the reasoning of cases such as *Wi Parata* and *Waipapakura* as well as the arguments of solicitors-general following in the footsteps of Salmond. It was said to be inconsistent with the reasoning in a number of more recent Court of Appeal decisions as well as Privy Council decisions in the past.[83] The protection of the Crown in the privative clauses of Salmond's *Native Land Act 1909* had been repealed in 1993 and replaced by limitation of actions protections to prevent historic customary rights land claims being relitigated. The Crown was thus left unprotected by the old *Wi Parata* and *Native Land Act 1909* doctrines with respect to any *new* claims that might arise based on tikanga Maori customary rights and on common law Aboriginal title doctrines. It was no doubt assumed in 1993 when the *Te Ture Whenua Maori Act 1993* was passed that all customary rights to dry land, the beds of inland waters, and (more recently) fisheries had been extinguished already.[84] There was thus thought to be no land resource of practical significance left for Aboriginal title doctrines to apply to. In the circumstances, it was politically desirable to accede to the submissions of the Maori Council and others by reframing Salmond's definition of "customary land." The former reference to such land being "vested in the Crown" was removed, and the new definition acknowledged an entirely different conceptual framework: "Land that is held in accordance with tikanga Maori shall have the status of Maori customary land."[85] This was the provision that was invoked by the seven *iwi* of the South Island in the Marlborough Sounds litigation in relation to foreshore and seabed lands.

In *Ngati Apa*, the unanimous decision was that *In Re the Ninety-Mile Beach* should be overruled. Justice Andrew Tipping, who was usually one of the more conservative figures on the Court of Appeal bench, began his judgment with these words:

When the common law of England came to New Zealand its arrival did not extinguish Maori customary title. Rather, such title was integrated into what then became the common law of New Zealand. Upon acquisition of sovereignty the Crown did not therefore acquire wholly unfettered title to all the land in New Zealand ...

It follows that as Maori customary land is an ingredient of the common law of New Zealand, title to it must be lawfully extinguished before it can be regarded as ceasing to exist ... Undoubtedly Parliament is capable of effecting such extinguishment but, again in view of the importance of the subject matter, Parliament would need to make its intention crystal clear. In other words Parliament's purpose would need to be demonstrated by express words or at least by necessary implication.

Justice Tipping went on to stress that "I have deliberately referred to the common law of New Zealand in this context to distinguish it from the common law of England which of course lacked any ingredient involving Maori customary title or land."[86] In the end, the court held that the *Foreshore and Seabed Endowment Revesting Act 1991*, numerous statutes on the territorial sea and exclusive economic zone, and many more statutes on empowering harbour boards and vesting land in them did not conclusively extinguish Maori customary title.[87] One judge, President Thomas Gault, expressed "real reservations about the ability of the appellants to establish that which they claim" in terms of an ownership interest under the *Te Ture Whenua Maori Act 1993*.[88] He agreed, however, that the appeal should be allowed so as to permit a Maori Land Court hearing to investigate the facts and assess the evidence.

With the court's emphasis on New Zealand common law, there was less emphasis on Canadian judgments in this case than had been a feature in President Cooke's judgments in the 1980s and 1990s. The first instance High Court decision of Justice Anthony Ellis in favour of the Crown was in error and had to be reversed, according to the court. Chief Justice Dame Sian Elias wrote:

> I consider that in starting with English common law, unmodified by New Zealand conditions (including Maori customary proprietary interests), and in assuming that the Crown acquired property in the land of New Zealand when it acquired sovereignty, the judgment in the High Court was in error. The transfer of sovereignty did not affect customary property. They are interests preserved by the common law until extinguished in accordance with law. I agree that the legislation relied on in the High Court does not extinguish any Maori property in the seabed or foreshore. I agree with Keith and Anderson JJ. and Tipping J. that *In Re the Ninety-Mile Beach* was wrong in law and should not be followed. *In Re the Ninety-Mile Beach* followed the discredited authority of *Wi Parata v Bishop of Wellington*, which was rejected by the Privy Council in *Nireaha Tamaki v Baker*. This is not a modern revision, based on developing insights since 1963. The reasoning the Court applied in *In Re the Ninety-Mile Beach* was contrary to other and higher authority and indeed was described at the time as "revolutionary."[89]

Further on in the decision, she stated:

> The applicable common law principle in the circumstances of New Zealand is that rights of property are respected on assumption of sovereignty. They

can be extinguished only by consent or in accordance with statutory authority. They continue to exist until extinguishment in accordance with law is established. Any presumption of the common law inconsistent with the recognition of customary property is displaced by the circumstances of New Zealand (see Roberts-Wray, at 635) ...

The approach adopted in the judgment under appeal in starting with the expectations of the settlers based on English common law and in expressing a preference for "full and absolute dominion" in the Crown pending a Crown grant is also the approach of *Wi Parata*. Similarly, the reliance by Turner J [in 1963] upon English law presumptions relating to ownership of the foreshore and seabed (an argument in substance re-run by the respondents in the present appeal) is misplaced. The common law as received in New Zealand was modified by recognising Maori customary property interests. If any such custom is shown to give interests in foreshore and seabed, there is no room for a contrary presumption derived from English common law. The common law of New Zealand is different.[90]

Despite the emphasis on the circumstances of New Zealand, Canadian influence is still readily apparent in the reasoning of the judges. Chief Justice Elias wrote:

As a matter of custom the burden on the Crown's radical title might be limited to use or occupation rights held as a matter of custom (as appears to be the position described in *St Catherine's Milling and Lumber Co v The Queen* ...) On the other hand, the customary rights might "be so complete as to reduce any radical right in the Sovereign to one which only extends to comparatively limited rights of administrative interference" (*Amodu Tijani v Secretary, Southern Nigeria* at 410). The Supreme Court of Canada has had occasion recently to consider the content of customary property interests in that country. It has recognised that, according to the custom on which such rights are based, they may extend from usufructuary rights to exclusive ownership with incidents equivalent to those recognised by fee simple title (see, for example, *Delgamuukw v British Columbia* [1997] 3 S.C.R. 1010 at paragraphs 110-119 per Lamer C.J.).[91]

Justice Sir Kenneth Keith (for himself and Justice Noel Anderson) emphasized the older United States cases, the 1847 New Zealand case *Symonds*, *Amodu Tijani*, and the Privy Council appeals from New Zealand and then wrote:

The protective approach adopted in the earlier American and Privy Council authorities is to be seen in more recent rulings of the Supreme Court of Canada, the High Court of Australia and this Court: the onus of proving extinguishment lies on the Crown and the necessary purpose must be clear and plain.[92]

The cases cited in support were *Sparrow, Mabo,* and *Te Runanga o Muriwhenua*. Cited with approval by Justice Keith from the latter case were President Cooke's remarks, already quoted earlier in this chapter, that New Zealand courts should "lean against any inference that in this democracy the rights of Maori people are less respected than the rights of aboriginal peoples are in North America."

History Rhymes

The *Ngati Apa* decision finally and conclusively overruled the *Wi Parata* approach. The latter no longer has any authority as a precedent in court proceedings. The decision also restores the Court of Appeal's 1980s reputation for being willing to move into unfamiliar legal territory for the benefit of Maori plaintiffs and their putative property rights, even if this is contrary to the position strongly advocated for by the Crown as being in the interest of all New Zealanders. Nevertheless, the chance to learn how the Canadian cases from *Calder* to *Delgamuukw* will be applied in the New Zealand context to foreshore and seabed claims is to be denied us. For, at the end of the day, the *Wi Parata* approach lives on, not in the courts, but in the government's response to the unexpected court decision. The government now insists, just as Chief Justice Prendergast had opined in 1877, that "the supreme executive Government must acquit itself as best it may, of its obligation to respect Native proprietary rights, and of necessity must be the sole arbiter of its own justice."[93] Again, the government in its 2003 consultations with the Maori approached the task in line with Salmond's advice that "when a dispute arises between Natives and the Crown as to the right to customary land, the dispute shall be settled by Parliament and not otherwise."[94] In a number of pan-tribal meetings and in the government-organized consultation meetings, the government's proposals were resoundingly rejected.[95] Despite this negative response, what the deputy prime minister said in late October 2003 was entirely consistent with Salmond's 1909 doctrine: "But in the end, this matter will be resolved in the legislative arena so any solution must be able to attract a Parliamentary majority."[96] The application of the common law to the circumstances of Aotearoa New Zealand as now understood by the courts gives much greater weight and credence to customary title rights than was permitted for most of New Zealand's legal history. Yet, in some respects, the colonialist assumptions accompanying the reception of English law in the British colonies remain powerful and persuasive for those acting on behalf of the Crown in right of New Zealand. As suggested in an aphorism attributed to Mark Twain (Samuel Clemens) "history does not repeat itself but it usually rhymes."

Grandstanding and posturing associated with the *Foreshore and Seabed Act 2004* continue to be a focus of national politics. Yet as I predicted when this chapter was first presented as a paper in 2003, the government made an offer in 2004 to vest in Maori interests a proportion of the marine aquaculture commercial licences – the practical issue that started the whole controversy over the foreshore and seabed lands. With only minimal political fuss, the *Maori Commercial Aquaculture Claims Settlement Act 2004* now provides for 20 percent of new space in aquaculture management areas to be allocated to a trustee company established under the *Maori Fisheries Act 2004*.[97] The pity is that this sensible settlement has been achieved only after a huge social and cultural chasm had been created by the foreshore and seabed customary rights debacle. Judicial due process was cast aside for the uncertain merits of a political and legal outcome imposed on the Maori rather than negotiated with them. I suspect that Frank Calder would have found much to criticize in the actions of the New Zealand government, which in 2003–4 ran so rough-shod over potential legal rights recognized in court proceedings. This was done without the courtesy of engaging in a "longer conversation" (as had been recommended by the Waitangi Tribunal) with the rights-holders – the indigenous people of Aotearoa New Zealand.

10
The Influence of Canadian and International Law on the Evolution of Australian Aboriginal Title
Garth Nettheim

Australia and Canada spring from similar roots. Both were settler colonies, established by the British Crown. Their periods of colonization overlapped substantially, the same individuals were often involved in setting colonial policy, and both countries drew on similar sources of immigrants. Both countries share the heritage of the common law, and both followed a similar path to political independence. Nevertheless, there are sharp distinctions between the historical and constitutional experiences of Canada and Australia in relation to indigenous peoples. They include, in the case of Canada, the history of treaty making, the Royal Proclamation of 1763,[1] and, upon Confederation, the conferment on the national government of primary legislative responsibility. In 1982, the "repatriated" constitution provided for the protection of "existing aboriginal and treaty rights." And it included a *Canadian Charter of Rights and Freedoms*.[2] The Australian experience has been markedly different and has provided little – and belated – recognition for the territorial rights of the prior inhabitants and even less for their governance rights.

In recent years, there have been significant cross-references in the developing jurisprudence of the courts in the two nations, particularly in relation to the territorial rights of Aboriginal peoples. The litigation in *Calder et al. v. Attorney-General of British Columbia*, in particular, shaped the principal Australian cases.[3] Yet there remain significant divergences. The approaches of the national legislatures to resolving issues over the past three decades have, again, differed markedly. And international law has been a more significant influence on the evolution, and on the assessment, of Australian law on these matters than it has been in Canada.

Recognition of Rights prior to the Nineteenth Century
I begin by going back to the times when what were to become the nations of Canada and Australia were at early stages of being constituted. The year 1763 represents a suitable starting point. In North America, the British had

had long experience in establishing settlements and in relating to the indigenous peoples. After New France fell to the British in 1759, the Crown issued its Royal Proclamation of 1763, setting out what had become the basic tenets of British policy towards the Indian nations. What were these tenets? Canada's Royal Commission on Aboriginal Peoples writes:

> Aboriginal/English relations had stabilised to the point where they could be seen to be grounded in two fundamental principles. Under the first principle, Aboriginal peoples were generally recognised as autonomous political units capable of having treaty relations with the Crown ... A second principle emerged from British practice. This acknowledged that Aboriginal nations were entitled to the territories in their possession unless, or until, they ceded them away.[4]

Much of these two basic tenets was retained after the United States won independence from Britain and received some judicial recognition in the US Supreme Court. However, the immediate point is that if British colonial policy had developed in this way in regard to North America, why did it not follow a similar development in Australia?

The critical times were close. The Royal Proclamation was issued in 1763. It was only five years later, in 1768, that the Admiralty issued its instructions to Lieutenant James Cook for his first great voyage into the Pacific. A primary task was to observe the transit of Venus from Tahiti, and there were a number of other scientific dimensions to the voyage. The search for the Great South Land was almost an afterthought. If he should find it, his instructions set out two alternatives:

> You are also *with the consent of the natives* to take possession of convenient situations in the country in the name of the King of Great Britain, or, if you find the country uninhabited take possession for His Majesty by setting up proper marks and inscriptions as first discoverers and possessors.[5]

This instruction is entirely consonant with the policy developed in relation to North America. However, when Cook sailed up the eastern coast of Australia in 1770, having some encounters with the "natives," he neither sought nor obtained their consent before proclaiming possession of "New South Wales," which then amounted to about half of the Australian continent, in the name of the Crown. And when, eighteen years later, the First Fleet sailed for Botany Bay, the commission that was issued to Governor Arthur Phillip said nothing about the rights of the Natives and authorized him to grant land to those who would "improve it," without any reference to Aboriginal consent.[6]

Had British policy changed so drastically in such a short period of time? It is clear that it had not when one refers to events after the 1770s. Historian Henry Reynolds refers to the North American experience and to British practice in Africa and the Pacific. He places the instructions issued to Cook in the context of later consideration by the House of Commons Committee on Transportation of possible locations for a penal settlement. The committee took it for granted that it would be necessary to have the agreement of the inhabitants. Britain wrote the principle into the 1790 agreement with Spain in relation to a possible settlement at Nootka Sound on the west coast of what is now Canada.[7] Later still, the principle was applied firmly in relation to New Zealand, culminating in the Treaty of Waitangi in 1840.[8] So why does the British settlement (invasion?) of the Australian colonies represent such an aberration from established policy and practice?

Reynolds sheds light on the critical factors. First, in 1785, when the House of Commons Committee on Transportation examined Sir Joseph Banks, who had sailed with Cook in 1770, he was asked whether the Aborigines would be willing to bargain their consent to settlement. Banks thought not, as Reynolds notes: "The real problem wasn't that the Aborigines had nothing to sell. They were unwilling to sell because the Europeans had nothing to tender which would be considered of value, apart from provisions which in 1770 had been too valuable to part with."[9] Second, there was a belief that Australia was *literally* uninhabited (*terra nullius*), apart from a few scattered groups along the coast. This notion, too, appears to have been derived from Banks' testimony. He reported that the people that he had encountered seemed to derive their sustenance from the sea and lacked the arts of cultivation. It would follow that the interior could provide no food and would, therefore, be uninhabited. Reynolds comments: "It all would have been so easy if Banks had been right ... But he wasn't."[10] A third factor may have arisen from the perceptions that the Australian Aborigines were less "advanced" than other Native peoples. In the hierarchy of land use, hunter-gatherers were regarded as being at a lower level than nomadic herders who were considered to be more "backward" than cultivators, let alone those peoples (such as Europeans) who had developed commercial societies. There was a tradition among scholars, such as Henry Home, John Locke, Sir William Blackstone, and Emerich de Vattel, which denied that the use of land by hunter-gatherers and herders merited recognition as property interests.[11]

This last point, of course, says more about the limitations of modern law's concept of property than any of the deficiencies in the relationship between indigenous peoples and their territories. David Williams refers to the "spiritual" dimensions of the Maori attachment to land.[12] Similarly, for Australia, anthropologist W.E.H. Stanner writes:

No English words are good enough to give a sense of the links between an Aboriginal group and its homeland. Our word "home," warm and suggestive though it be, does not match the Aboriginal word that may mean "camp," "hearth," "country," "everlasting home," "totem place," "life source," "spirit centre" and much else all in one. Our word "land" is too sparse and meagre. We can now scarcely use it except with economic overtones unless we happen to be poets.[13]

Whatever the reasons – and in stark contrast with the "two fundamental principles" referred to by Canada's Royal Commission on Aboriginal Peoples – the fact was that the colonization of Australia proceeded on the basis of non-recognition of the rights of Aboriginal peoples and the Torres Strait Islanders. There was no indigenous consent to the assertion of British sovereignty, and such consent has *still* not been given. And there was no recognition of territorial rights, although this situation did change in 1992 with the High Court's landmark decision in *Mabo v. Queensland (No. 2)* (*Mabo (No. 2)*).[14]

In his influential book, *Strange Multiplicity: Constitutionalism in an Age of Diversity*, James Tully has written about three conventions of common-law constitutionalism, which, if respected, can serve to offset "the empire of uniformity" that is a common feature of modern constitutionalism.[15] He names these as mutual recognition, continuity, and consent: "The first and most spectacular example is the mutual recognition and accommodation of the Aboriginal peoples of America and the British Crown as equal, self-governing nations."[16] His evidence draws from the history of treaty relations in North America with particular reference to the jurisprudence of the "Marshall cases," which also illustrate the conventions of consent and continuity.[17] Regrettably, there is little evidence for these three conventions to be found in the history of relations between the British and Aboriginal peoples in the Australian colonies.

Developments in the Nineteenth Century
In the United States Supreme Court, the "Marshall cases" in the 1820s and 1830s seemed to provide judicial underpinning to the legal principles that had emerged after some two centuries of settlement from Britain. Indeed, the Constitution itself appeared to recognize the political status of Indian nations, and the US Supreme Court has acknowledged that they enjoy a continuing, if subordinate, sovereignty.[18] Canadian jurisprudence, too, has built on these earlier "tenets" and also on the Royal Proclamation of 1763. Canada's recognition of territorial rights has also built on the history of treaty making, which continues to the present day. And the New Zealand experience in the early part of the nineteenth century, which built on the Treaty of Waitangi, has also provided some support for similar "tenets" and

for Tully's conventions.[19] However, in both Canada and the United States, the nineteenth century witnessed some erosion of Indian rights, which clearly related to changes in the power balance between settlers and the indigenous peoples and the growing pressure on Indian lands. Similar pressures developed in New Zealand, as David Williams notes in his chapter in this volume. They also occurred in Australia.

However, in contrast to North America and New Zealand, there had been no effective recognition of Aboriginal political or territorial rights in Australia. In regard to territorial rights, the best that the British government and the several colonial governments were able to achieve as the nineteenth century progressed was the establishment of a number of "reserves" for Aboriginal peoples and some provision that the vast pastoral leases granted for running cattle and sheep should not displace Aboriginal uses of the land and its resources.[20] Yet as far as the jurisprudence was concerned, on several occasions the Australian courts[21] and even the Judicial Committee of the Privy Council[22] declared that, on the settlement of the Australian colonies, the Crown acquired not only sovereignty but also the full beneficial ownership of all of the land, which it was then free to grant to settlers.

Another contrast between our two continents occurs at the constitutional level. With Confederation in 1867, the national Parliament in Canada was given primary responsibility for Indians and the land reserved for Indians, just as the United States Constitution conferred primary power on Congress. By contrast, the *Commonwealth of Australia Constitution Act 1900* expressly *denied* to the national parliament power to pass laws for Aborigines.[23] It took a referendum in 1967 for section 51(xxvi) of the Constitution to be amended to give the national Parliament a concurrent (but not exclusive) legislative power for Aboriginal people. And there has been a distinct tendency in the politics of Australian federalism for the national government to hesitate before over-riding state and territory governments on matters of "land management" and indigenous issues generally. (New Zealand, of course, does not need to be concerned about the niceties of such federal divisions of powers.) There are no provisions in the Commonwealth Constitution that specifically recognize and protect indigenous rights in Australia. The one provision in the Constitution that may offer some indirect protection for indigenous rights is section 51(xxxi), the "acquisitions power," insofar as it requires "just terms" for any Commonwealth law with respect to the acquisition of property. The *Native Title Act 1993* (*NTA*), therefore, makes some provision for compensation with regard to acts that affect Native title.[24]

The Recognition of the Territorial Rights of Indigenous Australians

The 1960s and 1970s marked a critical period in Australian developments, much as they did in Canada and New Zealand. As noted earlier, the long political struggle to amend section 51(xxvi) of the Constitution finally achieved success in the referendum of 1967. Yet the Constitution had always conferred on the Commonwealth Parliament plenary power to legislate for the territories. And it was in the vast Northern Territory that Aboriginal people launched two major campaigns for recognition of their land rights during the 1960s. These campaigns won significant support among non-indigenous Australians. One campaign was waged by the Gurindji people. In August 1966, led by Vincent Lingiari, they walked off the Wave Hill cattle station (ranch) in protest at their working and living conditions. They moved to Wattie Creek (Daguragu) in what became a seven-year struggle for the return of their lands. This struggle remained a political struggle and was ultimately successful.[25] Elsewhere in the Northern Territory, the Commonwealth government had granted a lease for extensive bauxite mining along the Gove Peninsula. The Yolgnu peoples protested that the land was theirs and that they had not been consulted. They, too, tried to win through political means, including the delivery of a famous "bark petition" to Parliament. Yet, eventually, they brought legal proceedings before a single judge of the Supreme Court of the Northern Territory in *Milirrpum v. Nabalco Pty Ltd* (*Gove Land Rights* case).[26]

The *Gove Land Rights* Case and Statutory Land Rights

Justice Richard Blackburn eventually delivered a learned judgment of more than 150 pages.[27] He acknowledged that the Yolgnu clans had a system of law but felt bound by the precedents to conclude that "the doctrine [of Native title] does not form, and never has formed, part of the law of any part of Australia."[28] He placed some reliance on Canadian judgments commencing with *St. Catherine's Milling & Lumber Co. v. R.*[29] In particular, he considered decisions of the courts of British Columbia, to this point unsuccessful, on the claim to Aboriginal title brought by the Nisga'a people in *Calder et al. v. Attorney-General of British Columbia*.[30] The first instance decision of Justice J. Gould had been argued before him. The dismissal of an appeal from this decision, by the British Columbia Court of Appeal, was a very recent development:

> Copies of the reasons for judgment were made available to me by counsel in this case; the appeal was not reported at the time when the case was cited to me ...

> I consider, with respect, that *Calder's* case, though it is not binding on this Court, is weighty authority for these propositions:

> 1 In a settled colony there is no principle of communal native title except such as can be shown by prerogative or legislative act, or a course of dealing.

2 In a settled colony a legislative and executive policy of treating the land and the colony as open to grant by the Crown, together with the establishment of native reserves, operates as an extinguishment of aboriginal title, if that ever existed.[31]

But, of course, the Nisga'a litigation went on to the Supreme Court of Canada, where their lordships took a very different view of the law from that taken in the lower courts. As to Justice Blackburn's judgment, some of his propositions were described in the Supreme Court of Canada as "wholly wrong."[32]

The initial response to the failure of litigation in Australia occurred at the political-legislative level. The Whitlam government, which took office in 1972, appointed Edward Woodward, QC (who had been senior counsel for the plaintiffs in the *Gove Land Rights* case), to conduct an inquiry and to report on how best to recognize Aboriginal land rights in the Northern Territory. Legislation based on Woodward's recommendations was finally enacted by the Commonwealth Parliament under the Fraser government as the *Aboriginal Land Rights (Northern Territory) Act 1976*.[33] Existing reserves were transferred to indigenous ownership as "inalienable Aboriginal freehold." Other areas could be subject to claims before an Aboriginal land commissioner. If the Aboriginal people could prove that it was their traditional land, it could be vested in them. Aboriginal people gained significant control over mining or other activity on their lands. Under the act, close to half of the land in the territory has been returned to Aboriginal ownership under Australian law or is subject to a Native title claim. (Aboriginal people constitute about 28 percent of the population of the territory.)

Land rights legislation was also enacted in most of the states (with notable variations among them). As of February 1994 (before determinations under the post-*Mabo (No. 2) NTA*[34] began to become significant), some 14.25 percent of Australia was held by indigenous Australians under legislation vesting freehold or leasehold titles or was occupied as Aboriginal or Torres Strait Islander reserves. Figures from 2003 put the percentage at 15.43 percent.[35] (The percentage of indigenous Australians compared to the total population of Australia is less than 3 percent.)

In the meantime, work began on gaining a higher-level reassessment of Australian common law and of the correctness of the *Gove Land Rights* decision. This process benefited immensely from the increasing number of exchanges between Canadian and Australian lawyers. Some of these exchanges occurred through visits by indigenous leaders and legal scholars. Canadians played an important part at a 1980 Symposium on Aboriginal Land Rights, which was held by the Australian Institute of Aboriginal and Torres Strait Islander Studies.[36] Brad Morse, from the University of Ottawa, visited the

University of New South Wales in 1982–83. From this base, he travelled widely and provided valuable perspectives on the way that Australian law had been perceived. In more recent times, Richard Bartlett, formerly from the University of Saskatchewan, moved to the University of Western Australia and has authored the leading text on Australian Native title law.[37] Jeremy Webber, following a sabbatical leave at the University of New South Wales, returned for several years as dean of the Sydney University Law School and wrote insightfully on the emerging Australian law. Kent McNeil from Osgoode Hall Law School also spent a period at the University of New South Wales and has written several cogent commentaries. And, of course, Australian scholars and indigenous leaders have spent considerable time in Canada.

In the latter part of 1981, following an influential conference in Townsville, work began on a challenge to the correctness of the *Gove Land Rights* decision. The case was brought by the Meriam people from the Torres Strait, which lies between the northern tip of Queensland and Papua New Guinea. This litigation was initiated in the original jurisdiction of the High Court of Australia in 1982 and culminated in what became known as the *Mabo (No. 2)* decision of 1992.[38] The lawyers conducting this litigation in Australia were able to draw on the Supreme Court of Canada's decision in *Calder* and other Canadian decisions. They also had useful exchanges of information and ideas with the lawyers running the Gitxsan-Wet'suwet'en litigation in *Delgamuukw v. British Columbia* in British Columbia.[39] Ultimately, as I understand it, argument before the BC Court of Appeal in *Delgamuukw* was reopened specifically to permit submissions based on the *Mabo (No. 2)* judgments. And, of course, when the litigation went on appeal, the Supreme Court of Canada finally had some high-level jurisprudence from Australia available for its own consideration.

The *Mabo (No. 2)* Case and Native Title

The judgments in *Mabo (No. 2)* occupy some 217 pages of the *Commonwealth Law Reports*, so what follows represents a very simple summary. The "lead" judgment is usually considered to be that of Justice Gerard Brennan, with which Chief Justice Anthony Mason and Justice Michael McHugh concurred. Justices William Deane and Mary Gaudron delivered a separate joint opinion. Justice John Toohey gave a separate judgment. Only Justice Daryl Dawson dissented. There are significant differences among the judgments, which otherwise held, six to one, that the Native title rights of the Meriam peoples had survived the extension of British sovereignty over their islands. The majority was able to recognize the possible survival of Native title, without disturbing two centuries of land grants, by drawing substantially on jurisprudence from the courts of the United States, Canada, and other lands colonized by the British. Canadian cases that were referred to in the case, apart from *Calder*, included *St. Catherine's Milling*,[40] *Guerin v. The Queen*,[41]

Eddie Mabo and his lawyers outside the High Court in Canberra in April 1991, waiting to commence final argument in the case. *From left to right:* Greg McIntyre, instructing solicitor; Ron Castan, QC; Eddie Mabo; and Bryan Keon-Cohen, junior counsel. *Courtesy of Bryan Keon-Cohen, photograph by Lindy Castan*

and the decision of the British Columbia Supreme Court in *Delgamuukw v. British Columbia.*[42]

By 1992, the High Court of Australia was no longer bound by decisions of the Judicial Committee of the Privy Council, let alone statements in prior Australian decisions that had affirmed the notion that when the Crown had acquired sovereignty it had also acquired beneficial title to all of the land. According to the High Court's majority judgments in *Mabo (No. 2)*, when the British asserted sovereignty over the Australian colonies they acquired "radical title," but not the "beneficial title," to the lands of indigenous peoples. The court held that Native title might be lost if the peoples concerned no longer retained their connection to the land in terms of their traditional laws and customs. Native title might be surrendered to the Crown, but it was otherwise inalienable outside the laws of the particular peoples. Native title might have been "extinguished," but for extinguishment to have occurred there needed to be established a "clear and plain" intention by the legislature that this should occur.

Canadian law had been highly influential. And the doctrine of Native title as set out in the leading judgment of Justice Brennan seemed fairly close to the Canadian doctrine of Aboriginal title. However, in later cases, notably in *Western Australia v. Ward,* a High Court majority stated that the "clear and plain intention" was not a matter of "the subjective thought

processes of those whose act is alleged to have extinguished native title."[43]
Rather,

> [a]s *Wik* and *Fejo* reveal, where, pursuant to statute, be it Commonwealth,
> State or Territory, there has been a grant of rights to third parties, the ques-
> tion is whether the rights are inconsistent with the alleged native title rights
> and interests. That is an objective inquiry which requires identification of
> and comparison between the two sets of rights.[44]

The High Court in *Mabo (No. 2)* itself held that extinguishment of Native
title might be effected by the action of the Crown in granting interests to
others or by appropriating land for public purposes, to the extent that such
grants and appropriations were inconsistent with the continued exercise
and enjoyment of Native title rights and interests. Such grants or appropriations might proceed without any requirement for the prior acquisition
of the Native title by the Crown. The High Court also said, by a four-to-
three majority, that extinguishment of Native title, as such, would not give
rise to any entitlement to compensation. These propositions represent clear
departures from fundamental principles that apply in regard to titles derived from the Crown grant.[45]

Kent McNeil found the Australian position at odds not only with Canadian law but also with American law that holds that government grants of
title, even freehold title, while valid, remain subject to the Indian right of
occupancy.[46] Yet in *Fejo v. Northern Territory*, the High Court held that a
grant of fee simple in 1882, without any reservation for indigenous use and
access, had extinguished Native title and had done so for all time, even
though in 1935 the Crown had re-acquired the title.[47] In the same case, the
High Court indicated that it was less disposed to follow Canadian and US
jurisprudence than it had been in *Mabo (No. 2)* and other cases:

> Although reference was made to a number of decisions in other common
> law jurisdictions about the effect of later grants of title to land on pre-exist-
> ing native title rights, we doubt that much direct assistance is to be had
> from these sources. It is clear that it is recognised in other common law
> countries that there can be grants of interests in land that are inconsistent
> with the continued existence of native title; the question in each case is
> whether the later grant has had that effect. In some cases the answer that
> has been given in other jurisdictions may have been affected by the exist-
> ence of a treaty or other like obligations.[48]

In relation to "other like obligations," another point to note was that few
of the justices in *Mabo (No. 2)* considered the fall-back argument raised by
the plaintiffs that the Crown owed a fiduciary duty to the Meriam people.

Justice Dawson considered the argument particularly in light of American cases and the Supreme Court of Canada decision in *Guerin,* but, given his conclusion that any Native title that the Meriam had had did not survive annexation by the Crown, he found no room for the application of any fiduciary or trust obligation. Only Justice Toohey considered the argument on the basis of the survival of Native title and concluded that a fiduciary duty would exist.[49] Native title, on these terms, was highly vulnerable.[50] State and territory governments could have proceeded, as they had in the past, to grant interests in land or to allocate land to public purposes, without any need even to inquire whether Native title rights might have survived. The only effective legal limitation on their powers to do so arose under international law.

The Influence of International Law

In 1975, Australia ratified the *International Convention on the Elimination of All Forms of Racial Discrimination*.[51] At the same time, the Commonwealth Parliament enacted the *Racial Discrimination Act 1975 (RDA)* to implement the terms of the convention in Australian law.[52] The constitutional validity of the *RDA* was called into question in the pre-*Mabo (No. 2)* case *Koowarta v. Bjelke-Petersen*.[53] The principal respondent was the premier of Queensland. The Winychanam people, led by Koowarta, had sought to acquire ownership of a cattle station (ranch) on their traditional land through purchase by the Aboriginal Land Fund Commission on their behalf. The Queensland minister for lands declined to approve the purchase of the lease on the basis of a cabinet policy not to approve acquisitions of further areas of land by Aborigines or Islanders. This decision was challenged by the plaintiffs as being contrary to the *RDA*. Queensland argued, in response, that the *RDA* was beyond the Commonwealth Parliament's legislative power. This issue came before the High Court. Three of the justices would have upheld validity on the basis of the power of the parliament to pass laws with respect to "external affairs," for the reason that the *RDA* was implementing obligations under a treaty that Australia had ratified.

Four of the justices held that this reason was insufficient and that an additional requirement was that the subject matter of the treaty itself must relate to Australia's relations with other nations. Three of the four justices held that this additional requirement was not satisfied by a law as to how Australians treat Australians within Australia. However, the fourth, Justice Ninian Stephen, held that the additional condition *was* satisfied on the basis that the prohibition of racial discrimination had become a principle of customary international law and that non-compliance would affect Australia's relations with other nations. His stance meant that the *RDA* was held valid by a narrow margin of four to three. (In later cases, the High Court moved to a more expansive reading of the external affairs power.)

The *RDA* proved to be critical to the progress of the *Mabo* case itself, when, in 1985, the Queensland Parliament legislated to extinguish retroactively any Native title that might have survived in the Torres Strait. In 1988, the High Court held, four to three, that the Queensland act was invalid for its inconsistency with the *RDA*.[54] Without the *RDA*, the substantive issue raised in the *Mabo* litigation would not have reached the High Court for determination. International law was also highly influential in the reasoning of the High Court in *Mabo (No. 2)*. The following passage from the judgment of Justice Brennan, writing with the concurrence of Chief Justice Mason and Justice McHugh, is indicative:

> Whatever the justification advanced in earlier days for refusing to recognise the rights and interests in land of the indigenous inhabitants of settled colonies, an unjust and discriminatory doctrine of that kind can no longer be accepted. The expectations of the international community accord in this respect with the contemporary values of the Australian people. The opening up of international remedies to individuals pursuant to Australia's accession to the Optional Protocol to the International Covenant on Civil and Political Rights brings to bear on the common law the powerful influence of the Covenant and the international standards it imparts. The common law does not necessarily conform to international law, but international law is a legitimate and important influence on the development of the common law, especially when international law declares the existence of universal human rights. A common law doctrine founded on unjust discrimination in the enjoyment of civil and political rights demands reconsideration. It is contrary both to international standards and to the fundamental values of our common law to entrench a discriminatory rule which, because of the supposed position on the scale of social organisation of the indigenous inhabitants of a settled colony, denies them a right to occupy their traditional lands.[55]

Responses to *Mabo (No. 2)*

When mining companies received advice from their lawyers that the decision might present problems, the mining industry launched a major campaign hostile to the newly discovered Native title. (The mining industry had, in previous years, expressed similar antipathy to land rights legislation that gave indigenous Australians any significant control over resource development on their lands.) What were the problems detected by the lawyers? One was the possibility that any mining leases or exploration licences granted since the commencement of the *RDA* in 1975 might be invalid. Under general Australian law (with some exceptions), minerals are owned by the Crown, and governments are able to authorize prospecting and extraction even over privately owned or leased lands, subject only to the title holder being notified and having an opportunity to object, plus an entitlement to be compensated for disturbance. The *RDA* would have required equal treatment for Native title holders. Yet Native title holders had not been given notice, an opportunity to object, or compensation when mining interests had been granted over their lands. It was arguable that many mining interests granted by governments since 1975 were invalid. Mining companies were also concerned about having to deal with Native title holders in regard to possible future interests, particularly when it might remain unclear for some time whether Native title survived over the land in question and, if it did, who the Native title holders might be.

In the heady debates that ran from the latter part of 1992 through 1993, some of the more excitable mining industry leaders and politicians called for the legislative overturning of the *Mabo (No. 2)* decision, or for the extinguishment of Native title, or for the repeal of the *RDA*.[56] Eventually, a less drastic solution to their concerns emerged in the form of a proposal that there should be legislative validation of "past acts" of governments that would be invalid because of the existence of Native title. Since such a validation would entail some rolling back of the consequences of the *RDA*, the necessary legislation had to be Commonwealth legislation. The legislation also set out to address other aspects of the belated recognition of Native title in Australia. The perceived need for legislation had clearly become part of the Australian experience after the *Gove Land Rights* case and the subsequent enactment of land rights acts for the Northern Territory and elsewhere.

This decision represented a marked departure from the experience in Canada. The balance of the judgments in *Calder* was such that the Supreme Court of Canada was unable to make a definitive decision as to the survival of Aboriginal title for the Nisga'a. Eventually, Canada turned to a policy of negotiating particular claims and chose not to enact detailed legislation for the ascertainment and protection of Aboriginal title.

The *NTA*: Challenges, Pastoral Leases, and Amendments

The *NTA* commenced operation on 1 January 1994. It had four principal objectives:

1 to recognize and protect native title
2 to provide for the validation of "past acts" of governments between 1975 and 1993 that might affect Native title
3 to provide, in respect of "future acts," that Native title generally should be accorded the same respect as freehold titles, and, in addition, in respect of proposals for mining on Native title land, or for compulsory acquisition for the benefit of a third party, Native title holders – and Native title claimants – should have an additional "right to negotiate"

4 to provide processes for the determination of Native title and/or compensation, involving a new National Native Title Tribunal (NNTT) and the Federal Court.

On this last point, the act followed the practice under some Australian land rights legislation of establishing a process, which is one step removed from the executive government, for dealing with particular claims. Aboriginal people were familiar with the different path taken by the Canadian government, after the *Calder* case, of attempting to resolve such matters by negotiated agreements, and they insisted that the Australian legislation should make provision for local and regional agreements. One of the few positive aspects of the 1998 amendments to the legislation under the Howard government, and one of the few points on which the government proceeded in accordance with indigenous proposals, was the enhanced provision for indigenous land use agreements (ILUAs). By 25 March 2003, some seventy-four ILUAs had been registered under the *NTA*.[57]

The processes got under way. Gradually, numbers of claims were settled by consent determinations, or decided by the courts, with appeals sometimes being taken all the way to the High Court. By 25 March 2003, there had been forty-five determinations: thirty-one had decided that Native title did exist, and fourteen had decided that it did not exist.[58] In the meantime, the law developed. One of the first significant High Court decisions after *Mabo (No. 2)* and the commencement of the *NTA* was *Western Australia v. Commonwealth*.[59] The government of Western Australia had attempted to head off the potential impact of the *NTA* by securing the prior enactment of the *Land (Titles and Traditional Usage) Act 1993*.[60] The act purported to extinguish Native title throughout the state and to substitute statutory "rights of traditional usage," which would be much more vulnerable than Native title would be under the *NTA*. Two Aboriginal groups challenged the constitutional validity of the *Land (Titles and Traditional Usage) Act 1993*, and the Western Australia government challenged the consitutional validity of the *NTA*. In a judgment that was effectively unanimous, the High Court rejected the challenge to the validity of the *NTA* and held that the *Land (Titles and Traditional Usage) Act 1993* was invalid for inconsistency with the *NTA* and the *RDA*.

Between 1994 and 1996, there were several decisions at the tribunal or Federal Court level that seemed to indicate the need for amendments to the *NTA*. The Keating Australian Labor Party government had not secured enactment of such legislation when, in the federal election of March 1996, it was replaced by the Howard Coalition government. During 1996, the new government proceeded to develop much more sweeping amendments to the *NTA* on the premise that the 1993 act had swung the pendulum too far in favour of indigenous Australians. The proposed amendments were with-drawn when, in December 1996, the High Court's decision in *Wik Peoples v. Queensland* led the government to conclude that more draconian amend-ments were needed.[61]

In brief, the High Court in *Wik Peoples* concluded, by a four-to-three major-ity, that pastoral leases (grazing leases) in Queensland, in contrast to com-mon law forms of leases, did not confer a right of exclusive possession and, accordingly, did not extinguish Native title on the lands in question, with the result that the two interests could co-exist. In the event of any incon-sistency, the rights of the pastoralist (the farmer) would prevail. The deci-sion related only to pastoral leases granted under Queensland law, but it seemed likely to apply to pastoral leases in other jurisdictions.[62] Some 42 percent of Australia is covered by pastoral leases. The decision produced a hostile response from farmers and another outbreak of "*Mabo* madness."[63] The eventual bill was twice enacted by the House of Representatives and was, on each occasion, subjected to amendments in the Senate that the government regarded as being unacceptable. There was a prospect that the impasse might be resolved by resort to the "double dissolution" election procedure, namely section 57 of the Constitution, which provides for re-solving deadlocks between the two houses. However, in mid-1998, the gov-ernment was able to negotiate a deal with two senators that gave the bill, the *Native Title Amendment Act 1998*, a bare majority in the Senate.[64] The NTA had been regarded as being long and complex, and this amended act was much longer and much more complex.

One target of the amended act had to do with mining rights. As noted earlier, the path-breaking *Aboriginal Land Rights (Northern Territory) Act 1976* followed recommendations from Edward Woodward, QC, to give Aborig-inal owners effective control over the mining on their lands. Woodward had reported: "I believe that to deny to Aborigines the right to prevent mining on their land is to deny the reality of their land rights."[65] Land rights legis-lation in some other parts of Australia had also given indigenous Austral-ians some say over mining on their lands. Mining companies and pro-development politicians had been unenthusiastic about having to deal with Aboriginal peoples on such projects. The original NTA had laid down a regime for "future acts," which required that Native title holders would have exactly the same rights as the holders of "ordinary title" (freehold, in most places). In addition, where mining was proposed (or compulsory ac-quisition for the benefit of a third party), the act had given Native title holders an additional, but time-limited, "right to negotiate." If agreement was not achieved, the matter would be determined by the NNTT. In the last resort, it might have to be determined by a minister. One of the major ele-ments in the *Native Title Amendment Act 1998* was to greatly reduce this "right to negotiate" (RTN). Entire categories of lands were exempted from the RTN, and, in some situations, states and territories were authorized to substitute reduced procedural rights.

In addition, a stiff and retrospective registration test was imposed on Native title claimants as a prerequisite to the RTN being available at all. Other features of the 1998 amendments included a further round of validation of "intermediate period acts" between 1994 and 1996 for governments that had chosen not to follow *NTA* requirements in their dealings with land, notably land that was (or had been) subject to pastoral leases. There was also an extraordinary provision authorizing states and territories to legislate to "confirm" the past extinguishment of Native title as a result of past grants of interests in land that are deemed to have conferred a right of exclusive possession. States and territories were empowered to enlarge the rights of pastoral leaseholders to include other forms of primary production.[66] It was these aspects of the 1998 amendments that caught the attention of international human rights committees over several years. In particular, from 1998 to 2000, there occurred several dialogues between the Committee on the Elimination of Racial Discrimination and the Australian government. In March 1999, the committee noted

> four specific provisions that discriminate against indigenous title holders under the newly amended Act. These include the Act's "validation" provisions; the "confirmation of extinguishment" provisions; the primary production upgrade provisions; and restrictions concerning the right of indigenous title holders to negotiate non-indigenous land uses.[67]

The Australian government expressed its disagreement with these and other critiques from the committee as well as from other human rights committees. And the *Native Title Amendment Act 1998* stood as amended.[68]

The Developing Jurisprudence of Native Title

Native title is defined in section 223 of the *NTA* as needing three prerequisites:

1. the rights and interests are possessed under the traditional laws acknowledged, and the traditional customs observed, by the Aboriginal peoples or Torres Strait Islanders; and
2. the Aboriginal peoples or Torres Strait Islanders, by those laws and customs, have a connection with the land or waters; and
3. the rights and interests are recognised by the common law of Australia.

Thus, the particular rights and interests being asserted have to be based on traditional laws and customs. Through these laws and customs, the people need to "have" a connection with the land or waters, and the rights and interests need to be recognized by the common law of Australia. Indigenous Australians need to demonstrate that, since the assertion of British sovereignty, their laws and customs have continued to provide a connection to the country. This assertion is difficult, particularly in the long-settled areas where so many people have long been displaced.

Section 223(1)(c) has long been regarded as a reference to the broad principles enunciated in *Mabo (No. 2)*, which could continue to provide guidance in the development of Native title law. However, in *Members of the Yorta Yorta Aboriginal Community v. Victoria*, the majority of the High Court effectively held that the Native title legislation is the primary point of reference for decisions and that there is little if any scope remaining to consider cases by reference to broad common law principles:

> [T]he reference in para (c) of s. 223 (1) to the rights and interests being *recognised* by the common law of Australia cannot be understood as a form of drafting by incorporation, by which some pre-existing body of the common law of Australia defining the rights or interests known as native title is brought into the Act. To understand para (c) as a drafting device of that kind would be to treat native title as owing its origins to the common law when it does not. And to speak of there being common law elements for the *establishment* of native title is to commit the same error. It is, therefore, wrong to read para (c) of the definition of native title as requiring reference to any such body of common law, for there is none to which reference could be made.[69]

Justice McHugh repeated his view from earlier cases that Parliament, in enacting both the 1993 *NTA* and the 1998 amendments, had believed that "the content of native title would depend on the developing common law." Yet he felt bound now to accept the narrower interpretation of recognition enunciated by the majority.[70]

The majority in *Western Australia v. Ward* largely resolved a disagreement among lower court justices by indicating that Native title was to be regarded less as a fundamental right to land than as a "bundle of rights," each one of which can be severally extinguished by acts of government.[71] This decision represented a more fragmented conception than what had been articulated in *Delgamuukw:*

> The respondents offer two alternative formulations: first, that aboriginal title is no more than a bundle of rights to engage in activities which are themselves aboriginal rights recognized and affirmed by s. 35 (1) and that the *Constitution Act, 1982,* merely constitutionalizes those individual rights, not the bundle itself, because the latter has no independent content; and, second, that aboriginal title, at most, encompasses the right to exclusive

use and occupation of land in order to engage in those activities which are aboriginal rights themselves, and that s. 35 (1) constitutionalises this notion of exclusivity.

The content of aboriginal title, in fact, lies somewhere in between these positions. Aboriginal title is a right in land and, as such, is more than a right to engage in specific activities which may themselves be aboriginal rights. Rather, it confers the right to use land for a variety of activities, not all of which need be aspects of practices, customs and traditions which are integral to the distinctive cultures of aboriginal societies. Those activities do not constitute the right *per se;* rather, they are parasitic on the underlying title.[72]

The "bundle of rights" approach, which was seemingly endorsed in *Ward*, may, in part, reflect section 62(2) of the *NTA*, which requires applicants, in effect, to itemize the Native title rights and interests being asserted, and also sections 94A and 225, which require that a Federal Court determination should specify the Native title rights and interests.

Recent cases have also addressed the survival of Native title. Section 223 of the *NTA* requires the continuation of the traditional basis for the connection with country, while leaving space for some modifications of these laws and customs, in accordance with Justice Brennan's comments in *Mabo (No. 2)*.[73] Justice Brennan did contemplate a point at which "the tide of history has washed away any real acknowledgment of traditional law and any real observance of traditional customs." At such a point, "the foundation of native title has disappeared" and Native title is lost forever.[74] In *Members of the Yorta Yorta Aboriginal Community v. Victoria,* Justice Howard Olney, at first instance, held that such a point had been reached with respect to this claim in the Murray and Goulburn Rivers area of Victoria and southern New South Wales.[75] The full Federal Court rejected, two to one, an appeal[76] and so, ultimately, did a majority in the High Court.[77]

If Native title can be established, it will permit traditional activities on the land or waters in question, but it does not preclude the use of modern technology to pursue such activities. The High Court so held in *Yanner v. Eaton* in upholding the Native title basis for the appellant's taking (without a permit) of an estuarine crocodile, using a dinghy powered by an outboard motor.[78] The High Court ruled that a Queensland statute that vested "property" of fauna in the Crown did not extinguish Native title rights to take such fauna but referred, rather, to the state's power to regulate. The effect of section 211 of the *NTA* was to override the requirement for a permit for someone exercising Native title hunting (and other) rights and to protect the exercise of such rights and activities when carried on "for the purposes of satisfying their personal, domestic or non-commercial communal needs."[79]

However, Native title rights and interests may not extend to the commercial exploitation of the resources of land and waters. With respect to mining, the High Court held in *Ward* that the applicants had not proved traditional rights in respect of minerals and petroleum and that, even if they had, any such rights had been extinguished by legislation vesting ownership in the Crown.[80] In regard to offshore rights, in *Commonwealth v. Yarmirr*, a majority of the High Court held that Native title rights were capable of being recognized by the common law with respect to the sea and seabed beyond the low water mark, but the court affirmed that claims to exclusive rights to fish and to navigate in offshore waters were overridden by the common law public rights of navigation and fishing, as well as by the right of innocent passage under international law.[81] Such outcomes contrast with Canadian experience, where some First Nations have prospered from the ownership of subsoil resources and where some have benefited from the recognition of fishing rights. New Zealand, too, has produced some winners in commercial terms. Again in *Ward*, the High Court majority affirmed that Native title rights do not extend to protecting cultural knowledge from exploitation.

This discussion is in no way comprehensive. It represents simply a sample of some of the decisions of the High Court on particular issues. There have been some wins in the Native title process in Australia. Mediation and agreements in some cases have produced consent determinations, particularly (though not exclusively) where indigenous people have continued to live on or near their country and where "extinguishing" acts have been non-existent or limited. Some of the cases that have gone through the courts have produced wins, or partial wins, for Native title holders, although others have not. However, generally, it seems fair to say that as the legislation has become more restrictive since 1998 so have at least some of the decisions in the courts. It seems appropriate to conclude this chapter with some comments from some of the High Court justices from decisions in late 2002.

Justice Kirby: [The] impenetrable jungle of legislation remains. But now it is overgrown by even denser foliage in the form of the *Native Title Act 1993* (Cth) ... and companion State legislation ... It would be easy for the judicial explorer to become confused and lost in the undergrowth to which rays of light rarely penetrate. Discovering the path through this jungle requires navigational skills of a high order. Necessarily, they are costly to procure and time consuming to deploy. The legal advance that commenced with *Mabo v Queensland (No. 2)*, or perhaps earlier, has now attracted such difficulties that the benefits intended for Australia's indigenous peoples in relation to native title to land and waters are being channelled into costs of administration and litigation that leave everyone dissatisfied and many disappointed.

The only way to pass through the jungle is to retain one's bearings, as the explorers of Australia have traditionally done, by keeping the eyes fixed on clear sources of light – like the rising sun in the morning or, at night, the constellation we call the Southern Cross.[82]

Justice McHugh: The dispossession of the Aboriginal peoples from their lands was a great wrong. Many people believe that those of us who are the beneficiaries of that wrong have a moral responsibility to redress it to the extent that it can be redressed. But it is becoming increasingly clear – to me, at all events – that redress cannot be achieved by a system that depends on evaluating the competing legal rights of landholders and native-title holders. The deck is stacked against the native-title holders whose fragile rights must give way to the superior rights of the landholders whenever the two classes of rights conflict. And it is a system that is costly and time-consuming. At present the chief beneficiaries of the system are the legal representatives of the parties. It may be that the time has come to think of abandoning the present system, a system that simply seeks to declare and enforce the legal rights of the parties, irrespective of their merits. A better system may be an arbitral system that declares what the rights of the parties *ought to be* according to the justice and circumstances of the individual case.[83]

Justice Callinan: The problems for the indigenous people were compounded by the difficulty of finding any conceptual common ground between the common and statutory law of real property and Aboriginal law with respect to land ...

And we now have a body of law that is so complicated, shifting and abstruse that it continues to require the intervention of this Court to resolve even the most basic issues ... [F]ew people, if any, have been able to thread this labyrinth of Minos unscathed ...

I do not disparage the importance to the Aboriginal people of their native title rights, including those that have symbolic significance. I fear, however, that in many cases because of the chasm between the common law and native title rights, the latter, when recognised, will amount to little more than symbols. It might have been better to redress the wrongs of dispossession by a true and unqualified settlement of lands or money than by an ultimately futile or unsatisfactory, in my respectful opinion, attempt to fold native title rights into common law.[84]

Negotiated Settlements

Increasingly, Native title holders are seeking to avoid the court process by negotiating agreements. Indeed, in South Australia, work has been proceeding for some time towards a statewide Native title agreement. And the Yorta Yorta Nation, whose application failed in the courts, signed in June 2004 a cooperative management agreement with the state of Victoria, quite outside the Native title process, to create a forum for the Yorta Yorta peoples to co-manage, with the state, parts of their traditional country. And further agreements are under consideration by the parties.[85] An interesting development over the years in Australia has been the negotiation of co-management regimes for national parks and similar areas. Indeed, the earlier agreements preceded the recognition in *Mabo (No. 2)* of Native title.

More generally, negotiated agreements appear certain to play a larger role in the future.[86] And it can be said that the belated recognition in *Mabo (No. 2)* of Native title established a legal basis from which indigenous Australians are increasingly regarded as being entitled to a seat at the table. Mining companies and other interest groups have moved on from the earlier antipathy to having to deal with indigenous Australians about development issues and are increasingly seeking out the people with credible claims to land in order to forge agreements and to develop good neighbourly relations. The idea of continuing Native title has finally, to some extent, begun to penetrate the national consciousness.

There has been a recurring debate in Australia about a possible treaty. Such a treaty (or treaties) could provide, belatedly, "the consent of the natives" to non-indigenous settlement and, thus, complete the "constituting" of the nation. Such a document might also address other items of "unfinished business" affecting indigenous Australians.[87] In the matter of treaties, as in matters of Native/Aboriginal title, Australia stands to benefit from an increased awareness of Canada's experience. And there may be some aspects of Australian experience that could be of interest in Canada. Despite the marked differences between our respective legal histories and constitutional arrangements, we have much to learn from each other's successes. And from our failures.

Part 5
The Future

11
Let Obligations Be Done
John Borrows

Upon meeting Frank Calder, I was impressed with how he placed issues in their broader context. We went out to lunch a few times and we visited with my students on other occasions. He was happy to talk about US politics, Canadian culture, and events in the Middle East, Africa, and Asia. Topics ranged from one subject to another. There was no particular order to our conversations. He was interested in the wider world. The exchange was inspiring. He seemed particularly drawn to the US civil rights movement. I think he believed this movement was as much about changing majority views as it was about empowering African-Americans. He also seemed to hold religion in high regard. His interests were also other-worldly. It was obvious he was a proud Anglican. It was refreshing to hear someone speak positively about their experiences with a church. He proudly told me about his time in residential school. The school's motto, "there is no backward step," seemed a guide for his walk through life. When he died in late 2006, I remembered his motto and thought of those next steps forward.

Frank Calder's forward-looking attitude embraced change and treasured tradition. He seemed to hold both in appropriate balance. Steps forward are easier when the best of your past can be carried into the future. He admired people who came to Canada from other parts of the world to improve their lives. While he said that some people might regard them as leaving their pasts behind, he saw things in a different light. Like them, he was not afraid to be true to himself and participate in Canadian life. He wanted Nisga'a and other Aboriginal people to do the same. He saw prosperity in being Nisga'a *and* in building Canada. He said his grandparents had prepared him to live his life with his language, customs, chieftainship, and identity and not to be afraid of getting involved with others who live in this land. He welcomed mutuality. In my view, he saw the world as one where rights and obligations could co-exist.

During the Calder conference, I sensed this wider view. As he spoke about the case that bears his name, he framed its implications broadly. He said the case was not just about himself, the Nisga'a, or Native people in Canada.[1] He said it was for the whole world. He seemed to feel that the case sent a message about overcoming oppression that everyone faced when injustice lives among us. He said that when a people are being held down it does not affect only those who are being held. Those who are doing the holding are also negatively impacted. When oppression is lifted from a people, those who were their captors are also suddenly free. They no longer have to be "down in the ditch" restraining others. *Calder et al. v. Attorney-General of British Columbia* bears this liberating message.[2] People exist within relationships of subjugation or degrees of freedom.

Our conversations confirmed my belief that Aboriginal peoples and other Canadians are related. When Aboriginal peoples are suppressed, Canadians are also entangled in this same suppression. When Aboriginal peoples are free, Canadians are also free. Past relationships between Aboriginal peoples and the Crown have domination and supremacy at their roots. This has negatively impacted all people in this land. Frank Calder's interpretation of his case can help us see Crown/Aboriginal relationships in a better light. Future relationships can move beyond repressive domination if they build on mutuality, balance, and symmetry in their interactions. This chapter will situate Crown/Aboriginal relationships in a reciprocal framework. It will suggest that the *Calder* case laid the foundation to consider Aboriginal rights in the context of Crown obligations.

From Political to Legal Obligations: The Road through *Calder*

It is now clear that the Crown has legally binding obligations towards Aboriginal peoples in Canada. Courts seemed unwilling to recognize this fact prior to the *Calder* case in 1973. For example, in 1887, Justice Henri-Elzéar Taschereau of the Supreme Court of Canada described the Crown's duty towards Aboriginal peoples as a "sacred political obligation, in the execution of which the state must be free from judicial control."[3] A year later, Lord Watson of the Judicial Committee of the Privy Council wrote that "the tenure of the Indians was a personal and usufructuary right, dependent upon the good will of the Sovereign."[4] In 1897, the Privy Council labelled treaty promises to Indians as "nothing more than a personal obligation."[5] Over sixty years later, Justice Ivan Rand found that the government had only political obligations to Aboriginal peoples.[6] The court's hesitancy to impose legal obligations on governments existed despite numerous promises to Aboriginal peoples, including executive proclamations,[7] treaties,[8] and the nature of the parties' relationship.[9]

In 1973, the situation seemingly changed.[10] Frank Calder's efforts to bring Canada's oppression to light made a real difference. As Michael Asch observes in this volume, it was a judgment so momentous it caused a reexamination of basic premises.[11] In *Calder,* the Supreme Court of Canada

The Nisga'a at the Parliament of Canada for the debate on their treaty in 1999. *From left to right: (front)* Nelson Leeson, Rod Robinson, Dr. Joseph Gosnell, Dr. Frank Calder, Edmond Wright; *(middle)* Harry Nyce, Sr., Herb Morven, Henry Moore, Gary Alexcee, Perry Azak; *(back)* Peter Squires, Eric Grandison, Edward Allen, Floyd Davis, Reg Percival, Bob Spence. *Photograph by Gary Fiegehen*

recognized that the Nisga'a had *legal* rights. As a result, in 2002, the Supreme Court of Canada wrote that "recognition of aboriginal rights could not be treated merely as an act of grace and favour on the part of the Crown."[12] The *Calder* case stands for the proposition that Aboriginal title is justiciable and, therefore, more than a moral or political claim.[13] The decision extends the rule of law in Canada because Aboriginal possession could be enforced by the courts and given the force of law if its constituent elements were proven.[14] The Court found the source of these rights originated from "the fact that when the settlers came, the Indians were there, organized in societies and occupying the land as their forefathers had done for centuries."[15] It found the scope of these rights depended upon historic use and the intention of the legislature to permit their continuance. These declarations brought Aboriginal rights squarely into Canada's legal structure. As British Columbia's lieutenant-governor, Iona Campagnolo observed, "Frank Calder and the Nisga'a People have increased the capacity of our capacious constitutional tent. We are all proud that the 'Rule of Law' under which we have chosen to live together, has been broadened sufficiently to include more of the diversity that so strengthens our national identity as Canadians."[16] Furthermore, the international implications of this framework extend far beyond the country's borders, as Stephen Haycox, David Williams, and Garth Nettheim note in earlier chapters in this volume.[17]

· Despite *Calder's* broad declarations and implications, the Nisga'a failed to secure recognition of their title because they did not have a fiat from the government of British Columbia that gave them permission to sue the Crown. The Supreme Court of Canada found it lacked jurisdiction to decide the case in the absence of the Crown's express willingness to be sued.[18] In these reasons, one can see how colonialism can create a relationship of mutual oppression. First Nations are obviously limited by their inferior legal status, but the Crown is also negatively impacted because it is robbed of important incentives to remedy the injustices it causes. Fortunately, the *Calder* case's requirement for permission squarely raised the notion that Aboriginal rights were related to Crown obligations. If the Crown did not give its consent it was not obliged to answer the case against it. The Nisga'a could not secure a declaration of title if the Crown would not allow itself to be held accountable. As Hamar Foster observes, the Crown was hesitant to grant a fiat to indigenous peoples in British Columbia because if the courts found in their favour it could drastically undermine Crown land claims and "jeopardize the very large sums of money already invested" in the province.[19] Despite this opinion, as Foster further argues, Aboriginal rights were an integral part of the legal framework of Canada.

While Aboriginal rights are now more firmly recognized, Crown obligations remain part of Canada's hidden constitution.[20] Commentators have largely overlooked them yet they lie on the frontier of Canada's constitutional development. In the spirit of innovation that animated the *Calder* decision, this fact can be highlighted and Canada's constitutional vision re-focused. As Frank Calder envisioned, there is a great need for a different level of legal analysis related to Aboriginal issues. This analysis can be extended further when one explicitly focuses on Crown obligations. The reciprocal relationship between Aboriginal rights and Crown obligations remains under-theorized and largely unrecognized. This needs to change because rights exist within relationships.[21] Frank Calder expressed this basic insight when he spoke of the possibility of Aboriginal/Crown relationships existing on an equal plane. He states: "To confine people inside that boundary, you have to be on top of them. You're both in the gutter. Right? If somebody's holding down that First Nation inside that reservation, somebody's got to be on his back and that guy on his back is controlling the law books. So the three to three decision meant that he had to get off my back and we'd turn around and face each other and talk."[22] Wherever a right exists, a correlative obligation can be found. As Wesley Hohfeld observes, "a duty is the invariable correlative of that legal relation which is most properly called a right or claim."[23] "A duty or a legal obligation is that which one ought or ought not to do. 'Duty' and 'right' are correlative terms. When a right is invaded, a duty is violated."[24] This is the case with Aboriginal and treaty rights in Canada. Wherever an Aboriginal or treaty right exists, a correlative governmental obligation can be found.

The Crown's Obligation under Section 35(1)

Frank Calder began his quest to improve relationships in the days when the Crown largely viewed itself as being above and beyond constraint. It spoke and acted as if its power was absolute and could not be questioned. In 1982, when Aboriginal and treaty rights were placed in section 35 of Canada's constitution, Crown obligations followed. Aboriginal and treaty rights did not enjoy strength until the government's legal duty to honour Aboriginal peoples' rights was recognized and affirmed. Since governments are interposed between Aboriginal peoples and others when it comes to dealing with Aboriginal rights,[25] they have the greatest potential to erode these rights if they do not possess firm legal obligations.[26] This has been the experience of the Nisga'a and numerous other First Nations across Canada. Historically, government power has led to the imposition of weakened government obligations in those situations where Aboriginal and treaty rights have been involved. The enactment of section 35(1) strengthened these obligations, and, in the words of Justice Ian Binnie, it converted them into "sterner stuff."[27] In *R. v. Sparrow*, the leading case interpreting section 35(1), the Court wrote that "recognition and affirmation [of Aboriginal rights] ... import some restraint on the exercise of sovereign power."[28] Governmental obligations flow from the limitations placed on Crown sovereignty under section 35(1).

There have been many governmental obligations recognized under section 35(1) that check the Crown's sovereignty. While the *Calder* case foreshadowed this growth, the judgments of Justices Emmett Hall and Wilfred

Judson could not anticipate their reach. The Crown's obligations towards Aboriginal peoples are now firmly part of Canada's constitutional fabric.[29] Crown obligations mirror the generic[30] and specific[31] nature of Aboriginal rights, as discussed by Brian Slattery.[32] First, there is a general obligation for the Crown to treat Aboriginal peoples fairly and honourably and to ensure that Aboriginal peoples are not exploited.[33] The Supreme Court of Canada has observed that "[t]he honour of the Crown exists as a source of obligation."[34] Second, there are also specific Crown obligations to protect particular Aboriginal rights. Sometimes these specific obligations are related to the Crown's fiduciary duties.[35] Other specific duties might be related to treaty promises, contracts, tort law, or statute. Specific obligations also operate both to prevent interference with Aboriginal and treaty rights and to ensure that if there is interference the Crown can constitutionally justify such actions. In the *Sparrow* case, the Supreme Court of Canada wrote that "federal power must be reconciled with federal duty and the best way to achieve that reconciliation is to demand the justification of any government interference that infringes upon or denies aboriginal rights."[36] The Crown's obligation to defend and protect Aboriginal and treaty rights, and justify its actions whenever these rights are diminished, constrains the Crown's sovereignty in order to preserve Canada's constitutional order.

It may be helpful to list Crown obligations relative to Aboriginal and treaty rights to gain a visual appreciation of their scope. They are numerous, although not presented in any particular order. Furthermore, the following list does not rank these obligations in order of their importance to Aboriginal peoples. The list is also limited to constitutional obligations and does not include other types of government obligations to Aboriginal peoples, such as contracts, torts, or statute. Despite these caveats, it can be said that Crown obligations with varied strength have been found to exist in relation to Aboriginal and treaty rights in the following matters:

- recognition
- affirmation
- reconciliation[37]
- non-extinguishment without consent[38]
- prevention of the perpetuation of "historic injustice suffered by Aboriginal Peoples at the hands of colonizers"[39]
- not imposing unjustifiably unreasonable limitations[40]
- not imposing unjustifiably undue hardships[41]
- not unjustifiably denying preferred means of Aboriginal people exercising rights[42]
- minimal impairment[43]
- allocating resources to Aboriginal peoples[44]
- conserving resources for Aboriginal peoples[45]

- protecting the safety of Aboriginal rights users[46]
- ensuring economic and regional fairness[47]
- measuring historic reliance on resource use for Aboriginal and non-Aboriginal people[48]
- structuring discretion[49]
- giving priority (which varies with nature of right)[50]
- providing for Aboriginal participation in resources development[51]
- government reducing economic barriers for Aboriginal peoples[52]
- managing change honourably[53]
- compensation[54]
- consultation[55]
- accommodation[56]
- administrative law procedural safeguards[57]
- legislative dispute resolution legislation[58]
- mitigation strategies[59]
- promoting federalism, democracy, rule of law, and protection of minorities[60]
- not violating Aboriginal individual's *Charter* rights[61]

This list is unique. It should give us pause. It bears repeated reading. I am not aware of any similar chronicle in Canada. None of these obligations existed when Frank Calder was born. They were not even on the horizon until the *Calder* case declared Aboriginal rights justiciable. The nature and scope of Crown obligations have only recently come to light. While the foregoing list is illustrative and not exhaustive, it does demonstrate a growing trend.[62] The list demonstrates that government obligations under section 35(1) are extensive and varied. These obligations may apply to both the federal and provincial governments,[63] though one should not lose sight of the special federal constitutional responsibility under section 91(24) of the *Constitution Act, 1867*.[64] The listed obligations are part of section 35(1)'s "general guiding principle," which is to ensure that the Crown fulfils its responsibility to act in a trust-like non-adversarial manner when dealing with Aboriginal peoples.[65] They must be generously understood and applied in all of the Crown's dealings with Aboriginal peoples to preserve its honour.[66] When I think about my time with Frank Calder, the word "honour" is at the forefront of my feelings towards him. It is fitting that honour is the primary principle that should motivate the Crown's actions towards Aboriginal peoples.

It is also fitting to remember that Frank Calder viewed the world broadly. I found him to be charitable towards others and concerned about seeing things in their most expansive light. It is encouraging that the standard for the reconciliation of rights and obligations required under section 35(1) partakes of this same spirit. Reconciliation is best obtained through a large, liberal, and generous conception of its constitutional purpose.[67] A broad conceptualization of section 35(1) is consistent with the Court's purposive approach to section 35(1): "[T]o reconcile the prior presence of aboriginal peoples in North America with the assertion of Crown sovereignty."[68] Mutual isolation is not the constitutional objective underlying section 35(1).[69] I am sure Frank Calder would have approved. Section 35(1) must be read in a way that incorporates reciprocity. Aboriginal rights have correlative legal consequences, as Hohfeld's theoretical framework suggests. Section 35(1) could thus be seen as incorporating Crown obligations. If this were the case, section 35(1) could be read as providing that the "existing *Crown* and treaty *obligations* of the *Crown in right of Canada and the provinces* are hereby recognized and affirmed."[70] Whenever the "rights" aspect of a stick is picked up, the "duties" aspect is lifted at the same moment. This broader conceptualization of section 35(1) places the Crown more squarely in the analysis. It appropriately shifts the focus from Aboriginal peoples to the Crown in a more significant way in working out the section's scope, content, and meaning. More relevant and wider remedies to implement Aboriginal rights can be canvassed when the Crown's obligations become more visible within section 35(1). These remedies should include a reciprocal obligation to recognize each party's governmental authority.

One can find mutuality in section 35(1) because of its government-to-government character. Section 35(1) focuses on "peoples," unlike individuated rights under the *Canadian Charter of Rights and Freedoms.*[71] The focus on peoples illustrates the section's governmental nexus and makes section 35(1) *sui generis:* unique.[72] Under the *Charter,* individuals are brought into relation with the government because their rights are "subject only to such reasonable limits prescribed by law as can be demonstrably justified in a free and democratic society."[73] In contrast, under section 35(1), group or peoples rights are brought into a *sui generis* relation with government and there is no such limitation. This should create a different interpretive dynamic than under the *Charter.*[74] Part of this difference is supported by the placement of section 35(1) in Part II of the *Constitution Act, 1982.*[75] There is no section 1 limitation under section 35(1) that hinders its reach.[76] Therefore, while section 35(1) has a rights component like the *Charter,* it goes much further. It has a governmental component since it deals with peoples and fosters the recognition and affirmation of political groups: *peoples.*

Sometimes the word "Aboriginal" is interpreted to the exclusion of the term "peoples" under section 35(1). For example, *R. v. Van der Peet* narrowly defined rights in relation to Aboriginality rather than qualifying and modifying Aboriginality by its relationship to the word "peoples."[77] Yet the term "peoples" holds the greatest significance for defining Aboriginal/Crown relationships. The word's content can draw great meaning from international law, although in a *sui generis* way.[78] The conception of peoples includes internal or external rights to self-determination,[79] depending upon the circumstances of the peoples' treatment by the state.[80] Self-determination should more thoroughly permeate section 35(1)'s rights/obligations matrix. This is the point made by Cathy Bell in a 1997 law review article.[81] She observes that section 35 came out of an international context where there was "[g]rowing activity at the United Nations aimed at ending colonial domination [which] resulted in increased international pressure on nation states to recognize and protect the human rights of colonized peoples."[82] When Aboriginal groups claim organizational rights as *peoples,* this represents a corresponding claim that the Crown has an obligation to recognize and affirm their governmental nature.[83] Section 35(1)'s focus on Crown obligations could bring the rights of Aboriginal *peoples* to life in Canadian law. This interpretation would take our focus beyond individuals such as Frank Calder, as good as he was, and recognize and affirm the indigenous collective context through which individuals like him take their language, customs, chieftainships, and identities.

Obligations and Their Relationship to Aboriginal Laws

It is significant that the *Calder* case seemed to accept the governmental nature of Aboriginal claims, even though it did not use the word "peoples." Kent McNeil has argued earlier in this volume that Aboriginal peoples' governmental rights seem to be implied in the Court's treatment of Aboriginal title in Canadian law.[84] He writes that "communal title necessarily entails authority within the community to make decisions about how the benefits of their title will be distributed within the community and how communal land will be regulated."[85] The characteristics of Aboriginal title necessitate a political structure.[86] In this vein, Justice Judson wrote that "when the settlers came, the Indians were there, organized in societies and occupying the land as their forefathers had done for centuries."[87] Aboriginal peoples remain organized as societies and occupy lands, and their laws continue to structure their relationships.[88] As such, indigenous laws can be relevant for the determination of Crown obligations.[89]

Frank Calder occupied an important position as a chief within Nisga'a law, which is called the *ayuukhl.*[90] It would have been good to see the *ayuukhl* form the standard by which Nisga'a title was judged in the *Calder* case. The *ayuukhl* is an ancient legal code that has guided Nisga'a social, economic, and political relationships from the "time of memory."[91] Centuries before Canada proclaimed itself a nation "founded upon the principles that recognize the supremacy of God and the rule of law," the people of the Nass River were living according to Ayuukhl Nisga'a, an ancient code of laws that "will stand comparison to any modern constitution or declaration of statehood and nationality."[92] Frank Calder had the benefit of his grandparents' knowledge of these laws. They governed land ownership, education, succession, citizenship, chiefs, education, marriage and divorce, war, peace, trading relationships, and restitution.[93] The *ayuukhl* operates in contemporary Canada through the Nisga'a Lisims government, which is recognized under treaty and the *Nisga'a Final Agreement Act*.[94] The knowledge that Frank Calder and his nation carry through the *ayuukhl* and other indigenous laws should influence section 35(1)'s contours. Within section 35(1), "[i]t is clear that a generous, liberal interpretation of the words in the constitutional provision is demanded."[95] A large, liberal, and generous interpretation of section 35(1) would recognize the continued existence of indigenous law and affirm its relevance for determining Crown obligations under Canada's constitutional order.

Aboriginal peoples such as the Nisga'a have perspectives on law, *and* they have law. Perspectives and law are very different things. Their classification within courts has significant implications for the recognition of obligations. In contrast to law, perspectives do not generally create strong obligations. Law exists for the purpose of determining binding obligations. The Supreme Court of Canada has not fully considered the implications of the distinction between Aboriginal perspectives and Aboriginal law in its legal reasoning. In the recent case of *R. v. Marshall; R. v. Bernard*, the majority spoke of Aboriginal perspectives with very little reference to Aboriginal law as a continuing force in Canada.[96] The minority took a different approach and recognized Aboriginal law as being distinct from Aboriginal perspectives. The courts have yet to fully reveal the multi-juridical nature of Canada's constitutional order over which they preside.[97]

In revealing indigenous laws, it might be recalled that the Supreme Court of Canada wrote that while Canada's constitution is "primarily a written one ... behind the written word is an historical lineage stretching back through the ages, which aids in the consideration of underlying constitutional principles.[98] Indigenous legal principles are part of this unwritten tradition.[99] These principles inform and sustain the constitutional text, and they can be regarded as part of the vital un-stated assumptions upon which the text is based.[100] The Court further noted that the constitution's unwritten principles are "not merely descriptive but are also invested with a powerful normative force, and are binding upon both courts and governments."[101] Indigenous legal traditions such as the *ayuukhl* have powerful normative force and could be employed to bind courts and governments. The constitution's unwritten postulates "form the very foundation of the Constitution of Canada."[102] Indigenous laws form part of the very foundation of the constitution in Canada. They reflect the constitution's underlying values in their own right[103] and, thus, could be referenced along with other sources to determine the content of the Crown's obligations.

These laws are also found in my First Nation. Obligations are central to relationships under Anishinabek law. When Anishinabek people historically met they would first ask one another: "*Weanaesh k'dodem?*" (what is your totem?).[104] Once a person's clan and family were determined, then they would be asked: "*Ahniish aen-anookeeyin?*" (what do you do for a living?). Both of these questions are related to a person's responsibility within the community. A person's *dodem* indicates more than their lineage because there are obligations attached to their clan affiliations. Like a *dodem*, a person's *anookeewin* also connotes ideas of duty and right (*daebinaewiziwin*). Anishinabek peoples have obligations (*daebizitawaugaewin*) to their families and community: to support them, to help them prosper, and to exercise their rights to live and work.[105] Rights and responsibilities are intertwined in an Anishinabek legal context. If these concepts were translated into Canadian constitutional law, we would see that section 35 could recognize *anookeewin*, with its attendant duties and responsibilities.[106] There are many stories with Anishinabek law that convey the importance and application of this principle, which could provide guidance to courts and others in determining Crown obligations under section 35(1).[107] While I never did take the opportunity to compare Nisga'a *ayuukhl* with Anishinabek laws in my conversations with Calder, I am confident from my research and conversations with other Nisga'a people that both could contribute to the contours of Crown obligations under section 35(1).

Aboriginal peoples also have obligations under these laws. The use of indigenous law would particularize and strengthen the content of obligations that Aboriginal peoples have to the Crown.[108] The mutuality of rights/obligations should remain the constitutional touchstone underlying this analysis. Aboriginal peoples can have obligations towards the Crown flowing from the parties' relationships that incorporate principles from indigenous law. Aboriginal peoples can also have obligations that are determined through treaties. For example, Aboriginal peoples promised to share their land with others in an atmosphere of peace, friendship, and respect under the numbered treaties.[109] These treaties were formed through Aboriginal peoples applying their laws to create and ratify legal relationships with others.[110] These laws can be referenced to construe past and present obligations. It is important that Aboriginal obligations are stressed when Crown obligations are discussed to avoid an inflated sense of personal entitlement. A number of Aboriginal people claim rights without responsibilities and this is harmful to a balanced outlook. If everyone acts as if they only have rights and do not affirm their obligations, society is in danger of coming apart at its seams.

Crown Obligations within Canada's Constitutional Tradition

Just as the recognition of the justiciability of Aboriginal rights in *Calder* was consistent with Canada's legal traditions, the recognition and affirmation of Crown obligations under section 35(1) does not represent a break with Canada's constitutional order. Constraints on Crown sovereignty are consistent with Canada's democratic traditions. The Crown's subjection to the rule of law is at the centre of the nation's political values. Constraints on Crown sovereignty have often been heralded as great breakthroughs for furthering human rights and liberty. For example, many proclaim the date 1215 as being significant because the issuance of the Magna Carta gave rights to certain classes of individuals relative to the Crown – rights that expanded through time.[111] Despite its limitations,[112] the Magna Carta has been applied and commemorated and is not seen as threatening, but as supporting, Canada's political order.[113] Similarly, the Glorious Revolution of 1688 in England, where the Crown's authority was made subject to Parliament, is held in high esteem in our democratic traditions. The English Bill of Rights, which flowed from the revolution, obligated the Crown to raise and spend money with the consent of elected parliamentary officials and not of its own accord.[114] Judges, lawyers, politicians, and the public often refer to the "glorious revolution" as an important source of political authority and regard it as a cornerstone of liberty. British North Americans enjoyed similar restraints on the exercise of the Crown prerogative when responsible government came to non-Aboriginal Canadians in the 1850s in the Canadian and the Atlantic colonies. Furthermore, the American and French revolutions of the late 1700s, which also purported to restrain Crown sovereignty relative to individual rights, are also regarded as being an essential step in democracy's development. Canada's own *Charter* is in this tradition.[115]

Constraints on Crown actions under section 35(1) should be seen as flowing from this same tradition. There are sound reasons for ensuring that political authority is subject to proper checks and balances. Recognizing Crown obligations relative to Aboriginal peoples is a part of this process. The Supreme Court of Canada has been clear that Crown constraints are a part of section 35(1)'s framework. As they observed in *Sparrow*, "Section 35 calls for a just settlement for aboriginal peoples. It renounces the old rules of the game under which the Crown established courts of law and denied those courts the authority to question sovereign claims made by the Crown."[116] Crown sovereignty is constrained under section 35(1) by its obligations to Aboriginal peoples. The Court has jurisdiction to question the Crown's actions, without an aggrieved party seeking permission from the Crown as required in the *Calder* case. These constraints on government action could be regarded in the same light as the Magna Carta, the Glorious Revolution, responsible government, and bills of rights. Each development significantly restricted the Crown's scope of authority relative to a significant section of the body politic. Freedom was increased when the Crown was obliged to observe constitutional limitations on its power. Section 35(1) falls within this tradition.

Despite the relevance of Canada's constitutional traditions for Aboriginal peoples, the Nisga'a had difficulty persuading the Court in the *Calder* case that their rights were enforceable without the Crown's permission. Section 35(1) and the enactment of the *Crown Proceedings Act* waiving sovereignty immunity from suit have eliminated this obstacle.[117] Despite these developments, it sometimes appears as though governments do not consider themselves as possessing significant obligations towards Aboriginal peoples. Aboriginal peoples persistently protest the Crown's approach to Aboriginal and treaty rights and yet the Crown often responds as if it does not have legal obligations to Aboriginal peoples.

The Crown's reluctance to recognize its obligations is curious. It may be related to a failure to accept that it has obligations.[118] Yet the law of obligations is a firmly established central axis of the law. Involuntary obligations are created, *inter alia*, through constitutional, statute, and tort law. They articulate standards of conduct that ensure that others are not harmed through unreasonable behaviour. Voluntary obligations also create standards recognized through constitutional, contractual, and other agreements. The Crown must do more to recognize this broader context, catalog its obligations, and take steps to operationalize them in practice.

The question of how the Crown can be encouraged to monitor and enforce its obligations may draw some insight from tort and contract law, although ultimate legal solutions lie in the constitutional realm. In tort law, involuntary obligations are often encouraged through standards of care that require reasonable behaviour. Behaviour is monitored and enforced by a legal system that has well-developed criteria for recognizing when behaviour has departed from a reasonable standard.[119] Constitutional obligations aimed at fairness, honour, and reconciliation are analogous to duties of care that regulate individual relationships in tort law.

The Crown also has many voluntary obligations owed to Aboriginal peoples assumed through agreements in treaties, interim measures, contracts, executive proclamations, and legislative provisions. Voluntary obligations are generally easier to encourage, monitor, and enforce because their adherents freely and consciously make them. One would expect that the Crown's conscious choice to undertake obligations would make their enforcement easier. However, this has not generally been the experience of Aboriginal peoples. This must change for Canada's democratic tradition to grow and become applicable to all the people living in this land. Without the glue of obligation, civil society fragments and conflict intensifies. I remember Frank Calder lamenting this fact in thinking about the Middle East and certain African countries.

Conclusion

The *Calder* case is important in Canada's legal history because it explicitly recognized that Aboriginal peoples possess justiciable rights. This case was also an important step on the road to recognizing the Crown's obligations towards Aboriginal peoples in Canada. The stronger integration of Aboriginal issues into Canadian law is an important legacy of the *Calder* case. It allows the courts to view Aboriginal peoples as political groups with their own legal systems that exist *in relation* to the Crown in Canada. This recognition may complete the process begun in *Calder* and guide judges in providing more appropriate remedies for purported breaches of the Crown's obligations towards them.

One of the main functions of legal systems is to authoritatively provide enforceable remedies for breaches (anticipated or otherwise) of the rights and obligations they confer. Law is an enforceable system of authority to which Aboriginal peoples belatedly have access, thanks to the *Calder* case. As a result, Aboriginal peoples are increasingly appealing to the law's principles to adjudicate the bounds of propriety in their interactions with the Crown. While justiciability in this sense can be beneficial for Aboriginal peoples, remedial access comes with a cost. The more Aboriginal peoples use the law, the more tightly they are drawn into a relationship with the Crown.[120] This result may not appeal to some Aboriginal peoples given their expressed desire for independence and a greater distance from the Canadian state. This group might want "obligations to be done" in a different sense: *they might want Crown obligations* to be *done away with* because they perceive autonomy may expand from having fewer ties with the Crown.

While *Calder* was successful in introducing legality to Aboriginal peoples' relationship with the Canadian state, it is important to remember that Canadian law is only one system of authority. Aboriginal peoples can and should continue to appeal to other sources of authority to press their ideas, including appeals to and within their own legal systems. It should not be forgotten that "authority" often exists in hierarchies, with some forms being privileged relative to others in public discourse. At present, it seems that Canadian law is often regarded as a source of authority that outranks all other sources in public affairs in Canada.[121] While the relative ranking of sources of authority is constantly shifting and can radically change over the course of time, Canadian law seems to be growing more dominant.

Aboriginal peoples should be concerned about the Canadian law's invidious influence. Its perceived paramountcy could prevent them from infusing Canada with different values that flow from appeals to their traditional authorities. Thus, even as Aboriginal peoples use Canadian law to speak to others, they should simultaneously highlight the fact that Canadian law is not the "only game in town." Aboriginal peoples could remind others that they should continue to reference other sources for authoritative answers to questions. There are religious, ethical, political, philosophical, moral, and cultural traditions that can also direct our relationships. Frank Calder spoke on many of these planes. Each of these traditions can be isolated, contextualized, compared, and contrasted with Canadian law to suggest answers to pressing questions. Sometimes, appeals to these different traditions give innovative answers to life's important questions. People look to many systems of authority to give them direction, and this should continue even as we use Canadian law to deal with our problems.

Canadian law's authority derives from appeals to consensus, reason, and consistency. It should also be remembered that Canadian law also derives its authority from force.[122] Its application can be hard to wrest from the biases of wealth, status, social convention, and established Western religious traditions. When Aboriginal peoples take advantage of the opportunity opened in *Calder*, to bring their issues before the courts, these cautions should be heeded. While busy working for victories in the courts, it must also be remembered that such victories can be hollow if Aboriginal peoples' own traditional authorities are permanently subjugated in the process. This warning is not to counsel against using Canadian law in every case but is meant to simultaneously keep our attention on its collateral consequences. Canadian law can sometimes be used with great effect but only if Aboriginal cultural values, traditions, and authorities are simultaneously brought forward.

Perhaps Frank Calder offers the best counsel on this issue, as he reflected on the perils and promise of using ideas and institutions from other peoples to advance Aboriginal issues. He said:

> There is a word going around these days, "globalization." Some are afraid of it. When I went to school I didn't lose anything. I kept my language. I kept my customs. I kept my chieftainship. I kept my identity. I did this because of my parents, God bless them. They told me to never forget who I was. We should not be afraid of getting involved with others. We can get involved with all those things out there, like lawyers, judges, and governments and still be ourselves.

The counsel for Aboriginal peoples to be themselves, even as their rights and the Crown's obligations interact on a more global basis, should be one of the primary lessons taken from the *Calder* case. It is also a lesson that I will continue to treasure from my conversations with Frank Calder himself. It is my hope that others will also take encouragement from his advice.

12
Closing Thoughts: Final Remarks from Iona Campagnolo, Lance Finch, Joseph Gosnell, and Frank Calder

The final event of the conference was the Gala Event held on the evening of Saturday, 15 November 2003. The gala, as it came to be known, was an event for conference participants and the general public. The evening, hosted by David Turpin, the president of the University of Victoria, opened with prayers and "good words" from Dr. Sammy Sam, a Tsartlip Elder. More than thirty Nisga'a Ts'amiks Dancers, from young children to Elders, performed in honour of Frank Calder's contributions to the Nisga'a people. Then, accompanied by "welcome" and honour songs performed by the Ts'amiks Dancers, the platform party came onto the stage in the order in which they would enter a Nisga'a bighouse on an important ceremonial occasion. The Nisga'a members of the party were dressed in their traditional regalia, adding to the importance of the occasion. It is impossible in mere words to adequately describe the respect with which Rob Robinson, Hubert Doolan, Frank Calder, and the other Nisga'a plaintiffs are held by the Nisga'a people. What follows are the remarks of the Honourable Iona Campagnolo (Lieutenant-Governor of British Columbia), the Honourable Lance Finch (Chief Justice of British Columbia), Dr. Joseph Gosnell (President of the Nishga Tribal Council), and Dr. Frank Calder (President Emeritus of the Nishga Tribal Council). It was a truly memorable occasion that was a fitting tribute to Frank Calder and all the Nisga'a people who worked with him so that right could be done.

The Honorable Iona Campagnolo, Lieutenant-Governor of British Columbia

Dr. Frank Calder, President Dr. David Turpin, Dr. Joseph Gosnell, Chief Justice Lance Finch, T'Secum Elder Dr. Samuel Sam, members of the Nisga'a Lisims government, Simoiget, Simmogetta, co-hosts, the University of Victoria Faculty of Law and International Indigenous Forum, distinguished jurists, honoured guests, Nisga'a Ts'amiks Dancers.

I acknowledge with respect the customs and traditions of the peoples of the Douglas Treaties, Coast Salish First Nation, in whose traditional territories we are gathered on this occasion. I also have the honour to represent

Her Majesty Queen Elizabeth, the Queen of Canada in British Columbia, and so bring special greetings to these proceedings in honour of Frank Calder, acknowledging his singular achievement during the long search for justice in the cause of his beloved Nisga'a people. Although I am at some disadvantage in these proceedings, being untrained in the law, my education concerning the Nisga'a began in childhood, when with other northern First Nations, we lived in the now lost world of a salmon cannery on the Skeena River.

We were separated into neo-colonial class and race divisions, but, as children, we overcame such barriers to hear each other's stories. Very early, I learned the legends of Eagle, Raven, Whale, Wolf, and Bear and some of the thrilling tales and formal customs of Royal Houses and Clans. At the cannery, there were also Haida, T'Simpsean [Tsimshian], and Gitxsan, Wet'suwet'en peoples, all of whom were richly diversified in languages, spiritual beliefs, and cultures, but, with the Nisga'a, they were all totally secure in the knowledge that since they had never surrendered their claims, they were owed justice due to their prior right in their territories, which they had occupied and used since "time immemorial." Subsequently, the thread of my life has unfolded in various posts and positions, and, along the way, the Nisga'a and I have shared much together.

It wasn't too long after that childhood that I was first made acquainted with the principles of the Royal Proclamation of 1763. In 1832, this proclamation was categorized by US Supreme Court Chief Justice John Marshall, as "British Policy, assuring Indian Nations were distinct, independent political communities with their own original natural rights as possessors of the soil since the beginning of time." The proclamation, along with a "fiduciary duty" of "the Crown" in the right of Canada, was deemed to assure the well-being of Aboriginal peoples and was regarded as the bedrock of their inherent rights. Naturally, Frank Calder was brought up on these promises of justice. But after generations of Nisga'a leaders succeeded each other in search of redress of their claims, without results, Frank Calder sought power to change things. As the first Aboriginal member of the British Columbia legislature in the Commonwealth, Frank took up the challenge of their claims in concert with the Nisga'a people.

We are all aware of the prejudice and injustices that stain our provincial history. In 1867, one of my least illustrious predecessors, first as premier and later as lieutenant-governor, Joseph Trutch, cemented a negative attitude against the search for justice in matters of Aboriginal rights and title that continued to haunt British Columbia for at least the next 120 years. But by the centennial year of 1967, things were starting to change, when the renowned T'sleil Watuth, Burrard Chief Dan George was able to give what was considered at the time to be a shocking, if memorable, speech on why he could not celebrate Canada's birthday. In spite of the ghost of Joseph Trutch, a good number of British Columbians of all heritages began working together towards a new day for First Nations and Aboriginal peoples, and things began to change a little more quickly!

It's a cliché to say that if you remember the 1960s you were not there, but, even without such impediments, it is becoming difficult now to recall how really promising the late 1960s were. In my opinion, it was a time of immense hopefulness, of infectious ferment directed towards resolving social inequities – all suffused with the conviction that we were on the road towards a "more just society" together. There seemed to be a whole new consciousness at play, supporting remedies to past injustices and embracing the possibility of a "new day" for Aboriginal peoples and all others who were oppressed. The sense of the times was manifest in many ways, perhaps among the most notable was the emergence of two great movements still shaking our universe with sweeping demands for women's equality and for a sustainable environment. It seems we were the first people to comprehend that our duty as citizens extended beyond respect for the past and an interest in our own survival and to understand that we were also responsible too for the well-being of all those who would follow us on this Earth! The legal expression of these hopes and dreams still echoes through the justice system today, but we have moved beyond rectifying past injustices towards insuring the fundamental human rights of every citizen.

Nisga'a leaders were inspired by the splendid spirit of those times as well and revived the work of their 1913 Land Claims Committee. Among so many others, I remember in addition to Frank Calder, the Nisga'a claim being recommenced by James Gosnell, who was later succeeded by his brother Joseph (with us today), Bill McKay, Maurice Nyce, Hubert Doolan, Harry Nyce, Bert McKay, Rod Robinson, and Alvin McKay (the latter two and I progressed from childhood through high school together). They formed the Nishga Tribal Council and formulated what was to become the *Calder* case in a suit against British Columbia seeking a declaration that the Aboriginal title of the Nisga'a people had never been extinguished. Led by the formidable Thomas Berger, and ultimately argued before the Supreme Court of Canada with Aboriginal title as the sole issue, justices deliberated on what soon became known simply as "Calder" – to be determined by seven of nine judges, with one ruling against the Nisga'a on technical grounds. The remaining six were equally divided with three in favour and three against. I hosted a radio show at that time and remember a quiet statement by Tom Berger observing that "sometimes a loss is almost as good as a win," and so it has proven to be.

It is generally agreed that the first significant outcome of *Calder* was the famous dissenting judgment of the gifted Saskatchewan jurist, Justice Emmett Hall, who unequivocally placed responsibility for action right back into the political sphere. The effect was to move Aboriginal rights and title onto Canada's agenda (and although denied for another twenty years) also onto

British Columbia's agenda. In 1973, Prime Minister Trudeau, who had long maintained that it was impossible to right historic wrongs, famously "changed his mind" and informed Canada's first Aboriginal member of parliament, future minister and senator Len Marchand that "your People have a lot more Rights than I thought you did, but it will take us a decade to define what they are."

By now, the Nisga'a were my Skeena constituents, and, on 26 January 1976, the Nishga Tribal Council and Canada gathered in New Aiyansh, on a basis of equal respect, to open negotiations on a treaty. Under Premier Bill Vander Zalm, British Columbia joined this negotiation in 1990. Twenty-four years after they had started, President Joseph Gosnell announced that the Nisga'a canoe had safely landed at last. On 12 September 2000, the Nisga'a Lisims government convened their first meeting in their own legislature. Every step along the way is recorded in history, providing other First Nations here at home and across the world with the confidence that it can be done.

As we mark this historic thirtieth anniversary together, we are also conscious that for the Nisga'a, the struggle began with the arrival of Captain Vancouver off the north coastal waters of the Nass River in their territory. We note with pride that although opposition was strong, during the course of this long struggle there have always been many descendants of those first European settlers who have given their strength and support to the Nisga'a cause. When, even at the eleventh hour in 2000, objections continued through the court, it was Frank Calder in his eighth decade, who stood firm in the witness box, supporting the contention that the "inherent right of self-government" had survived Confederation, and, once again led by Thomas Berger, the Court agreed that all of the rights set out in the Nisga'a treaty are treaty rights that are protected under the section 35(1) of Canada's 1982 constitution.

Few of us are privileged to change history; Frank Calder is one who has done so. Had there not been an Honourable Member for Atlin, elected in 1949, in the person of the "Little Chief," Frank Calder and for his presence in the legislature of British Columbia, we would all today, be the poorer. Without Frank Calder and the resulting *Calder* decision, the 1982 constitution of Canada would not now include a vital commitment to Indian, Inuit, and Métis peoples, as is contained in section 35 and described in *R. v. Sparrow*, which call for a just settlement for Aboriginal peoples. The section renounces the old (Trutch) rules of the game, under which the Crown established courts of law and then denied those courts the authority to question sovereign claims made by the Crown. Frank, through your actions and leadership, you have allowed us all to reinforce the dignity of this great country.

From the very beginning of this first delegation in the nineteenth century to Queen Victoria, the Nisga'a people always sought to enter into

Canada and not to separate from it. I rather think that those who suggest parallels between the Nisga'a and Québec often miss that most salient of points. Canada is always to remain a "work in progress." Through steady, generous, and reasoned negotiation, Frank Calder and the Nisga'a people have increased the capacity of our capacious constitutional tent. We are all proud that the "rule of law" under which we have chosen to live together and which has been broadened sufficiently to include more of the diversity that so strengthens our national identity as Canadians!

All Canadians and indigenous peoples around the planet have gained by this treaty. For the Nisga'a, as Joseph Gosnell has wisely said: "Now we are free to make our own mistakes." But, more than that, the Nisga'a are now legally able to exercise the right of self-government within the laws of Canada, derived not from delegation from the Crown but from the fact that they were self-governing at the time that the British claimed sovereignty over what is now British Columbia. For British Columbia, there is resolution in the great Nass Valley. For Canada, there is a new body of law built on the firm foundation of this successful search for justice. I submit that for Canada also there are less tangible but very valuable gifts deriving from this historic agreement that may prove to be even more rewarding over time. By embracing the Nisga'a people, confederation has gained the gifts of arts, music, languages, spiritual beliefs, customs, and culture that are the legacy of this ancient society with its roots deeply entrenched in the past and the future of this magnificent land. We have learned mighty lessons of respect and hospitality from First Nations, all of which have been reflected throughout the decades of the Nisga'a's search for justice. I still occasionally hear those voices questioning why throughout those excruciatingly long years of denial, frustration, and seemingly endless negotiations did the Nisga'a never once resort to hostility, anger, or even to discourtesy?

This question reminds me that in bringing the Nisga'a into honourable membership in our society, they have brought with them the timeless and priceless gift of their philosophy of the "common bowl." Older than time and rich in beliefs rooted in the realities of this land, the ethic of the "common bowl" has kept the Nisga'a people of the Nass Valley moving forward, through denial, disease, and death. It embraces a belief that all that ever has been, is now, or ever will be must be shared. Those who do not understand or who fear collectivities could benefit greatly from a greater application of the ethic of the common bowl, which through this treaty has now become an indivisible part of Canada's immeasurable plurality.

I submit that it is why Frank Calder, his fellow leaders, and his people always knew they would win when they started down this long, long road in 1967. I am so proud of what has been accomplished across our time. Most of us can look back now and see our younger selves in hopeful pursuit of change and now can rest assured that change has come about from the collective work of all of us. We acknowledge and remember our leaders and all those who did not live to see this time of fulfilment, and I know as we look ahead that we can see our shared society enriched by the addition of a timeless people with whom this favoured land is now justly shared.

To the new generation of Nisga'a leaders, even now progressing through Wilp Wilho'esk Nisga'a and other post-secondary institutions, when the reins of power are in your hands, I know you will continue to be inspired by the example that has been set by Dr. Frank Calder. We salute your courage, foresight, and determination, Frank, we also salute the great people from whom you come and who have supported and sustained you through all of the trials of the course of your life's dramatic journey. We especially thank all those in every part of our society, who saw, long before the law, that when the Nisga'a people at last became our fellow Canadians, we would all be enriched in the process. On behalf of our fellow citizens in British Columbia, I thank you, and I also bring a salute from that long ago group of "rag-tag" cannery kids, who few thought had much of a future but who grew up to become great Nisga'a chiefs, members of parliament, and the legislature, ministers of the Crown, and representatives of the Queen, knowing what an extraordinary country Canada really is when a "little chief" can do such big things!

The Honourable Lance Finch, Chief Justice of British Columbia
Your Honour, Mr. Attorney, President Turpin, Dr. Calder, Chief Gosnell, Dr. Sam, distinguished guests, ladies and gentlemen. Thank you for inviting me to say a few words at the conclusion of this conference on the *Calder* case and its impact on Aboriginal rights in Canada. I congratulate the law school at the University of Victoria and all others responsible for organizing this event, and I acknowledge with thanks the privilege of speaking on the traditional territories of the Aboriginal people of this area.

Your discussions over the last two days not only mark a significant legal anniversary but also emphasize and reinforce the importance of open, informed, and honest discourse among Aboriginal and non-Aboriginal peoples. Tonight, I wish to sound a note of optimism. My hope for the future is based on my belief of our collective capacity to learn, to change, and to grow. In turn, my belief in our ability to change is based on the events of the last thirty years. In 1969, the government of Canada issued a White Paper on Indian Policy. It refused to recognize Aboriginal title. Prime Minister Trudeau refused to entertain the possibility of negotiating land claims with Aboriginal peoples. I'm sorry I can't imitate his voice. Those of you who are old enough will remember that marvelous nasal twang and the passion with which he spoke. He said:

It's inconceivable, I think, that in a given society one section of the society should have a treaty with the other section of society. We must all be equal under the laws and we must not sign treaties amongst ourselves ... Our answer is "no." We can't recognize Aboriginal rights, because no society can be built on historical "might-have-beens."

A few years later, after the *Calder* decision in the Supreme Court of Canada, the prime minister admitted to the Nishga Tribal Council that Aboriginal peoples may have more legal rights in relation to their property than the government had earlier acknowledged. The federal government introduced its comprehensive land claims policy in 1973. Nine years later, in 1982, at the urging of Mr. Trudeau, Canada adopted the *Canadian Charter of Rights and Freedoms*. Section 35 of the *Charter*, as you all know, recognizes and affirms the existing Aboriginal and treaty rights of the Aboriginal peoples of Canada.

Thirty years after *Calder*, the Nisga'a peoples, the BC provincial government, and the federal government have finally settled claims, outstanding for more than a century, over title to the land in the Nass River Valley. This settlement, and other land claims agreements that have been reached or are currently under negotiation, find their genesis in *Calder*. I know that some have argued that the treaty negotiation process has been too long, too slow, and too costly, and there are others who maintain that the courts have been too timid, too tied to their common law roots, and too rigid in their perception of Aboriginal law. I admit that both criticisms can fairly be made. I would reply that, whatever disappointments litigants on all sides of these issues may have felt in particular cases, the courts have nevertheless played a useful role in the search for acceptable solutions. The courts have provided forums in which these controversial issues could be debated in a thoughtful and measured way, where parties' positions could be tested and evaluated, and where the broader communities could be encouraged to re-examine long-held views and deeply ingrained attitudes. It is also evident that the jurisprudence of the last thirty years has helped to inform the treaty-making process and the parties who are engaged in it. The legal discourse has not so much provided answers, as it has provided a framework for discussions outside the courtroom and at the negotiating tables. So I am encouraged by the events of the last thirty years, for which the *Calder* case can surely be said to be the seminal event.

The *Calder* case is a landmark not only in the field of Aboriginal law but also in the broader arena of human rights law. It belongs in the class of case described by Tom Berger in his book *Fragile Freedoms*. All such cases require courageous and committed litigants to pursue controversial claims and dedicated, imaginative lawyers to articulate new and unpopular arguments. For this, Mr. Calder and the Nishga Tribal Council, as well as Mr. Berger, deserve our recognition and our sincere thanks. These cases demonstrate how legal change has an iterative and cumulative effect on society. These cases mark starting points for the ongoing struggles to achieve further legal, political, and social recognition of a particular minority group's place in society.

From a jurisprudential perspective, *Calder* is very different from other landmark human rights cases. Unlike other human rights issues, which draw on principles long considered fundamental to the common law and now entrenched in the *Charter*, Aboriginal rights are based in the history of the Aboriginal peoples in Canada, living in distinctive cultures with their own social and legal systems prior to the arrival of Europeans. For this reason, *Calder*, and all subsequent Aboriginal title and Aboriginal rights cases, force us to confront not only the question of how to promote equality within Canadian society but also the unique question of how to achieve equality between or among societies within Canada.

One judicial answer to this dilemma may lie in the *sui generis* characterization of Aboriginal title, Aboriginal rights, and the relationship between Aboriginal peoples and the Crown. It is, to me at least, a curiosity that this uniquely "new world" problem should be labelled with a Latin phrase of uncertain meaning. But the *sui generis* suggests that Aboriginal rights are unique and cannot be fully explained by reference to common law principles. As Chief Justice Antonio Lamer observed in *R. v. Van der Peet*, the *sui generis* quality of Aboriginal rights makes them a form of "intersocietal law," which attempts to bridge both Aboriginal and non-Aboriginal cultures. True reconciliation therefore depends on the ability to define Aboriginal rights in a manner that gives equal weight to both Aboriginal perspectives and the perspective of the common law. Courts are therefore compelled to look beyond the common law and to consider Aboriginal legal perspectives to help determine the existence and nature of Aboriginal title and Aboriginal rights. I have suggested that the courts have played a useful role in developing our understanding of these issues, but I would like to conclude my remarks by emphasizing what the courts have said, over and over again, that the parties in these Aboriginal cases should seek to resolve their differences at the negotiating table and not in the law courts.

When I was a very young lawyer, the senior person in my firm told me that a bad settlement was better than a good lawsuit any day. This advice was sound then and it is still true today. How much better it is to resolve differences by compromise and conciliation, acceptable to all, than to resort to a solution imposed by a third party that is most likely to leave one, if not all, parties dissatisfied. The best solution is one where all parties recognize the dignity and autonomy of each other, where the inherent value of every group in our multicultural society is accepted, and in which every party has a stake. We are of course a long way from the end of this story. The great Canadian legal scholar Frank Scott said:

> If human rights and harmonious relations between cultures are forums of the beautiful, then the state is a work of art that is never finished.

Let us all, in whatever area we work, bend our best efforts to that unending task. Thank you.

Dr. Joseph Gosnell, President, Nishga Tribal Council

[Introduction in Nisga'a]. Her Honour the Lieutenant-Governor of the Province of British Columbia, Iona Campagnolo, Chief Justice Finch, Elders from the Nation on whose land that I stand today, ladies and gentlemen. I bring you greetings from the Nisga'a nation. What an appropriate theme for such a conference, as Dr. Calder indicated, "Let Right Be Done." I want to pay tribute to those men who led our nation back in the 1950s, Dr. Frank Arthur Calder, Hubert Doolan, Rod Robinson, Allan Moore, James Gosnell, William McKay, Alvin McKay, Henry McKay, Maurice Nyce, Harry Nyce, and Anthony Robinson. For those of you that have the program, their pictures are shown in this photograph taken in the Supreme Court of Canada in Ottawa, Thomas Berger, the women who stood behind these men, and the nation that stood behind them in the early days of the land question. We pay our homage to all of them – a tribute to their courage, determination, and steadfastness. I also would like to pay tribute to our church, the Anglican Church of Canada, who provided not only moral support and spiritual support but also, more importantly in the early days, financial support that was desperately needed to try and move this issue forward. We say thank you to our church, the Anglican Church. It is interesting to note, ladies and gentlemen, that those who came across the ocean and the hardships that they faced with their own governing bodies, it is interesting to note that they brought across with them the same thing that they left behind and imposed it upon our people. That was a long time ago. I recall Frank Calder's words and I want to quote them to you. In the early days of the argument leading up to the Supreme Court of Canada, he said, and I quote: "The Nisga'a people are not on trial. The Indian peoples are not on trial. British justice is on trial. I believe that British justice will prevail." Those were the words of our leader of that day, what he said.

So, what is it today that we have with the *Calder* decision that is not only recognized nationally here in Canada but internationally as well? What does it do for our people, the Nisga'a people? It provided hope when no hope existed – hope not only for the Nisga'a people but also for other indigenous peoples around the world. Today, since the coming on-stream of ·

the Nisga'a Final Agreement we have a continuous stream of visitors in the Nass Valley: people from across Canada, Alaska, the United States, Central and South America, New Zealand, Australia, and people from the Asian countries. We had a thirty-five-man delegation that came over not once, but twice, from Taiwan. We had a similar group from the Saami people in Western Europe, and they came over twice. The different consulates stationed in Vancouver came up to visit, and there is no end to the visitors that we have. They heard, no doubt, about the Nisga'a Final Agreement, the coming onstream of the treaty, and they wanted to see for themselves, with their own eyes, just what it was that we were trying to accomplish here. I recall the many, many conventions since the Nishga Tribal Council came to life. Dr. Calder and his colleagues revived the old Nisga'a Land Committee and renamed it the Nishga Tribal Council in the early fifties. Forty-three conventions we went through, forty-three years of annual gatherings of the Nisga'a people to talk about the land question – how we as a people would govern ourselves some day, once we got out from underneath the *Indian Act* and the Department of Indian Affairs. That's what they talked about.

I will read you a portion of a statement made many, many years ago, and this man spoke on behalf of the most senior chiefs of our nation and he said: "We are not opposed to the coming of the white people into our territory provided this be carried out justly in accordance with the British principles embodied in the Royal Proclamation. If therefore, as we expect, the Aboriginal rights which we claim should be established by the decision of His Majesty's Privy Council, we would be prepared to take a moderate and reasonable position in that event, while claiming the right to decide for ourselves the terms upon which we would deal with our territory." Ladies and gentlemen, the Nisga'a people did precisely that. We were told to go out and negotiate a treaty to the best of our ability, and, having done so, to bring it back to our people and they would be the ones to decide. They would decide whether or not they thought this treaty would be beneficial to our people. And regardless of the percentage of the vote, the ratification vote that took place, it was the will of the majority that prevailed. The will of the majority – not the will of the minority – because of the country that we live in. It's a democratic country, where the will of the majority prevails.

I recall that once our ratification process had been complete, the treaty was brought into the British Columbia legislature, and a great debate took place between the governing body of that day and the opposition party, which is now the governing body of British Columbia, as has been recalled over the past three days. I recall the debate in the House of Commons, the Standing Committee relating to that institution. I recall the 471 amendments that the Reform Party proposed with respect to the Nisga'a Final Agreement, and, if they were successful, it would have rendered the Nisga'a

Final Agreement completely useless. It would not be worth the paper it was written on. But, thank goodness, not one of those proposed amendments was approved by Parliament. I recall the treaty being taken into the Senate Chambers for further debate and further scrutiny and the Standing Committee that was associated with this governing body and the people who came forward and spoke for and against the Nisga'a treaty, including some of our own people. I recall standing up in the chambers in the Standing Committee and indicating to the senators as they debated the pros and cons of the Nisga'a Final Agreement that I challenged them to show me one perfect piece of provincial legislation. Show me one piece of perfect federal legislation. Show me a perfect international treaty – there aren't any because all of these things are a result of people sitting across a table negotiating. And there are no perfect pieces of legislation. That's the way the negotiations work.

Jim Aldridge, legal counsel for many, many years, since he came out of law school, recalls the day and his feelings when the Nisga'a Final Agreement was brought to a vote in the House of Commons. We were there: Rod Robinson, Frank, and Hubert Doolan. We sat up in the gallery. And I wanted to look into the faces of those elected members as they stood for or against the Nisga'a Final Agreement, to stand for or against the dreams of our people, and I watched with a great deal of enthusiasm and concern as the members stood as they were called by the chair. The Reform Party voted against the Nisga'a Final Agreement. The announcement was made by the chair that the document had passed. A great deal of clapping took place, handshaking, and, then – the first time that I have ever seen it in my life and I've watched the CPAC channel many, many times – someone on the floor of the House of Commons started to sing the national anthem, "O Canada." And people stood up, we stood up. The parties in the House did not want to stand up, which was all very interesting and comical in a sense. I never could fully describe how proud I was that day to stand in the gallery of the House of Commons and sing our national anthem. I was extremely proud – a proud Canadian. That was the way I felt.

I recall the time when we reached the agreement in principle, staying in the city of Vancouver. David Osborne was the chief federal negotiator at that time, and we knew we were coming down to the wire. And a determination was made that we would go around the clock if necessary, and we were prepared to sit in that room until the agreement had been reached. It was about four or five in the morning. We had not eaten properly. We were existing on Coca-Cola and pizza that was brought in periodically, and someone from the *Province* said: "You know, it would be a nice idea to take a break, and we're not going anywhere." Financial issues were the last thing to be removed from the table. And David Osborne came to me and asked what my thoughts were to adjourning the meeting until we could get some sleep, freshen up, have a decent meal, and I said: "No, David." I said: "My team will stay in the room until we reach that agreement." And we did. People got back together that morning in 1996. When someone said: "There is nothing left to talk about we have reached an agreement." I looked at my watch and my watch said 8:27 in the morning. And we stayed for a while, the three teams, just sort of reliving what we had gone through over so many, many, many years, and we let the media in. During the course of the night, the media, television cameras, and reporters camped outside the door and slept on the floor with their cameras and everything in Vancouver, including our own local members. When the door opened, it was just like an explosion of people jumping over tables and chairs, sticking microphones in your face. It was just amazing. I forgot about my tiredness and the fact that we hadn't eaten properly. And I was asked to do a live interview at 6:00 a.m. by the CBC, which I did. I went back to my room and tried to sleep. I couldn't. I went for a walk.

And these were just my recollections, never mind the recollections of the rest of our team or legal counsel. [Inaudible] ... the views and the feelings of the federal and provincial negotiator team. To us, ladies and gentlemen, the Nisga'a Final Agreement is no longer a theory that we talk about. It's reality. We willingly entered into this battle of words with the provincial government and the federal government. We knew who we were up against – the might of these two institutions, financial and legal. We knew that. We went in there with open minds. And the issue was to try and reconcile the rights of the Nisga'a people with the rights of other Canadians. How do we do that? The many, many pieces of federal and provincial legislation that we reviewed, the laws of this great land, the constitution, and the *Canadian Charter of Rights and Freedoms* were all scrutinized as to how the Nisga'a Final Agreement would be affected. We are now in a different phase, a different stage. We are in the process of reconciliation – the rebuilding of the tattered relationship that existed before. To me, a major part of this reconciliation will rest with the federal and provincial governments because they will have to fulfil the commitments that were made on the negotiation table. I recall the legal challenge to the Nisga'a Final Agreement by Gordon Campbell and two of his colleagues. He's now the premier. But Gordon Campbell was like Pierre Elliott Trudeau. Once the court decision was made, he too changed his mind. He came to our legislative house in New Aiyansh and spoke to our elected body, and he brought with him a message, saying that, despite our differences of opinion, legal or otherwise, the government would fulfil the commitments made in the Nisga'a Final Agreement.

Last night, I watched with a great deal of interest to the comments made by another individual who we will no doubt be dealing with, Paul Martin, the prime minister in waiting. I listened very keenly to what he had to say, and what caught my ear was a comment he made. His government will be committed to accountability. We are going to hold Mr. Martin accountable. So whether or not they, too, as a governing body will fulfil the commitments that the federal Crown made on the negotiation table remains to be seen. There have been many, many Supreme Court of Canada rulings over the years dealing with a whole range of issues, and I think that all too often the Aboriginal leadership just takes out what is good news to them. They don't read, or they overlook the entire text of these rulings that are made. Very seldom do I hear Aboriginal people describe in detail how the government has the ability to infringe on Aboriginal rights. All of these Supreme Court of Canada rulings have – *Delgamuukw* is the latest – and when you read what the justices have to say with respect to this area, where the government has the ability to infringe upon the rights of our people, it puts fear in my heart as a First Nations person – the original inhabitants of this land. And along this journey that we have made over many, many years, we ask questions. During the course of negotiations, I heard about the rule of law, the rule of law. And I must ask periodically, was there a failure to apply the rule of law to Aboriginal people? Was it applied fairly? Does the rule apply to one group of people and not to another group? Because we are talking about the lives of our people here, Aboriginal people, the first peoples of this land.

What are we doing today as a nation? We have no further need today to consult with, or seek, the consent of the minister of Indian Affairs. I listened to my own colleague Hubert Doolan this morning, and he asked when was the last revision of the *Indian Act*. I almost stood up and said, Hubert, we threw that thing out in 2000. [Laughter/clapping] And the Department of Indian Affairs went along with it. These are the things that ... major, major difference with the way things are being done today. Major difference here. It's as if we got back the power and the authority that our people exercised before the coming of the Europeans onto our territory – that's what we did. It wasn't something special that the senior and the provincial governments granted to us. It was something that we had before that was taken away. Taken away. And so we're in this aspect now to rebuild our nation. To rebuild our nation. To rebuild this relationship. One hundred and thirteen years it has taken us. I recall all of those many, many people who went before us and their dreams and their aspirations. They went to their graves with those dreams, talking about what we were going to do. They're gone. What an incredible journey this has been for the Nisga'a people. A journey filled with sorrow, a journey filled with heartache and tears. A journey filled with denial, a journey filled with shame. But still a journey filled with hope. That's why I indicated – what an appropriate theme for the conference: "Let Right Be Done." [Words in Nisga'a] Thank you.

Dr. Frank Calder, President Emeritus, Nishga Tribal Council
Master of Ceremonies, Dr. Turpin, Your Honour the Lieutenant-Governor
of British Columbia, Dr. Sam and the Coast Salish Nation, the Nisga'a
Ts'amiks Dancers, the participants to this great conference, the platform
party guests, ladies and gentlemen. First, I have to refer to the conference
that has just been concluded. It was a very successful three-day celebration
of the thirtieth anniversary of the *Calder* case. The presentations of present-
ers and the deliberations from the conference itself were very fruitful and
beneficial. I believe I speak for everyone in attendance during the conference and in attendance here when I say to the University of Victoria organizers this evening, thank you for a job well done. Second, as part of my
brief, short address to you, it is foremost in my mind, I reply to what Her
Honour Iona Campagnolo has said to you. She comes from the area, as
most of us know, which is considered by many to be the birthplace of the
British Columbia land question. She grew up in that area, and she's seen
with her own eyes exactly what was happening. She has witnessed and taken
part in the progress of this land question, especially during her term of
office as councillor in the city of Prince Rupert and as a federal member for
Skeena in the House of Commons. This, of course, took several years. Now
we listened carefully to her remarks. I am replying to those remarks as my
work this evening. Along with you, I treasure all of the words that she has
expressed to us. You're the witness when I say to her that I thank her with
all of our hearts. We remember the work she has done for us up north during her earlier years and during the time that she was elected as the people's
representative and her dedication and involvement and participation, which,
of course, benefit everyone, especially our people. We don't forget those
things. We thank her for that, and we thank her for her supportive remarks
that you have just heard. We thank her for those very encouraging words.
Iona, by your presence, we all feel at home here.

I went to a residential school for thirteen years. In 1924, I found out the
motto for that school, which is about three miles south of Chilliwack. It
says: "No backward steps." A lot of us, who recognize this motto, lived by it.
I still live by it today. I heard about that motto in 1924 when I was just
about nine years old. Seventy-nine years later, I heard another one today
from the University of Victoria and I am going to live by that. It said: "Let
right be done." There's another motto that I'll never forget, and I intend to
live by it because it is a good phrase and I hope you all remember it with
me. Once again, I would like to express a real deep appreciation and thank
you to the very words that have been expressed to all of us by Her Honour
the Lieutenant-Governor, and I would like to thank once again the university for this great event. But it is not only an event that the Nisga'a tribes
remember. I think the people who have studied the Nisga'a case know that
it has brought the people together into a room to negotiate and try to solve

their problems regardless of race, colour, or creed and for this I am very thankful.

I really admire a lot of people who are coming into this country. It seems to me that a lot of them that are coming into the country in Canada appear to have left their language and their culture behind from whence they came, and they seem to be flooding our schools and learning our language – the English – and our culture for one specific reason and that is to get a job and to live and to help build the country. And I don't think, and I'll say this very boldly, I don't think we as our own people, the first people in Canada known as the First Nations in this country, should be left behind. We should also participate and work in Canada along with the other races to keep up with the Joneses. I really believe that. Otherwise, we are going to be left behind. There is a new word being passed around. They call it globalization. I am not afraid to lose anything. After all of the years that I spent at Coqualeetza Residential School – thirteen years – I could still speak our language. I still know my customs. I know who my chief is. I know my identity. That school never took anything away from me and that's because my parents told me not to forget these things. God bless them. I am going to say that we are talking about the *Calder* case today. It is not just *Calder* – it's everybody's case. The decision of three to three has been adopted by all of the other races all over the world, especially people who have been oppressed, to try and work something out for themselves. To talk to the people who are more superior to them in their land and to try and work things out so that they can help build their respective countries.

I would like to conclude by saying that the whole *Calder* case, or whatever you call it, is to get rid of somebody that's holding you down. There was a very distinguished black man in the United States who once mentioned something about someone being on his back, that whoever was holding him down in the gutter, that person on his back, he was also in the gutter with him. And it's true. And the *Calder* case and many other cases, they are about negotiating on an equal base with the guy that used to be on your back and my back. That's why I just love that decision: three to three. So I push him off my back, and he faces me and we talk business. And, eventually, it will result in something worthwhile. This thought, my friends, I leave with you. Once again, my sincere thank you to the most encouraging words and comforting words produced by our very own Iona Campagnolo.

The proceedings were closed with an "encore" performance by the Nisga'a Ts'amiks Dancers and a closing prayer from Dr. Sam.

A Select Chronology

Stephanie Hanna and Hamar Foster

	British Columbia	The Nisga'a
Time immemorial		The Creator brings sun to the world, ending a time of hunger and war. The Creator's messenger, Txeemsim teaches the people how to live in the world in accordance with the cycle of life as well as how to build houses to survive the winter, how to defend their land, and how to organize their society.
ca. 1750		A volcanic eruption occurs in the Nass Valley, destroying two Nisga'a villages and becoming part of the Nisga'a oral tradition.
1763	A Royal Proclamation is issued by King George III on 7 October, reserving all tribal lands until they are purchased by the Crown according to the process outlined in the Proclamation.	
1778	The first Europeans (under Captain James Cook) land on the west coast of Vancouver Island.	
1793		Captain George Vancouver makes contact with the Nisga'a in the course of his surveying expedition.
1831		The Hudson's Bay Company (HBC) establishes Fort Simpson on the Nass River.
1834		The HBC relocates Fort Simpson south to the Skeena River.

▶

	British Columbia	The Nisga'a
1846	Great Britain and the United States sign the Treaty of Washington, agreeing that all territory south of the 49th parallel, except for Vancouver Island, will be American. First Nations are not consulted.	
1847	The Supreme Court of New Zealand decides *R. v. Symonds*, holding that imperial law had long recognized Aboriginal title.	
1849	The colony of Vancouver Island is established and title is temporarily granted to the HBC.	
1850–54	James Douglas, as agent of the HBC and then as governor, makes fourteen "Douglas Treaties" with First Nations at Fort Victoria, Nanaimo, and Fort Rupert on Vancouver Island. The treaties are based on New Zealand precedents.	
1858	The colony of British Columbia is established on the mainland, also with Douglas as governor.	
1859	Title to Vancouver Island reverts to the Crown, apparently with no further treaties made. No treaties are made in the mainland colony.	
1860		William Duncan makes the first missionary visit to the Nass River.
1863/1864	James Douglas retires as governor of both colonies.	Robert Doolan becomes the first resident missionary to the Nisga'a.
1866	The colonies of Vancouver Island and British Columbia merge. The legislature requires Aboriginal people to obtain the permission of the executive in order to pre-empt land.	
1868	Gilbert Malcolm Sproat publishes *Scenes and Studies of Savage Life*, probably the first book written about Aboriginal people in British Columbia.	
1870s		European settlers begin to pre-empt land in the Nisga'a territories.

►

	British Columbia	The Nisga'a
1871	British Columbia joins Confederation, ceding jurisdiction over "Indians, and lands reserved for the Indians," to the dominion government but retaining authority over lands and resources in the new province.	
	British Columbia provides the dominion with a list of Indian reserves in the province, revealing that there were none on the west coast of Vancouver Island, none on the east coast of Vancouver Island beyond Comox, and none beyond Burrard Inlet on the mainland.	
1875	Ottawa disallows British Columbia's *Crown Lands Act*, on the ground that it was beyond the jurisdiction of the province because it made no provision for Indian lands.	
1876	The first dominion *Indian Act* is enacted.	
	British Columbia's new *Crown Lands Act*, which continues to make no reference to Indian title, is reluctantly approved by Ottawa.	
	The Joint Indian Reserve Commission (JIRC) is established.	
	Gilbert Malcolm Sproat takes up the position of joint commissioner of the JIRC.	
1877	James Douglas dies.	
1878	The JIRC is replaced by the Indian Reserve Commission (IRC), and Sproat becomes the sole IRC commissioner. He resigns two years later and is replaced by Peter O'Reilly.	
1881		The first cannery is constructed on the Nass River.
		O'Reilly begins to impose the reserve system on the Nisga'a.
		A Nisga'a delegation, led by Chief Mountain, goes to Victoria to protest.

▶

	British Columbia	The Nisga'a
1884	The *Indian Act* is amended, outlawing ceremonies such as the potlatch.	
1886	Chief Justice Matthew Baillie Begbie decides *A.G. and I.B. Nash v. John Tait*, stating that Aboriginal peoples "had no rights to the land" other than occupation "at the will of the Crown."	The Nisga'a block attempts by Captain William Jemmett, the surveyor for the IRC, to draw reserve boundaries in their territory.
1887		A delegation of Nisga'a and Tsimshian chiefs travel to Victoria to ask for treaties that will recognize their title and a measure of self-governance.
		Later that year, a royal commission visiting the Nass Valley informs the Nisga'a that the government does not recognize any Nisga'a rights over their traditional territory.
1888	The Judicial Committee of the Privy Council (JCPC) decides *St. Catherine's Milling & Lumber Company v. R.*, holding that Aboriginal title is a legal interest in land.	
1890		According to some sources, the first Nisga'a Land Committee is established.
1899	The dominion makes Treaty 8, which extends into northeastern British Columbia. It is the first treaty in British Columbia since the Douglas Treaties and the last until the Nisga'a treaty in 2000.	
1906–07	A delegation of First Nations chiefs travels to London, England, to meet with King Edward VII in 1906.	Other sources indicate that the Land Committee is established in 1907 or perhaps in 1909.
1908	Ottawa and British Columbia reach a deadlock on reserve land issues so BC Premier Richard McBride suspends the work of the IRC.	Pre-emptions in the Nass Valley increase.
	Prime Minister Wilfrid Laurier meets with a delegation of chiefs in Ottawa, assuring them that their rights will be protected.	The Nisga'a Land Committee sends delegates to Ottawa.

▶

	British Columbia	The Nisga'a
1909–10	The Cowichan Petition, containing the first legal articulation of the doctrine of Aboriginal title in British Columbia, is conveyed to the Colonial Office in London by Arthur E. O'Meara. The Indian Rights Association, the Interior Tribes of British Columbia, and the Friends of the Indians of British Columbia are established.	
1910	The deputy minister of justice and British Columbia's deputy attorney general agree upon ten questions to be referred to the Supreme Court of Canada (SCC) respecting Indian lands in British Columbia. However, Premier McBride refuses to consent to the reference because three of the questions deal with Indian title.	
1911	Following British Columbia's refusal to consent to a reference to the courts, the dominion prepares to bring a lawsuit on its own against homesteaders on the Skeena River. However, the Laurier government is defeated and a new Conservative administration comes to power. Led by Sir Robert Borden, it is more sympathetic to the concerns of the Conservative McBride government in British Columbia.	A Nisga'a delegation goes to Victoria to inform the BC government of its intention to pursue its land claim and participates in a meeting of over 100 delegates and chiefs with the premier and members of the provincial cabinet.
1912	The McKenna-McBride Agreement is signed. In return for British Columbia giving up its claim to a reversionary interest in Indian reserve lands, the dominion agrees to shelve the question of Aboriginal title. The agreement also provides for a new Royal Commission on Indian Affairs for British Columbia.	
1913	The McKenna-McBride Commission (MMC) begins to examine the issue of reserves in British Columbia.	The Nisga'a Land Committee sends a petition to the Privy Council in England seeking recognition of the Nisga'a title.
1916	The MMC makes its report, which is not made public for several years. The Allied Indian Tribes of British Columbia is formed.	

▶

	British Columbia	The Nisga'a
1924		The MMC recommendation for Nisga'a reserves, as amended, is confirmed as 76 square kilometres.
1927	The *Indian Act* is amended to prohibit fundraising for the purpose of pursuing Aboriginal title claims without government consent. A joint committee of the Senate and House of Commons inquires into the claims of the Allied Indian Tribes. It recommends an annual payment of $100,000 in lieu of a treaty but holds that there is no valid claim for Aboriginal title.	The 1927 *Indian Act* amendment effectively puts an end to the Nisga'a Land Committee and the Allied Indian Tribes – groups that could not survive without fundraising.
1928		O'Meara, long-time legal counsel for the Nisga'a and the Allied Indian Tribes, dies of natural causes before the government is able to mount a case against him for contravening the 1927 *Indian Act* amendment.
1931	The Native Brotherhood of British Columbia is established.	
1932		Frank Calder joins the Native Brotherhood of British Columbia and is elected secretary.
1949	British Columbia extends the right to vote in provincial elections to status Indians.	Frank Calder is elected to the British Columbia legislature.
1951	The laws prohibiting the potlatch and land claims activity are not included in the revised *Indian Act*.	
1955		The Nisga'a Land Committee is re-established as the Nishga Tribal Council (NTC).
1960	The right to vote in federal elections is extended to status Indians.	
1967		The NTC hires Thomas Berger to take its case to court.
1968		The NTC initiates litigation in the BC Supreme Court (BCSC) on the land question in *Calder et al. v. Attorney-General of British Columbia*.

▶

	British Columbia	The Nisga'a
1969	The federal government issues a white paper recommending that the Indian Affairs Branch be dismantled, that the *Indian Act* be repealed, and that the so-called special status of Canada's Indians be removed. The paper is condemned by most Aboriginal groups and organizations. Only the Nisga'a support it on the condition that Canada recognize their land rights.	The BCSC rules against the Nisga'a in *Calder*.
1970		The BC Court of Appeal (BCCA) unanimously dismisses the Nisga'a appeal in *Calder*.
1973		The SCC decides the *Calder* case, recognizing that Aboriginal title is part of Canadian law, but dividing (three to three) as to whether or not the Nisga'a still have title. The appeal is dismissed, however, since four of the seven judges also rule that the Nisga'a should have obtained the Crown's permission to sue.
1974	A new BC *Crown Proceeding Act* is enacted, and, for the first time, the provincial Crown can be sued without obtaining the Crown's permission to do so – but it is too late for the Nisga'a.	
1976		The federal government begins negotiations with the NTC. British Columbia, however, refuses to participate in the negotiations.
1981	The federal government issues its comprehensive land claims policy, *In All Fairness*.	
1982	The Constitution of Canada recognizes and affirms *existing* Aboriginal treaty rights.	
1983	The Special Committee of the House of Commons on Indian Self-Government recommends the constitutional entrenchment of Aboriginal self-government.	

►

	British Columbia	The Nisga'a
1984	The Gitxsan and Wet'suwet'en issue the writ in *Delgamuukw v. British Columbia*. The SCC decides *R. v. Guerin*, confirming that Aboriginal title is a common law right that does not depend on government recognition.	
1985	The task force charged with reviewing comprehensive claims policy releases its report, *Living Treaties: Lasting Agreements*, proposing that major changes be made to the policy.	
1986	A self-government agreement is concluded with the Sechelt Indian Band. Canada releases its amended Comprehensive Land Claims Policy. This policy is still in force today.	
1989		The federal government and the NTC sign a bilateral framework agreement, setting out the scope, process, and topics for their negotiations.
1990	In *R. v. Sparrow*, the SCC rules that Aboriginal title could be extinguished before 1982 only by legislation evincing a clear and plain intention to do so, thereby adopting the views of Justice Emmett Hall in *Calder*. The federal government, the BC government, and the First Nations Summit (FNS) establish the BC Claims Task Force (BCCTF) to review Aboriginal claims in the province.	The BC government formally joins the Nisga'a negotiations.
1991	The BCCTF makes nineteen recommendations, including a six-step treaty negotiation process and the creation of the BC Treaty Commission (BCTC). All nineteen recommendations are accepted by Canada, British Columbia, and the FNS.	Canada, British Columbia, and the NTC sign a tripartite framework agreement, setting out the scope, process, and topics for their negotiations.
1992	The BCTC is established.	An interim protection measures agreement regarding resources and land use is signed by all parties involved in the Nisga'a negotiations.

▶

	British Columbia	The Nisga'a
1993–94	The BCTC begins treaty negotiations. It accepts statements-of-intent to negotiate from forty-two First Nations and conducts initial meetings.	
1994	Canada publicly acknowledges the existence of the Aboriginal right of self-government at a conference of federal and provincial ministers and Aboriginal leaders.	
1995	The federal government issues *Aboriginal Self-Government: The Government of Canada's Approach to Implementation of the Inherent Right and the Negotiation of Aboriginal Self-Government*, allowing for the negotiation of self-government arrangements.	
1996	The SCC decides a number of important Aboriginal rights cases, including *R. v. Van der Peet* and *R. v. Gladstone*.	The parties reach an agreement-in-principle (AIP) that is approved by the Nisga'a in a vote at New Aiyansh and by the BC and federal governments. Negotiations towards a final agreement begin.
1997	The SCC issues its judgment in *Delgamuukw v. British Columbia*, describing Aboriginal title as a unique property right that since 1982 cannot be unilaterally extinguished by legislation.	
1998		A final agreement is reached that includes 2,019 square kilometres of land and is ratified in a vote by the Nisga'a nation. Drafting begins on the *Nisga'a Final Agreement Act*.
1999	An AIP is signed with the Sechelt First Nation. It is the first to be signed in the BC treaty process (the Nisga'a treaty is outside this process).	British Columbia passes legislation ratifying the final agreement, and all three parties sign.
2000		Federal legislation ratifying the final agreement is passed.
		The BCSC rules in *Campbell v. British Columbia (Attorney General)* that the Nisga'a treaty and its enacting legislation are constitutionally valid.
		The Nisga'a begin implementing the treaty.

►

	British Columbia	The Nisga'a
2004	The SCC decides *Haida Nation v. British Columbia (Minister of Forests)* and *Taku River Tlingit First Nation v. British Columbia (Project Assessment Division)*, holding that governments have an obligation to consult with First Nations even where Aboriginal rights and title have not yet been proved in court.	
2007	The first treaty concluded since the BCTC was established in 1992 is ratified by the Tsawwassen First Nation.	

APPENDIX B
The Nisga'a Petition of 1913

IN THE MATTER OF THE TERRITORY OF THE
NISHGA NATION OR TRIBE OF INDIANS

To the King's Most Excellent Majesty in Council.

PETITION
OF
THE NISHGA NATION OR TRIBE OF
INDIANS.

FOX & PREECE,
15, Dean's Yard,
Westminster, S.W.

IN THE MATTER OF THE TERRITORY OF THE NISHGA NATION OR TRIBE OF INDIANS.

TO THE KING'S MOST EXCELLENT MAJESTY IN COUNCIL.

The HUMBLE PETITION of The Nishga Nation or Tribe of Indians

SHEWETH AS FOLLOWS:—

1. From time immemorial the said Nation or Tribe of Indians exclusively possessed, occupied and used and exercised sovereignty over that portion of the territory now forming the Province of British Columbia which is included within the following limits, that is to say:— Commencing at a stone situate on the south shore of Kinnamox or Quinamass Bay and marking the boundary line between the territory of the said Nishga Nation or Tribe and that of the Tsimpshean Nation or Tribe of Indians, running thence easterly along said boundary line to the height of land lying between the Naas River and the Skeena River, thence in a line following the height of land surrounding the valley of the Naas River and its tributaries to and including the height of land surrounding the north-west end of Mitseah or Meziadan Lake, thence in a straight line to the northerly end of Portland Canal, thence

southerly along the international boundary to the centre line of the passage between Pearse Island and Wales Island, thence south-easterly along said centre line to the centre line of Portland Inlet, thence north-easterly along said centre line to the point at which the same is intersected by the centre line of Kinnamox or Quinamass Bay, thence in a straight line to the point of commencement.

2. Your Petitioners believe the fact to be that, when sovereignty over the territory included within the aforesaid limits (hereinafter referred to as "the said territory") was assumed by Great Britain, such sovereignty was accepted by the said Nation or Tribe, and the right of the said Nation or Tribe to possess, occupy and use the said territory was recognised by Great Britain.

3. From time to time since assuming sovereignty over the said territory the Crown has by Proclamation and otherwise recognized the right of the said Nation or Tribe so to possess, occupy and use the said territory, and, in particular, by the Proclamation of His Majesty King George the Third issued on the 7th day of October, 1763, having the force and effect of a Statute of the Parliament of Great Britain, it was (amongst other things) enacted as follows:—

"And whereas it is just and reasonable, and essential to Our Interest and the Security of Our Colonies, that the several Nations or Tribes of Indians, with whom We are connected, and who live under Our Protection, should not be molested or disturbed in the Possession of such Parts of Our Dominions and Territories as, not having been ceded to, or purchased by Us, are reserved to them, or any of them, as their Hunting Grounds; We do therefore, with the Advice of Our Privy Council, declare it to be Our Royal Will and Pleasure that no Governor or Commander in Chief in any of Our Colonies of Quebec, East Florida, or West Florida, do presume, upon any Pretence whatever, to grant Warrants of Survey, or pass any Patents for Lands beyond the Bounds of their respective Governments, as described in their Commissions; as also, that no Governor or Commander in Chief in any of Our other Colonies or Plantations in America, do presume, for the present, and until Our further Pleasure be known, to grant Warrants of Survey, or pass Patents for any Lands beyond the Heads or Sources of any of the Rivers which fall into the Atlantick Ocean from the West and North West, or upon any Lands whatever, which, not having been ceded to, or purchased by Us as aforesaid, are reserved to the said Indians, or any of them.

"And We do further declare it to be Our Royal Will and Pleasure, for the present as aforesaid, to reserve under Our Sovereignty, Protection, and Dominion, for the Use of the said Indians all the Lands and Territories not included within the Limits of Our said Three New Governments, or within the Limits of the Territory granted to the Hudson's Bay Company, as also all the Lands and Territories lying to the Westward of the Sources of the Rivers which fall into the Sea from the West and North West as aforesaid; and We do hereby strictly forbid, on Pain of Our Displeasure, all Our loving Subjects from making any Purchases or Settlements whatever, or taking Possession of any of the Lands above reserved, without Our special Leave and License for that Purpose first obtained.

"And We do further strictly enjoin and require all Persons whatever, who have either wilfully or inadvertently seated themselves upon any Lands within the Countries above described, or upon any other Lands, which, not having been ceded to, or purchased by Us, are still reserved to the said Indians as aforesaid, forthwith to remove themselves from such Settlements.

"And whereas great Frauds and Abuses have been committed in the purchasing Lands of the Indians, to the great Prejudice of Our Interests, and to the great Dissatisfaction of the said Indians;

"In order therefore to prevent such Irregularities for the future, and to the End that the Indians may be convinced of Our Justice and determined Resolution to remove all reasonable Cause of Discontent, We do with the Advice of Our Privy

Council, strictly enjoin and require, that no private Person do presume to make any Purchase from the said Indians of any Lands reserved to the said Indians, within those Parts of Our Colonies where We have thought proper to allow Settlement; but that if, at any Time any of the said Indians should be inclined to dispose of the said Lands, the same shall be purchased only for Us, in Our Name, at some Publick Meeting or Assembly of the said Indians to be held for that Purpose by the Governor or Commander In Chief of Our Colonies respectively, within which they shall lie; and in case they shall lie within the Limits of any Proprietary Government they shall be purchased only for the Use and In the Name of such Proprietaries, conformable to such Directions and Instructions as We or they shall think proper to give for that Purpose: And We do, by the Advice of Our Privy Council, declare and enjoin, that the Trade with the said Indians shall be free and open to all Our Subjects whatever; provided that every Person, who may incline to trade with the said Indians, do take out a Licence for carrying on such Trade from the Governor or Commander in Chief of any of Our Colonies respectively, where such Persons shall reside; and also give Security to observe such Regulations as We shall at any Time think fit, by Ourselves or by Our Commissaries to be appointed for this Purpose, to direct and appoint for the Benefit of the said Trade; and We do hereby authorize, enjoin, and require the Governors and Commanders In Chief of all Our Colonies respectively, as well Those under Our Immediate Government as Those under the Government and Direction of Proprietaries, to grant such Licences without Fee or Reward, taking especial Care to insert therein a Condition, that such Licence shall be void, and the Security forfeited, in case the Person, to whom the same is granted, shall refuse or neglect to observe such Regulations as We shall think proper to prescribe as aforesaid.

"And We do further expressly enjoin and require all Officers whatever, as well Military as Those employed in the Management and Direction of Indian Affairs within the Territories reserved as aforesaid for the Use of the said Indians, to seize and apprehend all Persons whatever, who, standing charged with Treasons, Misprisions of Treason, Murders, or other Felonies or Misdemeanours, shall fly from Justice, and take Refuge in the said Territory, and to send them under a proper Guard to the Colony where the Crime was committed of which they stand accused, in order to take their Tryal for the same."

4. The said Nishga Nation or Tribe is one of the nations or tribes of Indians mentioned in the said Proclamation as being under the protection of the Sovereign, and all members thereof are Your Majesty's loyal subjects.

5. No part of the said territory has been ceded to or purchased by the Crown, and no part thereof has been purchased from the said Nation or Tribe by the Crown or by any person acting on behalf of the crown, at a public meeting or assembly or otherwise, or by any other person whomsoever.

6. No part of the said territory is within the limits of the territory granted to the Hudson's Bay Company.

7. By Statutes from time to time passed the Imperial Parliament, as Your Petitioners submit, recognized the territory now known as British Columbia as being part of the "Indian Territories," as appears from the Statute 12 and 13 Vict. cap. 48, entitled "An Act to provide for the Administration of Justice in Vancouver's Island," and earlier Statutes therein recited, and from the Statute 21 and 22 Vict., Cap. 99, entitled "An Act to provide for the Government of British Columbia."

8. From time to time the Government of the Province of British Columbia and various persons acting in the name of the Crown, under the assumed authority of the "Land Act" of British Columbia, have made surveys of, granted records of pre-emption of, sold and issued patents for, various parts of the said territory.

9. Together with this Petition are presented two blue prints taken from maps of the said territory prepared in the office of the Surveyor-General at Victoria, in the said Province, showing the various transactions which on the 26th day of September, 1912, had been so entered into in respect of portions of the said territory as aforesaid.

10. Your Petitioners allege that the said transactions and all other similar transactions which have been entered into in respect of any part of the said territory have been so entered into in violation of the provisions of the said Proclamation of King George the Third and without competent authority.

11. From time to time Your Petitioners have delivered to surveyors of the said Government entering the said territory for the purpose of surveying portions thereof, and to persons entering the said territory for the purpose of pre-empting or purchasing portions thereof under the assumed authority of the "Land Act," written notices of protest, of which the following is one:—

> "Whereas, we, the Indian people of the Aiyansh Valley, Naas River, British Columbia, being the lawful and original inhabitants and possessors of all the lands contained therein from time immemorial; and being assured in our possession of the same by the Proclamation of His Majesty, King George III, under date of October 7th, 1763, which Proclamation we hold as our Charter of Rights under the British Crown;
>
> "And whereas, it is provided in the said Proclamation that no private person do presume to make any purchase from us of any lands so reserved to us, until we have ceded the same to the representatives of the Crown in public meeting between us and them;
>
> "And whereas, up to the present time our lands have not been ceded by us to the Crown, nor in any way alienated from us by any agreement or settlement between the representatives of the Crown and ourselves;
>
> "And whereas, our case is now before the Privy Council in England and we are expecting a settlement of the difficulty at present existing between ourselves and the Government of this Province at an early date;
>
> "We do therefore, standing well within our constitutional rights, forbid you to stake off land in this valley, and do hereby protest against your proceeding further into our country with that end in view — until such time as a satisfactory settlement be made between the representatives of the Crown and ourselves.
>
> "Issued by the members of the Indian Land Committee elected by the Indians of the Upper Naas."

12. On the 3rd day of March, 1911, delegates representing the said Nishga Nation or Tribe waited upon the Government of British Columbia, asserted the title of the said Nation or Tribe in respect of the said territory, and protested against the refusal of that Government to recognize such title.

13. Notwithstanding the facts stated in the last preceding two paragraphs hereof the Government of British Columbia and the various persons to whom reference has above been made, have persisted in the course set forth in paragraph 8 hereof.

14. Your Petitioners are aware of the provisions of the agreement made in the year 1871 and set out in Article 13 of the "Terms of Union," and they are also aware of the provisions of an agreement made between a Special Commissioner of the Government of Canada and the Premier of British Columbia on the 24th day of September, 1912, relating to the matter of the so-called reserves, and approved by the Government of Canada on the 27th day of November, 1912, subject to a certain modification mentioned in the Order in Council made on that day. Your Petitioners humbly submit that nothing contained in either of the said two agreements does or can take away any of the rights which they claim.

15. In view of all that has been hereinbefore stated Your Petitioners, claiming to hold a tribal title to the whole of the said territory both by aboriginal right and under the said Proclamation, and having no other recourse for securing justice, humbly place this Petition before Your Majesty as the source and fountain of all justice, having supreme authority over all persons and matters within Your Majesty's dominions, and possessing and exercising upon and with the advice of Your Majesty's Privy Council original judicial jurisdiction.

Your Petitioners most humbly pray that Your Majesty in Council may be pleased to take into Your Most Gracious Consideration the matters hereinbefore set forth, and in exercise of the original jurisdiction to which reference has above been made and all other jurisdiction relating to such matters possessed by Your Majesty in Council, and upon report made to Your Majesty in Council by a Committee of the whole of Your Majesty's Privy Council, or upon report so made by the Judicial Committee or other Committee of the Council to which Your Majesty in Council may see fit to refer the same, may adjudge such matters and determine all questions arising therefrom for decision.

In particular Your Petitioners humbly pray that Your Majesty in Council may be pleased:—

(1) To adjudge and determine the nature and extent of the rights of the said Nishga Nation or Tribe in respect of the said territory.
(2) To adjudge and determine whether, as Your Petitioners humbly submit, the "Land Act" of British Columbia, now in force (Revised Statutes of British Columbia, 1911, Chapter 129), and any previous Land Act of that Province, in so far as the same purport to deal with lands thereby assumed to be the absolute property of the said Province and to confer title in such lands free from the right, title or interest of the Indian Tribes, notwithstanding the fact that such right, title or interest has not been in any way extinguished, are ultra vires of the Legislature of the said Province.

Your Petitioners also humbly pray that Your Majesty may be pleased, in pursuance of the above-mentioned provisions of the said Proclamation of King George the Third, to take such measures as may be found necessary for the protection of the said Nishga Nation or Tribe in the exercise and enjoyment of the right so adjudged and determined.

Your Petitioners also humbly pray that Your Majesty in Council may be pleased to grant to them such further or other relief in the premises as to Your Majesty in Your Great Wisdom shall seem meet.

Your Petitioners also humbly pray that all such orders or directions as to matters of practice or procedure may be made or given as to Your Majesty may seem meet.

Your Petitioners also humbly pray that upon consideration of this Petition by Your Majesty in Council or any Committee of the Privy Council Your Petitioners may be heard by their Counsel.

And Your Petitioners will ever pray, etc.

This Petition is presented by the Nishga Nation or Tribe of Indians through their Agents, Messrs. Fox and Preece, of 15, Dean's Yard, Westminster, Solicitors, in pursuance of a resolution passed at a meeting of the said Nishga Nation or Tribe, held at the Village of Kincolith, situated on the Naas River in the Province of British Columbia, on Wednesday, the 22nd day of January, 1913.

(Courtesy of the Public Record Office, Kew, England)

Notes

Chapter 1: The *Calder* Decision, Aboriginal Title, Treaties, and the Nisga'a

1 *Calder et al. v. Attorney-General of British Columbia,* [1973] S.C.R. 313, 34 D.L.R. (3d) 145 [*Calder,* cited to S.C.R.].

2 The different spellings (Nishga/Nisga'a) reflect different periods in the transliteration of the name of the people of the Nass Valley. "Nishga" was popularized by missionary J.B. McCullagh. The now-current "Nisga'a" is derived from a new system of transliteration invented by linguist Bruce Rigsby in the 1960s to better reflect the proper pronunciation of the word (roughly nis-GA-a). This latter spelling was adopted first by Nisga'a language educators in 1974 and somewhat later by the Nishga Tribal Council itself. The authors would like to thank Dr. Marie-Lucie Tarpent for her generous help in providing this information.

3 See generally Edwin Peter May, "The Nishga Land Claim, 1873-1973" (MA thesis, Simon Fraser University, 1979); E.P. Patterson, "A Decade of Change: Origins of the Nisga'a and Tsimshian Land Protests in the 1880's" (1983) 18 Journal of Canadian Studies 40; Daniel Raunet, *Without Surrender, Without Consent: A History of the Nisga'a Land Claims* (Vancouver: Douglas and McIntyre, 1996); H. Foster, "Honouring the Queen's Flag: A Legal and Historical Perspective on the Nisga'a Treaty" (1998–99) 120 BC Studies 27; T. Molloy, *The World Is Our Witness: The Historic Journey of the Nisga'a into Canada* (Calgary: Fifth House, 2000); Alex Rose, *Spirit Dance at Meziadin: Chief Joseph Gosnell and the Nisga'a Treaty* (Madeira Park, BC: Harbour Publishing, 2000); and Thomas R. Berger, *One Man's Justice: A Life in the Law* (Vancouver: Douglas and McIntyre, 2002).

4 See Paul Tennant, *Aboriginal Peoples and Politics: The Indian Land Question in British Columbia, 1849-1989* (Vancouver: UBC Press, 1990); Robert Galois, "The Indian Rights Association, Native Protest Activity and the 'Land Question' in British Columbia, 1903-1916" (1992) 8(2) Native Studies Review 1. For further information on the history of indigenous advocacy in British Columbia, see A. Morley, *Roar of the Breakers: A Biography of Peter Kelley* (Toronto: Ryerson, 1967); F.E. LaViolette, *The Struggle for Survival: Indian Cultures and the Protestant Ethic in British Columbia* (Toronto: University of Toronto Press, 1973); Norman Klippenstein, "The Haida Struggle for Autonomy on the Haida Gwaii, 1966-1990" (PhD diss., University of Manitoba, 1991; reproduced by UMI Dissertation Services, Ann Arbor, MI, 1995); and Peter McFarlane, *Brotherhood to Nationhood: George Manuel and the Making of the Modern Indian Movement* (Toronto: Between the Lines, 1993).

5 See Donald Craig Mitchell, *Sold American: The Story of Alaska Natives and Their Land, 1867-1959* (Hanover: Dartmouth College, University Press of New England, 1997); and Stephen Haycox, *Alaska: An American Colony* (Seattle: University of Washington Press, 2002).

6 For the text of the Nisga'a treaty, background information, and the four side agreements to the treaty (Own Source Revenue, Fiscal Financing, Taxation, and Harvest Agreements), see the website of the Department of Indian and Northern Affairs, Canada, http://www.ainc-inac.gc.ca/pr/agr/nsga/. For a summary, see British Columbia Ministry of Aboriginal Affairs, *The Nisga'a Final Agreement in Brief: Bringing BC Together* (Victoria: British Columbia Ministry of Aboriginal Affairs, 1999). See also Neil J. Sterritt et al., *Tribal Boundaries in the*

Nass Watershed (Vancouver: UBC Press, 1998); C. Taylor, "On the Nisga'a Treaty" (1999) 120 BC Studies 37; Molloy, *supra* note 3; D. Sanders, "'We Intend to Live Here Forever': A Primer on the Nisga'a Treaty" (2000) 33 UBC Law Review 103; P. Rynard, "'Welcome In, But Check Your Rights at the Door': The James Bay and Nisga'a Agreements in Canada" (2000) 33(2) Canadian Journal of Political Science 211; J. Bowering, "Certainty and Finality in the Nisga'a Agreement" (2002) 11 Dalhousie Journal of Legal Studies 1; and L. Dufraimont, "Continuity and Modification of Aboriginal Rights in the Nisga'a Treaty" (2002) 35 UBC Law Review 455.

7 For example, at a speech in Vancouver delivered in 1969, Pierre Trudeau said: "Aboriginal rights, this really means saying, 'We were here before you. You came and you took the land from us and perhaps you cheated us by giving us some worthless things in return for vast expanses of land and we want to reopen this question. We want you to preserve our aboriginal rights and to restore them to us.' And our answer – it may not be the right one and may not be one which is accepted ... our answer is 'No.'" Reprinted in Peter A. Cumming and Neil H. Mickenberg, eds., *Native Rights in Canada,* 2nd edition (Toronto: Indian-Eskimo Association of Canada and General Publishing, 1972) at 331. Trudeau is also credited with the austere pronouncement, "We say we won't recognize aboriginal rights." See Michael Asch, *Home and Native Land: Aboriginal Rights and the Canadian Constitution,* revised edition (Vancouver: UBC Press 1993) at 9.

8 Canada, Department of Indian Affairs and Northern Development, *Statement of the Government of Canada on Indian Policy* (Ottawa: Queen's Printer, 1969). See Peter H. Russell, "High Courts and the Rights of Aboriginal Peoples: The Limits of Judicial Independence" (1998) 61 Saskatchewan Law Review 247 at 260; and S. Weaver, *Making Canadian Indian Policy: The Hidden Agenda 1968-70* (Toronto: University of Toronto Press, 1981).

9 Including *Sioui v. Quebec (Attorney General),* [1990] 1 S.C.R. 1025, 70 D.L.R. (4th) 427 [*Sioui*]; *R. v. Sparrow,* [1990] 1 S.C.R. 1075, 46 B.C.L.R. (2d) 1 [*Sparrow,* cited to S.C.R.]; *R. v. Van der Peet,* [1996] 2 S.C.R. 507, 137 D.L.R. (4th) 289 [*Van der Peet,* cited to S.C.R.]; and *Delgamuukw v. British Columbia,* [1997] 3 S.C.R. 1010, 153 D.L.R. (4th) 193 [*Delgamuukw,* cited to S.C.R.]. Gérard La Forest's path-breaking study of natural resources law is *Natural Resources and Public Property under the Canadian Constitution* (Toronto: University of Toronto Press, 1969).

10 See also Berger, *supra* note 3.

11 For example, *R. v. Sikyea* (1964), 43 D.L.R. (2d) 150, 46 W.W.R. 65 (N.W.T. C.A.); *R. v. White and Bob* (1964), 50 D.L.R. (2d) 613, 52 W.W.R. 193 (B.C.C.A), aff'd (1965), 52 D.L.R. (2d) 481 (SCC).

12 Russell, *supra* note 8 at 260.

13 Ralph W. Johnson, "Fragile Gains: Two Centuries of Canadian and United States Policy toward Indians" (1991) 66 Washington Law Review 643 at 675. See also the works cited in note 56 later in this chapter.

14 *Calder, supra* note 1 at 317.

15 *Ibid.* at 328.

16 *Ibid.* at 337.

17 *Ibid.* at 404.

18 *Crown Proceedings Act,* S.B.C. 1974, c. 24. See Peter W. Hogg and Patrick J. Monahan, *Liability of the Crown,* 3rd edition (Toronto: Carswell, 2000) at 7-9.

19 *Delgamuukw v. British Columbia* (1991), 79 D.L.R. (4th) 185, [1991] 3 W.W.R. 97 (B.C.S.C.).

20 Task Force to Review Comprehensive Claims Policy, *Living Treaties, Lasting Agreements* (Ottawa: Department of Indian Affairs and Northern Development, 1985) at 12. See also Peter A. Cumming, "Native Land Rights and Northern Development" (1974) 12 Alberta Law Review 57 at 59.

21 Cumming, *supra* note 20 at 59. See also "Indians Have More Land Rights Than He Thought, Trudeau Says" *Globe and Mail,* 8 February 1973, 8.

22 "Statement made by the Honourable Jean Chrétien, minister of Indian Affairs and Northern Development, on claims of Indian and Inuit people, 8 August 1973" (1973) [unpublished, on file with author].

23 Canada, *In All Fairness* (Ottawa: Department of Indian Affairs and Northern Development, 1981).

24 Cited in notes 58-61 later in this chapter.

25 *Mabo v. Queensland (No. 2)* (1992), 175 C.L.R. 1 (H.C. Aust.).

26 Jack Woodward, *Native Law* (Toronto: Carswell, 1989); Shin Imai, *Aboriginal Law Handbook* (Scarborough, ON: Carswell, 1993); D.W. Elliot, ed., *Law and Aboriginal Peoples of Canada,* 3rd edition (North York, ON: Captus Press, 1997); Thomas F. Isaac, *Aboriginal Law: Cases, Materials, and Commentary* (Saskatoon: Purich Publishing, 1995); Robert Alan Reiter, *The Law of First Nations* (Edmonton: Juris Analytica Publishing, 1996); and John J. Borrows and Leonard I. Rotman, *Aboriginal Legal Issues: Cases, Materials and Commentary* (Toronto: Butterworths, 1998).

27 The conference was entitled "'Let Right be Done': *Calder*, Aboriginal Rights and the Treaty Process" and was held at the University of Victoria on 13-15 November 2003.

28 See Dufraimont, *supra* note 6 especially at 465 and 508-9.

29 The final report of the Royal Commission on Aboriginal Peoples was issued in 1996 and can be accessed online at http://www.ainc-inac.gc.ca/ch/rcap/index_e.html. Royal Commission on Aboriginal Peoples, *Report of the Royal Commission on Aboriginal Peoples* (Ottawa: Minister of Supply and Services Canada, 1996). All of the commission's reports and the extensive supporting documentation were published on CD-ROM: Royal Commission on Aboriginal Peoples, *For Seven Generations: An Information Legacy of the Royal Commission on Aboriginal Peoples* (Ottawa: RCAP, 1997). For the federal government's principal response to the Royal Commission on Aboriginal Peoples, see Government of Canada, *Gathering Strength: Canada's Aboriginal Action Plan* (Ottawa: Minister of Indian Affairs and Northern Development, 1997).

30 Brian Slattery, "Understanding Aboriginal Rights" (1987) 66(4) Canadian Bar Review 727; Jeremy Webber, "Relations of Force and Relations of Justice: The Emergence of Normative Community between Colonists and Aboriginal Peoples" (1995) 33 Osgoode Hall Law Journal 623; Royal Commission on Aboriginal Peoples, *Report of the Royal Commission on Aboriginal Peoples, supra* note 29, volume 1 at 99-132; and John Borrows and Leonard Rotman, "The *Sui Generis* Nature of Aboriginal Rights: Does It Make a Difference?" (1997) 36 Alberta Law Review 9.

31 See especially Ingebord Marshall, *A History and Ethnography of the Beothuk* (Montreal and Kingston: McGill-Queen's University Press, 1996); and Ralph T. Pastore, "Archaeology, History and the Beothuks" (1993) Newfoundland Studies 260. Further readings are listed at http://www2.marianopolis.edu/nfldhistory/Beothukbibliography.htm.

32 Ethno-historical studies of colonial relations have therefore been fundamental to our understanding of the emergence of the law of Aboriginal title. The literature is now voluminous, and what follows provides only a selection of the principal book-length works. On pre-contact Aboriginal societies, see Wilson Duff, ed., *Histories, Territories and Laws of the Kitwancool* (Victoria: British Columbia Provincial Museum, 1959); Harold Edson Driver, *Indians of North America,* 2nd edition (Chicago: University of Chicago Press, 1969); Bruce Trigger, *The Children of Aataentsic: A History of the Huron People to 1660* (Montreal and Kingston: McGill-Queen's University Press, 1976); Diamond Jenness, *The Indians of Canada,* 7th edition (Toronto: University of Toronto Press, 1977); Tom McFeat, *Indians of the North Pacific Coast* (Ottawa: Carleton University Press, 1987); Wayne Suttles and William C. Sturtevant, eds., *Handbook of North American Indians,* vol. 7: *Northwest Coast* (Washington: Smithsonian Institution, 1990); Bruce Trigger, *The Huron: Farmers of the North,* revised edition (New York: Holt, Rinehart and Winston, 1990); Bruce Trigger, *The Cambridge History of the Native Peoples of the Americas,* vol. 1: *North America* (New York: Cambridge University Press, 1996); Arthur J. Ray, *I Have Lived Here Since the World Began: An Illustrated History of Canada's Native Peoples* (Toronto: Lester Publishing, 1996); and Olive Dickason, *Canada's First Nations: A History of Founding Peoples from Earliest Times,* 2nd edition (Toronto: Oxford University Press, 1997).

For descriptions of the early years of colonial contact, see Wilson Duff, *The Indian History of British Columbia,* vol. 1: *The Impact of the White Man* (Victoria: British Columbia Provincial Museum, 1965); Bruce Trigger, *The Impact of Europeans on Huronia* (Toronto: Copp Clark, 1969); Leslie F.S. Upton, *Micmacs and Colonists: Indian-White Relations in the Maritimes, 1713-1867* (Vancouver: UBC Press, 1979); Bruce Trigger, *Natives and Newcomers: Canada's "Heroic Age" Reconsidered* (Montreal and Kingston: McGill-Queen's University Press,

1985); Denys Delâge, *Le pays renversé: Amérindiens et Européens en Amérique du Nord-Est, 1600-1664* (Montréal: Boréal Express, 1985), translated by Jane Brierley as *Bitter Feast: Amerindians and Europeans in Northeastern North America, 1600-64* (Vancouver: UBC Press, 1993); William C. Sturtevant, ed., *Handbook of North American Indians*, vol. 4: *History of Indian-White Relations* (Washington: Smithsonian Institution, 1988); Richard White, *The Middle Ground: Indians, Empires, and Republics in the Great Lakes Region, 1650-1815* (Cambridge: Cambridge University Press, 1991); J.R. Miller, *Skyscrapers Hide the Heavens: A History of Indian-White Relations in Canada* (Toronto: University of Toronto Press, 1991); James R. Gibson, *Otter Skins, Boston Ships and China Goods: The Maritime Fur Trade of the Northwest Coast, 1785-1841* (Montreal and Kingston: McGill-Queen's University Press, 1992); Robin Fisher, *Contact and Conflict: Indian-European Relations in British Columbia, 1774-1890*, 2nd edition (Vancouver: UBC Press, 1992); Anthony Pagden, *European Encounters with the New World: From Renaissance to Romanticism* (London: Yale University Press, 1993); Royal Commission on Aboriginal Peoples, *supra* note 29; National Archives of Canada, *Aboriginal Peoples and Archives: A Brief History of Aboriginal and European Relations in Canada* (Ottawa: National Archives of Canada, 1997); Richard Mackie, *Trading beyond the Mountains: The British Fur Trade on the Pacific, 1793-1843* (Vancouver: UBC Press, 1997); Richard C. Harris and Jean Barman, eds., *Native Peoples and Colonialism* (Vancouver: UBC Press, 1997); Sarah Carter, *Aboriginal People and Colonizers of Western Canada to 1900* (Toronto: University of Toronto Press, 1999); Julie Evans et al., *Equal Subjects, Unequal Rights: Indigenous Peoples in British Settler Colonies, 1830-1910* (New York: Manchester University Press, 2003); John C. Weaver, *The Great Land Rush and the Making of the Modern World, 1650-1900* (Montreal and Kingston: McGill-Queen's University Press, 2003); Gilles Havard, *Empire et métissages: Indiens et Français dans le Pays d'en Haut, 1660-1715*.(Sillery, QC: Septentrion, 2003); and Stuart Banner, *How the Indians Lost Their Land: Law and Power on the Frontier* (Cambridge, MA: Belknap Press of Harvard University Press, 2005).

33 Royal Proclamation of 7 October 1763, R.S.C. 1985, App. II, No. 1. For discussion of the nature and impact of the proclamation, see Brian Slattery, *The Land Rights of Indigenous Canadian Peoples, as Affected by the Crown's Acquisition of Their Territories* (Saskatoon: Native Law Centre, University of Saskatchewan, 1979); Jack Stagg, *Anglo-Indian Relations in North America to 1763 and an Analysis of the Royal Proclamation of 7 October 1763* (Ottawa: Research Branch, Indian and Northern Affairs Canada, 1981); and John Borrows, "Constitutional Law from a First Nation Perspective: Self-Government and the Royal Proclamation" (1994) 28 UBC Law Review 1.

34 Which in turn have much in common with other British colonies. See Hamar Foster, "Indigenous Peoples and the Law: The Colonial Legacy in Australia, Canada, New Zealand and the United States," in D. Johnston and G. Ferguson, eds., *Asia Pacific Legal Development* (Vancouver: UBC Press, 1998), 466-500; Weaver, *supra* note 32; and the chapters of Garth Nettheim and David Williams in this book.

35 *Fletcher v. Peck*, 10 U.S. 97 (1810); *Johnson and Graham's Lessee v. M'Intosh*, 8 Wheaton 543, 21 U.S. 543 (1823); *Cherokee Nation v. State of Georgia*, 5 Pet. 1, 30 U.S. 1 (1831); and *Worcester v. State of Georgia*, 6 Pet. 515, 31 U.S. 515 (1832).

36 For discussion of the Marshall judgments and their impact, see, for example, Felix S. Cohen, "Original Indian Title" (1947) 32 Minnesota Law Review 28; H.R. Berman, "The Concept of Aboriginal Rights in the Early Legal History of the United States" (1978) 27 Buffalo Law Review 637; C. Wilkinson, *American Indians, Time and the Law* (New Haven: Yale University Press, 1987); and Eric Kades, "History and Interpretation of the Great Case of *Johnson v. M'Intosh*" (2001) 19 Law and History Review 67.

37 Royal Proclamation of 1763, *supra* note 33.

38 See, for example, *R. v. Marshall; R. v. Bernard*, 2005 SCC 43 at para. 70.

39 See Jeremy Webber, "Beyond Regret: *Mabo's* Implications for Australian Constitutionalism," in Duncan Ivison, Paul Patton, and Will Sanders, eds., *Political Theory and the Rights of Indigenous Peoples* (Cambridge: Cambridge University Press, 2000), 60 at 70-72; and Kent McNeil, "Aboriginal Rights in Canada: From Title to Land to Territorial Sovereignty," in Kent McNeil, ed., *Emerging Justice? Essays on Indigenous Rights in Canada and Australia* (Saskatoon: Native Law Centre, University of Saskatchewan, 2001), 58 at 89-95.

40 *Indian Act*, R.S.C. 1985, c. I-5.
41 Dawnis Kennedy, "Reconciliation without Respect? Section 35 and Indigenous Legal Orders" (paper presented to "Law's Empire: The Annual Conference of the Canadian Law and Society Association," Harrison Hot Springs, 25-29 June 2005).
42 McNeil, *supra* note 39 at 95.
43 For an overview of the different periods of treaty making, see Miller, *supra* note 32; and Hamar Foster, "Canadian Indians, Time and the Law" (1994) 7 Western Legal History 69. See also Darlene Johnston, *The Taking of Indian Lands in Canada: Consent or Coercion?* (Saskatoon: Native Law Centre, University of Saskatchewan, 1989).
44 For early treaties in eastern Canada, see Canada, Department of Indian Affairs, *Indian Treaties and Surrenders from 1680 to 1890 in Two Volumes* (Ottawa: Queen's Printer, 1891; Coles reprint 1971); Stagg, *supra* note 33; Ian Getty and Robert J. Surtees, "Indian Land Cessions in Ontario, 1763-1862: The Evolution of a System" (PhD diss., Carleton University, 1983); W. Dougherty, *Maritime Indian Treaties in Historical Perspective* (Ottawa: Treaties and Historical Research Centre, Department of Indian and Northern Affairs Canada, 1983); Robert J. Surtees, *Treaty Research Report: The Robinson Treaties* (Ottawa: Department of Indian Affairs and Northern Development, 1986), http://www.ainc-inac.gc.ca/pr/trts/hti/trob/trerob_e.pdf; Stewart C. Paul and Ronald E. Gaffney, *As Long as the Sun and Moon Shall Endure: A Brief History of the Maritime First Nations Treaties, 1675-1783* (Fredericton: Paul and Gaffney and Associates, 1986); MAWIW District Council and Indian and Northern Affairs Canada, *"We Should Walk in the Tract Mr. Dummer Made": A Written Joint Assessment of Historical Materials ... Relative to Dummer's Treaty of 1725 and All Other Related or Relevant Maritime Treaties and Treaty Negotiations* (Ottawa: Department of Indian and Northern Affairs Canada, 1992); Gilles Havard, *La Grande Paix de Montréal de 1701: Les voies de la diplomatie franco-amérindienne* (Montreal: Recherches amérindiennes au Québec, 1992), translated by Phyllis Aronoff and Howard Scott as *The Great Peace of Montreal of 1701: French-Native Diplomacy in the Seventeenth Century* (Montreal and Kingston: McGill-Queen's University Press, 2001); and Daniel N. Paul, *We Were Not the Savages: A Micmac Perspective on the Collision of European and Aboriginal Civilizations* (Halifax: Nimbus Publishing, 1993), esp. chapters 5-8.
      For primary materials on the Douglas Treaties, including the text of the treaties themselves, see Hartwell Bowsfield, ed., *Fort Victoria Letters, 1846-1851* (Winnipeg: Hudson's Bay Record Society, 1979); and *Papers Connected with the Indian Land Question, 1850-1875* (Victoria: Queen's Printer, 1875; repr. 1987). For analysis of the Douglas Treaties, see Wilson Duff, "The Fort Victoria Treaties" (1969) 1 BC Studies 3; Dennis Madill, *British Columbia Indian Treaties in Historical Perspective* (Ottawa: Indian and Northern Affairs Canada, 1981); James E. Hendrickson, *The Aboriginal Land Policy of Governor James Douglas, 1849-1864* (Burnaby, BC: Simon Fraser University, 1988); Hamar Foster, "The Saanichton Bay Marina Case: Imperial Law, Colonial History, and Competing Theories of Aboriginal Title," (1989) 23 UBC Law Review 629-50; Dave Elliott, Sr., and Janet Poth, *Saltwater People*, 2nd edition (Saanichton, BC: School District No. 63, 1990); Cole Harris, *Making Native Space: Colonialism, Resistance, and Reserves in British Columbia* (Vancouver: UBC Press, 2002), chapter 2; and Hamar Foster and Alan Grove, "'Trespassers on the Soil': *United States v. Tom* and a New Perspective on the Short History of Treaty Making in Nineteenth Century British Columbia" (2003) 138-39 BC Studies 51.
45 *R. v. Bartleman* (1984), 55 B.C.L.R. 78, 12 D.L.R. (4th) 73 (B.C.C.A.); *Saanichton Marina Ltd. v. Claxton* (1989), 36 B.C.L.R. (2d) 79, 57 D.L.R. (4th) 161 (B.C.C.A); *Sioui, supra* note 9; *R. v. Marshall (No. 1)*, [1999] S.C.R. 456, 177 D.L.R. (4th) 513; and *R. v. Marshall; R. v. Bernard, supra* note 38.
46 *R. v. White and Bob, supra* note 11. For background and discussion see Berger, *supra* note 3 at 87ff.
47 The text of the principal treaties can be found in: Alexander Morris, *The Treaties of Canada with the Indians of Manitoba and the North-West Territories* (Toronto: Belfords, Clarke and Company, 1880; Coles reprint 1979); Canada, Department of Indian Affairs, *supra* note 44; and at http://www.ainc-inac.gc.ca/pr/trts/hti/site/guindex_e.html. For analysis, see Surtees, *supra* note 44; Bruce W. Hodgins and Jamie Benidickson, *The Temagami Experience:*

Recreation, Resources and Aboriginal Rights in the Northern Ontario Wilderness (Toronto: University of Toronto Press, 1989); James Morrison, "The Robinson Treaties of 1850: A Case Study," reprinted in a CD-ROM: *For Seven Generations: An Information Legacy of the Royal Commission on Aboriginal Peoples* (Ottawa: Canada Communications Group, 1996); and Janet E. Chute, *The Legacy of Shingwaukonse: A Century of Native Leadership* (Toronto: University of Toronto Press, 1998), especially chapter 5.

48 Morris, *supra* note 47; Rene Fumoleau, *As Long as This Land Shall Last: A History of Treaty 8 and Treaty 11, 1870-1939* (Toronto: McClelland and Stewart, 1973); R. Price, ed., *The Spirit of the Alberta Indian Treaties*, 3rd edition (Edmonton: University of Alberta Press,1999); John Leonard Taylor, *Treaty Research Report: Treaty Four (1874)* (Ottawa: Indian Affairs and Northern Development, 1987); Wendy Aasen, *The Spirit and Intent of Treaty 8 in the Northwest Territories: As Long As the Sun Shines, the River Flows, and the Grass Grows* (Yellowknife: Treaty 8 Tribal Council, 1994); Sharon Venne, "Understanding Treaty 6: An Indigenous Perspective," in Michael Asch, ed., *Aboriginal and Treaty Rights in Canada: Essays on Law, Equality and Respect for Difference* (Vancouver: UBC Press, 1997); Mike Robinson, ed., *In the Spirit of Inistisinni: Exploratory Discussions on the Spirit and Intent of Treaty 7* (Calgary: Arctic Institute of North America, 1998); Arthur J. Ray, Jim Miller, and Frank Tough, *Bounty and Benevolence: A History of Saskatchewan Treaties* (Montreal and Kingston: McGill-Queen's University Press, 2000); and R. Metcs and C. Devlin, "Land Entitlement under Treaty 8" (2004) 41(4) Alberta Law Review 951.

49 See Government of Canada, Indian and Northern Affairs, Treaty Guide to the Williams Treaties, http://www.ainc-inac.gc.ca/pr/trts/hti/guid/twil_e.html.

50 For a discussion of the status and interpretation of treaties generally, see Price, *supra* note 48; Sébastien Grammond, *Les Traités entre l'Etat Canadien et les Peuples Autochtones* (Cowansville: Editions Yvon Blais, 1994); Robert Alan Reiter, *The Law of Canadian Indian Treaties* (Edmonton: Juris Analytica, 1995); Treaty 7 Elders and Tribal Council with Walter Hildebrandt, Dorothy First Rider, and Sarah Carter, *The True Spirit and Original Intent of Treaty 7* (Montreal and Kingston: McGill-Queen's University Press, 1996); James (Sákéj) Youngblood Henderson, "Interpreting Sui Generis Treaties" (1997) 36 Alberta Law Review 46; Leonard I. Rotman, "Taking Aim at the Canons of Treaty Interpretation in Canadian Aboriginal Rights Jurisprudence" (1997) 46 University of New Brunswick Law Journal 11; Michael Enright, *Whose Country Is It? Law, Politics and Indian Rights* (Ottawa: Bowdens Media Monitoring, 1999); Gordon Christie, "Justifying Principles of Treaty Interpretation" (2000) 26 Queen's Law Journal 143; and Harold Cardinal and Walter Hildebrandt, *Treaty Elders of Saskatchewan: Our Dream Is That Our Peoples Will One Day Be Clearly Recognized as Nations* (Calgary: University of Calgary Press, 2000).

51 Canada, Department of Indian Affairs and Northern Development, *Outstanding Business: A Native Claims Policy: Specific Claims* (Ottawa: Minister of Supply and Services Canada, 1982). This policy was revised in 1991, but a new document was not published.

52 *Indian Act*, *supra* note 40. For an annotated version, see Shin Imai, *The 1997 Annotated Indian Act* (Toronto: Carswell Thomson, 1996). For history and discussion, see E. Brian Titley, *A Narrow Vision: Duncan Campbell Scott and the Administration of Indian Affairs in Canada* (Vancouver: UBC Press, 1986); Richard H. Bartlett, *Indian Act of Canada*, 2nd edition (Saskatoon: Native Law Centre, University of Saskatchewan, 1988); John S. Molloy, "The Early Indian Acts: Developmental Strategy and Constitutional Change," in J.R. Miller, ed., *Sweet Promises: A Reader on Indian-White Relations in Canada* (Toronto: University of Toronto Press, 1991), 145; Larry Gilbert, *Entitlement to Indian Status and Membership Codes in Canada* (Scarborough: Carswell, 1996); Royal Commission on Aboriginal Peoples, *supra* note 29 at 255-332; Cathy Plewes, *First Nations, the Church, State and Image: Policy and Ideals Reflected in the Indian Act of 1876* (Ann Arbor, MI: University of Michigan, 1999); and Kent McNeil, "Aboriginal Title and Section 88 of the Indian Act" (2001) 34 UBC Law Review 159-194.

53 For more on the restriction of Aboriginal access to resources and the reserve system, see Robert J. Surtees, "The Development of an Indian Reserve Policy in Canada" (1969) 61 Ontario History 87; Robert E. Cail, *Land, Man and the Law: The Disposal of Crown Lands in British Columbia* (Vancouver: UBC Press, 1974); Richard H. Bartlett, *Indian Reserves and*

Aboriginal Lands in Canada: A Homeland: A Study in Law and History (Saskatoon: Native Law Centre, University of Saskatchewan, 1990); Ken S. Coates, *Best Left as Indians: Native-White Relations in the Yukon Territory, 1840-1973* (Montreal and Kingston: McGill-Queen's University Press, 1991); Peter Carstens, *The Queen's People: A Study of Hegemony, Coercion, and Accommodation among the Okanagan of Canada* (Toronto: University of Toronto Press, 1991); Dianne Newell, *Tangled Webs of History: Indians and the Law in Canada's Pacific Coast Fisheries* (Toronto: University of Toronto Press, 1993; Duane Thomson, "The Response of the Okanagan Indians to European Settlement" (1994) 101 BC Studies 96; Douglas C. Harris, *Fish, Law, and Colonialism: The Legal Capture of Salmon in British Columbia* (Toronto: University of Toronto Press, 2001); and Harris, *supra* note 44.

54 For an introduction to these issues, see Royal Commission on Aboriginal Peoples, *supra* note 29, especially volume 1, Part II, and volumes 3 and 4; and Emma D. LaRocque, "Violence in Aboriginal Communities," in Royal Commission on Aboriginal Peoples, ed., *The Path to Healing: Report of the Round Table on Aboriginal Health and Social Issues* (Ottawa: Minister of Supply and Services, 1993). In recent years, there has been a growing literature focusing on the situation of women. For work on these issues by Aboriginal authors, see Patricia Monture, "Ka-Nin-Geh-Heh-Gah-E-Sa-Nonh-Yah-Gah" (1988) 2 Canadian Journal of Women and the Law 159; Mary Ellen Turpel, "Home/Land" (1991) 10 Canadian Journal of Family Law 17; Patricia Monture-Okanee, "The Roles and Responsibilities of Aboriginal Women: Reclaiming Justice" (1992) 56 Saskatchewan Law Review 237; Mary Ellen Turpel, "Patriarchy and Paternalism: The Legacy of the Canadian State for First Nations Women" (1993) 6 Canadian Journal of Women and the Law 174; Teressa Nahanee, "Dancing with a Gorilla: Aboriginal Women, Justice and the Charter," in Royal Commission on Aboriginal Peoples, ed., *Aboriginal Peoples and the Justice System: Report of the National Round Table on Aboriginal Justice Issues* (Ottawa: Minister of Supply and Services, 1993); Sharon McIvor, "The Indian Act as Patriarchal Control Of Women" (1994) 1 Aboriginal Women's Law Journal 41; Christina Miller and Patricia Chuchryk, eds., *Women of the First Nations: Power, Wisdom, Strength* (Winnipeg: University of Manitoba Press, 1996); Venne, *supra* note 48; and Teressa Nahanee, "Indian Women, Sex Equality and the Charter," in Caroline Andrew and Sandra Rodgers, eds., *Women and the Canadian State* (Montreal and Kingston: McGill-Queen's University Press, 1997) at 89.

55 *St. Catherine's Milling & Lumber Co. v. R.*, 14 App. Cas. 46 (P.C.) (1888).

56 Canada, Department of Indian Affairs and Northern Development, *supra* note 8. For important contributions from, and overviews of, this era, see Harold Cardinal, *The Unjust Society: The Tragedy of Canada's Indians* (Edmonton: Hurtig, 1969); Indian-Eskimo Association of Canada, *Native Rights in Canada* (Toronto: n.p., 1970) (although, in this case, the most influential edition may have been the second); Cumming and Mickenberg, eds., *supra* note 7; George Manuel and Michael Posluns, *The Fourth World: An Indian Reality* (Don Mills: Collier-Macmillan, 1974); Harold Cardinal, *The Rebirth of Canada's Indians* (Edmonton: Hurtig, 1977); Ian A.L. Getty and Antoine S. Lussier, eds., *As Long as the Sun Shines and the Water Flows* (Vancouver: UBC Press, 1983); and Weaver, *supra* note 8.

57 See, for example, Hugh Brody, *Maps and Dreams: Indians and the British Columbia Frontier* (Vancouver: Douglas and McIntyre, 1981); James B. Waldram, *As Long as the Rivers Run: Hydroelectric Development and Native Communities in Western Canada* (Winnipeg: University of Manitoba Press, 1988); Boyce Richardson, *Strangers Devour the Land* (Post Mills, VT: Chelsea Green Publishing, 1991); Ken S. Coates, ed., *Aboriginal Land Claims in Canada: A Regional Perspective* (Toronto: Copp Clark Pitman, 1992).

58 *James Bay and Northern Quebec Agreement and Complementary Agreements* (Sainte-Foy: Gouvernement du Québec, 1998) *[JBNQA]*. See Richard F. Salisbury, *A Homeland for the Cree: Regional Development in James Bay, 1971-1981* (Montreal and Kingston: McGill-Queen's University Press, 1986); Sylvie Vincent and Garry Bowers, eds., *Baie James et Nord Québécois: Dix Ans Après* (Montreal: Recherches amérindiennes au Québec, 1988); Roy MacGregor, *Chief: The Fearless Vision of Billy Diamond* (Markham, ON: Viking, 1989); Richardson, *supra* note 57; Colin H. Scott, ed., *Aboriginal Autonomy and Development in Northern Quebec and Labrador* (Vancouver: UBC Press, 2001); and Toby Morantz, *The White Man's Gonna Getcha: The Colonial Challenge to the Crees in Quebec* (Montreal and Kingston: McGill-Queen's

University Press, 2002). At roughly the same time as the *JBNQA* was being negotiated, Thomas Berger (counsel in *Calder* and, by 1974, a justice of the Supreme Court of British Columbia), conducted a highly publicized inquiry into a proposal to build a pipeline down the Mackenzie Valley in the Northwest Territories. Both the inquiry and its report (the chief recommendation of which was the imposition of a moratorium until Aboriginal title had been dealt with – a recommendation that was accepted) did much to sensitize the Canadian public to issues of Aboriginal title. See Thomas R. Berger, *Northern Frontier, Northern Homeland: The Report of the Mackenzie Valley Pipeline Inquiry* (Toronto: James Lorimer and Company, 1977).

59 *Chief Max "One-Onti" Gros-Louis c. Société de développement de la Baie James*, [1974] R.P. 38 (Superior Court); and *Société de développement de la Baie James c. Kanatewat*, [1975] C.A. 166 (Court of Appeal).

60 *Northeastern Quebec Agreement*, cited in *JBNQA, supra* note 58.

61 For the text of these agreements and others, see the website of the Department of Indian and Northern Affairs, http://www.ainc-inac.gc.ca/pr/agr/index_e.html#FinalAgreements2.

62 See the website of the Department of Indian and Northern Affairs, http://www.ainc-inac.gc.ca/bc/treapro/ston/nwdev/nwdev_e.html. On the BC treaty process, see Christopher McKee, *Treaty Talks in British Columbia: Negotiating a Mutually Beneficial Future*, 2nd edition (Vancouver: UBC Press, 2000); British Columbia Treaty Commission, *What's the Deal with Treaties? A Lay Person's Guide to Treaty Making in British Columbia* (Vancouver: BC Treaty Commission, 2003); Andrew Woolford, *Between Justice and Certainty: Treaty Making in British Columbia* (Vancouver: UBC Press, 2005); and the report that is the foundation of the BC treaty process, *The Report of the British Columbia Claims Task Force* (Vancouver: British Columbia Claims Task Force, 1991). See also the materials on the Nisga'a treaty, *supra* note 6.

63 Indian and Northern Affairs, Canada, "Nisga'a Final Agreement Act Issue Papers," http://dsp-psd.pwgsc.gc.ca/Collection/R72-289-2000-3E.pdf, especially at 3.2, 23.1, and 23.4. Note that this is calculated on the basis of payments to be made over fifteen years, the last seven of which will involve re-calculations based on indices of inflation. This sum is therefore approximate, as is the estimate of the Nisga'a population.

64 For a comprehensive and balanced overview of the cases to date, see, for example, McNeil, *Emerging Justice, supra* note 39; and Peter W. Hogg, *Constitutional Law of Canada: 2005 Student Edition* (Scarborough, ON: Thomson Carswell, 2005) at 619ff.

65 For consideration of the relative role of courts and negotiations in Aboriginal/non-Aboriginal relations, see Mary Ellen Turpel, "Aboriginal Peoples and the Canadian Charter: Interpretive Monopolies, Cultural Difference" (1989–90) 6 Canadian Human Rights Yearbook 3; Russell, *supra* note 8; P. Macklem and R. Townshend, "Resorting to Court: Can the Judiciary Deliver Justice for First Nations?" in D. Engelstad and J. Bird, eds., *Nation to Nation: Aboriginal Sovereignty and the Future of Canada* (Concord: Anansi Press, 1992); Webber, *supra* note 39; Ross Poole, "Justice or Appropriation? Indigenous Claims and Liberal Theory" (2001) 101 Radical Philosophy 5; Gordon Christie, "Judicial Justification of Recent Development in Aboriginal Law" (2002) 17 Canadian Journal of Law and Society 41; Gordon Christie, "Law, Theory and Aboriginal Peoples" (2003) 2 Indigenous Law Journal 67; and Kerry Wilkins, "Conclusion: Judicial Aesthetics and Aboriginal Claims," in Kerry Wilkins, ed., *Advancing Aboriginal Claims: Visions/Strategies/Directions* (Saskatoon: Purich, 2004), 288.

66 For comprehensive discussions of the law of Aboriginal title, see Cumming and Mickenberg, eds., *supra* note 7; Slattery, *supra* note 30; Kent McNeil, *Common Law Aboriginal Title* (Oxford: Clarendon Press, 1989); Woodward, *supra* note 26; Shin Imai, Katharine Logan, and Garry Stein, *Aboriginal Law Handbook* (Scarborough, ON: Carswell Thomson, 1993); Elliot, *supra* note 26; Kent McNeil, *Defining Aboriginal Title in the 90's: Has the Supreme Court Finally Got It Right?* (Toronto: Robarts Centre for Canadian Studies, York University, 1998); and McNeil, *Emerging Justice, supra* note 39.

For historical discussions of Aboriginal title in Canada, see Louis A Knafla, ed., *Law and Justice in a New Land: Essays in Western Canadian Legal History* (Toronto: Carswell, 1986) at 79-164; Paul Tennant, "Aboriginal Rights and the Canadian Legal System: The West Coast Anomaly," in John McLaren, Hamar Foster, and Chet Orloff, eds., *Law for the Elephant, Law for the Beaver: Essays in the Legal History of the North American West* (Regina, SK: Canadian

Plains Research Centre, 1992), 106; and Wesley Pue, DeLloyd J. Guth, and Christopher John Basil English, eds., *Canada's Legal Inheritances* (Winnipeg: Canadian Legal History Project, 2001), especially sections I, X, and XI.

For discussions of Aboriginal title in its social and political context, see Asch, *supra* note 7; Menno Boldt, Anthony Long, and Leroy Little Bear, eds., *Quest for Justice: Aboriginal Rights in Canada* (Toronto: University of Toronto Press, 1985); Donald J. Purich, *Our Land: Native Rights in Canada* (Toronto: James Lorimer and Company, 1986); Frank Cassidy, ed., *Aboriginal Title in British Columbia: Delgamuukw v. The Queen* (Montreal: Institute for Research on Public Policy, 1992); M. Asch and N. Zlotkin, "Affirming Aboriginal Title: A New Basis for Comprehensive Claims Negotiations," in M. Asch, ed., *supra* note 48, 208; Patrick Macklem, "What's Law Got to Do with It? The Protection of Aboriginal Title in Canada" (1997) 35 Osgoode Hall Law Journal 125.

For comparison with other common law jurisdictions, see A. Fleras and J.E. Elliot, *The Nations Within: Aboriginal-State Relations in Canada, the United States and New Zealand* (Toronto: Oxford University Press, 1992); Paul Havemann, ed., *New Frontiers? First Nations' Rights in the Settler Dominions: Australia, Canada and New Zealand/Aotearoa 1975-1995* (Auckland: Oxford University Press, 1999); and P.G. McHugh, *Aboriginal Societies and the Common Law: A History of Sovereignty, Status and Self-determination* (Oxford: Oxford University Press, 2004).

67   *Delgamuukw, supra* note 9. For the text of this decision in non-law libraries, see *Delgamuukw: The Supreme Court of Canada Decision on Aboriginal Title* (Vancouver: Greystone Books, 1998), with introduction by Stan Persky. For discussion, see N. Bankes, "*Delgamuukw,* Division of Powers and Provincial Land and Resource Laws: Some Implications for Provincial Resource Rights" (1998) 32 UBC Law Review 317-51; Hamar Foster, "Aboriginal Title and the Provincial Obligation to Respect It: Is *Delgamuukw v. British Columbia* 'Invented Law'?" (1998) 56 The Advocate 221; Melvin H. Smith, *The Delgamuukw Case: What Does It Mean and What Do We Do Now?* (Vancouver: Fraser Institute, 1998); Richard H. Bartlett and Jill Milroy, *Native Title Claims in Canada and Australia: Delgamuukw and Miriuwung Gajerrong* (Perth: University of Western Australia, 1999); John Borrows, "Sovereignty's Alchemy: An Analysis of *Delgamuukw v. British Columbia*" (1999) 37 Osgoode Hall Law Journal 537-96; Gordon Christie, "*Delgamuukw* and the Protection of Aboriginal Land Interests" (2001) 32 Ottawa Law Review 85-115; B. Donovan, "The Evolution and Present Status of Common Law Aboriginal Title in Canada: The Law's Crooked Path and the Hollow Promise of *Delgamuukw*" (2002) 35 UBC Law Review 43; and Val Napoleon, "*Delgamuukw:* A Legal Straightjacket for Oral Histories?" (2005) 20 Canadian Journal of Law and Society 123.

For background, see *Spirit in the Land: Statement of the Gitksan and Wetsuweten Hereditary Chiefs in the Supreme Court of British Columbia, 1987-1990* (Gabriola, BC: Reflections, 1992); Don Monet and Ardyth Wilson, *Colonialism on Trial: Indigenous Land Rights and the Gitksan-We'Suwet'En Sovereignty Case* (Philadelphia: New Society Publishers, 1992); Antonia Mills, *Eagle Down Is Our Law: Witsuwit'en Law, Feasts, and Land Claims* (Vancouver: UBC Press, 1994); Sterritt et al., *supra* note 6; Dara Culhane, *The Pleasure of the Crown: Anthropology, Law and First Nations* (Burnaby, BC: Talonbooks, 1998); and Richard Daly, *Our Box Was Full: An Ethnography for the Delgamuukw Plaintiffs* (Vancouver: UBC Press, 2005). The discussion that follows is largely drawn from *Delgamuukw.*

68   *Delgamuukw, supra* note 9 at para. 125.

69   Some scholarly writing does deal directly with the law of the Aboriginal peoples themselves. For examples, see H.G. Barnett, *The Coast Salish of British Columbia* (Eugene: University of Oregon Press, 1955); Duff, ed., *Kitwancool, supra* note 32; Trigger, *Children of Aataentsic, supra* note 32, especially chapter 2; Adrian Tanner, *Bringing Home Animals: Religious Ideology and Mode of Production of the Mistassini Cree Hunters* (New York: St. Martin's Press, 1979); Brody, *supra* note 57; E.Y. Arima, *The West Coast People: The Nootka of Vancouver Island and Cape Flattery* (Victoria: British Columbia Provincial Museum, 1983); Douglas R. Hudson, "The Okanagan Indians of British Columbia," in Jean Webber and the En'owkin Centre, eds., *Okanagan Sources* (Penticton: Theytus Books, 1990); Mills, *supra* note 67; B. Bryan "Property as Ontology: On Aboriginal and English Understandings of Ownership" (2000)

13 Canadian Journal of Law and Jurisprudence 3; Bruce G. Miller, *The Problem of Justice: Tradition and Law in the Coast Salish World* (Lincoln, NB: University of Nebraska Press, 2001); and Kiera L. Ladner, "Governing within an Ecological Context: Creating an AlterNative Understanding of Blackfoot Governance" (2003) 70 Studies in Political Economy 125.

These works have traditionally been written by anthropologists, but increasingly legal scholars too are exploring Aboriginal law. A pioneering and still fascinating example is Karl Llewellyn and E. Adamson Hoebel, *The Cheyenne Way: Conflict and Case Law in Primitive Jurisprudence* (Norman: University of Oklahoma Press, 1941). For a more modern example, see John Borrows, *Recovering Canada: The Resurgence of Indigenous Law* (Toronto: University of Toronto Press, 2002); John Borrows, "Creating an Indigenous Legal Community" (2005) 50 McGill Law Journal 172. There is also a voluminous literature on Aboriginal sentencing and conflict resolution, for example, Leroy Little Bear, "Dispute Settlement among the Naidanac," in Richard Devlin, ed., *Introduction to Jurisprudence* (Toronto: Emond Montgomery, 1990); Emily Mansfield, "Balance and Harmony: Peacemaking in Coast Salish Tribes of the Pacific Northwest" (1993) 10 Mediation Quarterly 339; Rupert Ross, *Returning to the Teaching: Exploring Aboriginal Justice* (New York: Penguin, 1996); R.G. Green, *Justice in Aboriginal Communities: Sentencing Alternatives* (Saskatoon: Purich, 1998); and Catherine Bell, *Contemporary Metis Justice: The Settlement Way* (Edmonton: Metis Settlement Appeals Tribunal, 1999).

70 *Van der Peet, supra* note 9, at para. 46.

71 *Ibid.* at para 59.

72 *Ibid.* For discussions of this case, see Russel L. Barsh and James (Sákéj) Youngblood Henderson, "The Supreme Court's *Van Der Peet* Trilogy: Naïve Imperialism and Ropes of Sand" (1997) 42 McGill Law Journal 993; Eric Clemont, "La Trilogie *Van Der Peet, Gladstone, Smokehouse* et la Droit Autochone" (1997) 28 Revue Generale de Droit 89; Kent McNeil, "Aboriginal Title and Aboriginal Rights: What's the Connection?" (1997) 36 Alberta Law Review 759; Leonard I. Rotman, "Hunting for Answers in a Strange Kettle of Fish: Unilateralism, Paternalism and Fiduciary Rhetoric in *Badger* and *Van der Peet*" (1997) 8 Constitutional Forum 40; Anna Zalewski, "From *Sparrow* to *Van Der Peet*: The Evolution of a Definition of Aboriginal Rights" (1997) 55 University of Toronto Faculty Law Review 435; John Borrows, "Frozen Rights in Canada: Constitutional Interpretation and the Trickster" (1997–98) 22 American Indian Law Review 37; Douglas Lambert, "*Van Der Peet* and *Delgamuukw*: Ten Unresolved Issues" (1998) 32 UBC Law Review 249; Jonathan Rudin, "One Step Forward, Two Steps Back: The Political and Institutional Dynamics behind the Supreme Court of Canada's Decisions in *R. v. Sparrow, R. v. Van der Peet* and *Delgamuukw v. British Columbia*" (1998) 13 Journal of Law and Social Policy 67. The discussion that follows is largely drawn from *Van der Peet*, as modified by *Delgamuukw, supra* note 9.

73 See Barsh and Henderson, Borrows, McNeil, Rotman, and Zalewski, all *supra* note 71.

74 *Van der Peet, supra* note 9 at para. 54.

75 *Sparrow, supra* note 9.

76 This was the conclusion of the BC Court of Appeal in *Delgamuukw v. British Columbia* (1993), 104 D.L.R. (4th) 470. See also Hamar Foster, "It Goes without Saying: Precedent and the Doctrine of Extinguishment by Implication in *Delgamuukw v. The Queen*," in Cassidy, ed., *supra* note 66 at 133. The New Democratic Party had formed a new government in British Columbia following the decision of the BC Supreme Court in *Delgamuukw, supra* note 9. It abandoned the previous government's position that Aboriginal title had been extinguished prior to Confederation. The Supreme Court of Canada therefore did not address the issue.

77 *Sparrow, supra* note 9 at 1097.

78 *Delgamuukw, supra* note 9 at para. 175. For discussion generally of the balance between federal and provincial authority with respect to Aboriginal peoples, see Hogg, *supra* note 64 at 602ff; David C. Hawkes, ed., *Aboriginal Peoples and Government Responsibility: Exploring Federal and Provincial Roles* (Ottawa: Carleton University Press, 1989); and Kent McNeil, "Aboriginal Title and the Division of Powers: Rethinking Federal and Provincial Jurisdiction" (1998) 61 Saskatchewan Law Review 431.

79 For discussions of the fiduciary duty, see Hawkes, ed., *supra* note 78; Brian Slattery, "First Nations and the Constitution: A Question of Trust" (1992) 71 Canadian Bar Review 261; Leonard I. Rotman, *Parallel Paths: Fiduciary Doctrine and the Crown-Native Relationship in Canada* (Toronto: University of Toronto Press, 1996); Mary C. Hurley, *The Crown's Fiduciary Relationship with Aboriginal Peoples* (Ottawa: Parliamentary Research Branch, 2000); Kent McNeil, "Fiduciary Obligations and Federal Responsibility for the Aboriginal Peoples," in McNeil, *Emerging Justice, supra* note 39, 309; Michael Coyle, "Loyalty and Distinctiveness: A New Approach to the Crown's Fiduciary Duty toward Aboriginal People" (2002–3) 40 Alberta Law Review 841; Thomas Isaac and A. Knox, "The Crown's Duty to Consult Aboriginal People" (2003–4) 41 Alberta Law Review 49; and James I. Reynolds, *A Breach of Fiduciary Duty: Fiduciary Obligations and Aboriginal Peoples* (Saskatoon: Purich Publishing, 2005).
80 *Guerin v. The Queen,* [1984] 2 S.C.R. 335, 13 D.L.R. (4th) 321.
81 *Wewaykum Indian Band v. Canada,* [2002] 4 S.C.R. 245, 220 D.L.R. (4th)1 at para. 83 [*Wewaykum,* cited to S.C.R.].
82 *Sparrow, supra* note 9 at 1110; *Wewaykum, supra* note 81 at para 80; and *Mikisew Cree First Nation v. Canada (Minister of Canadian Heritage),* 2005 SCC 69 [*Mikisew*].
83 *Haida Nation v. British Columbia (Minister of Forests),* [2004] 3 S.C.R. 511, 245 D.L.R. (4th) 33 at paras. 57-59 [*Haida,* cited to S.C.R.].
84 *Sparrow, supra* note 9; and *Haida, supra* note 83.
85 For example, *Haida, supra* note 83 at paras. 16-20; *Taku River Tlingit First Nation v. British Columbia (Project Assessment Director),* 2004 SCC 74, [2004] 3 S.C.R. 550, 245 D.L.R. (4th) 193 at para. 24 [*Taku River,* cited to S.C.R.]; and *Mikisew, supra* note 82.
86 On the meaning and effect of the constitutional protection of Aboriginal and treaty rights, see Hogg, *supra* note 64 at 619-49; Brian Slattery, "The Hidden Constitution: Aboriginal Rights in Canada" (1984) 32 American Journal of Comparative Law 361; Slattery, *supra* note 30; James (Sákéj) Youngblood Henderson, Marjorie L. Benson, and Isobel M. Findlay, *Aboriginal Tenure in the Constitution of Canada* (Toronto: Carswell, 2000); Patrick Macklem, *Indigenous Difference and the Constitution of Canada* (Toronto: University of Toronto Press, 2001); Ardith Walkem and Halie Bruce, eds., *Box of Treasures or Empty Box: Twenty Years of Section 35* (Penticton: Theytus Books, 2003); Kirsten Matoy Carlson, "Does Constitutional Change Matter: Canada's Recognition of Aboriginal Title" (2005) 22 Arizona Journal of International and Comparative Law 455. For an overview of the movement towards constitutional recognition of Aboriginal peoples generally, see Douglas E. Sanders, "The Renewal of Indian Special Status," in Anne F. Bayefsky and Mary Eberts, eds., *Equality Rights and the Canadian Charter of Rights and Freedoms* (Toronto: Carswell, 1985), 529.
87 *Canadian Charter of Rights and Freedoms,* Part 1 of the *Constitution Act 1982,* being Schedule B to the *Canada Act, 1982* (U.K.), 1982, c. 11.
88 Delia Opekokew, *The First Nations: Indian Government and the Canadian Federation* (Saskatoon: Federation of Saskatchewan Indians, 1980); National Indian Brotherhood, *Constitutional Strategies for Entrenchment of Treaty and Aboriginal Rights: Transcript* (Ottawa: Assembly of First Nations Constitutional Conference, 1980); W. Many Fingers and G. Dacks, "Aboriginal Peoples and the Constitution: Comment" (1981) 19 Alberta Law Review 428, as a response to Douglas E. Sanders, "Aboriginal Peoples and the Constitution" (1981) 19 Alberta Law Review 410; Douglas E. Sanders, "The Indian Lobby," in Keith Banting and Richard Simeon, eds., *And No One Cheered: Federalism, Democracy and the Constitution Act* (Toronto: Methuen, 1983), 301; Douglas E. Sanders, "The Rights of the Aboriginal Peoples of Canada" (1983) 61 Canadian Bar Review 314; Douglas E. Sanders, "Prior Claims: Aboriginal People in the Constitution of Canada," in S.M. Beck and I. Bernier, eds., *Canada and the New Constitution: The Unfinished Agenda,* volume 1 (Montreal: Institute for Research on Public Policy, 1983), 227; and Roy Romanow, John Whyte, and Howard Leeson, *Canada ... Notwithstanding: The Making of the Constitution 1976-1982* (Toronto: Carswell/Methuen, 1984), *passim,* but especially 121-22. In addition to section 35 of the *Constitution Act, 1982,* section 25 of this act stated that *Charter* rights should not be construed so as to derogate from "aboriginal, treaty or other rights or freedoms that pertain to the aboriginal peoples

of Canada." See William Pentney, "The Rights of the Aboriginal Peoples of Canada and the *Constitution Act, 1982:* Part I: The Interpretive Prism of Section 25" (1988) 22 UBC Law Review 21.

89 See Norman K. Zlotkin, "The 1983 and 1984 Constitutional Conferences: Only the Beginning" (1984) 3 Canadian Native Law Reporter 3; David C. Hawkes, *Negotiating Aboriginal Self-Government: Developments Surrounding the 1985 First Ministers' Conference* (Kingston: Institute of Intergovernmental Relations, 1985); Bryan Schwartz, *First Principles, Second Thoughts: Aboriginal Peoples, Constitutional Reform and Canadian Statecraft* (Montreal: Institute for Research on Public Policy, 1986); Douglas E. Sanders, "An Uncertain Path: The Aboriginal Constitutional Conferences," in Joseph M. Weiler and Robin M. Elliot, eds., *Litigating the Values of a Nation: The Canadian Charter of Rights and Freedoms* (Toronto: Carswell, 1986), 63; Norman K. Zlotkin, ed., "Documents from the 1987 First Ministers' Conference on Aboriginal Matters" (1987) 3 Canadian Native Law Reporter 1; and David C. Hawkes, *Aboriginal Peoples and Constitutional Reform: What Have We Learned?* (Kingston: Institute of Intergovernmental Relations, 1989).

90 For discussion of the Aboriginal provisions of the Charlottetown Accord, see K. McRoberts and P.J. Monahan, eds., *The Charlottetown Accord, the Referendum, and the Future of Canada* (Toronto: University of Toronto Press, 1993) at 117ff; Jeremy Webber, *Reimagining Canada: Language, Culture, Community and the Canadian Constitution* (Montreal and Kingston: McGill-Queen's University Press, 1994) at 170-72; Kent McNeil, "The Decolonization of Canada: Moving toward Recognition of Aboriginal Governments" (1994) 7 Western Legal History 113; Peter H. Russell, *Constitutional Odyssey: Can Canadians Become a Sovereign People?* 3rd edition (Toronto: University of Toronto Press, 2004), chapters 10-12. For an argument for constitutional reform in the interest of Aboriginal peoples, co-authored by the then head of the Assembly of First Nations in the wake of the Charlottetown Accord, see Ovide Mercredi and Mary Ellen Turpel, *In the Rapids: Navigating the Future of First Nations* (Toronto: Penguin Books, 1994).

91 The decision that established the fundamental structure of section 35 analysis was *Sparrow*, *supra* note 9. The phrase "compelling and substantial" was used in *Sparrow* at 1113.

92 Conservation, resource management, and the prevention of harm to users were given as examples in *Sparrow*, *supra* note 9 at 1113, economic development and settlement in *Delgamuukw*, *supra* note 9 at para. 165.

93 *Delgamuukw*, *supra* note 9 at paras. 162, 169.

94 The court in *Van der Peet*, *supra* note 9 at para. 29, stated that the Aboriginal interests protected by section 35 "must be identified through an explanation of the basis for the legal doctrine of aboriginal rights, not through an explanation of why that legal doctrine now has constitutional status." But the pre-section 35 authorities canvassed by the court do not emphasize cultural difference as the foundation for the rights. Justice Antonio Lamer adopts this emphasis when he comes to define the distinctive role of section 35 (at para. 44ff).

95 For general discussions of modern treaty making, see Hamar Foster and Alan Grove, "Looking behind the Masks: A Land Claims Discussion Paper for Researchers, Lawyers and Their Employers" (1993) 27 UBC Law Review 213; Royal Commission on Aboriginal Peoples, *Treaty-Making in the Spirit of Co-Existence: An Alternative to Extinguishment* (Ottawa: Minister of Supply and Services Canada, 1995); Royal Commission on Aboriginal Peoples, *Report of the Royal Commission on Aboriginal Peoples*, vol. 2: *Restructuring the Relationship* (Ottawa: Minister of Supply and Services Canada, 1996) at 9-104; Robert Mainville, *An Overview of Aboriginal and Treaty Rights and Compensation for Their Breach* (Saskatoon: Purich, 2001); British Columbia Treaty Commission/Canada Law Commission, *Speaking Truth to Power: A Treaty Forum* (Canada, 2001); Sharon Venne, "Treaty-Making with the Crown," in J. Bird et al., eds., *Nation to Nation: Aboriginal Sovereignty and the Future of Canada* (Toronto: Irwin, 2002).

96 On extinguishment and its alternatives, see Patricia E. Doyle-Bedwell, "The Evolution of the Legal Test of Extinguishment: From *Sparrow* to *Gitskan*" (1993) 6 Canadian Journal of Women and the Law 193; Royal Commission on Aboriginal Peoples, *Treaty Making, supra*

note 95; P. Joffe and M.E. Turpel, *Extinguishment of the Rights of Aboriginal People: Problems and Alternatives*, 3 volumes, June 1995, on CD-ROM: *For Seven Generations: An Information Legacy of the Royal Commission on Aboriginal Peoples* (Ottawa: Royal Commission on Aboriginal Peoples, 1997); Kent McNeil, "Extinguishment of Aboriginal Title in Canada: Treaties, Legislation, and Judicial Discretion" (2001-2) 33 Ottawa Law Review 301; and Kent McNeil, "Racial Discrimination and Unilateral Extinguishment of Native Title" in McNeil, *Emerging Justice, supra* note 39, 357.

97   On co-management arrangements, see E. Pinkerton, ed., *Co-operative Management of Local Fisheries* (Vancouver: UBC Press, 1989); Harry Bombay and John MacTavish, *Co-Management and Other Forms of Agreement in the Forest Sector* (Ottawa: National Aboriginal Forestry Association, 1997); Deborah Curran and Michael M'Gonigle, "Aboriginal Forestry: Community Management as Opportunity and Imperative" (1999) 37 Osgoode Hall Law Journal 731; Donna Craig, "Recognising Indigenous Rights through Co-Management Regimes: Canadian and Australian Experiences" (2002) 6 New Zealand Journal of Environmental Law 211; Paul Nadasdy, *Hunters and Bureaucrats: Power, Knowledge, and Aboriginal-State Relations in the Southwest Yukon* (Vancouver: UBC Press, 2003). For materials on self-government, see notes 104-10 later in this chapter.

98   See, for example, the complex arrangements provided in chapter 16 of the Nisga'a treaty and the Nisga'a Nation Taxation Agreement, *supra* note 6.

99   Royal Commission on Aboriginal Peoples, *supra* note 95, volume 2 at 65-69, 177-84, and 310-21.

100   See Patricia A. Monture-Okanee, "Alternative Dispute Resolution: A Bridge to Aboriginal Experience?" in Catherine Morris and Andrew Pirie, eds., *Qualifications for Dispute Resolution: Perspectives on the Debate* (Victoria, BC: University of Victoria Institute for Dispute Resolution, 1994); Catherine Morris, ed., *Making Peace and Sharing Power: A National Gathering on Aboriginal Peoples and Dispute Resolution, April 30-May 3, 1996, Victoria, British Columbia* (Victoria: University of Victoria Institute for Dispute Resolution, 1997); James Tully, "Aboriginal Peoples: Negotiating Reconciliation," in J. Biderton and A.-G. Gagnon, eds., *Canadian Politics* (Toronto: Broadview Press, 1999); and Catherine Bell and David Kahane, *Intercultural Dispute Resolution in Aboriginal Contexts* (Vancouver: UBC Press, 2004).

101   On the BC treaty process, see the materials cited at note 61 earlier in this chapter. On the Yukon process, see Kirk Cameron and Graham White, *Northern Governments in Transition: Political and Constitutional Development in the Yukon, Nunavut and the Western Northwest Territories* (Montreal: Institute for Research on Public Policy, 1995); Steven M. Cohn, "Competing Claims, Uncertain Sovereignties: Resource Conflict and Evolving Tripartite Federalism in Yukon Territory, Canada" (PhD diss., University of California, Berkeley, 2001); Nadasdy, *supra* note 97; Andrew R. Thompson and Nancy A. Morgan, "Water Issues and Treaty Negotiations: Lessons from the Yukon Experience," in Robert B. Anderson and Robert M. Bone, eds., *Natural Resources and Aboriginal People in Canada* (Concord, ON: Captus, 2003); and Timothy Dickson, "Self-Government by Side Agreement?" (2004) 49 McGill Law Journal 419.

102   Examples of discussion of these challenges in the BC context include McKee, *supra* note 62; and Woolford, *supra* note 62.

103   Royal Commission on Aboriginal Peoples, *supra* note 95, volume 2 at 587-89. See also *Report of the British Columbia Claims Task Force* (Vancouver: British Columbia Claims Task Force, 1991), http://www.bctreaty.net/files_3/pdf_documents/bc_claims_task_force_report.pdf.

104   *Haida, supra* note 83. See Mark Rappaport, "Bringing Meaning to First Nations Consultation in the British Columbia Salmon Aquaculture Industry" (2005) 14 Dalhousie Journal of Legal Studies 149; Timothy Huyer, "Honour of the Crown: The New Approach to Crown-Aboriginal Reconciliation" (2006) 21 Windsor Review of Legal and Social Issues 34. Not everyone agrees that this is a large step forward: see Gordon Christie, "A Colonial Reading of Recent Jurisprudence: *Sparrow, Delgamuukw* and *Haida Nation*" (2005) 23 Windsor Yearbook of Access to Justice 18.

105   Descriptions of and documents relating to the "new relationship" can be found at http://www.gov.bc.ca/arr/popt/the_new_relationship.htm.

106 Webber, *supra* note 90 at 72-73; and Kent McNeil, "Aboriginal Rights in Canada: From Title to Land to Territorial Sovereignty" (1998) 5 Tulsa Journal of Comparative and International Law 253. See also Bird et al., eds., *supra* note 95.

107 For principles and models of Aboriginal self-government, see Menno Boldt, Anthony Long, and Leroy Little Bear, eds., *Pathways to Self Determination: Native Indian Leaders' Perspectives on Self-Government* (Toronto: University of Toronto Press, 1984); F. Cassidy and R.L. Bish, *Indian Government: Its Meaning in Practice* (Lantzville: Oolichan Books, 1989); M. Boldt, *Surviving as Indians: The Challenge of Self-Government* (Toronto: University of Toronto Press, 1993); John M. Olynyk, "Approaches to Sorting Out Jurisdiction in a Self-Government Context" (1995) 53 University of Toronto Faculty of Law Review 235; S. Weaver, "An Assessment of the Federal Self-Government Policy," in A. Morrison and I. Cotler, eds., *Justice for Natives: Searching for Common Ground* (Montreal and Kingston: McGill-Queen's University Press, 1997), 111; Michael Murphy, ed., *Canada: The State of the Federation: Reconfiguring Aboriginal-State Relations* (Montreal and Kingston: Institute of Intergovernmental Relations, 2003); and John Borrows, "Tracking Trajectories: Aboriginal Governance as an Aboriginal Right" (2005) 38 UBC Law Review 293.

108 Bill C-7, *An Act Respecting Leadership Selection, Administration and Accountability of Indian Bands, and to Make Related Amendment to Other Acts*, 2nd Sess., 37th Parl. (First Reading 9 October 2002), http://www.parl.gc.ca/37/2/parlbus/chambus/house/bills/government/C-7/C-7_2/90192bE.html [*First Nations Governance Act*]. For criticisms, see John Borrows, "Stewardship and the First Nations Governance Act" (2003) 29 Queen's Law Journal 103; Kiera Ladner and Michael Orsini, "The Persistence of Paradigm Paralysis: The *First Nations Governance Act* as the Continuation of Colonial Policy," in Murphy, ed., *supra* note 107, 185; and John Provart, "Reforming the *Indian Act:* First Nations Governance and Aboriginal Policy in Canada" (2003) 2 Indigenous Law Journal 117.

109 *Delgamuukw, supra* note 9 at 115; *R. v. Pamajewon*, [1996] 2 S.C.R. 821, 138 D.L.R. (4th) 204; *Campbell v. British Columbia*, [2000] 4 C.N.L.R. 1 at 30, 189 D.L.R. (4th) 333 (B.C.S.C); and *Mitchell v. M.N.R.*, [2001] 1 S.C.R. 911, 199 D.L.R. (4th) 385. For arguments in favour of a constitutional right of self-government, see Bruce Clark, *Native Liberty, Crown Sovereignty: The Existing Aboriginal Right of Self-Government in Canada* (Montreal and Kingston: McGill-Queen's University Press, 1990); Patrick Macklem, "First Nations Self-Government and the Borders of the Canadian Legal Imagination" (1990-91) 36 McGill Law Journal 382; and Macklem, *supra* note 86.

110 For a wonderful bibliographical compilation of the voluminous literature on this topic, see Steven Perkins' website at http://intelligent-internet.info/law/ipr2.html. Leading works and Canadian-focused contributions include Darlene M. Johnston, "The Quest of the Six Nations Confederacy for Self-Determination" (1986) 44 University of Toronto Faculty of Law Review 1; Ruth Thompson, ed., *The Rights of Indigenous People in International Law: Selected Essays on Self-Determination* (Saskatoon: Native aw Centre, University of Saskatchewan, 1987); Mary Ellen Turpel, "Indigenous People's Rights of Political Participation and Self-Determination: Recent International Legal Developments and the Continuing Struggle for Recognition" (1992) 25 Cornell International Law Journal 579; Olive Dickason with Leslie Green, *The Law of Nations and the New World* (Edmonton: University of Alberta Press, 1993); David Steadman Berry, *Aboriginal Self-Determination under International Law* (Ottawa: National Library of Canada, 1994); Jeff J. Corntassel and T.H. Primeau, "'Indigenous Sovereignty' and International Law: Revised Strategies for Pursuing 'Self-Determination'" (1995) 17 Human Rights Quarterly 343; S. James Anaya, *Indigenous People in International Law*, 2nd edition (Oxford: Oxford University Press, 2004); Garth Nettheim, "The Practical Relevance of International Law, CERD and the UN Draft Declaration on the Rights of Indigenous Peoples," in Bryan Keon-Cohen, ed., *Native Title in the New Millennium* (Canberra: Aboriginal Studies Press, 2001), 391; Ross Poole, "The Nation-State and Aboriginal Self-Determination," in Michel Seymour, ed., *The Fate of the Nation-State* (Montreal: McGill-Queen's University Press, 2004); and Chidi Oguamanam, "Indigenous Peoples and International Law: The Making of a Regime" (2004–5) 30 Queen's Law Journal 353.

111 See, for example, Alan C. Cairns, "Ritual, Taboo, and Bias in Constitutional Controversies in Canada, or Constitutional Talk Canadian Style," in Alan C. Cairns, *Disruptions:*

Constitutional Struggles, from the Charter to Meech Lake (Toronto: McClelland and Stewart, 1991), 199 at 212ff; and M. Smith, *Our Home or Native Land? What Governments' Aboriginal Policy Is Doing to Canada* (Victoria: Crown Western, 1995).

112 See Opekokew, *supra* note 88; Royal Commission on Aboriginal Peoples, *Partners in Confederation: Aboriginal Peoples, Self-Government, and the Constitution* (Ottawa: Minister of Supply and Services Canada, 1993); James (Sákéj) Youngblood Henderson, "Empowering Treaty Federalism" (1994) 58 Saskatchewan Law Review 241; Royal Commission on Aboriginal Peoples, *supra* note 95, volume 2 at 163-245; Kent McNeil, "Envisaging Constitutional Space for Aboriginal Governments," in McNeil, *Emerging Justice, supra* note 39, 184; Borrows, *Recovering Canada, supra* note 69; Kiera L. Ladner, "Treaty Federalism: An Indigenous Vision of Canadian Federalisms," in F. Rocher and M. Smith, eds., *New Trends in Canadian Federalism*, 2nd edition (Peterborough: Broadview, 2003), 167; Val Napoleon, "Aboriginal Self Determination: Individual Self and Collective Selves" (2005) 29(2) Atlantis 31. Some indigenous scholars do, however, reject a federal model, at least as the starting point in the analysis of indigenous self-determination. See, for example, Gerald R. Alfred, *Heeding the Voices of Our Ancestors: Kahnawake Mohawk Politics and the Rise of Native Nationalism* (Toronto: Oxford University Press, 1995); Taiaiake Alfred, *Peace, Power, Righteousness: An Indigenous Manifesto* (Don Mills, ON: Oxford University Press, 1999); and Taiaiake Alfred, *Wasa'se: Indigenous Pathways of Action and Freedom* (Peterborough, ON: Broadview Press, 2005).

113 See Harry W. Daniels, *The Forgotten People: Métis and Non-Status Indian Land Claims* (Ottawa: Native Council of Canada, 1979); Métis Association of Alberta, *Métis Land Rights in Alberta: A Political History* (Edmonton: Métis Association of Alberta, 1981); Jacqueline Peterson and Jennifer S.H. Brown, eds., *The New Peoples: Being and Becoming Métis in North America* (Winnipeg: University of Manitoba Press, 1985); Paul Chartrand, *Manitoba's Métis Settlement Scheme of 1870* (Saskatoon: Native Law Centre, University of Saskatchewan, 1991); Thomas Flanagan, *Métis Lands in Manitoba* (Calgary: University of Calgary Press, 1991); and Paul Chartrand and Albert Peeling, "Sovereignty, Liberty, and the Legal Order of the Freemen (Otipahemsu'uk): Towards a Constitutional Theory of Metis Self-Government" (2004) 67 Saskatchewan Law Review 339. The Supreme Court of Canada has begun to address Métis issues in *R. v. Powley*, [2003] 2 S.C.R. 205, 2003 SCC 43, which dealt with hunting rights.

114 See Robert Groves, *Re-fashioning the Dialogue: Urban Aboriginal Governance in Canada* (Ottawa: National Association of Friendship Centres, 1999); Paul Chartrand, *Who Are Canada's Aboriginal Peoples? Recognition, Definition and Jurisdiction* (Saskatoon: Purich, 2002); Chris Andersen, "Residual Tensions of Empire: Contemporary Métis Communities and the Canadian Judicial Imagination" and the papers in Part II of Murphy, ed., *supra* note 107. Alan Cairns has been particularly insistent in asking these questions: Cairns, *supra* note 111 at 212-13; and Alan C. Cairns, *First Nations and the Canadian State: In Search of Coexistence* (Kingston: Institute of Intergovernmental Relations, 2005).

115 John Borrows, "Fourword: Issues, Individuals, Institutions and Ideas" (2002) 1 Indigenous Law Journal vii; Borrows, *Recovering Canada, supra* note 69. See also Patricia Monture-Angus, *Journeying Forward: Dreaming First Nations' Independence* (Halifax: Fernwood, 1999); Alfred, *Peace, Power, Righteousness, supra* note 112; James (Sákéj) Youngblood Henderson, "Ayukpachi: Empowering Aboriginal Thought," in Marie Battise, ed., *Reclaiming Indigenous Voice and Vision* (Vancouver: UBC Press, 2000), 248; Mariano Aupilaarjuk et al., *Interviewing Inuit Elders: Perspectives on Traditional Law* (Iqaluit: Nunavut Arctic College, 2000); James (Sákéj) Youngblood Henderson, "Postcolonial Indigenous Legal Consciousness" (2002) 1 Indigenous Law Journal 1; Ladner, *supra* note 69; Christie, "Law, Theory," *supra* note 67; Val Napoleon, "Who Gets to Say What Happened? Reconciliation Issues for the Gitxsan," in Catherine Bell and David Kahane, eds., *Intercultural Dispute Resolution in Aboriginal Contexts* (Vancouver: UBC Press, 2004), 176; Kennedy, *supra* note 41; Perry Shawana, "Carrier Medicine Knowledge, Ethics and Legal Processes" (paper presented to "Law's Empire: The Annual Conference of the Canadian Law and Society Association," Harrison Hot Springs, 25-29 June 2005); and Dale Turner, *This Is Not a Peace Pipe: Towards a Critical Indigenous Philosophy* (Toronto: University of Toronto Press, 2006).

116 Philip Awashish, "From Board to Nation Governance: The Evolution of Eeyou Tapay-Tah-Jeh-Souwin (Eeyou Governance) in Eeyou Istchee," in Murphy, ed., *supra* note 107, 165 at 179.

117 The most prominent of these was the Oka crisis of 1990, which contributed to the establishment of the Royal Commission on Aboriginal Peoples. See C. MacLaine, M. Baxendale, and R. Galbraith, *This Land Is Our Land: The Mohawk Revolt at Oka* (Montreal: Optimum, 1990); Jacques Lamarche, *L'été des Mohawks: Bilan des 78 Jours* (Montreal: Stanké, 1990); Gerald R. Alfred, "From Bad to Worse: Internal Politics in the 1990 Crisis at Kahnawake" (1991) 8 Northeast Indian Quarterly 23; Francois Dallarie, *Oka: La hache de guerre* (Sainte-Foy, QC: Editions la Liberté, 1991); Maurice Tugwell and John Thompson, *The Legacy of Oka* (Toronto: Mackenzie Institute, 1991); Geoffrey York and Loreen Pindera, *People of the Pines: The Warriors and the Legacy of Oka* (Boston: Little, Brown, 1991); Patricia Begin, Wendy Moss, and Peter Niemczak, *The Land Claim Dispute at Oka* (Ottawa: Library of Parliament, Research Branch, 1992); Lisa Austin. and Christina Boyd, *The Oka Crisis* (Dundas: Peace Research Institute, 1994); John Ciaccia, *The Oka Crisis: A Mirror of the Soul* (Dorval, QC: Maren Publications, 2000); Bruce Hodgins, Ute Lischke, and David McNab, *Blockades and Resistance: Studies in Actions of Peace and the Temagami Blockades of 1988-89* (Waterloo, ON: Wilfrid Laurier University Press, 2002); and Andrew J. Orkin, "When the Law Breaks Down: Aboriginal Peoples in Canada and Governmental Defiance of the Rule of Law" (2003) 41 Osgoode Hall Law Journal 445.

118 A.V. Dicey, *Introduction to the Study of the Law of the Constitution*, 10th edition (London: Macmillan, 1959) at 72ff.

Chapter 2: Frank Calder and Thomas Berger: A Conversation

1 *Calder et al. v. Attorney-General of British Columbia*, [1973] S.C.R. 313, 34 D.L.R. (3d) 145.

2 The responses of Thomas Berger and Frank Calder have been very lightly edited. For example, punctuation and sentence breaks are added, some redundant words have been removed, and three minor errors on dates have been corrected. Jeremy Webber's questions have been abbreviated. Only the interview and the first ten minutes of the question period were recorded. A video recording of the interview is available from the Priestly Law Library in the Faculty of Law at the University of Victoria, British Columbia.

3 *R. v. White and Bob* (1964), 50 D.L.R. (2d) 613 (B.C.C.A.); aff'd (1965), 52 D.L.R. (2d) 481 (SCC).

4 *Campbell v. British Columbia (Attorney General)* (2000), 79 B.C.L.R. (3d) 122 (B.C.S.C.).

5 In 1927, the *Indian Act* was amended (S.C. 1927, c. 32, s. 6) to add section 141, which prohibited the receiving of money for the prosecution of any claim of an Indian, band, or tribe (*Indian Act*, R.S.C. 1927, c. 98, s. 141). Section 141 was removed from the *Indian Act* in 1952 (R.S.C. 1952, c. 149).

6 This passage is lightly amended from the original interview. At the conference, Mr. Berger made an initial error in the judges hearing the appeal but immediately realized the error and corrected his mistake. This version reproduces only his corrected version.

7 The petition was based on the Cowichan Petition of 1909 and was filed with the Privy Council in London. In March 1918, Fox and Preece was dissolved, and the firm of Smith, Fox and Sedgewick took over the file. In 1929, the files were transferred to Waterhouse and Company when Fox joined that firm. In 1989, the firm became Field Fisher Waterhouse. Regrettably, the files appear to have been destroyed during the London Blitz of 1940.

Chapter 3: Reminiscences of Aboriginal Rights at the Time of the *Calder* Case and Its Aftermath

1 *Calder et al. v. Attorney-General of British Columbia*, [1973] S.C.R. 313, 34 D.L.R. (3d) 145 [*Calder*, cited to S.C.R].

2 W.H.P. Clement, *The Law of the Canadian Constitution*, 3rd edition (Toronto: Carswell, 1916) at 633-38.

3 *St. Catherine's Milling & Lumber Co. v. R.*, (1888), 14 App. Cas. 46 (P.C.).

4 *Constitution Act, 1867*, 30 & 31 Victoria, c. 3.

5   *Rupert's Land and North-Western Territory Order*, (U.K.), 23 June 1870, reprinted R.S.C. 1985, App. II, No. 9, s. 14; *Manitoba Act, 1870* (Can.), R.S.C. 1985, App. II, No.8, s. 31, s. 32(3) and s. 32(4); *Ontario Boundaries Extension Act*, S.C. 1912, c. 40, s. 2(c); *Quebec Boundaries Extension Act*, S.C. 1912, c. 45, s. 2(e); and *British Columbia Terms of Union, 1871* (U.K.), R.S.C. 1985, Appendix II, No. 10, s. 13.

6   *Indian Act*, R.S.C. 1927, c. 28, s. 141.

7   Gérard V. La Forest, *Natural Resources and Public Property under the Canadian Constitution*, (Toronto: University of Toronto Press, 1969).

8   *R. v. Sikyea*, (1964), 43 D.L.R. (2d) 150 (N.W.T. C.A.), aff'd [1964] S.C.R. 642; *R. v. White and Bob* (1964), 50 D.L.R. (2d) 613 (B.C.C.A.), aff'd (1965), 52 D.L.R. (2d) 481n (SCC).

9   Canada, Department of Indian Affairs and Northern Development, *Statement of the Government of Canada on Indian Policy* (Ottawa: Queen's Printer, 1969).

10 *Calder, supra* note 1.

11 *Campbell v. Hall* (1774), 1 Cowp. 204, 98 E.R. 1045, [1558-1774] All E.R. Rep. 252 (K.B.).

12 *Calder, supra* note 1, especially at 404.

13 *Canadian Pacific Ltd. v. Paul* (1983), 2 D.L.R. (4th) 22 (N.B.C.A.); and *R. v. Sparrow*, [1990] 1 S.C.R. 1075.

14 The Cree and Inuit plaintiffs were successful at trial, although the injunction was set aside on appeal: *Chief Max "One-Onti" Gros-Louis c. Société de développement de la Baie James*, [1974] R.P. 38 (Sup. Ct.); and *Société de développement de la Baie James c. Kanatewat*, [1975] C.A. 166.

15 *Re Paulette* (1973), 39 D.L.R. (3d) 45.

16 Hon. J. Chrétien, "Statement Made by the Hon. Jean Chrétien, Minister of Indian Affairs and Northern Development, on Claims of Indian and Inuit People, 8 August 1973," 1973 [unpublished, on file with author].

17 *James Bay and Northern Quebec Agreement and Complementary Agreements* (Sainte-Foy: Gouvernement du Québec, 1998).

Chapter 4: We Are Not O'Meara's Children

1   *Calder et al. v. Attorney-General of British Columbia*, [1973] S.C.R. 313, 34 D.L.R. (3d) 145 [*Calder*, cited to S.C.R]. For my account of *Calder*, see Hamar Foster, "Law, History and Aboriginal Title: *Calder v. Attorney General of British Columbia*," in Bob Hesketh and Chris Hackett, eds., *Canada: Confederation to Present* (Edmonton: Chinook Multimedia, 2001), http://www.chinookmultimedia.com.

2   To an important extent, this is true even *before* title was established. See *Haida Nation v. British Columbia (Minister of Forests)*, [2004] 3 S.C.R. 511, 245 D.L.R. (4th) 33.

3   Royal Proclamation of 7 October, 1763, R.S.C. 1985, App. II, No. 1. The only other BC treaties are Treaty 8 (1899) and the recent Nisga'a treaty.

4   See generally Hamar Foster, "Litigation and the BC Treaty Process: Some Recent Cases in Historical Perspective" (a contribution to the third "Speaking Truth to Power" conference, Vancouver, March 2002, http://www.bctreaty.net/files_2/pdf_documents/truth_3_book.pdf.

5   One of these obstacles was the 1927 law (section 141 of the *Indian Act*, which is discussed in the text accompanying note 43). It was dropped in 1951. The Nishga Tribal Council was established in 1955.

6   See *R. v. White and Bob* (1964), 50 D.L.R. (2d) 613 (B.C.C.A.); aff'd (1965), 52 D.L.R. (2d) 481n (SCC); and *Calder, supra* note 1. In chapter 4 of his book, *One Man's Justice* (Vancouver: Douglas and McIntyre, 2002), Thomas Berger describes his introduction to the Douglas Treaties in *White and Bob*.

7   When the claims of the Allied Indian Tribes of British Columbia came before a joint committee of Parliament in 1927, the committee noted that "the aboriginal title claimed was first presented as a legal claim against the Crown about fifteen years ago." But, of course, the claim itself dated from the 1850s. The lawyers simply put it into acceptable legal language. See *Special Committees of the Senate and House of Commons Meeting in Joint Session to Inquire into the Claims of the Allied Indian Tribes of British Columbia, as Set Forth in Their Petition Submitted to Parliament in June 1926: Proceedings, Report and the Evidence* (Ottawa: King's Printer, 1927) at viii [*Joint Committee Report*]; and the newspaper story in the *Victoria Daily Colonist, infra* note 21.

8 See Hamar Foster and Alan Grove, "'Trespassers on the Soil': *United States v. Tom* and a New Perspective on the Short History of Treaty Making in Nineteenth-Century British Columbia" (2003) 138-39 BC Studies 51 at 58-63. Until 1866, there were two colonies in British territory on the northwest coast of Canada: the proprietary colony of Vancouver's Island (1849-66) and the Crown colony of British Columbia (1858-71), which absorbed Vancouver Island in 1866. The united colony became the province of British Columbia in 1871.

9 Generally speaking, the Roman Catholic missionaries did not play the sort of role in the land question that many Methodist and some Anglican missionaries did. However, there were exceptions. See, for example, Lynn A. Blake, "Oblate Missionaries and the 'Indian Land Question'" (1998) 119 BC Studies 27.

10 The commissioners noted that if "an Indian conceives he has been ill-treated, if he thinks he has a right which is unrecognized, or which he is restrained from exercising, he becomes morose, unyielding on the subject, as the Scotch say, a 'dour' feeling with reference to the matter takes possession of him, and no amount of reasoning with him will enable him to disabuse his mind of his *possibly* ill-conceived convictions" [emphasis added]. "Papers Relating to the Commission appointed to enquire into the state and condition of the Indians of the North-West Coast of British Columbia," *BC Session Papers*, 1888, 415 at 416 and 422-23.

11 *Ibid.* at 432-33.

12 Commissioner Clement F. Cornwall told Charles Russ that "there is no probability of your views as to the land being entertained." Commissioner Joseph Phrys Planta explained that "the whole question of the Indian lands in British Columbia was settled long ago by the law," citing the *British North American Act*, 30 & 31 Victoria, c. 3, and the Terms of Union, R.S.C. 1985, App. II, No. 10, Article 13 (*ibid.* at 433).

13 To give a simple example, after the United States purchased the Louisiana Territory from France in 1803 for $15,000,000, it subsequently spent more than twenty times that much purchasing the land within the territory from its tribal owners. Felix S. Cohen, "Original Indian Title" (1947) 32 Minnesota Law Review 28 at 34-35. The Treaty of Washington is reproduced in Clive Parry, ed., *The Consolidated Treaty Series* (Dobbs Ferry: Oceana Publications, 1969), vol. 100 at 39-42.

14 See Hamar Foster, "Honouring the Queen's Flag: A Legal and Historical Perspective on the Nisga'a Treaty" (1998-99) 120 BC Studies 11. Nor did it mean that the Nisga'a had lost all of their own powers of self-governance. *Campbell v. British Columbia (Attorney General)* (2000), 79 B.C.L.R. (3d) 122 (B.C.S.C.). As Jeremy Webber has argued, the struggle for Aboriginal title is really about recognizing separate societies as possessing their own bodies of law and negotiating an accommodation. Jeremy Webber, "Beyond Regret: *Mabo's* Implications for Australian Constitutionalism," in Duncan Ivison, Paul Patton, and Will Sanders, eds., *Political Theory and the Rights of Indigenous Peoples* (Cambridge: Cambridge University Press, 2000) at 60-88.

15 *The British Columbian*, 14 April 1866, quoted in Julie Evans et al., *Equal Subjects, Unequal Rights: Indigenous Peoples in British Settler Colonies, 1830-1910* (New York: Manchester University Press, 2003) at 55.

16 In addition to the Royal Proclamation of 7 October, 1763, R.S.C. 1985, App. II, No. 1 [Royal Proclamation of 1763], a number of decisions in the United States Supreme Court and, only two years before the colony of Vancouver's Island was established, one in the Supreme Court of New Zealand all supported the idea of Indian or Native title as a legal right. As the New Zealand Court put it, such title had been recognized by the common law quite apart from treaty, and it was nothing new. *R. v. Symonds*, [1847] N.Z.P.C.C. 387 (P.C.).

17 *A.G. and I.B. Nash v. John Tait* [unreported], cited in Begbie Bench Books, 28 October 1886, British Columbia Archives and Records Services (BCARS), Vol. 13 at 446, discussed in Foster and Grove, *supra* note 8 at 52, 76, and 80-81.

18 See generally Cole Harris, *Making Native Space: Colonialism, Resistance, and Reserves in British Columbia* (Vancouver: UBC Press 2002).

19 Peter Kelly attended the Coqualeetza Institute, the Methodist residential school at Sardis, from 1900 to 1903 and Columbian College from 1913 to 1916, after which he was ordained a Methodist minister. Alan Morley, *Roar of the Breakers: A Biography of Peter Kelly* (Toronto: Ryerson Press, 1967) at 58-59, 86, and 90. Andy Paull went to the Roman Catholic

school at the Mission reserve between 1899 and 1907 and then spent a number of years working in the law office of Hugh Cayley. E. Palmer Patterson, II, "Andrew Paull (1892-1959): Finding a Voice for the 'New Indian'" (1976) 6 Western Canadian Journal of Anthropology 63 at 63 and 64.

20 On Aboriginal participation in the work force, see Rolf Knight, *Indians at Work: An Informal History of Native Labour in British Columbia 1858-1930*, 2nd edition (Vancouver: New Star Books, 1996). In April 1911, the lawyer for the Nisga'a told Prime Minister Wilfrid Laurier that he had recently been to the Land Office in Victoria and had been astonished at the "scores of applications for purchase" of land in Nisga'a territory. Edwin Peter May, "The Nishga Land Claim, 1873-1973" (MA thesis, Simon Fraser University, 1979) at 28.

21 *Victoria Daily Colonist*, 19 June 1910.

22 Donald J. Bourdon, *The Boom Years: G.G. Nye's Photographs of North Vancouver, 1905-1909* (North Vancouver: Hancock House, 1981) at 50.

23 Superintendent F.S. Hussey of the BC Provincial Police reported that Joe Capilano was "a dangerous man ... very likely to cause some serious trouble in the Naas and Skeena districts as well as in other unsettled portions of this Province." Hussey therefore recommended his early arrest and prosecution. F.S. Hussey to Attorney General Bowser, 3 November 1908, BCARS, GR 429, Box 15, File 5.

24 *Criminal Code*, R.S.C. 1906, ss. 109 and 110. A number of Gitxsan were convicted in 1909, one of whom received a sentence of ninety days in prison. See Robert Galois, "The History of the Upper Skeena Region, 1850 to 1927" (1993–94) 9 Native Studies Review 113 at 146-47. There were also prosecutions in Kitwancool (Gitanyow) territory in the 1920s.

25 See generally Robert Galois, "The Indian Rights Association, Native Protest Activity and the 'Land Question' in British Columbia, 1903-1916" (1992) 8 Native Studies Review 1.

26 See the very sketchy record of this case in "Re Indian Land," BCARS, GR 1727, Vols. 504 and 525. T.R.E. MacInnes provided more detail in his 1909 report for the dominion government, *Report on the Indian Title in Canada with Special Reference to British Columbia, infra* note 35.

27 There is a copy at BCARS, F/52/C83.

28 To date, there are only two published articles on Arthur O'Meara: E. Palmer Patterson, II, "Arthur E. O'Meara, Friend of the Indians" (1967) 58 Pacific Northwest Quarterly 90, and the recent, much fuller account in Mary Haig-Brown, "Arthur Eugene O'Meara: Servant, Advocate, Seeker of Justice," in Celia Haig-Brown and David A. Nock, eds., *With Good Intentions: Euro-Canadian and Aboriginal Relations in Colonial Canada* (Vancouver: UBC Press, 2006), 258. Tate has attracted even less attention, but it seems that he may have drafted an earlier petition for the Cowichan in 1901, which was sent to King Edward VII. See Galois, *supra* note 25 at 28.

29 This biographical information is based on Patterson, *supra* note 28, and my own archival research.

30 John Clark was "one of the leaders of the bar" whose praises are sung in, *inter alia*, Hector Charlesworth, ed., *A Cyclopaedia of Canadian Biography* (Toronto: Hunter-Rose Company, 1919) at 78-79. His entry is as long as those allotted to Sir Robert Borden and Sir Wilfrid Laurier.

31 Late in 1908, O'Meara reported to his bishop that he had recently become aware of the Royal Proclamation of 1763, *supra* note 16, and it seems likely that Clark was the source of this information. O'Meara to Bishop Isaac Stringer, 1 December 1908, BCARS, Add. MSS 1950, Box 141, File 7.

32 "Statement of Facts and Claims on Behalf of the Indians of British Columbia," BCARS, NWP 970.5 C593s.

33 *Delgamuukw v. British Columbia*, [1997] 3 S.C.R. 1010, 153 D.L.R. (4th) 193.

34 I have bored readers with this opinion before. See, for example, "Aboriginal Title and the Provincial Obligation to Respect It: Is *Delgamuukw v. British Columbia* 'Invented Law'?" (1998) 54 The Advocate 221.

35 *Report on the Indian Title in Canada with Special Reference to British Columbia*, 20 August 1909, Library and Archives Canada (LAC), RG 10, Ser. B-8, Vol. 11/208, File 1 [*Report on the Indian Title*]. There is also a copy in the National Library.

36 *Report of Deputation before Sir Wilfrid Laurier*, 26 April 1911, BCARS, F/52/C16 at 51.

37 *A.-G. Ont. v. A.-G. Can.*, [1912] A.C. 571 (J.C.P.C.) [*A.-G. Ont.*]. This meant that Ottawa could "force" British Columbia into court by referring the land title issue to the Supreme Court of Canada because the province would then be obliged to appear in order to defend its position.

38 *Report of Deputation before Sir Wilfrid Laurier, supra* note 36 at 51.

39 See *Indian Act,* S.C. 1910, c. 28, s. 1; and *Indian Act,* S.C. 1911, c. 14, s. 4. These statutes and the aborted 1910 reference are discussed later in this chapter.

40 *Prince Rupert News,* 29 April 1911, LAC, RG 10, Ser. C-II-3, Vol. 11/047, File 33/General, Part 6.

41 In a letter to McBride, dated 29 July 1912, the dominion negotiator, J.A.J. McKenna, noted that British Columbia "would not deviate "from its position that there was no Aboriginal title in the province and that having a court decide this matter was unacceptable. Accordingly, he assured McBride, "it is dropped." This letter is reproduced in part in the 1927 *Joint Committee Report, supra* note 7 at 8-9. For more detail, see Hamar Foster, "A Romance of the Lost: The Role of Tom MacInnes in the History of the British Columbia Indian Land Question," in G. Blaine Baker and Jim Phillips, eds., *Essays in the History of Canadian Law,* vol. 8: *In Honour of RCB Risk* (Toronto: Osgoode Society, 1999) at 171; and Hamar Foster, "Letting Go the Bone: The Idea of Indian Title in British Columbia, 1849-1927," in Hamar Foster and John McLaren, eds., *Essays in the History of Canadian Law,* vol. 6: *British Columbia and the Yukon* (Toronto: Osgoode Society, 1995) at 28.

42 A copy of the Nisga'a Petition is reprinted in the MA thesis by Edwin May, *supra* note 20.

43 *Indian Act,* R.S.C. 1927, c. 28, s. 141 at s. 149A. It became section 141 in the 1927 consolidated statutes (R.S.C. 1927, c. 98).

44 *Indian Act,* R.S.C. 1952, c. 149.

45 The "friends" were non-Aboriginal and made up primarily (but not exclusively) of clergy and missionaries. They were not unlike the "friends" that flourished in the 1880s and 1890s in the United States. Key figures in British Columbia included O'Meara, F.C. Wade, KC, a prominent Liberal lawyer and newspaperman, and the Reverend Dr. L. Norman Tucker of the Moral and Social Reform Council of Canada. The Indian Rights Association (IRA), unlike the American body of the same name, was an Aboriginal organization with some non-Aboriginals on the executive, including missionary Charles Tate. Their legal counsel was Clark. The Interior Tribes of British Columbia were a loose grouping that, like the IRA, was more or less superseded by the Allied Indian Tribes of British Columbia in 1916. Another key non-Aboriginal figure in the campaign for title was James A. Teit, who worked first with the Interior Tribes of British Columbia and then with the Allied Indian Tribes of British Columbia until his death in 1922. The Nisga'a tended to go it alone, but, on occasion, they joined forces with other groups, and by 1916 O'Meara was representing both the Nisga'a, with whom he had worked since 1910, and the Allied Indian Tribes of British Columbia. On the American "Friends of the Indians" phenomenon generally, see Francis Paul Prucha, *Americanizing the American Indians: Writings by the "Friends of the Indian," 1880-1900* (Lincoln: University of Nebraska Press, 1973). On Teit, see Wendy Wickwire, "'We Shall Drink from the Stream and So Shall You': James A. Teit and Native Resistance in British Columbia, 1908-22" (1998) 79 Canadian Historical Review 199.

46 The trial would be in the Supreme Court of British Columbia, and appeals would lie to the recently established BC Court of Appeal, then to the Supreme Court of Canada, and finally to the Judicial Committee. However, in those days, it was possible to appeal directly – *per saltum* – to the Judicial Committee from a provincial appellate court. (This is probably one of the reasons why the dominion would not go along with British Columbia's attempt – see text accompanying note 26 earlier in this chapter – to refer the status of British Columbia's Indian reserves to the provincial courts in 1908. If the province lost, it could avoid the Supreme Court of Canada by appealing directly to the Judicial Committee.)

47 *Crown Proceeding Act,* S.B.C. 1974, c. 24. Now see *Crown Proceeding Act,* R.S.B.C. 1996, c. 89.

48 The classic text on such petitions is probably Walter Clode, *The Law and Practice of Petition of Right* (London: William Clowes and Sons, 1887).

49 McBride to Laurier, 19 November 1910, BCARS, GR 441, Box 149, cited in Jeannie L. Kanakos, "The Negotiations to Relocate the Songhees Indians, 1843-1911" (MA thesis, Simon Fraser University, 1974) at 71 [emphasis added].

50 *St. Catherine's Milling & Lumber Co. v. R.* (1888) 14 App. Cas. 46 at 59 [emphasis added], citing section 109 of the *British North American Act, supra* note 12. The McBride government, of course, maintained that there was no Aboriginal title in British Columbia to be disencumbered and that this was not a justiciable issue.

51 Minister Charles Stewart, reported in *House of Commons Debates* (26 June 1925) at 4994.

52 A dominion fiat would have allowed a suit confined to the federal lands in the Railway belt and the Peace River block, which were not reconveyed to British Columbia until 1930. But dominion land legislation had acknowledged the issue of Aboriginal title from the beginning. See, for example, the first *Dominion Land Act*, 35 Victoria, c. 23, s. 42. The real issue was title to *provincial* land.

53 Since *Dyson v. Attorney General*, [1911] 1 K.B. 410 (C.A.), it had been possible to get around the fiat requirement by suing the attorney general instead of the Crown, so long as the only relief requested was a declaration, which is what Berger and Calder had done. According to Peter W. Hogg and Patrick J. Monahan, *Liability of the Crown*, 3rd edition (Toronto: Carswell, 2000) at 27, *Calder* may be the law in Canada but elsewhere the question is unsettled. The Canadian position, as laid down in *Calder*, is therefore controversial.

54 *Calder, supra* note 1 at 226.

55 The critical three questions are reproduced, with some editing, in George Edgar Shankel, "The Development of Indian Policy in British Columbia" (PhD diss., University of Washington, 1945) at Appendix F. An unedited copy is available in BCARS, F/52/C16 at 91-95.

56 *A.-G. Ont., supra* note 37. The Judicial Committee ruled that Ottawa's authority to refer questions to the Supreme Court of Canada was an incident of self-government and was based on the committee's own reference jurisdiction (for more information on this jurisdiction, see the fourth strategy, discussed later in this chapter).

57 *Report on the Indian Title, supra* note 35. There appears to be no legal, as opposed to political, reason why Ottawa could not employ the "MacInnes gambit" today.

58 *Indian Act, supra* note 39. These amendments provided, *inter alia*, that the Exchequer Court had jurisdiction where the claim was for Indian reserve land or for land in respect of which Indians claimed "possession or any right of possession." This was, no doubt, seen as necessary because the provincial supreme court would otherwise have exclusive jurisdiction over a lawsuit respecting land title in British Columbia.

59 See "Certified Copy of a Report of the Committee of the Privy Council, approved by His Excellency the Governor General on the 17th May, 1911," PC 1081, reproduced in Appendix E to *Joint Committee Report, supra* note 7 at 52.

60 Chief Gdansk (Amos Russ) told Chairman Wetmore, who later that year would resign from the McKenna-McBride Commission because he found his duties too onerous, that "lawyer Clark" was taking their claims to the Privy Council in England. Wetmore responded that this could not be so. Transcript of the McKenna-McBride Commission's Meeting at Skidegate, 13 September 1913, at 35 [on file with the author].

61 See Morley, *supra* note 19 at 106. In *Cultures of the North Pacific Coast* (New York: Harper and Row 1965) at 229, Philip Drucker describes the Aboriginal title claim as "singularly weak and faulty." Earlier in *The Native Brotherhoods: Modern Intertribal Organizations on the Northwest Coast*, Bulletin 168 (New York: Smithsonian Institution, Bureau of American Ethnology, 1958) at 86ff, he makes similar comments. Yet it is clear that neither author really understood the legal issues involved.

62 *An Act for the Better Administration of Justice in His Majesty's Privy Council*, 3 & 4 William IV (1833), c. 41 (UK).

63 J.M. Clark to F.C. Wade, 4 April 1913, VCA, Add. MSS 44, Vol. 18, File 9. Clark was probably referring to the Cowichan Petition because by then he had opposed the filing of separate tribal petitions. See Galois, *supra* note 25 at 21. (Indeed, it seems that Clark and O'Meara fell out over this issue, among others.) On the same day, Clark sent a telegram to Andy Paull, advising the Kitsilano and the tribes on the Skeena that they should stand fast and avoid resort to force because "justice will be done." Three years earlier, Clark had told Wade that he was pleased that they both agreed that the Royal Proclamation of 1763 applied to British Columbia. J.M. Clark to F.C. Wade, 4 May 1910, VCA, Add. MSS 44, Vol. 18, File 9. With respect to Wade, see note 45 earlier in this chapter.

64 *Ontario Mining Company v. Seybold*, [1903] A.C. 73 (J.C.P.C.).

65 The case is *Attorney General for Ontario v. Hamilton Street Railway*, [1903] A.C. 524 (J.C.P.C.), in which O'Meara was counsel for the Ontario Lord's Day Alliance. In 1890–91, the published law lists show him as practising in the firm of Macdonald, Marsh and O'Meara at 25 Toronto Street, and the senior partner is described as "The Right Hon. Sir John A. Macdonald, GCB, QC" (information supplied by Ms. Susan Lewthwaite of the Law Society of Upper Canada, January 2001).

66 Terms of Union, *supra* note 12.

67 Briefly, the problem was that the dominion government had assured the Imperial Privy Council that all of the issues in the Nisga'a Petition were within the mandate of the McKenna-McBride Commission, which began its work in 1913, so any reference of the Aboriginal title question to the Judicial Committee was premature. However, the premise was not true. Aboriginal title had been specifically *excluded* from the mandate of the commission (see note 41 earlier in this chapter and the accompanying text), and, when Aboriginal people tried to raise it, the commission either told them to desist or explained that it was not within its mandate. The relevant documentation is in Public Record Office (PRO), PC 8/1240, and an example of the commission taking this position may be found in the transcript of the hearings at Skidegate referred to in note 60 earlier in this chapter. As a result, the Skidegate people refused to talk to the commission.

68 The bad news was conveyed to the London solicitors for the Nisga'a in a letter from Almeric FitzRoy at the Privy Council Office. See A. FitzRoy to Smiths, Fox and Sedgwick, 16 December 1918, reproduced in the *Joint Committee Report, supra* note 7 at 61 (Appendix G). Before making this decision, however, the lord president of the Privy Council, concerned about the allegations of bad faith made by counsel for the Nisga'a against Ottawa, had consulted Baron Finlay, the lord chancellor, who advised against the referral. Lord Chancellor to FitzRoy, 11 December 1918, PRO, PC 8/1240.

69 See *A.-G. Ont., supra* note 37.

70 Lieutenant-Colonel Ed. S. Stanton, secretary to the governor general, to O'Meara, 25 September 1916, reproduced in the *Joint Committee Report, supra* note 37 at 63 (Appendix G).

71 Perhaps it should be added that Baron Finlay, who as lord chancellor advised against the reference, was a man who not only appears to have been past his. prime but also was counsel in *A.-G. Ont., supra* note 37, where he represented the provincial side. He was also counsel in *Corinthe v. Ecclesiastics of the Seminary of St. Sulpice*, [1912] A.C. 872, successfully arguing against the Mohawk claim to Oka. For information on Finlay at this late stage of his career, see R.F.V. Heuston, *Lives of the Lord Chancellors, 1885-1940* (Oxford: Clarendon Press, 1964) at 335 and 340; and Robert Stevens, *Law and Politics: The House of Lords as a Judicial Body, 1800-1976* (Chapel Hill: University of North Carolina Press, 1978) at 229.

72 Galois, *supra* note 25 at 20-22. Clark, as lawyer for the Indian Rights Association, had recommended acceptance of a proposal put forward by the dominion in 1914 (see note 84 later in this chapter and the accompanying text), which O'Meara regarded as totally inadequate. This caused a split among BC's First Nations that ended rather confusingly, with Tate, O'Meara, and Clark all acting independently. In the end, both Clark and Tate were eased out. With respect to fees, the balance sheets for the Indian Rights Association (1909–14) show Clark billing $2,570 in this period and O'Meara only $750, of which $250 was a loan. *Petition of the Allied Indian Tribes of British Columbia to the Senate of Canada*, 9 June 1920, LAC, RG 10, Ser. C-II-3, Vol. 11/047, File 33/General, Part 6.

73 Even Shankel, *supra* note 55 at 200, concedes that the Indians were "not altogether wrong" in thinking that their petition was before the Privy Council and that only procedural problems were delaying the hearing.

74 *In re Southern Rhodesia*, [1919] A.C. 211 (J.C.P.C.) [*Southern Rhodesia*].

75 Smiths, Fox and Sedgwick to the Clerk of the Privy Council, 27 May 1918, PRO, PC 8/1240. O'Meara had been in contact with the Anti-Slavery and Aborigines Protection Society since at least 1909, when he went to London to file the Cowichan Petition. So he would have been aware of the *Southern Rhodesian* case, *supra* note 74, and would have instructed his London solicitors to track its progress.

76 The British South Africa Company had originally objected to the Anti-Slavery and Aborigines Protection Society appearing on behalf of the indigenous peoples, mainly the Matabele and the Mashona, without a power of attorney to show their authority. Although this objection was eventually dropped, it appears that the company nevertheless made it very difficult for the society to get any sort of instructions, and it therefore did not appear. Indeed, it seems its representative may have run into the same sort of official attitude to Aboriginal land rights advocates as that expressed by BC Superintendent of Police Hussey (see note 23 earlier in this chapter). See *Anti-Slavery Reporter and Aborigines' Friend*, 1915, University of Toronto, Microfilm Collection, HT 851.A682 MICR, Ser. 5, Vol. 5, No. 1 at 1; and Robin Palmer, *Land and Racial Domination in Rhodesia* (London: Heinemann, 1977) at 112. I am indebted to David Yarrow for drawing this source to my attention.

77 The Judicial Committee decided only that the company was entitled to compensation. A subsequent commission of inquiry decided the amount. Lord Loreburn had dissented vigorously, but dissenting opinions in the Judicial Committee were never made public. Heuston, *supra* note 71 at 178 and 422.

78 Lord Sumner was obviously unaware of allegations (see *Southern Rhodesia, supra* note 74) that the British South Africa Company had hindered efforts by the Anti-Slavery and Aborigines Protection Society to discuss the litigation with the "natives."

79 *Southern Rhodesia, supra* note 74 at 230, 232, and 248. The native title claim in the case was disposed of without a single precedent cited in support. Although this might suggest that the Nisga'a may have had a narrow escape, their case would have been much more fully argued.

80 But not for long, I hope. The research is done.

81 See text accompanying note 36 in this chapter. An example of Aboriginal disunity that is especially pertinent here is a protest by the Tsimshian against the Nisga'a Petition. See letter, Henry D. Price, Port Simpson, to Privy Council, 7 April 1919, PRO, PC8/1240. Today, the Nisga'a and the Gitanyow disagree about the boundaries of the Nisga'a territory: see Neil J. Sterritt et al., eds., *Tribal Boundaries in the Nass Watershed* (Vancouver: UBC Press, 1998).

82 O'Meara to Wade, 21 June 1913, VCA, Add. MSS 44, Vol. 18, File 9.

83 This, at any rate, is how McBride subsequently described his remarks to a delegation of the Friends of the Indians, which met with him later that year. See *British Columbia Indian Situation: Report of Interview had with the Government of British Columbia at Victoria, on 23rd January, 1912*, VCA, PAM 1912-2 at 3. When McBride was informed that a stenographer would record this interview, he at first demurred but eventually acquiesced.

84 See "Certified Copy of a Report of the Committee of the Privy Council, approved by His Royal Highness the Governor General on the 20th June, 1914," PC 751, 20 June 1914, reproduced in the *Joint Committee Report, supra* note 7 at 55 (Appendix F).

85 A.E. O'Meara, *Memorandum No. 2 for the Lord President of H.M. Privy Council*, 30 June 1927, PRO 8/1240 at 7. He was quoting from an "explanatory statement," which was issued in October 1915 and sent to the tribes by Dr. L. Norman Tucker, chairman of the Indian Affairs Committee of the Social Service Council of Canada and P.D. McTavish, chairman of the Society of Friends of the Indians.

86 As to which, see note 72 earlier in this chapter.

87 Edited typescript of an interview with the Executive Council, 3 March 1911, BCARS, GR 3074, File 1/1. The chiefs had come from all over the province to meet with McBride, and Kelly had travelled from Hartley Bay on the central coast, where he was a lay preacher at the Methodist Church.

88 In 1920, during the hearings on the bill that dealt with implementing the report of the McKenna-McBride Commission, the Allied Indian Tribes of British Columbia petitioned to be heard. This was discussed in the House of Commons, and Colonel Cyrus Peck, member of parliament, described O'Meara as an "agitator" and "sea lawyer." Another member of parliament speculated that, given his name, O'Meara was "an Italian, apparently." When Peck was told the names of the Nisga'a, Tsimshian, Haida, and Shuswap representatives who wished to be heard, his response was, "I know them all; they are all O'Meara's children." See *House of Commons Debate* (20 March 1920) at 792-93.

89 See, for example, Morley's assessment, in the text accompanying note 61 earlier in this chapter.

90 *Joint Committee Report, supra* note 7 at 215-17. In 1995, Peter Kelly's son, Reginald Kelly, described Stevens as a "rough speaking politician ... accustomed to shouting down opposition" (taped interview with the author, 21 November 1995).

91 *House of Commons Debates* (20 March 1920) at 792-93. The member of parliament was Colonel Peck (see note 88 earlier in this chapter).

92 *House of Commons Debates* (15 February 1927) at 324-25. Harry Stevens, the member of parliament for Vancouver Centre, interjected to say: "Hear, hear."

93 Galois, *supra* note 25 at 31, citing "Notes of an Interview with Honourable Doctor Roche," 17 February 1915, LAC, RG 10, Vol. 7781, File 27150-3-4. The position that this put O'Meara in obliged him to borrow from his increasingly anxious relatives. See, for example, Thomas O'Meara to Charles O'Meara, 29 June 1916, O'Meara Papers, 1916–1918 Correspondence, Wycliffe College, Toronto.

94 O'Meara to Treasurer Albert Allen, 20 September 1927, LAC, RG 10, Vol. 3823, File 59/335-5.

95 Deputy Superintendent General Duncan Campbell Scott to William Ditchburn, 3 February 1928, and Scott to Indian Agent W.E. Collison, 16 February 1928, LAC, RG 10, Vol. 3823, File 59, 335-5.

96 Probate files, BCARS, GR 2205. I am grateful to Mary Haig-Brown for providing me with a copy.

97 Shankel, *supra* note 55 at 258. Kanakos, *supra* note 49 at 75, says that H.D. Helmcken got much more – $75,000 – and that S.H. Matson, who owned the *Victoria Times Colonist* newspaper, was paid (depending on the source) either $75,000 or $150,000 for his services.

98 Frank Leonard, *A Thousand Blunders: The Grand Trunk Pacific Railway and Northern British Columbia* (Vancouver: UBC Press, 1996) at 172, quoting from letters. The priest also submitted an extravagant bill for expenses.

99 O'Meara had the bad luck to be attracting the Department of Indian Affairs' attention at the same time that a real charlatan, John Robert Ockleshaw-Johnson, was active among the Six Nations. For details about Ockleshaw-Johnson and others, see E. Brian Titley, *A Narrow Vision: Duncan Campbell Scott and the Administration of Indian Affairs in Canada* (Vancouver: UBC Press, 1986), chapters 6 and 7.

100 Information kindly supplied by Gail Gatehouse, O'Meara's granddaughter.

101 Morley, *supra* note 19 at 116. Reginald Kelly, *supra* note 90, confirmed to me that Kelly might have felt that way at the end. But he added that his father credited O'Meara with the idea of petitioning Parliament to get around all the roadblocks that the government had erected against the Allied Indian Tribes of British Columbia getting a hearing (taped interview, 14 November 1995).

102 *Joint Committee Report, supra* note 7 at 146. On this occasion, Kelly had objected to a committee member referring to the representatives of the Allied Indian Tribes of British Columbia as O'Meara's "people." He saw this as code for what was implied when someone referred to them as O'Meara's children.

103 This is also Palmer Patterson's view, *supra* note 28, although he presses it more than I would.

104 *Joint Committee Report, supra* note 7 at 161.

Chapter 5: Then Fight For It

1 *Tlingit and Haida Indians of Alaska v. U.S.*, 177 F. Supp. 452 (Ct. Cls. 1959) at 388-92 [*Tlingit and Haida*].

2 "Official Returns ... Vote of November 4, 1924 (Territory of Alaska – First Division)," Alaska State Archives (ASA), Records of the Office of the Governor of Alaska, 1924, Voting Statistics, Box 47, File 14.

3 "Notice of Appointment," 12 November 1920, Robert W. Jennings, Alaska District Court, William Paul Papers, Box 2, File "Biography," Manuscripts Division, University of Washington Library.

4 Donald Craig Mitchell, *Sold American: The Story of Alaska Natives and Their Land, 1867-1959* (Hanover: University Press of New England, 1997) at 215; and *Mason v. Churchill*, US District Court for the District of Alaska, 1st Division, No. 2242-A (1922), ASA, Judicial Records Series, Box 23.

5 *Davis v. Sitka School Board*, 3 Alaska 481 (1908).

6 *Indian Reorganization Act*, 25 U.S.C.A. 461 et seq., 48 Stat. 984 (1934).

7 *Tlingit and Haida*, supra note 1.

8 *Tee-Hit-Ton Indians v. U.S.*, 348 U.S. 272 (1955).

9 *Alaska Native Claims Settlement Act*, 43 U.S.C. 33 (1971) [*ANCSA*].

10 See Robert D. Arnold, *Alaska Native Land Claims* (Anchorage: Alaska Native Foundation, 1976).

11 Mitchell, *supra* note 4 at 383-86.

12 Brian W. Dippie, *The Vanishing Indian: White Attitudes and U.S. Indian Policy* (Lawrence: University Press of Kansas, 1982), passim and 243ff.

13 William Paul Autobiography, William Paul Papers, Box 2, File "Biography," Manuscripts Division, University of Washington Library; and Mitchell, *supra* note 4 at 193-210.

14 Lawrence Baca, "The Legal Status of American Indians," in William C. Sturtevant and Wilcomb E. Washburn, eds., *Handbook of North American Indians*, vol. 4: *History of Indian-White Relations* (Washington, DC: Smithsonian Institution, 1988), 232; and Felix S. Cohen, *Handbook of Federal Indian Law* (Albuquerque, NM: University of New Mexico Press, 1945) at 153.

15 *Indian Citizenship Act*, 8 U.S.C. 1201 (1924).

16 *General Allotment Act*, 24 U.S.C. 388 (1887).

17 Mitchell, *supra* note 4 at 388-91.

18 Act of February 23, 1871 (Indian Appropriations), 25 U.S.C.A. 71; and William C. Canby, Jr., *American Indian Law* (St. Paul: West Publishing, 1981) at 16-17.

19 *Treaty Concerning the Cession of the Russian Possessions in North America by His Majesty the Emperor of All the Russias to the United States of America*, 15 Stat. 539 (1867).

20 James Wickersham Diary, 30 November 1929, Manuscripts Division, Rasmuson Library, University of Alaska (Fairbanks).

21 Mitchell, *supra* note 4 at 228-31.

22 *Act Authorizing the Tlingit and Haida Indians of Alaska to Bring Suit in the United States Court of Claims, and Conferring Jurisdiction upon Said Court to Hear, Examine, Adjudicate, and Enter Judgment upon Any and All Claims which Said Indians May Have, or Claim to Have, against the United States, and For Other Purposes* [*Tlingit-Haida Jurisdictional Act*], Act of June 19, 1935, 49 Stat. 388, as amended by Act of June 5, 1942, 56 Stat. 323, and Act of June 4, 1945, 59 Stat. 231.

23 Peter M. Metcalfe, *An Historical and Organizational Profile: The Central Council of the Tlingit and Haida Indian Tribes of Alaska* (Juneau: Central Council of the Tlingit and Haida Indian Tribes of Alaska, 1981).

24 *United States ex rel G.W. Folta v. William Paul*, US District Court for the District of Alaska, 1st Division, No. 3918A (16 October 1936), ASA, Judicial Records Series, Box 23.

25 Philip Drucker, *The Native Brotherhoods: Modern Inter-tribal Organizations on the Northwest Coast*, Bureau of American Ethnology Bulletin No. 168 (Washington, DC: Smithsonian Institution, 1958), 38.

26 Mitchell, *supra* note 4 at 310-19; and David Morgan to Alaska Native Brotherhood Local Camps (chapters), 30 March 1940, William Paul Papers, Box 44, File "Correspondence," Manuscripts Division, University of Washington Library.

27 Mitchell, *supra* note 4 at 310ff.

28 *Tlingit and Haida*, supra note 1.

29 "Economic Development and Indian Land Rights in Modern Alaska: The 1947 Tongass Timber Act" (1990) 21 *Western Historical Quarterly* 21-46.

30 *Tee-Hit-Ton Indians v. U.S.* 120 Fed. Supp. 202 (Ct. Cl. 1954), 384 U.S. 272 (1955) [*Tee-Hit-Ton Indians*].

31 *Tlingit and Haida*, supra note 1.

32 The US Supreme Court had found for the validity of Aboriginal title in 1941 in *Hualapai Indians v. Santa Fe Railroad*, 314 U.S. 339 (1941) [*Hualapai Indians*].

33 *Tlingit and Haida, supra* note 1.
34 *An Act Providing a Civil Government for Alaska*, 23 Stat. 24, sec. 8 (1884).
35 *Tlingit and Haida Indians of Alaska*, 79 Stat. 543 (1865).
36 *Tlingit and Haida Indians of Alaska et al. v. U.S.*, 389 Fed. 2nd 778 (Ct. Cls 1968).
37 Robert D. Arnold, *Alaska Native Land Claims* (Anchorage: Alaska Native Foundation, 1976) at 277.
38 *Alaska Statehood Act*, Pub. L. 85-508, 72 Stat. 339 (1958).
39 *Hualapai Indians, supra* note 32.
40 *Alaska Statehood Act, supra* note 38.
41 The reserve was renamed National Petroleum Reserve. *Alaska in the Alaska National Interest Lands Conservation Act*, of 2 December 1980, 94 Stat. 2371 (1980).
42 *State of Alaska v. Udall*, 420 F.2d 938 (Ninth Circuit 1969), cert. denied, 397 U.S. 1076, 90 S. Ct. 1522 (1970). The secretary's action is *Alaska Lands Order*, Public Order No. 4582, 34 Fed. Reg. 1025 (1969).
43 *ANCSA, supra* note 9.
44 Donald Craig Mitchell, *Take My Land, Take My Life: The Story of Congress's Historic Settlement of Alaska Native Land Claims, 1960-71* (Fairbanks: University of Alaska Press, 2001). Environmental suits filed by three conservation organizations led to an injunction halting construction of the Alaska pipeline until Congress passed the *Trans-Alaska Pipeline Authorization Act* (43 U.S.C. 1651 [1973]). A provision in the claims settlement act committed Congress to comprehensive environmental legislation for Alaska, which passed in 1980 as the *Alaska National Interest Lands Conservation Act*, 94 Stat. 2371 (1980).
45 Mitchell, *supra* note 4 at 385.

Chapter 6: *Calder* and the Representation of Indigenous Society in Canadian Jurisprudence

1 *Brown v. Board of Education*, 347 U.S. 483 (1954).
2 *Mabo v. Queensland (No. 2)* (1992), 175 C.L.R. 1 (H.C. Aust.) [*Mabo*].
3 *Alexkor Ltd. v. Richtersveld Community and Others*, C.C.T. 19/03 (S. Afr. S.C.).
4 *Calder et al. v. Attorney-General of British Columbia*, [1973] S.C.R. 313, 34 D.L.R. (3d) 145 [*Calder*, cited to D.L.R.].
5 Canada, Department of Indian Affairs and Northern Development, *Statement of the Government of Canada on Indian Policy* (Ottawa: Queen's Printer, 1969) at 11.
6 Canada, Task Force to Review Comprehensive Claims Policy, *Living Treaties, Lasting Agreements, Report of the Task Force to Review Comprehensive Claims Policy* (Ottawa: Department of Indian Affairs and Northern Development, 1985) at 12.
7 *Calder et al. v. Attorney General of British Columbia* (1970), 74 W.W.R. 481 at 483 (B.C.C.A.).
8 *In re Southern Rhodesia*, (1919), A.C. 210 (P.C.) [*Southern Rhodesia*].
9 *Calder, supra* note 4 at 169ff.
10 *Ibid.* at 169.
11 In this regard, Justice Emmett Hall's definition of society conforms to the following from the *Oxford English Dictionary*: "[A] collection of individuals composing a community or living under the same organization of government" (*Oxford English Dictionary*, 1989, *s.v.* "society") and "the community of people living in a particular country or region and having shared customs, laws, and organizations" (*New Oxford American Dictionary*, 2001, *s.v.* "society").
12 It is important to emphasize that Justice Hall used the word "standards" rather than "understanding," as it is certainly true that the standards through which the hegemonic discourse comparing different societies have changed. However, the representation of indigenous peoples in Western thought of the kind proposed by Hall is one that even pre-dates 1858 (see the 1830 speech that US Senator Frelinghuysen gave on the removal of the Cherokee (cited in Michael Asch, *Home and Native Land: Aboriginal Rights and the Canadian Constitution*, revised edition [Vancouver: UBC Press, 1993]).
13 *Calder, supra* note 4 at 190.
14 *Ibid.* at 156.

15 Michael Asch, "From Calder to Van der Peet: Aboriginal Rights and Canadian Law, 1973-1996," in P. Havemann, ed., *Indigenous Peoples' Rights in Australia, Canada, and New Zealand* (Melbourne: Oxford University Press, 1999), 428 at 437.

16 *Ibid.* at 438.

17 See Catherine Bell and Michael Asch, "Challenging Assumptions: The Impact of Precedent in Aboriginal Rights Litigation," in Michael Asch, ed., *Aboriginal and Treaty Rights in Canada: Essays on Law, Equality, and Respect for Difference* (Vancouver: UBC Press, 1997), 38. See also Michael Asch and Patrick Macklem, "Aboriginal Rights and Canadian Sovereignty: An Essay on *R. v. Sparrow*" (1991) 29 Alberta Law Review 498.

18 *Hamlet of Baker Lake v. Minister of Indian Affairs and Northern Development* (1979), 107 D.L.R. (3d) 513 (F.C.T.D.) [*Baker Lake*]; and *R. v. Sparrow,* [1990] 1 S.C.R. 1075 [*Sparrow*].

19 *Baker Lake, supra* note 18.

20 *Ibid.* at 542.

21 Although it has not been raised explicitly in recent judgments, the rationale that lies behind the *Baker Lake* test is commonly found in the reasoning used in judgments at all levels of the judiciary.

22 *Baker Lake, supra* note 18 at 542.

23 *Southern Rhodesia, supra* note 8 at 233.

24 *Baker Lake, supra* note 18 at 543.

25 *Ibid.* at 544.

26 *Delgamuukw v. British Columbia* (1991), 79 D.L.R. (4th) 185 (B.C.S.C.) [*Delgamuukw*].

27 Specifically, he asserted: "I do not accept the ancestors 'on the ground' behaved as they did because of 'institutions.' Rather I find they more likely acted as they did because of survival instincts which varied from village to village." *Delgamuukw, supra* note 26 at 441.

28 *Ibid.* at 1208.

29 *Ibid.* at 452ff.

30 *Ibid.* at 452.

31 *Ibid.* at 455.

32 *Ibid.* at 462.

33 *Ibid.* at 455.

34 *R. v. Van der Peet,* [1996] 2 S.C.R. 507 [*Van der Peet*].

35 Specifically, they concluded that the Stó:lō were at a band level and not a tribal level of society. As they state: "[T]he Sto:lo were at a band level of social organization rather than at a tribal level. As noted by the various experts, one of the central distinctions between a band society and a tribal society relates to specialization and division of labour. In a tribal society there tends to be specialization of labour – for example, specialization in the gathering and trade of fish – whereas in a band society division of labour tends to occur only on the basis of gender or age. The absence of specialization in the exploitation of the fishery is suggestive, in the same way that the absence of regularized trade or a market is suggestive, that the exchange of fish was not a central part of Sto:lo culture. I would note here as well Scarlett Prov. Ct. J.'s finding that the Sto:lo did not have the means for preserving fish for extended periods of time, something which is also suggestive that the exchange or trade of fish was not central to the Sto:lo way of life." *Ibid.* at para. 90.

36 *Sparrow, supra* note 18 at 1103. For a commentary on this passage in *Sparrow,* see Hamar Foster, "Forgotten Arguments: Aboriginal Title and Sovereignty in Canada Jurisdiction Act Cases" (1992) 21 Manitoba Law Journal 343.

37 Asch and Macklem, *supra* note 17 [emphasis added].

38 The "settlement thesis" also provides the most "cogent" explanation in English law to explain the presumption that sovereignty and jurisdiction were acquired legitimately by the Crown in regions of the country, such as most of the territory of British Columbia, where treaties that purport to include provisions ceding rights to the Crown were not negotiated.

Chapter 7: A Taxonomy of Aboriginal Rights

1 *Constitution Act, 1982,* being Schedule B to the *Canada Act 1982* (U.K.), 1982, c. 11.

2 *Calder et al. v. Attorney-General of British Columbia,* [1973] S.C.R. 313, 34 D.L.R. (3d) 145.

3 *R. v. Van der Peet,* [1996] 2 S.C.R. 507 (SCC) *[Van der Peet].*

4 *Delgamuukw v. British Columbia,* [1997] 3 S.C.R. 1010 (SCC) *[Delgamuukw].*

5 This section draws on Brian Slattery, "Making Sense of Aboriginal and Treaty Rights" (2000) 79 Canadian Bar Review 196 at 211-13.

6 *Van der Peet, supra* note 3. See also the summary of the test in *Mitchell v. M.N.R.,* [2001] 1 S.C.R. 911 (SCC) at paras. 12-13 *[Mitchell].*

7 *Van der Peet, supra* note 3 at paras. 46 and 60.

8 *Ibid.* at paras. 55-56. In *R. v. Sappier; R. v. Gray,* 2006 SCC 54 *[Sappier],* the Supreme Court of Canada stressed that this criterion should be applied flexibly "because the object is to provide cultural security and continuity for the particular aboriginal society" (at para. 33). It does not mean that the pre-contact practice has to go to the "core of the society's identity" in the sense of constituting its single most important defining character (at para. 40). Nor should the notion that the practice must be a "defining feature" of the Aboriginal society be used "to create artificial barriers to the recognition and affirmation of aboriginal rights" (at para. 41). The purpose is "to understand the way of life of the particular aboriginal society, pre-contact, and to determine how the claimed right relates to it" (at para. 40).

9 *Van der Peet, supra* note 3 at paras. 71-72. The point is reiterated and sharpened in *Sappier, supra* note 8 at paras. 42-46.

10 *R. v. Gladstone,* [1996] 2 S.C.R. 723 (SCC).

11 *Van der Peet, supra* note 3 at para. 69.

12 *Delgamuukw, supra* note 4. For discussion, see Owen Lippert, ed., *Beyond the Nass Valley: National Implications of the Supreme Court's Delgamuukw Decision* (Vancouver: Fraser Institute, 2000); Kent McNeil, *Emerging Justice? Essays on Indigenous Rights in Canada and Australia* (Saskatoon: Native Law Centre, University of Saskatchewan, 2001) at 58-160. The concept of Aboriginal title is analyzed in Brian Slattery, "Understanding Aboriginal Rights" (1987) 66 Canadian Bar Review 727; Kent McNeil, *Common Law Aboriginal Title* (Oxford: Clarendon Press, 1989); Patrick Macklem, "What's Law Got to Do with It? The Protection of Aboriginal Title in Canada" (1997) 35 Osgoode Hall Law Journal 125; Kent McNeil, "Aboriginal Title and the Supreme Court: What's Happening?" (2006) 69 Saskatchewan Law Review 282; and Brian Slattery, "The Metamorphosis of Aboriginal Title" (2006) 85 Canadian Bar Review 255.

13 *Delgamuukw, supra* note 4 at paras. 110-11.

14 *Ibid.* at paras. 116-32.

15 *Van der Peet, supra* note 3.

16 The capacity of Indian nations to conclude treaties with the Crown is comprehensively reviewed in *R. v. Sioui,* [1990] 1 S.C.R. 1025 (SCC) at 1037-43.

17 *Constitution Act, 1982, supra* note 1.

18 For discussion of the inter-societal character of this law, see Slattery, "Understanding Aboriginal Rights," *supra* note 12 at 736-41 and 744-45; Slattery, "Making Sense of Aboriginal and Treaty Rights," *supra* note 5 at 198-206; Slattery, "The Metamorphosis of Aboriginal Title," *supra* note 12. For parallel approaches, see Mark D. Walters, "British Imperial Constitutional Law and Aboriginal Rights: A Comment on *Delgamuukw v. British Columbia*" (1992) 17 Queen's Law Journal 350; Jeremy Webber, "Relations of Force and Relations of Justice: The Emergence of Normative Community between Colonists and Aboriginal Peoples" (1995) 33 Osgoode Hall Law Journal 623; John Borrows, "With or Without You: First Nations Law (in Canada)" (1996) 41 McGill Law Journal 629; John Borrows and Leonard I. Rotman, "The *Sui Generis* Nature of Aboriginal Rights: Does It Make a Difference?" (1997) 36 Alberta Law Review 9; and Mark D. Walters, "The 'Golden Thread' of Continuity: Aboriginal Customs at Common Law and under the *Constitution Act, 1982*" (1999) 44 McGill Law Journal 711.

19 *Constitution Act, 1867,* 30 & 31 Victoria (U.K.), c. 3, s. 91(24).

20 On the constitutional effects of federal-provincial agreements, see *Reference Re Canada Assistance Plan (B.C.),* [1991] 2 S.C.R. 525; and discussion in Peter W. Hogg, *Constitutional Law of Canada,* 3rd edition (Scarborough, ON: Carswell, 1992) at 12.3(a).

21 See *Connolly v. Woolrich* (1867), 17 R.J.R.Q. 75 (Que. S.C.); *Casimel v. Insurance Corp. of British Columbia,* [1994] 2 C.N.L.R. 22 (B.C.C.A.); *Van der Peet, supra* note 3 at paras. 38-40; *Delgamuukw, supra* note 4 at paras. 146-48; *Campbell v. British Columbia (Attorney General)*

[2000] 4 C.N.L.R. 1 (B.C.S.C.) at paras. 83-136; and *Mitchell, supra* note 6 at paras. 9-10, 61-64, and 141-54.

22 *Van der Peet, supra* note 3 at para. 263. Justice McLachlin was dissenting, but not on this point.

23 Section 129, *Constitution Act, 1867, supra* note 19.

24 See *Guerin v. The Queen,* [1984] 2 S.C.R. 335 (SCC); *R. v. Sparrow,* [1990] 1 S.C.R. 1075 (SCC) [*Sparrow*]; *Van der Peet, supra* note 3 at paras. 24-25; and *Wewaykum Indian Band v. Canada,* [2002] S.C.R. (SCC) [*Wewaykum*].

25 *Sparrow, supra* note 24 at 1108.

26 *Wewaykum, supra* note 24 at paras. 79-80.

27 *Mitchell, supra* note 6 at para. 9.

28 *Haida Nation v. British Columbia (Minister of Forests),* [2004] 3 S.C.R. 511 (SCC) at paras. 16-25.

29 *Wewaykum, supra* note 24 at para. 83.

30 *Ibid.* at paras. 86-104.

31 *Delgamuukw, supra* note 4.

32 See Slattery, "The Metamorphosis of Aboriginal Title," *supra* note 12 and other references in the same note.

33 *Van der Peet, supra* note 3 at paras. 270-72.

34 Royal Proclamation of 7 October, 1763, R.S.C. 1985, App. II, No. 1. The most accurate printed text is found in Clarence S. Brigham, ed., *British Royal Proclamations Relating to America* (Worcester, MA: American Antiquarian Society, 1911) at 212.

35 *Van der Peet, supra* note 3 at para. 272.

36 *R. v. Marshall (No. 1),* [1999] 3 S.C.R. 456 (SCC).

37 *Ibid.* at para. 25. See also *Mikisew Cree First Nation v. Canada (Minister of Canadian Heritage),* [2005] 3 S.C.R. 388 (SCC) at para. 26.

38 *Sappier, supra* note 8 at especially paras. 37-40 and 45.

39 Royal Commission on Aboriginal Peoples, *Report of the Royal Commission on Aboriginal Peoples* (Ottawa: Minister of Supply and Services Canada, 1996); *Campbell v. British Columbia (Attorney General),* [2000] 4 C.N.L.R. 1 (B.C.S.C.); and Brian Slattery, "First Nations and the Constitution: A Question of Trust" (1992) 71 Canadian Bar Review 261 at 278-87.

40 *R. v. Sioui,* [1990] 1 S.C.R. 1025 (SCC) at 1054-55 [emphasis added].

41 The following discussion draws on Brian Slattery, "Making Sense of Aboriginal and Treaty Rights," *supra* note 5 at 213-14.

42 *R. v. Pamajewon,* [1996] 2 S.C.R. 821 (SCC) at 832-33.

43 *Delgamuukw, supra* note 4 at 1115; see also Royal Commission on Aboriginal Peoples, *supra* note 39, volume 2, part 1, especially at 163-280. On the right of self-government, see Patrick Macklem, "First Nations Self-Government and the Borders of the Canadian Legal Imagination" (1991) 36 McGill Law Journal 382; Slattery, *supra* note 39 at 278-87; and Patrick Macklem, "Distributing Sovereignty: Indian Nations and Equality of Peoples" (1993) 45 Stanford Law Review 1311.

44 *Delgamuukw, supra* note 4 at 1114-15.

45 As the Court states: "The broad nature of the claim [of self-government] at trial also led to a failure by the parties to address many of the difficult conceptual issues which surround the recognition of aboriginal self-government ... We received little in the way of submissions that would help us to grapple with these difficult and central issues. Without assistance from the parties, it would be imprudent for the Court to step into the breach" (*ibid.* at 1115).

46 See *R. v. Côté,* [1996] 3 S.C.R. 139 (SCC) at paras. 42-54; *R. v. Adams* [1996] 3 S.C.R. 101 (SCC) at paras. 31-33 [*Adams*]; and Brian Slattery, "Understanding Aboriginal Rights," *supra* note 12 at 736-41.

47 See *Adams, supra* note 46; *R. v. Marshall; R. v. Bernard,* [2005] 2 S.C.R. 220 (SCC) at paras. 58-59 and 66. For discussion, see B. J. Burke, "Left Out in the Cold: The Problem with Aboriginal Title under Section 35(1) of the *Constitution Act, 1982* for Historically Nomadic Aboriginal Peoples" (2000) 38 Osgoode Hall Law Journal 1; and Brian Slattery, "The Metamorphosis of Aboriginal Title," *supra* note 12.

48 For a discussion of indigenous rights in international law, see S. James Anaya, *Indigenous Peoples in International Law* (New York: Oxford University Press, 1996).
49 *Delgamuukw, supra* note 4 at paras. 143-45.
50 The Royal Proclamation of 1763's text is found in Brigham, ed., *supra* note 34 at 212. For detailed discussion, see Brian Slattery, "The Land Rights of Indigenous Canadian Peoples, As Affected by the Crown's Acquisition of Their Territories" (D.Phil. diss., Oxford University, 1979; reprinted in Saskatoon: Native Law Centre, University of Saskatchewan, 1979) at 204-82; Brian Slattery, "The Hidden Constitution: Aboriginal Rights in Canada" (1984) 32 American Journal of Comparative Law 361 at 368-72; and Brian Slattery, "The Legal Basis of Aboriginal Title," in Frank Cassidy, ed., *Aboriginal Title in British Columbia: Delgamuukw v. The Queen* (Lantzville, BC: Oolichan Books, 1992) at 121-29.
51 See Slattery, "The Land Rights of Indigenous Canadian Peoples," *supra* note 50 at 175-90.
52 See *Delgamuukw, supra* note 4 at paras. 197-98 (per La Forest J.); and Slattery, "Understanding Aboriginal Rights," *supra* note 12 at 741-44 and 755-69.
53 For a good survey, see Colin G. Calloway, *New Worlds for All: Indians, Europeans, and the Remaking of Early America* (Baltimore, MD: Johns Hopkins University Press, 1997).
54 See Bruce G. Trigger and William R. Swagerty, "Entertaining Strangers: North America in the Sixteenth Century," in B.G. Trigger and W.E. Washburn, eds., *The Cambridge History of the Native Peoples of the Americas*, vol. 1: *North America*, Part 1 (Cambridge: Cambridge University Press, 1996) at 363. Syphilis was probably carried back to Europe as early as 1493.
55 *R. v. Powley*, [2003] 2 S.C.R. 207 (SCC) at para. 18.
56 On the evolution of Aboriginal rights, see especially *Sparrow, supra* note 24 at 1093; and *Sappier, supra* note 8 at paras. 48-49.
57 However, the various *Indian Acts* passed by the federal government, notoriously, did not respect this basic principle.
58 *Van der Peet, supra* note 3.

Chapter 8: Judicial Approaches to Self-Government since *Calder*

1 *Calder et al. v. Attorney-General of British Columbia*, [1973] S.C.R. 313, 34 D.L.R. (3d) 145 [*Calder*, SCC].
2 For example, see the *Manitoba Act*, 33 Victoria (Can.), c. 3, s. 31; *Rupert's Land and North-Western Territory Order* (U.K.), 23 June 1870, reprinted in R.S.C. 1985, App. II, No. 9, s. 14. The Royal Proclamation of October 7, 1763 is reprinted in R.S.C. 1985, App. II, No. 1.
3 *James Bay and Northern Quebec Agreement and Complementary Agreements* (Sainte-Foy: Gouvernement du Québec, 1998) [*JBNQA*].
4 *Indian Act*, R.S.C. 1927, c. 98, s.141, enacted as S.C. 1926-27, c. 32, s. 6. See Paul Tennant, *Aboriginal Peoples and Politics: The Indian Land Question in British Columbia, 1849-1989* (Vancouver: UBC Press, 1990) at 111-13.
5 Canada, Department of Indian Affairs and Northern Development, *Statement of the Government of Canada on Indian Policy* (Ottawa: Queen's Printer, 1969) [*Statement on Indian Policy*]. For background and analysis, see Sally M. Weaver, *Making Canadian Indian Policy: The Hidden Agenda 1968-1970* (Toronto: University of Toronto Press, 1981).
6 *Statement on Indian Policy, supra* note 5 at 11. See also Prime Minister Pierre Trudeau's speech in Vancouver, British Columbia, on 8 August 1969, excerpted in Peter A. Cumming and Neil H. Mickenberg, eds., *Native Rights in Canada*, 2nd edition (Toronto: Indian-Eskimo Association of Canada and General Publishing, 1972) at 331.
7 Jean Chrétien retracted the white paper in a speech at Queen's University on 17 March 1971, entitled "The Unfinished Tapestry – Indian Policy in Canada." See Weaver, *supra* note 5 at 184-89.
8 *Constitution Act, 1867*, 30 & 31 Victoria (U.K.), c. 3, s. 91(24).
9 *Calder et al. v. Attorney-General of British Columbia* (1969), 8 D.L.R. (3d) 59 at 62 [*Calder*, BCSC].
10 See generally Robin Fisher, *Contact and Conflict: Indian-European Relations in British Columbia, 1774-1890*, 2nd edition (Vancouver: UBC Press, 1992); Hamar Foster, "Letting Go the Bone: The Idea of Indian Title in British Columbia, 1849-1927," in Hamar Foster and John McLaren, eds., *Essays in the History of Canadian Law: British Columbia and the Yukon*, volume

6: *British Columbia and the Yukon* (Toronto: University of Toronto Press, 1995), 28; and Tennant, *supra* note 4.

11 The exceptions are the Vancouver Island treaties of the 1850s, which were entered into by Governor James Douglas pursuant to his more liberal policy, and Treaty 8 (1899), which was extended into northeastern British Columbia by the federal government without provincial participation or, apparently, opposition. See Tennant, *supra* note 4 at 65-67, where it is explained that the federal government was able to create reserves there using its own lands from the Peace River Block.

12 While *R. v. White and Bob* (1964), 50 D.L.R. (2d) 613 (B.C.C.A.), aff'd (1965), 52 D.L.R. (2d) 481 (SCC), had been a major victory, it was a treaty case involving hunting rights that did not present any challenge to British Columbia's assertion of ownership of unpatented lands in the province.

13 *Calder*, BCSC, *supra* note 9; and *Calder et al. v. Attorney-General of British Columbia* (1970), 13 D.L.R. (3d) 64 (B.C.C.A.).

14 *Calder*, SCC, *supra* note 1.

15 *St. Catherine's Milling & Lumber Co. v. R.* (1888), 14 App. Cas. 46 (J.C.P.C.) [*St. Catherine's*].

16 Self-government had, nonetheless, long been a goal of the Nisga'a. See Joseph Gosnell, "Speech to the British Columbia Legislature, December 2, 1998" (Winter 1998-99) 120 BC Studies 5; and Hamar Foster, "Honouring the Queen's Flag: A Legal and Historical Perspective on the Nisga'a Treaty" (1998-99) 120 BC Studies 9 (especially at 10 on Charles Russ's statement to the royal commissioners who visited the Nass Valley in 1887).

17 This is not to say that there was no judicial recognition of this right prior to *Calder*. In *Connolly v. Woolrich* (1867), 17 R.J.R.Q. 75 at 87 (Que. S.C.), Justice Monk stated that, even after French and British assertions of sovereignty in the interior of North America, "the Indian political and territorial right, laws and usages remained in full force." See discussion in Royal Commission on Aboriginal Peoples, *Partners in Confederation: Aboriginal Peoples, Self-Government, and the Constitution* (Ottawa: Minister of Supply and Services Canada, 1993), 5-8 [*Partners in Confederation*]. Statutory acknowledgment can also be found in certain legislative provisions, past and present (see *ibid.* at 33-35). See also *Indian Act*, R.S.C. 1985, c. I-5, s. 2(1) (definition of "council of the band" includes a "council chosen according to the custom of the band," which the Federal Court, Trial Division, has interpreted to mean that bands have inherent authority to choose their leaders by custom. See *Bone v. Sioux Valley Indian Band No. 290 Council*, [1996] 3 C.N.L.R. 54 at 65; *Jock v. Canada (Minister of Indian and Northern Affairs)*, [1992] 1 C.N.L.R. 103; *Sparvier v. Cowessess Indian Band #73*, [1994] 1 C.N.L.R. 182; *Crow v. Blood Indian Band Council*, [1997] 3 C.N.L.R. 76; *McLeod Lake Indian Band v. Chingee*, [1999] 1 C.N.L.R. 106; *Francis v. Mohawk Council of Kanesatake*, [2003] 3 C.N.L.R. 86; and *Salt River First Nation 195 (Council) v. Salt River First Nation* [2003] 3 C.N.L.R. 332.

18 On the need for strategic approaches to Aboriginal rights litigation, see Kerry Wilkins, "Conclusion: Judicial Aesthetics and Aboriginal Claims," in Kerry Wilkins, ed., *Advancing Aboriginal Claims: Visions/Strategies/Directions* (Saskatoon: Purich, 2004), 288. See also Peter H. Russell, "High Courts and the Rights of Aboriginal Peoples: The Limits of Judicial Independence" (1998) 61 Saskatchewan Law Review 247.

19 On this point, Justices Wilfred Judson and Emmett Hall agreed, moving Canadian law beyond the *St. Catherine's* decision, *supra* note 15, in which the Privy Council had based Aboriginal title on the Royal Proclamation, *supra* note 2.

20 Justice Judson, Justices Martland and Ritchie concurring, was of the view that the title had been unilaterally extinguished by legislation prior to Confederation, whereas Justice Hall, Justices Laskin and Spence concurring, was of the view that it had not. Justice Pigeon, with whom Justice Judson (and therefore Justices Martland and Ritchie, making a majority) agreed, did not deal with extinguishment, as he concluded that the Nisga'a's action failed because they had not obtained permission from the provincial Crown to bring the action against it.

21 *JBNQA*, *supra* note 3, s. 9.0.1. See also the *Sechelt Indian Band Self-Government Act*, S.C. 1986, c. 27, discussed in John P. Taylor and Gary Paget, "Federal/Provincial Responsibility and

the Sechelt," in David C. Hawkes, ed., *Aboriginal Peoples and Government Responsibility: Exploring Federal and Provincial Roles* (Ottawa: Carleton University Press, 1989), 297.

22 *Cree-Naskapi (of Quebec) Act*, S.C. 1984, c.18.

23 *Constitution Act, 1982*, Schedule B to the *Canada Act 1982*, (U.K.) 1982, c. 11.

24 See Kent McNeil, "The Decolonization of Canada: Moving Toward Recognition of Aboriginal Governments" (1994) 7 Western Legal History 113 at 120-26, republished in Kent McNeil, *Emerging Justice? Essays on Indigenous Rights in Canada and Australia* (Saskatoon: Native Law Centre, University of Saskatchewan, 2001), 161 at 167-71.

25 *Ibid.* at 128-41.

26 See Minister of Indian Affairs and Northern Development, *Aboriginal Self-Government* (Ottawa: Public Works and Government Services Canada, 1995). See also Minister of Indian Affairs and Northern Development, *Gathering Strength: Canada's Aboriginal Action Plan* (Ottawa: Public Works and Government Services Canada, 1997) at 13. For discussion, see Bradford W. Morse, "Permafrost Rights: Aboriginal Self-Government and the Supreme Court in *R. v. Pamajewon*" (1997) 42 McGill Law Journal 1011 at 1038-40.

27 For further affirmation of the inherent right of self-government and discussion of its implementation, see *Partners in Confederation, supra* note 17; Royal Commission on Aboriginal Peoples, *Report of the Royal Commission on Aboriginal Peoples*, vol. 2: *Restructuring the Relationship* (Ottawa: Minister of Supply and Services, 1996) at 105-382.

28 *R. v. Sparrow*, [1990] 1 S.C.R. 1075 [*Sparrow*].

29 *Ibid.* at 1102 (Dickson C.J. and La Forest J.).

30 *Ibid.*

31 *R. v. Sparrow* (1986), 36 D.L.R. (4th) 246 (B.C.C.A.) at 272 [emphasis added].

32 *Sparrow, supra* note 28 at 1103. For critical commentary, see Michael Asch and Patrick Macklem, "Aboriginal Rights and Canadian Sovereignty: An Essay on *R. v. Sparrow*" (1991) 29 Alberta Law Review 498.

33 *Sparrow, supra* note 28 at 1109.

34 For further discussion of this aspect of the *Sparrow* decision, see Kent McNeil, "Envisaging Constitutional Space for Aboriginal Governments" (1993) 19 Queen's Law Journal 95, republished in McNeil, *Emerging Justice, supra* note 24 at 184.

35 *R. v. Pamajewon*, [1996] 2 S.C.R. 821 [*Pamajewon*, SCC].

36 *Criminal Code*, R.S.C. 1985, c. C-46.

37 Justice L'Heureux-Dubé delivered her own judgment, in which she characterized the alleged right differently from, while arriving at the same result as, the chief justice.

38 *Pamajewon*, SCC, *supra* note 35 at para. 24.

39 *Ibid.* at para. 27.

40 *Ibid.*

41 *R. v. Van der Peet*, [1996] 2 S.C.R. 507 [*Van der Peet*].

42 *Pamajewon*, SCC, *supra* note 35 at para. 26.

43 *Van der Peet, supra* note 41 at para. 46. For critical commentary on this test, see John Borrows, "Frozen Rights in Canada: Constitutional Interpretation and the Trickster" (1997–98) 22 American Indian Law Review 37; Russel Lawrence Barsh and James (Sákéj) Youngblood Henderson, "The Supreme Court's *Van der Peet* Trilogy: Naïve Imperialism and Ropes of Sand" (1997) 42 McGill Law Journal 993; and Catherine Bell, "New Directions in the Law of Aboriginal Rights" (1998) 77 Canadian Bar Review 36 at 44-50.

44 *Pamajewon*, SCC, *supra* note 35 at para. 24.

45 *Ibid.* at paras. 28 and 29.

46 *R. v. Pamajewon* (1994), 21 O.R. (3d) 385, esp. at 400 (Ont. C.A.) [*Pamajewon*, OCA].

47 See also Morse, *supra* note 26; Michael Coyle, "Loyalty and Distinctiveness: A New Approach to the Crown's Fiduciary Duty toward Aboriginal Peoples" (2003) 40 Alberta Law Review 841 at 846-47; Doug Moodie, "Thinking Outside the Twentieth-Century Box: Revisiting *Mitchell* – Some Comments on the Politics of Judicial Law-Making in the Context of Aboriginal Self-Government" (2003–4) 35 Ottawa Law Review 1 at 18-21.

48 *Pamajewon*, OCA, *supra* note 46 at 396 and 400 [italics removed].

49 *Ibid.* at 396.

50 *Delgamuukw v. British Columbia* (1993), 104 D.L.R. (4th) 470 [*Delgamuukw,* BCCA].
51 *Delgamuukw v. British Columbia,* [1997] 3 S.C.R. 1010 at para. 117 (Lamer C.J.) [*Delgamuukw,* SCC]. This general description of Aboriginal title is nonetheless subject to an inherent limit that prevents the lands from being used in ways that are irreconcilable with the attachment to the land that forms the basis of the title (*ibid.* at paras. 125-32). For critical commentary on this limit, see Kent McNeil, "The Post-*Delgamuukw* Nature and Content of Aboriginal Title," in McNeil, *Emerging Justice, supra* note 24, 102 at 116-22.
52 *Pamajewon,* SCC, *supra* note 35 at para. 29, quoting *Pamajewon,* OCA, *supra* note 46 at 400. See text accompanying notes 45-46 in this chapter.
53 An answer to this might be that gambling is a use of land that is too indirect to be properly classified as land use in the sense that Chief Justice Lamer had in mind in *Delgamuukw,* SCC, *supra* note 51. See text accompanying notes 86-89 in this chapter. However, neither Justice Osborne nor Chief Justice Lamer articulated a distinction between direct and indirect land uses in their judgments in *Pamajewon,* OCA, *supra* note 46, and SCC, *supra* note 35.
54 See text accompanying note 32 in this chapter.
55 This raises the vital issue, which cannot be dealt with here, of whether federal interference with a certain element of Aboriginal self-government should be classified as extinguishment of this element or infringement of a broader self-government right.
56 *Pamajewon,* OCA, *supra* note 46 at 400.
57 See text accompanying note 45 in this chapter.
58 Fishing rights can also be public. See *Gann v. Free Fishers of Whitstable* (1865), 11 H.L.C. 192; *A.G. of British Columbia v. A.G. of Canada,* [1914] A.C. 153 at 169-70 (P.C.); and *R. v. Gladstone,* [1996] 2 S.C.R. 723 at para. 67.
59 See *Attorney-General for Canada v. Attorney-General for Ontario,* [1898] A.C. 700 at 709 (P.C.), where Lord Herschell said in the context, *inter alia,* of fisheries: "It must also be borne in mind that there is a broad distinction between proprietary rights and legislative jurisdiction." This is the classic distinction between *dominium* and *imperium* made in Roman law, obscured in feudal Europe, and reasserted with the emergence of nation states. See Sir John Salmond, *Jurisprudence,* 7th edition (London: Sweet and Maxwell, 1924) at 554. For critical assessment in light of the growth of corporate power, see Morris R. Cohen, "Property and Sovereignty" (1927–28) 13 Cornell Law Quarterly 8. For more recent analyses beyond the domestic sphere, see David J. Elkins, *Beyond Sovereignty: Territory and Political Economy in the Twenty-First Century* (Toronto: University of Toronto Press, 1995); and A. Claire Cutler, *Private Power and Global Authority: Transnational Merchant Law in the Global Political Economy* (Cambridge: Cambridge University Press, 2003).
60 For example, section 92(13) of the *Constitution Act, 1867, supra* note 8, gives the provinces jurisdiction over "Property and Civil Rights" within their boundaries, but these rights are generally derived from other sources such as gifts, deeds, wills, bills of sale, and so on.
61 In *St. Catherine's, supra* note 15, where Lord Watson distinguished between the provinces' underlying title to Indian lands, which entitles the provinces to the natural resources after the burden of Aboriginal title has been removed, and Parliament's jurisdiction over those lands.
62 *Pamajewon,* SCC, *supra* note 35 at para. 24. See text accompanying note 44 in this chapter. See also Coyle, *supra* note 47 at 846.
63 *Pamajewon,* SCC, *supra* note 35 at para. 24.
64 *Van der Peet, supra* note 41 at para. 31.
65 *Delgamuukw,* SCC, *supra* note 51.
66 Even the test for Aboriginal resource rights was modified somewhat in the case of Métis claims in *R. v. Powley,* [2003] 2 S.C.R. 207, where the Court used effective European control rather than contact as the appropriate time for determining the validity of these claims.
67 See text accompanying notes 45 and 56-57 in this chapter.
68 See generally Russel Lawrence Barsh, "The Nature and Spirit of North American Political Systems" (1986) 10 American Indian Quarterly 181; Menno Boldt and J. Anthony Long, "Tribal Traditions and European-Western Political Ideologies: The Dilemma of Canada's Native Indians," in Menno Boldt and J. Anthony Long, eds., *The Quest for Justice: Aboriginal*

Peoples and Aboriginal Rights (Toronto: University of Toronto Press, 1985), 333; and Gordon Christie, "Law, Theory and Aboriginal Peoples" (2003) 2 Indigenous Law Journal 67.

69 See text accompanying notes 47-56 in this chapter.
70 *Campbell v. British Columbia (Attorney General)*, [2000] 4 C.N.L.R 1 [*Campbell*].
71 See Morse, *supra* note 26 at 1036; and Coyle, *supra* note 47 at 847.
72 *Delgamuukw*, SCC, *supra* note 51 at para. 7.
73 *Delgamuukw v. British Columbia* (1991), 79 D.L.R. (4th) 185 at 452-55. For critical commentary, see Mark D. Walters, "British Imperial Constitutional Law and Aboriginal Rights: A Comment on *Delgamuukw v. British Columbia*" (1992) 17 Queen's Law Journal 350.
74 *Delgamuukw v. British Columbia* (1993), 104 D.L.R. (4th) 470 at para. 171 (Macfarlane J.A., Taggart J.A. concurring; see also Wallace J.A. at paras. 470-85) [*Delgamuukw*, BCCA]. Justices Lambert and Hutcheon wrote separate dissenting judgments.
75 *Delgamuukw*, SCC, *supra* note 51 at para. 170.
76 Royal Commission on Aboriginal Peoples, *supra* note 27.
77 *Delgamuukw*, SCC, *supra* note 51 at para. 171.
78 *Ibid.* at para. 170.
79 Wilkins, *supra* note 18 at 307, note 19. As this appears to be primarily a question of law, it does not depend on the trial judge's findings of fact that were held by the Supreme Court of Canada to be tainted by his failure to give independent weight to the oral histories of the Gitxsan and Wet'suwet'en.
80 This was the conclusion reached by Justice Williamson in *Campbell*, *supra* note 70 at para. 133. Chief Justice Lamer's reference in this context to the Royal Commission on Aboriginal Peoples, *supra* note 27, might hint at the same conclusion, as the commissioners concluded at 199-213 that an inherent right of self-government is an existing section 35(1) right.
81 See text accompanying notes 28-32 and 47-57 in this chapter.
82 *Delgamuukw*, SCC, *supra* note 51 at para. 115 [emphasis in original].
83 Chief Justice Lamer said that "aboriginal title encompasses within it a right to choose to what ends a piece of land can be put" (*ibid.* at para. 168).
84 For more detailed discussion, see Kent McNeil, "Aboriginal Rights in Canada: From Title to Land to Territorial Sovereignty" (1998) 5 Tulsa Journal of Comparative and International Law 253 at 286-91, republished in McNeil, *Emerging Justice*, *supra* note 24, 58 at 89-95.
85 See text accompanying notes 49-53 in this chapter.
86 Quoting *Delgamuukw*, SCC, *supra* note 51 at para. 117. See text accompanying note 51 in this chapter.
87 *Ibid.* at para. 122. This is subject to the inherent limit (see *supra* note 51), which would prevent, for example, strip mining of a hunting ground (*ibid.* at para. 128).
88 In municipal law, authority to make by-laws regulating use of land does not include authority to regulate businesses operating on the land and *vice versa*. See *Jensen v. Corporation of Surrey* (1989), 47 M.P.L.R. 192 (B.C.S.C.); *Texaco Canada v. Corporation of Vanier*, [1981] 1 S.C.R. 254; and *Re Cities Service Oil Co. and the City of Kingston* (1956), 5 D.L.R. (2d) 126 (Ont. H.C.).
89 For more detailed discussion, see McNeil, "Aboriginal Rights in Canada," *supra* note 84 at 283-85. As I pointed out in that article, this may be a way of distinguishing *Pamajewon* from claims to self-government powers over direct uses of Aboriginal title lands such as resource extraction. See also Kerry Wilkins, "Negative Capacity: Of Provinces and Lands Reserved for the Indians" (2002) 1 Indigenous Law Journal 57 at 92-97, discussing the related issue of classification of provincial laws as laws in relation to land for division-of-powers purposes.
90 *Campbell*, *supra* note 70.
91 Initialled 4 August 1998. *Nisga'a Final Agreement Act*, S.C. 2000, c. 7; *Nisga'a Final Agreement Act*, S.B.C. 1999, c. 2.
92 The plaintiffs also argued that the treaty violated the constitution by allowing the Nisga'a nation to make laws without royal assent and denying voting rights to non-Nisga'a residents of Nisga'a territory.

93 See text accompanying notes 78-80 in this chapter.

94 *Campbell, supra* note 70, especially at paras. 58-59 and 71-72.

95 *Constitution Act, 1867, supra* note 8. The preamble states in part that Canada shall have "a Constitution similar in Principle to that of the United Kingdom," which of course is an unwritten constitution.

96 Specifically in *Reference Re Remuneration of Judges of the Provincial Court of Prince Edward Island,* [1997] 3 S.C.R. 3 [*Remuneration of Judges*]; and *Reference Re Secession of Quebec,* [1998] 2 S.C.R. 217.

97 *Campbell, supra* note 70 at para. 68, quoting from Chief Justice Lamer's judgment in *Remuneration of Judges, supra* note 96 at 69.

98 *Campbell, supra* note 70 at para. 81. See also *Partners in Confederation, supra* note 17, especially at 31-36.

99 *Campbell, supra* note 70 at para. 82.

100 *Johnson and Graham's Lessee v. M'Intosh,* 8 Wheaton 543, 21 U.S. 543 (1823) [*Johnson*]; *Cherokee Nation v. State of Georgia,* 5 Pet. 1, 30 U.S. 1 (1831) [*Cherokee*]; and *Worcester v. State of Georgia,* 6 Pet. 515, 31 U.S. 515 (1832) [*Worcester*]. These cases and references to them by the Supreme Court of Canada are discussed in the text accompanying notes 127-40 and 150-53 in this chapter.

101 See also note 17 in this chapter.

102 *Constitution Act, 1982, supra* note 23.

103 *Sparrow, supra* note 28; and *R. v. Badger,* [1996] 1 S.C.R. 771 [*Badger*].

104 *Campbell, supra* note 70 at para. 128.

105 *Ibid.* at para. 114.

106 See text accompany note 82 in this chapter.

107 *Campbell, supra* note 70 at paras. 137-38, quoting from *Delgamuukw,* SCC, *supra* note 51 at para. 133. At paragraphs 138-39, Justice Williamson found additional support for his conclusion that treaties can contain self-government arrangements in the statement by Justice Lamer (as he then was) in *R. v. Sioui,* [1990] 1 S.C.R. 1025 at 1043 [*Sioui*], that "[t]here is no reason why an agreement concerning something other than a territory, such as an agreement about political or social rights, cannot be a treaty within the meaning of s. 88 of the *Indian Act.*"

108 See text accompanying note 82 in this chapter.

109 See generally Dennis Lloyd, *The Law Relating to Unincorporated Associations* (London: Sweet and Maxwell, 1938); Harold A.J. Ford, *Unincorporated Non-Profit Associations: Their Property and Their Liability* (Oxford: Clarendon Press, 1959); and S.J. Stoljar, *Groups and Entities: An Enquiry into Corporate Theory* (Canberra: Australian National University Press, 1973).

110 See generally Eileen E. Gillese, *Property Law: Cases, Text and Materials,* 2nd edition (Toronto: Emond Montgomery, 1990) at 18:11-33.

111 For more detailed discussion, see McNeil, "The Post-*Delgamuukw* Nature," *supra* note 51 at 122-27. On the distinction between "collective entities" that exist in their own right and have legal, moral, and, in some instances, political rights and mere "aggregations of individuals," see Vernon Van Dyke, "Collective Entities and Moral Rights: Problems in Liberal-Democratic Thought" (1982) 44 Journal of Politics 21 especially at 21-23. See also Frances Svensson, "Liberal Democracy and Group Rights: The Legacy of Individualism and Its Impact on American Indian Tribes" (1979) 37 Political Studies 421; Robert N. Clinton, "The Rights of Indigenous Peoples as Collective Group Rights" (1990) 32 Arizona Law Review 739; and Darlene M. Johnston, "Native Rights as Collective Rights: A Question of Group Self-Preservation" (1989) 2 Canadian Journal of Law and Jurisprudence 19.

112 See McNeil, "Aboriginal Rights in Canada," *supra* note 84 at 285-91. Note that this governmental dimension of Aboriginal title also helps explain another *sui generis* aspect of it, namely inalienability other than by surrender to the Crown, because a title that has jurisdictional elements cannot be converted into a mere property right by transfer to private persons. See Kent McNeil, "Self-Government and the Inalienability of Aboriginal Title" (2002) 47 McGill Law Journal 473.

113 *Campbell, supra* note 70 at para. 130, quoting from *Delgamuukw,* SCC, *supra* note 51 at para. 170.

114 *Campbell, supra* note 70 at para. 131.
115 For example, see *Sioui, supra* note 107; *Badger, supra* note 103; and *R. v. Marshall (No. 1)*, [1999] 3 S.C.R. 456.
116 See text accompanying notes 106-8 in this chapter.
117 See text accompanying notes 49-53 in this chapter.
118 See text accompanying notes 47-57 in this chapter.
119 See text accompanying notes 108-12 in this chapter. For more detailed arguments, see McNeil, "The Post-*Delgamuukw* Nature," *supra* note 51 at 122-27; and McNeil, "Aboriginal Rights in Canada," *supra* note 84 at 286-91.
120 See text accompanying notes 75-77 in this chapter.
121 *Sparrow, supra* note 28 at 1112. See also *R. v. Sappier; R. v. Gray*, 2006 SCC 54 at paras. 26, 31, and 74.
122 *R. v. Marshall (No. 2)*, [1999] 3 S.C.R. 533 at para. 17 [emphasis added]; see also paras. 37-38 [*Marshall (No. 2)*].
123 See text accompanying notes 86-89 in this chapter.
124 Royal Commission on Aboriginal Peoples, *supra* note 27.
125 A pre-1982 example is the *Calder* case, itself, *supra* note 1, where both Justices Judson and Hall relied on American law.
126 *Sioui, supra* note 107.
127 *Indian Act*, R.S.C. 1985, c. I-5.
128 *Sioui, supra* note 107 at 1054, quoting *Worcester, supra* note 100 at 548-49 [Lamer's emphasis].
129 *Sioui, supra* note 107 at 1052-53.
130 *Van der Peet, supra* note 41 at para. 35, quoting from Brian Slattery, "Understanding Aboriginal Rights" (1987) 66 Canadian Bar Review 727 at 759.
131 *Johnson, supra* note 100; and *Worcester, supra* note 100.
132 *Johnson, supra* note 100 at 574, quoted in *Van der Peet, supra* note 41 at para. 36.
133 Relating this quotation to the constitutional entrenchment of Aboriginal and treaty rights in Canada, Chief Justice Lamer said: "It is, similarly, the reconciliation of pre-existing Aboriginal claims to the territory that now constitutes Canada, with the assertion of British sovereignty over that territory, to which recognition and affirmation of Aboriginal rights in s. 35(1) is directed." *Van der Peet, supra* note 41 at para. 36.
134 *Ibid.* at para. 37.
135 *Ibid.*, quoting *Worcester, supra* note 100 at 542-43 and 559 [Lamer's emphasis].
136 Later in his judgment in *Worcester, supra* note 100 at 560-61, Chief Justice Marshall stated that even when they entered into treaties with Great Britain and then the United States, the Indian nations did not give up their independence: "[T]he settled doctrine of the law of nations is, that a weaker power does not surrender its independence – its right to self government, by associating with a stronger, and taking its protection."
137 See text accompanying notes 35-46 in this chapter.
138 For example, see Ardith Walkem and Halie Bruce, eds., *Box of Treasures or Empty Box: Twenty Years of Section 35* (Penticton: Theytus Books, 2003).
139 See Rennard Strickland, ed., *Felix S. Cohen's Handbook of Federal Indian Law* (Charlottesville: Michie Bobbs-Merrill, 1982) at 229-57. See also Frank Pommersheim, *Braid of Feathers: American Indian Law and Contemporary Indian Life* (Berkeley: University of California Press, 1995) at 50-56, criticizing the power of Congress to limit Indian sovereignty unilaterally.
140 See William C. Canby, Jr., *American Indian Law*, 2nd edition (St. Paul: West Publishing, 1988) at 71-72. The application of this presumption is revealed in part by the rule of statutory interpretation that Acts of Congress are to be construed if possible in favour of Indian sovereignty. See *Santa Clara Pueblo v. Martinez*, 436 U.S. 49 (1978); *United States v. Wheeler*, 435 U.S. 313 (1978) [*Wheeler*]; and *Bryan v. Itasca County*, 426 U.S. 373 (1976).
141 Recall that the Ontario Court of Appeal rejected this argument, not because it lacked merit, but because the court concluded that the uses First Nations can make of their Aboriginal title lands do not include gambling. See text accompanying notes 48-53 in this chapter. As outlined earlier, I think the Supreme Court of Canada's treatment of this argument was inadequate. See text accompanying notes 35-71 in this chapter.
142 *Mitchell v. M.N.R.*, [2001] 1 S.C.R. 911 [*Mitchell*].

143 This was a recharacterization of the claim as pleaded and argued by Grand Chief Michael Mitchell and dealt with by the lower courts. See Peter W. Hutchins and Anjali Choksi, "From *Calder* to *Mitchell:* Should the Courts Control Cultural Borders?" (2002) 16 Supreme Court Law Review (2d) 241 at 251-57; and Coyle, *supra* note 47 at 848-51.

144 *Mitchell, supra* note 142 at paras. 61-64.

145 See Hutchins and Choksi, *supra* note 143 at 260-66; Leonard I. Rotman, "Developments in Aboriginal Law: The 2000-2001 Term" (2001) 15 Supreme Court Law Review (2d) 1 at 20-28; and Gordon Christie, "The Court's Exercise of Plenary Power: Rewriting the Two-Row Wampum" (2002) 16 Supreme Court Law Review (2d) 285.

146 Justice Binnie relied specifically on American law in this regard, especially *Wheeler, supra* note 140: see *Mitchell, supra* note 142 at paras. 165-69. See also Strickland, *supra* note 139 at 232-35 and 244-46; and text accompanying notes 131-40 in this chapter.

147 See Moodie, *supra* note 47. As a consequence of this, one should not expect the courts to rearrange the political or economic power structures in Canada too radically. See Russell, *supra* note 18; and Kent McNeil, "The Vulnerability of Indigenous Land Rights in Australia and Canada" (2004) 42 Osgoode Hall Law Journal 271.

148 In addition to the issue of which adjudicative bodies have jurisdiction, any assessment of the legality of Crown acquisition of sovereignty raises the complex question of which legal system can appropriately be used to assess the matter. See Brain Slattery, "Aboriginal Sovereignty and Imperial Claims" (1991) 29 Osgoode Hall Law Journal 681.   ·

149 This is commonly regarded as an aspect of the act of state doctrine. For an explicit application of it to the Crown assertion of sovereignty in Australia, see *Mabo v. Queensland (No. 2)* (1992), 175 C.L.R. 1 at 31-32 (Brennan J.). However, it needs to be emphasized that, when relying on this doctrine, common law courts do not rule on the legitimacy or even the legality of Crown sovereignty. Rather, they simply admit their incapacity to deal with the matter.

150 *Mitchell, supra* note 142 at para. 165 [emphasis in original].

151 *Cherokee, supra* note 100 at 17.

152 *Wheeler, supra* note 140 at 322, quoting from Felix S. Cohen, *Handbook of Federal Indian Law,* reprint (Washington, DC: US Department of Interior, 1945) at 122 [Cohen's emphasis].

153 *Mitchell, supra* note 142 at para. 169 [emphasis in original].

154 *Ibid.* at para. 156.

155 *Ibid.* at para. 158; see also para. 172, where Binnie J. referred to "the transition to non-Mohawk sovereignty."

156 *Ibid.* at paras. 161-63.

157 Apparently this happened despite the Two-Row Wampum treaty between the Haudenosaunee and the Crown. See *ibid.* at paras. 127-30. For critical commentary, see Christie, *supra* note 145.

158 Royal Commission on Aboriginal Peoples, *supra* note 27.

159 *Mitchell, supra* note 142 at para. 129 [emphasis in original].

160 Royal Commission on Aboriginal Peoples, *supra* note 27 at 240.

161 *Ibid.* at 240-41, quoted in *Mitchell, supra* note 142 at para. 130.

162 Royal Commission on Aboriginal Peoples, *supra* note 27 at 241, relying on *R. v. Secretary of State for Foreign and Commonwealth Affairs, ex parte Indian Association of Alberta,* [1982] 2 All E.R. 118.

163 Royal Commission on Aboriginal Peoples, *supra* note 27 at 241.

164 For example, the federal and provincial governments act in right of, and on behalf of, the Crown. If the Crown is "the symbol of the constitutional relationship among various autonomous political communities" (as the commissioners stated in the passage just quoted), do Aboriginal governments as one of the three orders of government in Canada also act in right of, and on behalf of, the Crown? I suspect that many Aboriginal people would be startled and disturbed if this were so. It might also entail a requirement for royal assent for laws made by Aboriginal governments, which Justice Williamson rejected in *Campbell, supra* note 70 at paras. 144-66. However, if Aboriginal governments do not act in right of, and on behalf of, the Crown, how do they fit into the federal arrangement and what is

their relationship with the Crown that exercises authority almost exclusively through the federal and provincial governments?

165 See also Moodie, *supra* note 47 at 27-39.
166 With respect to these matters, Justice Binnie thought that Aboriginal persons, as citizens of Canada, are fully represented by the Canadian government. *Mitchell, supra* note 142 at para. 164.
167 Justice Binnie explicitly included armed forces within the scope of sovereign incompatibility (*ibid.* at paras. 152-53).
168 *Ibid.* at paras. 151 and 154.
169 *Ibid.* at para. 165 [emphasis in original].
170 *Ibid.* See text accompanying note 150 in this chapter.
171 *Delgamuukw*, SCC, *supra* note 51; and *Marshall (No. 2), supra* note 122.

Chapter 9: Customary Rights and Crown Claims

1 The explorer, Abel Tasman, assumed that he had seen part of a great South land lying east of Tierra del Fuego and known to the Dutch as "Staten Landt." Later, when it transpired that there was no such continent, Dutch map makers substituted "Zeelandia Nova" for Tasman's discovery (after Zeeland province in the Netherlands). It became known in English as "New Zealand": A. Salmond, *Two Worlds: First Meetings between Maori and Europeans 1642-1772* (Auckland: Viking, 1991) at 24 and 437. "Aotearoa" was the name applied by some Maori to part or all of the North Island in the nineteenth century. It became the common Maori language name for the whole country during the twentieth century (including in the Maori version of the national anthem now commonly in use and in numerous Maori and government publications). The origins of this usage have been traced to a school bulletin in 1913. M. King, *Penguin History of New Zealand* (Wellington: Penguin, 2003) at 69.
2 Government of New Zealand, *Facsimiles of the Declaration of Independence* [1835] *and the Treaty of Waitangi* [1840] (Wellington: Government Printer, 1976).
3 See C. Orange, *The Treaty of Waitangi* (Wellington: Allen and Unwin/Port Nicholson Press, 1987) (texts and translations of the treaty are included at 255-66); and M. Durie, *Te Mana, Te Kawanatanga: The Politics of Maori Self-Determination* (Auckland: Oxford University Press, 1998).
4 D.V. Williams, "The Annexation of New Zealand to New South Wales in 1840: What of the Treaty of Waitangi?" (1985) 2 Australian Journal of Law and Society 41.
5 *Native Rights Act 1865* (N.Z.), 1865/71.
6 P. Hohepa and D.V. Williams, *The Taking into Account of Te Ao Maori in Relation to the Reform of the Law of Succession* (Wellington: New Zealand Law Commission, 1996) at 10. See T.A. Royal, ed., *The Woven Universe: Selected Writings of Rev. Maori Marsden* (Otaki: Te Wananga-a-Raukawa, 2003).
7 *Land Claims Ordinance 1841* (N.Z.), 1841, Sess. 1, No. 2.
8 Earl Grey to George Grey, 23 December 1846, *British Parliamentary Papers: Colonies New Zealand*, vol. 5 (Shannon: Irish University Press, 1969) at 524. This is a direct quotation by Earl Grey of "a passage from the works of Dr. Arnold which I think may safely be accepted as of authority upon this subject."
9 *Ibid.* at 523-25. See D.V. Williams, *"Te Kooti tango whenua": The Native Land Court 1864-1909* (Wellington: Huia, 1999) at 108-14.
10 The Supreme Court (re-named the High Court in 1980) was the first instance superior court established by the *Supreme Court Ordinance 1841* (N.Z.) Sess. 2, No. 1. Confusingly, the Supreme Court is now a new second tier appellate body established on the abolition of appeals to the Privy Council. *Supreme Court Act 2003* (N.Z.), 2003/53.
11 *The Queen v. Symonds* [1847] N.Z.P.C.C. 387 (SC) [*Symonds*], reprinted in H.F. von Haast, ed., *New Zealand Privy Council Cases, 1840-1932* (Wellington: Butterworth, 1938) 387. This is a report of an 1847 Supreme Court case that remained unreported until it was included in this volume. See D.V. Williams, "*Queen v. Symonds* Reconsidered" (1989) 19 Victoria University of Wellington Law Review 385. The *Symonds* approach was affirmed in *Re Lundon and Whitaker Claims Act 1871* (N.Z.), (1872), 2 N.Z.C.A. 41 at 49.

12 *Symonds* at 390 (per Chapman J. citing James Kent, "Commentaries on American Law [1826–30]," vol. 3, lecture 51); at 393 (per Martin C.J., citing Kent, "Commentaries," vol. 3, p. 379). See Chancellor James Kent, "Commentaries on American Law (1826-30)": http://www.lonang.com/exlibris/kent/index.html.

13 See J. Belich, *Making Peoples: A History of the New Zealanders from Polynesian Settlement to the End of the Nineteenth Century* (Auckland: Penguin, 1996).

14 *Wi Parata v. Bishop of Wellington* (1877), 3 N.Z. Jur. 72 (N.S.) (S.C.) [*Wi Parata*]; and *Symonds*, *supra* note 9.

15 *Ibid.* at 77.

16 *Ibid.* at 78.

17 *Ibid.* at 77-80 discussing the *Native Rights Act 1864* (N.Z.), 1854/11. See P.G. McHugh, "Tales of Constitutional Origin and Crown Sovereignty in New Zealand" (2002) 52 University of Toronto Law Journal 69 at 77-82.

18 *Nireaha Tamaki v. Baker*, [1901] A.C. 561 [*Nireaha Tamaki*]; and *Wallis v. Solicitor-General*, [1903] A.C. 173 [*Wallis*].

19 *Hohepa Wi Neera v. Bishop of Wellington* (1902), 21 N.Z.L.R. 655 (C.A.).

20 *Land Titles Protection Act 1902* (N.Z.), 1902/37; and *Maori Land Claims Adjustment and Laws Amendment Act 1904* (N.Z.), 1904/49 at s. 4.

21 "Protest of Bench and Bar, 25 April 1903," in von Haast, *supra* note 11, Appendix, 730-60 at 732.

22 *Native Land Act 1909* (N.Z.), 1909/15.

23 These sections were re-enacted in the 1931 and 1953 consolidations of Salmond's Maori affairs code, and they remained in force until the passage of *Te Ture Whenua Maori Act / Maori Land Act 1993* (N.Z.), 1993/4.

24 A. Frame, *Salmond: Southern Jurist* (Wellington: Victoria University Press, 1995) at 114 (citing John Salmond to Apirana Ngata, 22 December 1909, Crown Law Office, Wellington, Case File 84).

25 J. Salmond, "Memorandum: Notes on the History of Native-Land Legislation." Much of this memorandum was published with the 1931 consolidation, H.A. Palmer and J. Christie, eds., *The Public Acts of New Zealand (Reprint) 1908-1931*, volume 6 (Wellington: Government Printer, 1932) at 87-94. The words quoted in the text were omitted in this volume but are in H. Bassett, R. Steel, and D.V. Williams, *The Maori Land Legislation Manual* (Wellington: Crown Forestry Rental Trust, 1994), Appendix C, 95-6.

26 *Native Land Act 1909* (N.Z.), 1909/15. A full list of statutory definitions of "land" in the many Native land acts passed from 1862 to 1909 is set out in Williams, *supra* note 9 at Appendix 3, 255-59.

27 Williams, *supra* note 9 at 59.

28 *Tamihana Korokai v. Solicitor-General* (1912), 32 N.Z.L.R. 321 (C.A.).

29 Frame, *supra* note 24 at 115-28.

30 *Ibid.* at 127. See also *In Re the Bed of the Wanganui River*, [1962] N.Z.L.R. 600 (C.A.); and E.J. Haughey, "Maori Claims to Lakes, River Beds and the Foreshore" (1966) 2 New Zealand Universities Law Review 29.

31 A. Ward, *A Show of Justice: Racial "Amalgamation" in Nineteenth Century New Zealand*, 2nd edition (Auckland: Auckland University Press, 1995); P. Adams, *Fatal Necessity: British Intervention in New Zealand 1830-1847* (Auckland: Auckland/Oxford University Press, 1977); and D.V. Williams, *Crown Policy Affecting Maori Knowledge Systems and Cultural Practices* (Wellington: Waitangi Tribunal, 2001).

32 See J. Belich, *Paradise Reforged: A History of the New Zealanders from the 1880s to the Year 2000* (Auckland: Penguin, 2001).

33 *Treaty of Waitangi Act 1975* (N.Z.), 1975/114.

34 D.V. Williams, "Te Tiriti o Waitangi – Unique Relationship between Crown and Tangata Whenua?" in I.H. Kawharu, ed., *Waitangi* (Auckland: Oxford University Press, 1989), 84-89.

35 *Calder et al. v. Attorney-General of British Columbia*, [1973] S.C.R. 313, 34 D.L.R. (3d) 145 [*Calder*].

36 H. Foster, "Honouring the Queen's Flag: A Legal and Historical Perspective on the Nisga'a Treaty" (1998-99) 120 BC Studies 11 at 25-26.

37 Waitangi Tribunal, *Motunui Waitara Report* (Wellington: Waitangi Tribunal, 1983) at para. 10.1. The *Calder* citation should be: (1973) 34 D.L.R. (3d) 145. Chief Judge Durie was the first Maori lawyer to be appointed chief judge of the Maori Land Court, and he was later appointed a High Court judge.

38 *Te Weehi v. Regional Fisheries Officer,* [1986] 1 N.Z.L.R. 680 (H.C.) [*Te Weehi*].

39 *Waipapakura v. Hempton,* [1914] 33 N.Z.L.R. 1065.

40 *Fisheries Act 1908* [N.Z.], 1908/65, s. 77. See Frame, *supra* note 24 at 104-6.

41 The Canadian cases cited, in addition to *Calder,* were *Kruger and Manuel v. The Queen,* [1978] 1 S.C.R. 104 [*Kruger*]; *Hamlet of Baker Lake v. Minister of Indian Affairs and Northern Development* (1979), 107 D.L.R. (3d) 513 (F.C.T.D.) [*Baker Lake*]; and *Guerin v. The Queen,* [1984] 13 D. L. R (4th) 321 [*Guerin*]. See P.G. McHugh, "The Legal Status of Maori Fishing Rights in Tidal Waters" (1984) 14 Victoria University of Wellington Law Review 247; McHugh, "Aboriginal Title in New Zealand Courts" (1984) 2 Canterbury Law Review 235; and McHugh, "Maori Fishing Rights and the North American Indian" (1985) 6 Otago Law Review 62. Dr. McHugh, now of Cambridge University, has a LL.M. from the University of Saskatchewan, Saskatoon.

42 Waitangi Tribunal, *Muriwhenua Fishing Claims Report,* Record of Inquiry Doc. B21 (Wellington: Waitangi Tribunal, 1988) [*Muriwhenua Fishing Claims Report*]. The Canadian cases in addition to *Calder* were *Baker Lake, supra* note 41; *Kruger, supra* note 41; *Guerin, supra* note 41; and *Bolton v. Forest Pest Management Institute* (1985), 21 D.L.R. (4th) 242.

43 *Muriwhenua Fishing Claims Report, supra* note 42 at 172, 234-35, and 208-9.

44 *Amodu Tijani v. Secretary, Southern Nigeria,* [1921] 2 A.C. 399 [*Amodu Tijani*].

45 *Muriwhenua Fishing Claims Report, supra* note 42 at 209.

46 Waitangi Tribunal, *Kaituna River Claim Report* (Wellington: Waitangi Tribunal, 1984) at s. 5.6-5.12.

47 *Te Runanga o Muriwhenua v. Attorney-General,* [1990] 2 N.Z.L.R. 641 (C.A.) [*Te Runanga o Muriwhenua*].

48 *Ibid.* at 654. *Amodu Tijani supra* note 44.

49 *St. Catherine's Milling & Lumber Co. v. R.* (1888), 14 App. Cas. 46 (U.K.P.C.).

50 *Te Runanga o Muriwhenua, supra* note 47 at 65, citing *Guerin, supra* note 41; and *Simon v. R.* (1985), 24 D.L.R. (4th) 390. In all, six Canadian cases were cited in this judgment. Earlier, at 645 he cited *R. v. Sparrow,* (1986) 3 D.L.R (4th) 246 (B.C. C.A.), noting "a decision of the Supreme Court of Canada is at present awaited." See *R. v. Sparrow,* [1990] 1 S.C.R. 1075 [*Sparrow*].

51 J. Webber, "Beyond Regret: *Mabo's* Implications for Australian Constitutionalism," in D. Ivison, P. Patton, and W. Sanders, eds., *Political Theory and the Rights of Indigenous Peoples* (Cambridge: Cambridge University Press, 2000), 72.

52 E. Durie, "Constitutionalising Maori," in G. Huscroft and P. Rishworth, eds., *Litigating Rights: Perspectives from Domestic and International Law* (Oxford: Hart, 2002), 262.

53 *State-Owned Enterprises Act 1986* (N.Z.), 1986/124 at s. 9; *NZ Maori Council v. Attorney-General,* [1987] 1 N.Z.L.R. 641 (C.A.) (State-Owned Enterprise lands); *NZ Maori Council v. Attorney-General,* [1989] 2 N.Z.L.R. 142 (C.A.) (forests); and *Tainui Maori Trust Board v. Attorney-General,* [1989] 2 N.Z.L.R. 513 (C.A.) (coal). See also *Huakina Development Trust v. Waikato Valley Authority,* [1987] 2 N.Z.L.R. 188, where the High Court held the Treaty of Waitangi to be relevant to an assessment of "public interest" even when interpreting a statute containing no references to the treaty or to Maori values.

54 New Zealand Law Commission, *Maori Custom and Values in New Zealand Law,* Study Paper 9 (Wellington: New Zealand Law Commission, 2001) at 83-84; and Te Puni Kokiri/Ministry of Maori Development, *He Tirohanga o Kawa ki te Tiriti o Waitangi/A Guide to the Principles of the Treaty of Waitangi as Expressed by the Courts and the Waitangi Tribunal* (Wellington: Te Puni Kokiri/Ministry of Maori Development, 2001).

55 Department of Justice, *Principles for Crown Action on the Treaty of Waitangi* (Wellington: Department of Justice, 1989); Office of Treaty Settlements, *Crown Proposals for the Settlement of*

Treaty of Waitangi Claims, Detailed Proposals (Wellington: Office of Treaty Settlements, 1994); and Office of Treaty Settlements, *Healing the Past, Building a Future: A Guide to Treaty of Waitangi Claims and Direct Negotiations with the Crown*, 2nd edition (Wellington: Office of Treaty Settlements, 2002).

56 *Ngai Tahu Trust Board v. Attorney-General*, 2 November 1987, Doc. CP 559/87, Wellington (unreported but appended to the Waitangi Tribunal's *Muriwhenua Fishing Claims Report, supra* note 42, Appendix 5, at 307-14.

57 *Maori Fisheries Act 1989* (N.Z.), 1989/159; and *Maori Fisheries Act 1983* (N.Z.), 1983/14.

58 *Te Runanga o Muriwhenua, supra* note 47 at 656.

59 *Ibid.* See *United States v. State of Washington* 384 F.Supp. 312 (1974).

60 *Treaty of Waitangi (Fisheries Claims) Settlement Act 1992* (N.Z.), 1992/121.

61 *Te Runanga o Wharekauri Rekohu v. Attorney-General*, [1993] 2 N.Z.L.R. 301 (C.A.) at 306 [*Te Runanga o Wharekauri Rekohu*].

62 *Mabo v. Queensland (No. 2)*, (1992) 175 C.L.R. 1 (H.C.) [*Mabo*].

63 *Te Runanga o Wharekauri Rekohu supra* note 61 at 306. The *Treaty of Waitangi (Fisheries Claims) Settlement Act 1992, supra* note 60 was duly enacted very shortly after the court delivered its *Te Runanga o Wharekauri Rekohu* decision.

64 *Te Runanganui o Te Ika Whenua Inc. v. Attorney-General*, [1994] 2 N.Z.L.R. 20 (C.A.) [*Te Runanganui o Te Ika Whenua*].

65 *Energy Companies Act 1992* (N.Z.), 1992/56.

66 Waitangi Tribunal, *Te Ika Whenua – Energy Assets Report* (Wellington: Waitangi Tribunal, 1993); and Waitangi Tribunal, *Mohaka River Report* (Wellington: Waitangi Tribunal, 1992). For an exposition on the meaning and essence of *taonga*, see *Muriwhenua Fishing Claims Report, supra* note 42 at s. 10.3.2.

67 *Te Runanganui o Te Ika Whenua, supra* note 64 at 26, doubting *In re the Bed of the Wanganui River,* [1962] N.Z.L.R. 600 (C.A.).

68 *Baker Lake, supra* note 41; *Guerin, supra* note 41; and *Sparrow, supra* note 50.

69 *Te Runanganui o Te Ika Whenua, supra* note 64 at 27.

70 *Te Runanganui o Te Ika Whenua, supra* note 64 at 24. The Canadian cases cited with approval were *Eastmain Band v. James Bay and Northern Quebec Agreement (Administrator)* (1992), 99 D.L.R. (4th) 16; and *Apsassin v. Canada (Department of Indian Affairs and Northern Development)* (1993), 100 D.L.R. (4th) 504.

71 Waitangi Tribunal, *Radio Frequencies Report* (Wellington: Waitangi Tribunal, 1990) at 42-43.

72 See *New Zealand Maori Council v. Attorney-General*, [1994] 1 N.Z.L.R. 513 (P.C.); and Waitangi Tribunal, *Radio Spectrum Final Report* (Wellington: Waitangi Tribunal, 1999). Information on Maori radio stations can be accessed at http://www.tmp.govt.nz/radio/radio.html.

73 Waitangi Tribunal, *Whanganui River Report* (Wellington: Waitangi Tribunal, 1999) at 294. Whanganui is the correct Maori spelling of the name of the river; it is the same Wanganui River whose bed was the subject of the 1962 Court of Appeal decision cited earlier. See F.M. Brookfield, "The Waitangi Tribunal and the Whanganui River-Bed," (2000) New Zealand Law Review 1.

74 Court of Appeal of New Zealand, "Media Release: Seabed Case," 19 June 2003 [on file with author].

75 *Attorney-General v. Ngati Apa & Others*, [2003] 3 N.Z.L.R. 643 (C.A.) [*Ngati Apa*].

76 "Seabed Owned by the Crown Says PM" *New Zealand Herald*, 23 June 2003.

77 Department of the Prime Minister and Cabinet, *The Foreshore and Seabed of New Zealand: Protecting Public Access and Customary Rights: Government Proposals for Consultation* (Wellington: Department of the Prime Minister and Cabinet, 2003).

78 Waitangi Tribunal, *Report on the Crown's Foreshore and Seabed Policy* (Wellington: Waitangi Tribunal, 2004).

79 *Foreshore and Seabed Act 2004* (N.Z.), 2004/93. The scale of Maori protests may be gleaned from photographs in A. Harris, *Hikoi: Forty Years of Maori Protest* (Wellington: Huia, 2004) at 144-55.

80 The *Foreshore and Seabed Act 2004, ibid.,* provides for negotiated redress in relation to "territorial customary rights" (at ss. 32-45) following High Court proceedings and non-exclusive

"customary rights orders" (at ss. 46-65) in Maori Land Court hearings. See also T. Bennion, M. Birdling, and R. Paton, *Making Sense of the Foreshore and Seabed* (Wellington: Maori Law Review, 2004).

81 *In Re the Ninety-Mile Beach,* [1963] N.Z.L.R. 461 (C.A.).

82 K. Roberts-Wray, *Commonwealth and Colonial Law* (London: Stevens, 1966) at 626-35; F.M. Brookfield, "The New Zealand Constitution: The Search for Legitimacy," in Kawharu, ed., *supra* note 34 at 10-12; R.P. Boast, "*In Re the Ninety-Mile Beach* Revisited" (1993) 23 Victoria University of Wellington Law Review 145; and P.G. McHugh, *The Maori Magna Carta: New Zealand Law and the Treaty of Waitangi* (Auckland: Oxford University Press, 1991) at 117-26. See *Ngati Apa, supra* note 75 at para. 87 (per Elias C.J.).

83 Recent Court of Appeal decisions include *Te Runanga o Muriwhenua, supra* note 47; and *Te Runanganui o Te Ika Whenua, supra* note 64. Relevant Privy Council cases on appeals from New Zealand include *Nireaha Tamaki, supra* note 18; *Wallis, supra* note 18; and *Manu Kapua v. Para Haimona,* [1913] A.C. 761. A later Nigerian appeal to the Privy Council, *Amodu Tijani supra* note 44 was crucial to the reasoning of the judges in *Ngati Apa, supra* note 75.

84 *Te Ture Whenua Maori Act 1993* (N.Z.), 1993/4.

85 *Ibid.* at s. 129 (2)(a). For a list of some seventeen statutes in force that explicitly mention *tikanga,* see A. Frame, *Grey and Iwikau: A Journey into Custom* (Wellington: Victoria University Press, 2002) at 90, n. 102.

86 *Ngati Apa, supra* note 75 at paras. 183, 185, and 212.

87 *Foreshore and Seabed Endowment Revesting Act 1991* (N.Z.), 1991/103, s. 5.

88 *Ngati Apa, supra* note 75 at para. 106.

89 *Ibid.* at para. 13 [case citations omitted].

90 *Ibid.* at paras. 85-86.

91 *Ibid.* at para. 31; see also para. 87.

92 *Ibid.* at paras. 148-49.

93 *Wi Parata, supra* note 14 at 78.

94 See Frame, *supra* note 24 at 114, quoting Salmond.

95 Te Ope Mana a Tai, "Discussion Framework on Customary Rights to the Foreshore and Seabed," August 2003, see http://www.teope.co.nz; and Indigenous Research Institute, *Te Takutai Moana: Economics, Politics and Colonisation,* volume 5, 2nd edition (Auckland: Indigenous Research Institute, 2003).

96 M. Cullen, "Government Aiming for Foreshore Policy Statement by Xmas," 23 October 2003 Media Statement, attached to Memorandum (No. 3) of Counsel (TJ Castle) for Ngati Rarua and Ngati Apa, 24 October 2003, Doc. 2.142 (Wai 1071), Waitangi Tribunal, Wellington.

97 *Maori Commercial Aquaculture Claims Settlement Act 2004* (N.Z.), 2004/107; and *Maori Fisheries Act 2004* (N.Z.), 2004/78.

Chapter 10: The Influence of Canadian and International Law on the Evolution of Australian Aboriginal Title

The early section of this chapter draws in part from a paper delivered at the 2002 conference of the Association for Canadian Studies in Australia and New Zealand and published as "Constitutional Comparisons: Canadian Dimensions on Australia's Experience with Native Title" (2003) 21(1) Australian Canadian Studies 101.

1 Royal Proclamation of 7 October, 1763, R.S.C. 1985, App. II, No. 1.

2 *Canadian Charter of Rights and Freedoms,* Part 1 of the *Constitution Act, 1982,* being Schedule B to the *Canada Act, 1982* (U.K.), 1982, c. 11.

3 *Calder et al. v. Attorney-General of British Columbia,* [1973] S.C.R. 313, 34 D.L.R. (3d) 145.

4 Royal Commission on Aboriginal Peoples, *Report of the Royal Commission on Aboriginal Peoples,* vol. 1: *Looking Forward, Looking Back* (Ottawa: Minister of Supply and Services Canada, 1996) at 114.

5 J.M. Bennett and A.C. Castles, *A Source Book of Australian Legal History* (Sydney: Law Book Company, 1982) at 253-54 [emphasis added].

6 G. Barton, *History of New South Wales from the Records,* vol. 1: *Governor Phillip* (Sydney: Charles Potter, 1889) at 481, 483, 485, and 486.

7   H. Reynolds, *The Law of the Land* (Ringwood, Victoria: Penguin Australia, 1987) at 51-52. J. Simsarian, "The Acquisition of Legal Title to *Terra Nullius*" (1938) 53 Political Science Quarterly 111 at 121-23.

8   Government of New Zealand, *Facsimiles of the Declaration of Independence* [1835] *and the Treaty of Waitangi* [1840] (Wellington: Government Printer, 1976).

9   Reynolds, *supra* note 7 at 54.

10 *Ibid.* at 32.

11 See Henry Home, *Historical Law Tracts*, 2nd edition (Edinburgh: A Kincaid, King's Printer, 1761) at 94-95; John Locke, *Two Treatises of Government*, 4th edition (London, 1713) at 15; Sir William Blackstone, *Commentaries on the Laws of England*, 18th edition (London, 1923) at 3, 5, 8, 261; Emerich de Vattel, *The Laws of Nations* (London, 1760), facsimile version, Carnegie Institute, Washington, 1916, 3, at 84.

12 See the chapter by David V. Williams in this volume.

13 W.E.H. Stanner, *White Man Got No Dreaming: Essays 1938-1973* (Canberra: Australian National University Press, 1979) at 230.

14 *Mabo v. Queensland (No. 2)* (1992), 175 C.L.R. 1.

15 James Tully, *Strange Multiplicity: Constitutionalism in an Age of Diversity* (Cambridge: Cambridge University Press, 1995).

16 *Ibid.* at 117.

17 *Johnson and Graham's Lessee v. M'Intosh*, 8 Wheaton 543, 21 U.S. 543 (1823); *Cherokee Nation v. State of Georgia*, 5 Pet. 1, 30 U.S. 1 (1831); and *Worcester v. State of Georgia* 31 U.S. (6 Pet.) 530 (1832).

18 US Constitution, Art. 1, s. 8(3).

19 See the chapter by David V. Williams in this volume.

20 *Wik Peoples v. Queensland* (1996), 187 C.L.R. 1 [*Wik Peoples*].

21 *Attorney-General (NSW) v. Brown* (1847), 1 Legge 312; *Williams v. Attorney-General (NSW)* (1913), 16 C.L.R. 404; *Randwick Corporation v. Rutledge* (1959), 102 C.L.R. 54; and *New South Wales v. The Commonwealth* (1975), 135 C.L.R. 337.

22 *Cooper v. Stuart*, [1889] 14 App. Cas. 286.

23 *Commonwealth of Australia Constitution Act 1900* (Imp.).

24 *Native Title Act 1993* (Cth.) [*NTA*].

25 The story was recounted in 1996 by then governor-general Sir William Deane, in the inaugural Vincent Lingiari Memorial Lecture, "Some Signposts from Dagaragu" (Council for Aboriginal Reconciliation), http://www.austlii.edu.au/au/other/IndigLRes/car/1996/2208.html.

26 *Milirrpum v. Nabalco Pty Ltd* (1971), 17 F.L.R. 141 [*Gove Land Rights*].

27 *Ibid.*

28 *Ibid.* at 244-45.

29 *St. Catherine's Milling & Lumber Co. v. R.* (1888), 14 App. Cas. 46 (U.K.P.C.) [*St. Catherine's Milling*].

30 *Calder et al. v. Attorney-General of British Columbia* (1969), 8 D.L.R. (3d) 59; (1970) 13 D.L.R. (3d) 64.

31 *Gove Land Rights, supra* note 26 at 221 and 223.

32 *Calder et al. v. Attorney-General of British Columbia* (1973), 34 D.L.R. (3d) 145 at 218 (Hall J., Laskin and Spence JJ. concurring).

33 *Aboriginal Land Rights (Northern Territory) Act 1976* (Cth.).

34 *NTA, supra* note 24.

35 For detail of statutory land rights regimes, see H. McRae, G. Nettheim, L. Beacroft, and L. McNamara, *Indigenous Legal Issues: Commentary and Materials*, 3rd edition (Sydney: Law Book Company, 2003) at chapters 4 and 5.

36 The proceedings were published as Nicolas Peterson and Marcia Langton, eds., *Aborigines, Land and Land Rights* (Canberra: Australian Institute of Aboriginal Studies, 1980) and contain chapters by Noel Dyke, Harvey Feit, and Constance Hunt from Canada.

37 Richard H. Bartlett, *Native Title in Australia*, 2nd edition (Sydney: LexisNexis Butterworths, 2004).

38 *Mabo v. Queensland (No. 2)* (1992), 175 C.L.R. 1 [*Mabo (No. 2)*].

39 *Delgamuukw v. British Columbia*, [1997] 3 S.C.R. 1010 (SCC) [*Delgamuukw*].
40 *St. Catherine's Milling, supra* note 29.
41 *Guerin v. The Queen* (1984), 13 D.L.R. (4th) 321.
42 *Delgamuukw v. British Columbia* (1991), 79 D.L.R. (4th) 185.
43 *Western Australia v. Ward* (2002), 213 C.L.R. 1.
44 *Ibid.* at 89.
45 Kent McNeil, "Racial Discrimination and Unilateral Extinguishment of Native Title" (1996) 1 Australian Indigenous Law Reporter 181; reproduced in Kent McNeil, *Emerging Justice? Essays on Indigenous Rights in Canada and Australia* (Saskatoon: Native Law Centre, University of Saskatchewan, 2001) at 357.
46 Kent McNeil, "Extinguishment of Native Title: The High Court and American Law" (1997) 2 Australian Indigenous Law Reporter 366; reproduced in McNeil, *Emerging Justice, supra* note 45 at 409.
47 *Fejo v. Northern Territory* (1998), 195 C.L.R. 96.
48 *Ibid.* at 130 (per Gleeson C.J., Gaudron, McHugh, Gummow, Hayne, and Callinan JJ.). For a fuller statement leading to a similar conclusion, see Justice Kirby (at 148-50 and 154).
49 Generally, and in contexts not relating particularly to indigenous peoples, the High Court has also expressed caution about following Canadian and US decisions on fiduciary obligations. *Hospital Products Ltd. v. United States Surgical Corporation* (1984), 156 C.L.R. 41 at 96-97 (especially per Mason J.); *Breen v. Williams* (1996), 186 C.L.R. 71; and *Pilmer v. Duke*, [2001] H.C.A. 31. The issue of fiduciary obligation has been raised in other cases involving indigenous Australians and is likely to be argued in forthcoming litigation. The following represents a selection of Australian writings on the matter: C. Hughes, "The Fiduciary Obligations of the Crown to Aborigines: Lessons from the United States and Canada" (1993) 16(1) University of New South Wales Law Journal 71; D. Sweeney, "Broken Promises: The Crown's Fiduciary Duty to Aboriginal Peoples" (1995) 3(75) Aboriginal Law Bulletin 4; L. Behrendt, "Bargaining on More Than Good Will: Recognising a Fiduciary Obligation in Native Title" (2000) 2(4) Land, Rights, Laws: Issues of Native Title 1; G. McIntyre, "Fiduciary Obligations of Governments towards Indigenous Minorities," in Bryan Keon-Cohen, ed., *Native Title in the New Millennium* (Canberra: Aboriginal Studies Press, 2001) at 305; and L. Behrendt, "Responsibility in Governance: Implied Rights, Fiduciary Obligation and Indigenous Peoples" (2002) 61(2) Australian Journal of Public Administration 106. See also Richard H. Bartlett, *Native Title in Australia*, 2nd edition (Sydney: LexisNexis Butterworths, 2004) at chapter 24.
50 Kent McNeil, "The Vulnerability of Indigenous Land Rights in Australia and Canada" (2004) 42 Osgoode Hall Law Journal at 271-301.
51 *International Convention on the Elimination of All Forms of Racial Discrimination* (1966), United Nations, *Treaty Series*, vol. 660 at 195, entered into force on 4 January 1969, [1] and [2].
52 *Racial Discrimination Act 1975* (Cth.).
53 *Koowarta v. Bjelke-Petersen* (1982), 153 C.L.R. 168.
54 *Mabo v. Queensland (No. 1)* (1988), 166 C.L.R. 186. See also *Western Australia v. Commonwealth* (1995), 183 C.L.R. 373 [*Western Australia*].
55 *Mabo (No. 2), supra* note 38 at 42. I have discussed the role of international law in "'Retreat from Injustice': The High Court of Australia and Native Title," in M. Gibney and S. Frankowski, eds., *Judicial Protection of Human Rights: Myth or Reality?* (Westport, CT: Praeger, 1999), 163; and in "The Practical Relevance of International Law, CERD and the UN Draft Declaration on the Rights of Indigenous Peoples," in Bryan Keon-Cohen, ed., *Native Title in the New Millennium* (Canberra: Aboriginal Studies Press, 2001), 391.
56 A summary of the debate is provided in McRae, Nettheim, Beacroft, and McNamara, *supra* note 35 at 242-53. See also Bartlett, *supra* note 49 at chapter 3.
57 McRae, Nettheim, Beacroft, and McNamara, *supra* note 35 at 371.
58 It is possible under the *NTA* for people or governments to lodge a non-claimant application seeking a determination that Native title does not exist.
59 *Western Australia, supra* note 54.
60 *Land (Titles and Traditional Usage) Act 1993* (W.A.).
61 *Wik Peoples, supra* note 20.

62 Later decisions reached a similar conclusion for the Northern Territory and Western Australia: *Hayes v. Northern Territory* (1997), F.C.R. 32; *Western Australia v. Ward* (2002), 213 C.L.R. 1 *[Ward]*. However, the High Court also decided that pastoral leases in the western division of New South Wales granted exclusive possession and therefore extinguished Native title. *Wilson v. Anderson* (2002), 213 C.L.R. 401.

63 McRae, Nettheim, Beacroft, and McNamara, *supra* note 35 at 258-62.

64 *Native Title Amendment Act 1998* (Cth.).

65 Aboriginal Land Rights Commission, *Second Report* (Canberra: Australian Government Publishing Service, 1974) at para. 568.

66 I have given an overview of the extraordinarily long and complex 1998 amendments in G. Nettheim, "The Search for Certainty and the *Native Title Amendment Act 1998* (Cth.)" (1999) 22 University of New South Wales Law Journal 564.

67 Committee on the Elimination of Racial Discrimination, *Decision on Australia,* Doc. CERD/C/54/Misc. 40/Rev 2 (18 March 1999); reproduced in (1999) 4(2) Australian Indigenous Law Reporter 140.

68 Greg Marks, "Avoiding the International Spotlight: Australia, Indigenous Rights and the United Nations Treaty Bodies" (2002) 2(1) Human Rights Law Review 19; and McRae, Nettheim, Beacroft, and McNamara, *supra* note 35 at 263-77.

69 *Members of the Yorta Yorta Aboriginal Community v. Victoria* (2002), 194 A.L.R. 538 at 560-61 (per Gleeson C.J., Gummow and Hayne JJ).

70 *Ibid.* at 572-73.

71 *Ward, supra* note 62 at 89 and 95 (per Gleeson C.J., Gaudron, Gummow and Hayne JJ.) *[Ward]*. Justices McHugh, Kirby, and Callinan, in separate opinions, appeared to concur with the majority opinion, although Justice Kirby gave his view that "the object of the NTA is the recognition of 'native *title,*' rather than the provision of a list of activities" (at 243).

72 *Delgamuukw, supra* note 39 at 240-41 (per Lamer C.J.).

73 *Mabo (No. 2), supra* note 38 at 61.

74 *Ibid.* at 60.

75 *Members of the Yorta Yorta Aboriginal Community v. Victoria,* [1998] F.C.A. 1606.

76 *Members of the Yorta Yorta Aboriginal Community v. Victoria* (2001), 110 F.C.R. 244.

77 *Members of the Yorta Yorta Aboriginal Community v. Victoria* (2002), 194 A.L.R. 538 (Gleeson C.J., McHugh, Gummow, Hayne, and Callinan JJ.; Gaudron and Kirby JJ. dissenting).

78 *Yanner v. Eaton* (1999), 201 C.L.R. 351 (Gleeson C.J., Gaudron, Gummow, Kirby, and Hayne JJ.; McHugh and Callinan JJ. dissenting).

79 *NTA, supra* note 24, s. 211.

80 *Ward, supra* note 62.

81 *Commonwealth v. Yarmirr* (2001), 208 C.L.R. 1.

82 *Wilson v. Anderson* (2002), 213 C.L.R. 401 at 453-54.

83 *Ward, supra* note 62 at 240-41.

84 *Ibid.* at 397-99.

85 Peter Seidel and Julian Hetyey, "Summary of the Yorta Yorta Nation Aboriginal Corporation/State of Victoria Co-operative Management Agreement" (2004) 6(4) Indigenous Law Bulletin 15.

86 Marcia Langton and Lisa Palmer, "Modern Agreement Making and Indigenous People in Australia: Issues and Trends" (2003) 8(1) Australian Indigenous Law Reporter 1; Marcia Langton, Maureen Tehan, Lisa Palmer, and Kathryn Shain, eds., *Honour among Nations? Treaties and Agreements with Indigenous People* (Carlton: Melbourne University Press, 2004); Garth Nettheim, Gary D. Meyers, and Donna Craig, *Indigenous Peoples and Governance Structure: A Comparative Analysis of Land and Resource Management Rights* (Canberra: Aboriginal Studies Press, 2002) especially at chapters 14 and 15.

87 See Sean Brennan, Larissa Behrendt, Lisa Strelein, and George Williams, eds., *Treaty* (Sydney: Federation Press, 2005).

Chapter 11: Let Obligations Be Done

1 I find myself agreeing with Frank Calder. I have always regarded my academic field's focus on Aboriginal peoples as being exceedingly narrow. The Supreme Court of Canada has

fallen into this trap by obsessing over the "Aboriginal" in section 35(1). Others have ignored the histories, ideas, environments, and economies we share together on this continent. An exclusive focus on Aboriginal peoples can treat us as if we were, are, or should be outside of history, politics, or contemporary culture. In my opinion, this slender view is not healthy or helpful in generating holistic relationships.

2 *Calder et al. v. Attorney-General of British Columbia*, [1973] S.C.R. 313, 34 D.L.R. (3d) 145 [*Calder*, cited to S.C.R.].

3 *St. Catherine's Milling & Lumber Co. v. R.* (1887), 13 S.C.R. 577 at 649 (SCC).

4 *St. Catherine's Milling & Lumber Co. v. R.* (1888), 14 App. Cas. 46 (J.C.P.C.).

5 "Their Lordships have had no difficulty in coming to the conclusion that, under the treaties, the Indians obtained no right to their annuities, whether original or augmented, beyond a promise and agreement, which was nothing more than a personal obligation by [the] governor." *Attorney-General of Ontario v. Attorney General of Canada: Re Indian Claims*, [1897] A.C. 199 at 213 (J.C.P.C.).

6 "The language of the statute [*Indian Act*, R.S.C. 1985, c. I-5] embodies the accepted view that these aborigines are, in effect, wards of the State, whose care and welfare are a political trust of the highest obligation." *St. Ann's Island Shooting and Fishing Club Ltd. v. The King*, [1950] S.C.R. 211 at 219.

7 Despite this line of cases, it appears as though the Crown's relationship to Aboriginal peoples has long involved issues of obligations. The Royal Proclamation of 7 October, 1763, R.S.C. 1985, App. II, No. 1, is a good illustration. The Crown promised Indian nations they would remain "unmolested" and "undisturbed" in their territories. It obligated itself to secure Indian title by consent, secured by the Imperial government, rather than through local colonies or settlers. It later recognized and affirmed this position through treaty. The effect of the Royal Proclamation was to initiate an era of wider peace between First Nations and the Crown in the Great Lakes region. The proclamation became central to the party's relationship for many years. The obligation the government assumed became the right Indians claimed. See John Borrows, "Wampum at Niagara: First Nations Self-Government and the Royal Proclamation," in Michael Asch, ed., *Aboriginal and Treaty Rights in Canada: Essays on Law, Equality, and Respect for Difference* (Vancouver: UBC Press, 1997).

8 Justice Gwynne, of the Supreme Court of Canada, recognized the obligatory nature of treaties when he wrote in dissent in *Province of Ontario v. Dominion of Canada and Province of Quebec; In re Indian Claims* (1895), 25 S.C.R. 434 at 511-12: "[T]he terms and conditions expressed in those instruments as to be performed by or on behalf of the Crown, have always been regarded as involving a trust graciously assumed by the Crown to the fulfilment of which with the Indians the faith and honour of the Crown is pledged, and which trust has always been most faithfully fulfilled as a treaty obligation of the Crown."

9 See *Mitchell v. M.N.R.*, [2001] 1 S.C.R. 911 at para. 9 [*Mitchell*]: "With this assertion [sovereignty] arose an obligation to treat aboriginal peoples fairly and honourably, and to protect them from exploitation."

10 See *R. v. Sparrow*, [1990] 1 S.C.R. 1075 at 1104 [*Sparrow*]: "It took a number of judicial decisions and notably the *Calder* case ... to prompt a reassessment of the position."

11 See the chapter by Michael Asch in this volume.

12 *Wewaykum Indian Band v. Canada*, [2002] 4 S.C.R. 245 at 282.

13 *Calder*, supra note 2 at 404. Justice Hall wrote: "The Court of Appeal also erred in holding that there 'is no Indian Title capable of judicial interpretation unless it has previously been recognized either by the Legislature or the Executive Branch of Government.'"

14 For explanations about proof of title, see *Delgamuukw v. British Columbia*, [1997] 3 S.C.R. 1010 [*Delgamuukw*].

15 *Calder*, supra note 2 at 328.

16 Iona Campagnolo, in "Closing Thoughts" at the end of this volume.

17 See the chapters by Stephen Haycox, David V. Williams, and Garth Nettheim all in this volume.

18 *Calder*, supra note 2. Justice Pigeon wrote for the majority: "The substance of the claim is that the Crown's title to the subject land is being questioned, its assertion of an absolute title in fee being challenged on the basis of an adverse title which is said to be a burden on

the fee ... I have to hold that the preliminary objection that the declaration prayed for, being a claim of title against the Crown in the right of the Province of British Columbia, the Court has no jurisdiction to make it in the absence of a fiat of the Lieutenant-Governor of that Province. I am deeply conscious of the hardship involved in holding that the access to the Court for the determination of the plaintiffs' claim is barred by sovereign immunity from suit without a fiat. However, I would point out that in the United States, claims in respect of the taking of lands outside of reserves and not covered by any treaty were not held justiciable until legislative provisions had removed the obstacle created by the doctrine of immunity. In Canada, immunity from suit has been removed by legislation at the federal level and in most Provinces. However, this has not yet been done in British Columbia" (at 225-26).

19 See the chapter by Hamar Foster in this volume.

20 Brian Slattery, "The Hidden Constitution: Aboriginal Rights in Canada" (1984) 32 American Journal of Comparative Law 361.

21 Jennifer Nedelsky, "Reconceiving Rights as Relationship" (1993) 1 Review of Constitutional Studies 1; and Joseph Singer, "The Legal Rights Debate in Analytical Jurisprudence from Bentham to Hohfeld" (1982) Wisconsin Law Review 975.

22 See the conversation between Frank Calder and Thomas Berger in the second chapter of this volume.

23 Wesley Newcomb Hohfeld, *Fundamental Legal Conceptions*, edited by Walter Wheeler Cook (New Haven, CT: Yale University Press, 1919) at 35-64.

24 *Lake Shore & M.S.R. Co. v. Kurtz*, (1894) 10 Ind. App., 60, 37 N.E., 303 and 304, cited in Hohfeld, *supra* note 23.

25 *Johnson v. M'Intosh* (1823), 8 Wheaton 543, 21 U.S. 543 (1823) at 573-74: "Those relations which were to exist between the discoverer and the natives, were to be regulated by themselves. The rights thus acquired being exclusive, no other power could interpose between them." See also *Osoyoos Indian Band v. Oliver (Town)*, [2001] 3 S.C.R. 746 at para. 154: "In *Guerin v. The Queen*, [1984] 2 S.C.R. 335, at p. 383, the Court noted that the purpose of requiring Crown consent was not to substitute the Crown's decision for the band's decision but rather to prevent exploitation in the bargaining process. Thus as Dickson J. (as he then was) noted in *Guerin*: 'The purpose of this surrender requirement is clearly to interpose the Crown between the Indians and prospective purchasers or lessees of their land, so as to prevent the Indians from being exploited.'"

26 *Canadian Pacific Ltd. v. Paul*, [1988] 2 S.C.R. 654 at 677.

27 *R. v. Marshall (No. 1)*, [1999] 3 S.C.R. 456 at para. 48 [*Marshall*].

28 *Sparrow, supra* note 10 at 1109.

29 This argument mirrors Brian Slattery's thesis that there are general and specific Aboriginal rights within section 35(1). See Brian Slattery, "Making Sense of Aboriginal and Treaty Rights" (2000) 79 Canadian Bar Review 196; and his chapter in this volume, though I am focusing on obligations.

30 Generic Aboriginal rights are of a uniform character and do not vary according to factors particular to any Aboriginal group.

31 Specific Aboriginal rights are defined by factors pertaining to a particular Aboriginal group and thus can vary from group to group.

32 See the chapter by Brian Slattery in this volume.

33 See *Mitchell, supra* note 9. See also *Haida Nation v. British Columbia (Minister of Forests)*, [2004] 3 S.C.R. 511 at para. 16 [*Haida Nation*]: "The honour of the Crown is always at stake in its dealings with Aboriginal peoples." See, for example, *R. v. Badger*, [1996] 1 S.C.R. 771 at para. 41; and *Marshall, supra* note 27. It is not a mere incantation but, rather, a core precept that finds its application in concrete practices.

34 *Mikisew Cree First Nation v. Canada (Minister of Canadian Heritage)*, 2005 SCC 69 at para. 51, [2005] 3 S.C.R. 388 [*Mikisew Cree*].

35 Leonard I. Rotman, *Parallel Paths: Fiduciary Doctrine and the Crown-Native Relationship in Canada* (Toronto: University of Toronto Press, 1996).

36 *Sparrow, supra* note 10 at 1109.

37 *See Mikisew Cree, supra* note 34: "The fundamental objective of the modern law of aborigi-
    nal and treaty rights is the reconciliation of aboriginal peoples and non-aboriginal peoples
    and their respective claims, interests and ambitions" (at para. 1). Reconciliation comes
    from the Latin roots *re,* meaning "again"; *con,* meaning "with"; and *sella,* meaning "seat."
    Reconciliation, therefore, literally means "to sit again with."
38 *R. v. Marshall; R. v. Bernard,* 2005 SCC 43 at para. 39 (Can. LII) [*Marshall*]: "Prior to
    constitutionalization of aboriginal rights in 1982, aboriginal title could be extinguished by
    clear legislative act (see *R. v. Van der Peet,* [1996] 2 S.C.R. 507). Now that is not possible." See
    also Kent McNeil, "Extinguishment of Aboriginal Title in Canada: Treaties, Legislation,
    and Judicial Discretion" (2001-2) 33 Ottawa Law Review 301.
39 See *R. v. Côté,* [1996] 3 S.C.R. 139 at para. 59: "[A] static and retrospective interpretation of
    s. 35(1) cannot be reconciled with the noble and prospective purpose of the constitutional
    entrenchment of aboriginal and treaty rights in the *Constitution Act, 1982.* Indeed, the
    respondent's proposed interpretation risks undermining the very purpose of s. 35(1) by
    perpetuating the historical injustice suffered by aboriginal peoples at the hands of colonizers
    who failed to respect the distinctive cultures of pre-existing aboriginal societies. To quote
    the words of Brennan J. in *Mabo v. Queensland (No. 2)* (1992), 175 C.L.R. 1 (H.C. Aust.) at
    42: 'Whatever the justification advanced in earlier days for refusing to recognize the rights
    and interests in land of the indigenous inhabitants of settled colonies, an unjust and dis-
    criminatory doctrine of that kind can no longer be accepted.'"
40 *Sparrow, supra* note 10 at 1112.
41 *Ibid.*
42 *Ibid.*
43 *Ibid.* See also generally *Osoyoos Indian Band v. Oliver (Town),* [2001] 3 S.C.R. 746.
44 *Sparrow, supra* note 10 at 1117. "The appellants have, to employ the words of their counsel,
    a 'right to share in the available resource.' *Delgamuukw, supra* note 14 at para. 167: "[T]hat
    the conferral of fee simples for agriculture, and of leases and licences for forestry and min-
    ing reflect the prior occupation of aboriginal title lands."
45 *Ibid.* at 1115-17.
46 *R. v. Sundown,* [1999] 1 S.C.R. 393 at para. 26; and *R. v. Badger,* [1996] 1 S.C.R. 771 at paras.
    88-92.
47 *Delgamuukw, supra* note 14 at para. 161, quoting *R. v. Gladstone,* [1996] 2 S.C.R. 723 at para.
    75 [*Gladstone*]: "Legitimate government objectives also include 'the pursuit of economic
    and regional fairness' and 'the recognition of the historical reliance upon, and participa-
    tion in, the fishery by non-aboriginal groups.'"
48 *Gladstone, supra* note 47.
49 "In light of the Crown's unique fiduciary obligations towards aboriginal peoples, Parlia-
    ment may not simply adopt an unstructured discretionary administrative regime which
    risks infringing aboriginal rights in a substantial number of applications in the absence of
    some explicit guidance." *R. v. Adams,* [1996] 3 S.C.R. 101 at para. 54.
50 *Gladstone, supra* note 47 at paras. 59-80
51 *Delgamuukw, supra* note 14 at para. 167.
52 *Ibid.*
53 *Mikisew Cree, supra* note 34 at para. 31.
54 *Ibid.* at para. 169: "The economic aspect of aboriginal title suggests that compensation is
    relevant to the question of justification as well, a possibility suggested in *Sparrow* and which
    I repeated in *Gladstone.* Indeed, compensation for breaches of fiduciary duty are a well-
    established part of the landscape of aboriginal rights: *Guerin.* In keeping with the duty of
    honour and good faith on the Crown, fair compensation will ordinarily be required when
    aboriginal title is infringed. The amount of compensation payable will vary with the na-
    ture of the particular aboriginal title affected and with the nature and severity of the in-
    fringement and the extent to which aboriginal interests were accommodated." See also
    Sparrow, supra note 10 at 1119.
55 "The government's duty to consult with Aboriginal peoples and accommodate their inter-
    ests is grounded in the honour of the Crown." *Haida Nation, supra* note 33 at para. 16.

56 *Ibid.* at para. 49-50. "The terms 'accommodate' and 'accommodation' have been defined as to 'adapt, harmonize, reconcile' ... 'an adjustment or adaptation to suit a special or different purpose ... a convenient arrangement; a settlement or compromise." *Concise Oxford Dictionary of Current English,* 9th edition (Oxford: Oxford University Press, 1995) at 9. The Court's decisions confirm this vision of accommodation. The Court in *Sparrow, supra* note 10, raised the concept of accommodation, stressing the need to balance competing societal interests with Aboriginal and treaty rights. In *R. v. Sioui,* [1990] 1 S.C.R. 1025 at 1072, the Court stated that the Crown bears the burden of proving that its occupancy of lands "cannot be accommodated to reasonable exercise of the Hurons' rights." And in *R. v. Côté,* [1996] 3 S.C.R. 139 at para. 81, the Court spoke of whether restrictions on Aboriginal rights "can be accommodated with the Crown's special fiduciary relationship with First Nations." Balance and compromise are inherent in the notion of reconciliation.

57 *Haida Nation, supra* note 33 at para. 51. See also *R. v. Adams,* [1996] 3 S.C.R. 101 at para. 5.

58 *Paul v. British Columbia (Forest Appeals Commission),* [2003] 2 S.C.R. 585 [*Paul*]; and *Haida Nation, supra* note 33 at para. 44: "The government may wish to adopt dispute resolution procedures like mediation or administrative regimes with impartial decision-makers in complex or difficult cases."

59 *Taku River Tlingit First Nation v. British Columbia (Project Assessment Director),* [2004] 3 S.C.R. 550 at para. 44.

60 *Reference re Secession of Quebec,* [1998] 2 S.C.R. 217 at para. 82: "[T]he framers of the *Constitution Act, 1982* included in s. 35 explicit protection for existing aboriginal and treaty rights, and in s. 25, a non-derogation clause in favour of the rights of aboriginal peoples. The 'promise' of s. 35, as it was termed in *R. v. Sparrow,* [1990] 1 S.C.R. 1075, at p. 1083, recognized not only the ancient occupation of land by aboriginal peoples, but their contribution to the building of Canada, and the special commitments made to them by successive governments. The protection of these rights, so recently and arduously achieved, whether looked at in their own right or as part of the larger concern with minorities, reflects an important underlying constitutional value." For further commentary about the potential significance of the Québec secession reference to Aboriginal peoples, see John Borrows, "Sovereignty's Alchemy: An Analysis of *Delgamuukw v. British Columbia*" (1999) 37 Osgoode Hall Law Journal 537 at 537.

61 *Corbiere v. Canada (Minister of Indian and Northern Affairs),* [1999] 2 S.C.R. 203. *Canadian Charter of Rights and Freedoms,* Part 1 of the *Constitution Act, 1982,* being Schedule B to the *Canada Act, 1982* (U.K.), 1982, c. 11.

62 *Delgamuukw, supra* note 14 at para. 167.

63 *Paul, supra* note 58 at para. 24: "Section 35 therefore applies to both provinces and the federal government."

64 *Constitution Act, 1867,* 30 & 31 Victoria, c. 3. Under section 91(24), the federal government has exclusive legislative authority in relation to "Indians and lands reserved for Indians." These provisions should be interpreted in light of the human rights values in the *Charter, supra* note 61. See *R. v. Demers,* [2004] 2 S.C.R. 489 at para. 85: "Since the promulgation of the *Charter* in 1982, the provisions set out therein have resulted in fructifying contact with the other elements of our constitution. Thus, the human rights and freedoms expressed in the *Charter,* while they do not formally modify the scope of the powers in ss. 91 and 92 of the *Constitution Act, 1867,* do provide a new lens through which those powers should be viewed. In choosing one among several possible interpretations of powers that implicate human rights, the interpretation that best accords with the imperatives of the *Charter* should be adopted."

65 *Sparrow, supra* note 10 at 1108.

66 *Haida Nation, supra* note 33.

67 There are, however, different ways to construe reconciliation: see Kent McNeil, "Reconciliation and the Supreme Court: The Opposing Views of Chief Justices Lamer and McLachlin" (2003) 2 Indigenous Law Journal 1.

68 *Delgamuukw, supra* note 14 at 141.

69 *Mitchell, supra* note 9 at para. 133.

70 Section 35(1) reads, "The existing Aboriginal and treaty rights of the Aboriginal peoples of Canada are hereby recognized and affirmed."

71 *Charter, supra* note 61.

72 Their *sui generis* designation is a signal that the common law can be inappropriate as a measure for determining Aboriginal interests. It developed from a different cultural context and has not always recognized and affirmed distinct ways of Aboriginal organization. For further analysis, see John Borrows and Leonard Rotman, "The Sui Generis Nature of Aboriginal Rights: Does It Make a Difference?" (1997-98) 36 University of Alberta Law Review 9.

73 *Constitution Act, 1982*, being Schedule B to the *Canada Act, 1982* (U.K.), 1982, c. 11, s. 1.

74 However, see *Paul, supra* note 58 at para. 38: "[T]here is no principled basis for distinguishing s. 35 rights from other constitutional questions." However, it should be remembered that the argument in *Paul* was directed to the point that provincial tribunals had authority to consider Aboriginal rights questions and not to the *sui generis* nature of Aboriginal rights.

75 *Constitution Act, 1982, supra* note 73.

76 John Borrows, "Uncertain Citizens: Aboriginal Peoples and the Supreme Court" (2001) 80 Canadian Bar Review 15.

77 John Borrows, "The Trickster: Integral to a Distinctive Culture" (1997) Constitutional Forum 29. *Van der Peet, supra* note 38.

78 The Supreme Court of Canada has written that international law is helpful by way of analogy when dealing with Aboriginal issues, though it is not determinative. See *Simon v. R.*, [1985] 2 S.C.R. 387 at para. 33: "While it may be helpful in some instances to analogize the principles of international treaty law to Indian treaties, these principles are not determinative."

79 *Reference re Secession of Quebec, supra* note 60 at para. 114: "The existence of the right of a people to self-determination is now so widely recognized in international conventions that the principle has acquired a status beyond 'convention' and is considered a general principle of international law."

80 *Ibid.* at paras. 126-34.

81 Catherine Bell, "Métis Constitutional Rights in Section 35(1)" (1997) 36 Alberta Law Review 180, 189-92, and 194-95.

82 *Ibid.* at 183. Furthermore, the Supreme Court of Canada has observed: "The right to self-determination has developed largely as a human right." *Reference re Secession of Quebec, supra* note 60 at para. 124.

83 Section 35(1)'s purpose is partially constructed on the fact of the organized nature of Aboriginal societies written about in *Calder*. See *Van der Peet, supra* note 38 at para. 33.

84 See the chapter by Kent McNeil in this volume.

85 *Ibid.*

86 *Ibid.*

87 *Calder, supra* note 2 at 328.

88 John Borrows, "Tracking Trajectories: Aboriginal Governance as an Aboriginal Right" (2005) 38 UBC Law Review 285.

89 John Borrows, "Creating an Indigenous Legal Community" (2005) 50 McGill Law Journal 153.

90 A. Rose, ed., *Nisga'a: People of the Nass River* (Vancouver: Douglas and McIntyre, 1993) at 22.

91 *Ibid.* at 15.

92 T. Molloy, *The World Is Our Witness: The Historic Journey of the Nisga'a into Canada* (Calgary: Fifth House, 2000) at 121.

93 For a summary of *Ayuukhl Nisga'a* by Nisga'a Elder Bert McKay, see Rose, ed., *supra* note 90 at 125-29.

94 *Nisga'a Final Agreement Act*, R.S.C. 2000, c. 7, S.B.C. 1999, c. 2. Within the Nisga'a Lisims government, there is a legislative house knows as Wilp Si'ayuukhl Nisga'a and the Nisga'a Lisims.

95 *Sparrow, supra* note 10 at 1106.

96 *Marshall, supra* note 38 at para. 130; see also para. 139: "The aboriginal perspective on the occupation of their land can also be gleaned in part, but not exclusively, from pre-sovereignty systems of aboriginal law."

97 John Borrows, "Indigenous Legal Traditions in Canada," Washington Journal of Law and Policy [forthcoming].
98 See *R. v. Demers*, [2004] 2 S.C.R. 489 at para. 83: These unwritten elements are aids in the interpretation of the text of our constitutional documents and can fill gaps in the text. *Reference re Secession of Quebec, supra* note 60 at paras. 53-54. They may also, in certain circumstances, give rise to substantive legal obligations, which themselves are limitations on government and courts (at para. 55).
99 *Campbell et al. v. AG BC/AG Cda & Nisga'a Nation et al.* (2000), 189 D.L.R. (4th) 333 at paras. 65-81.
100 *Reference re Secession of Quebec, supra* note 60 at para. 50.
101 *Ibid.* at para. 54.
102 *Ibid.*
103 *Ibid.* at para. 82.
104 Basil Johnston, *Ojibway Heritage* (Toronto: McClelland and Stewart, 1976) at 59.
105 Basil Johnston [correspondence with author].
106 *Ibid.*
107 Johnston, *supra* note 104 at 61-79.
108 See *Haida Nation, supra* note 33 at paras. 42 and 48. In the case of consultation, Aboriginal obligations include a duty to act in good faith, to not frustrate the Crown's reasonable good faith attempts, to not take unreasonable positions to thwart the government from acting, and to define the claim and concerns as clearly as possible.
109 Harold Cardinal and Walter Hildebrandt, eds., *Treaty Elders of Saskatchewan: Our Dream Is That Our Peoples Will One Day Be Clearly Recognized as Nations* (Calgary: University of Calgary Press, 2000).
110 John Borrows, "Ground Rules: Indigenous Treaties in Canada and New Zealand" (2006) 22 New Zealand Universities Law Review 188.
111 See *Reference re Secession of Quebec, supra* note 60 at para. 63: "The evolution of our democratic tradition can be traced back to the Magna Carta (1215) and before, through the long struggle for Parliamentary supremacy which culminated in the English *Bill of Rights* of 1689, the emergence of representative political institutions in the colonial era, the development of responsible government in the 19th century, and eventually, the achievement of Confederation itself in 1867 ... [T]he Canadian tradition ... is one of evolutionary democracy moving in uneven steps toward the goal of universal suffrage and more effective representation."
112 See *R. v. Rahey*, [1987] 1 S.C.R. 588 at para. 98: "The great defect of Magna Carta, however, lay in its failure to provide adequate mechanisms for the enforcement of the rights it purported to guarantee."
113 See Kent McNeil, "Aboriginal Title as a Constitutionally Protected Aboriginal Right," in Owen Lippert, ed., *Beyond the Nass Valley: National Implications of the Supreme Court's Delgamuukw Decision* (Vancouver: Fraser Institute, 2000): "*Magna Carta* would have been received as part of the applicable statute law in all the common law provinces. As a fundamental part of the British constitution, no doubt it applies in Quebec as well, despite the reintroduction of French civil law by the *Quebec Act*, 14 Geo. III (1774), c. 83 (U.K.). The preamble to the *Constitution Act, 1867, supra* note 64, provides that Canada shall have "a Constitution similar in Principle to that of the United Kingdom."
114 *An Act Declaring the Rights and Liberties of the Subject and Settling the Succession of the Crown, 1688,* (U.K.) 1 Will. & Mary, c. 2.
115 The *Charter* constrains the Crown relative to individual citizens and obligates it to respect enumerated rights in the document.
116 *R. v. Sparrow*, 70 D.L.R. (4th) 385 at 412.
117 *Crown Proceedings Act*, R.S.B.C. 1996, c. 89.
118 Furthermore, the Crown may have worries related to the fiscal burden such responsibilities might entail. The Crown may also be hesitant to recognize its obligations because they constrain its sovereignty whenever they are in operation. These objections should not stand in the way of recognizing governmental obligations under section 35(1).

119 Insurance is often taken out to compensate groups or individuals who are harmed by those who fail to meet appropriate standards. In applying these insights to involuntary obligations that the government has towards Aboriginal peoples, Aboriginal peoples might often feel as though they are the victims of a rogue tortfeasor. Some governments seem unwilling to take reasonable care and ensure that Aboriginal and treaty rights are recognized and affirmed. Aboriginal peoples thereby experience harm. There is no insurance that Aboriginal peoples can purchase to compensate against this harm. The entity with the involuntary obligation often does not seem to want to admit to its obligation.

120 John Borrows, "Measuring a Work in Progress: Canada, Constitutionalism, Citizenship and Aboriginal Peoples," in Ardith Walkem and Halie Bruce, eds., *Box of Treasures or Empty Box: Twenty Years of Section 35* (Penticton, BC: Theytus Books, 2003).

121 For many years, religion provided the most prominent source of guidance for most people in this country. As religion has faded from public discourse, other systems of traditional authority have competed for the public's loyalty.

122 Austin Sarat, ed., *Law, Violence and the Possibility of Law* (Princeton: Princeton University Press, 2001).

Bibliography

Books and Articles

Aasen, Wendy. *The Spirit and Intent of Treaty 8 in the Northwest Territories: As Long As the Sun Shines, the River Flows, and the Grass Grows* (Yellowknife, NWT: Treaty 8 Tribal Council, 1994).

Adams, P. *Fatal Necessity: British Intervention in New Zealand 1830-1847* (Auckland: Auckland/ Oxford University Press, 1977).

Alfred, Gerald R. "From Bad to Worse: Internal Politics in the 1990 Crisis at Kahnawake" (1991) 8 Northeast Indian Quarterly 23.

–. *Heeding the Voices of Our Ancestors: Kahnawake Mohawk Politics and the Rise of Native Nationalism* (Toronto: Oxford University Press, 1995).

Alfred, Taiaiake. *Peace, Power, Righteousness: An Indigenous Manifesto* (Don Mills, ON: Oxford University Press, 1999).

–. *Wasa'se: Indigenous Pathways of Action and Freedom* (Peterborough, ON: Broadview Press, 2005).

Anaya, S. James. *Indigenous Peoples in International Law* (New York: Oxford University Press, 1996).

–. *Indigenous Peoples in International Law*, 2nd edition (Oxford: Oxford University Press, 2004).

Andersen, Chris. "Residual Tensions of Empire: Contemporary Métis Communities and the Canadian Judicial Imagination." In Michael Murphy, ed., *Canada: The State of the Federation: Reconfiguring Aboriginal-State Relations* (Montreal and Kingston: Institute of Intergovernmental Relations, 2003).

Anderson, Robert B., and Robert M. Bone, eds. *Natural Resources and Aboriginal People in Canada* (Concord, ON: Captus, 2003).

Andrew, Caroline, and Sandra Rodgers, eds. *Women and the Canadian State* (Montreal and Kingston: McGill-Queen's University Press, 1997).

Arima, E.Y. *The West Coast People: The Nootka of Vancouver Island and Cape Flattery* (Victoria: British Columbia Provincial Museum, 1983).

Arnold, Robert D. *Alaska Native Land Claims* (Anchorage: Alaska Native Foundation, 1976).

Asch, Michael, *Home and Native Land: Aboriginal Rights and the Canadian Constitution*, revised edition (Vancouver: UBC Press, 1993).

–. "From *Calder* to *Van der Peet*: Aboriginal Rights and Canadian Law, 1973–96." In P. Havemann, ed., *Indigenous Peoples' Rights in Australia, Canada, and New Zealand* (Melbourne: Oxford University Press, 1999).

–, ed. *Aboriginal and Treaty Rights in Canada: Essays on Law, Equality, and Respect for Difference* (Vancouver: UBC Press, 1997).

Asch, Michael, and Patrick Macklem. "Aboriginal Rights and Canadian Sovereignty: An Essay on *R. v. Sparrow*" (1991) 29 Alberta Law Review 498.

Asch, M., and N. Zlotkin. "Affirming Aboriginal Title: A New Basis for Comprehensive Claims Negotiations." In M. Asch, ed., *Aboriginal and Treaty Rights in Canada: Essays on Law, Equality and Respect for Difference* (Vancouver: UBC Press, 1997).

Aupilaarjuk, Mariano et al. *Interviewing Inuit Elders: Perspectives on Traditional Law* (Iqaluit: Nunavut Arctic College, 2000).

Austin, Lisa, and Christina Boyd. *The Oka Crisis* (Dundas: Peace Research Institute, 1994).

Awashish, Philip. "From Board to Nation Governance: The Evolution of Eeyou Tapay-Tah-Jeh-Souwin (Eeyou Governance) in Eeyou Istchee." In Michael Murphy, ed., *Canada: The State of the Federation: Reconfiguring Aboriginal-State Relations* (Montreal and Kingston: Institute of Intergovernmental Relations, 2003).

Baca, Lawrence. "The Legal Status of American Indians." In William C. Sturtevant and Wilcomb E. Washburn, eds. *Handbook of North American Indians*. Vol. 4: *History of Indian-White Relations* (Washington, DC: Smithsonian Institution, 1988).

Bankes, N. "*Delgamuukw*, Division of Powers and Provincial Land and Resource Laws: Some Implications for Provincial Resource Rights" (1998) 32 UBC Law Review 317.

Banner, Stuart. *How the Indians Lost Their Land: Law and Power on the Frontier* (Cambridge, MA: Belknap Press of Harvard University Press, 2005).

Banting, Keith, and Richard Simeon, eds. *And No One Cheered: Federalism, Democracy and the Constitution Act* (Toronto: Methuen, 1983).

Barnett, H.G. *The Coast Salish of British Columbia* (Eugene: University of Oregon Press, 1955).

Barsh, Russel Lawrence. "The Nature and Spirit of North American Political Systems" (1986) 10 American Indian Quarterly 181.

Barsh, Russel L., and James (Sákéj) Youngblood Henderson. "The Supreme Court's *Van Der Peet* Trilogy: Naïve Imperialism and Ropes of Sand" (1997) 42 McGill Law Journal 993.

Bartlett, Richard H. *Indian Act of Canada*, 2nd edition (Saskatoon: University of Saskatchewan Native Law Centre, 1988).

–. *Indian Reserves and Aboriginal Lands in Canada: A Homeland: A Study in Law and History* (Saskatoon: University of Saskatchewan Native Law Centre, 1990).

–. *Native Title in Australia*, 2nd edition (Sydney: LexisNexis Butterworths, 2004).

Bartlett, Richard H., and Jill Milroy. *Native Title Claims in Canada and Australia*: Delgamuukw *and* Miriuwung Gajerrong (Perth: University of Western Australia, 1999).

Barton, G. *History of New South Wales from the Records*. Vol. 1: *Governor Phillip* (Sydney: Charles Potter, 1889).

Bassett, H., R. Steel, and D.V. Williams. *The Maori Land Legislation Manual* (Wellington: Crown Forestry Rental Trust, 1994).

Bayefsky, Anne F., and Mary Eberts. *Equality Rights and the Canadian Charter of Rights and Freedoms* (Toronto: Carswell, 1985).

Beck, S.M., and I. Bernier, eds. *Canada and the New Constitution: The Unfinished Agenda*. Vol. 1 (Montreal: Institute for Research on Public Policy, 1983).

Begin, Patricia, Wendy Moss, and Peter Niemczak. *The Land Claim Dispute at Oka* (Ottawa: Library of Parliament, Research Branch, 1992).

Behrendt, L. "Bargaining on More Than Good Will: Recognising a Fiduciary Obligation in Native Title" (2000) 2(4) Land, Rights, Laws: Issues of Native Title: http://ntru.aiatsis.gov.au/ntpapers/IPv2n4.pdf.

–. "Responsibility in Governance: Implied Rights, Fiduciary Obligation and Indigenous Peoples" (2002) 61(2) Australian Journal of Public Administration 106.

Belich, J. *Making Peoples: A History of the New Zealanders from Polynesian Settlement to the End of the Nineteenth Century* (Auckland: Penguin, 1996).

–. *Paradise Reforged: A History of the New Zealanders from the 1880s to the Year 2000* (Auckland: Penguin, 2001).

Bell, Catherine. *Contemporary Metis Justice: The Settlement Way* (Edmonton, AB: Metis Settlement Appeals Tribunal, 1999).

–. "Metis Constitutional Rights in Section 35(1)" (1997) 36 Alberta Law Review 180.

–. "New Directions in the Law of Aboriginal Rights" (1998) 77 Canadian Bar Review 36.

Bell, Catherine, and Michael Asch. "Challenging Assumptions: The Impact of Precedent in Aboriginal Rights Litigation." In Michael Asch, ed., *Aboriginal and Treaty Rights in Canada: Essays on Law, Equality and Respect for Difference* (Vancouver: UBC Press, 1997).

Bell, Catherine, and David Kahane, eds. *Intercultural Dispute Resolution in Aboriginal Contexts* (Vancouver: UBC Press, 2004).

Bennett, J.M., and A.C. Castles, *A Source Book of Australian Legal History* (Sydney: Law Book Company, 1982).

Bennion, T., M. Birdling, and R. Paton, *Making Sense of the Foreshore and Seabed* (Wellington: Maori Law Review, 2004).

Berger, Thomas R. *Northern Frontier, Northern Homeland: The Report of the Mackenzie Valley Pipeline Inquiry* (Toronto: James Lorimer and Company, 1977).

–. *One Man's Justice: A Life in the Law* (Vancouver: Douglas and McIntyre, 2002).

Berman, H.R. "The Concept of Aboriginal Rights in the Early Legal History of the United States" (1978) 27 Buffalo Law Review 637.

Berry, David Steadman. *Aboriginal Self-Determination under International Law* (Ottawa: National Library of Canada, 1994).

Biderton, J., and A.-G. Gagnon, eds. *Canadian Politics* (Toronto: Broadview Press, 1999).

Bird, J. et al., eds. *Nation to Nation: Aboriginal Sovereignty and the Future of Canada* (Toronto: Irwin, 2002).

Blackstone, Sir William. *Commentaries on the Laws of England.* 18th edition (London, 1923).

Blake, Lynn A. "Oblate Missionaries and the 'Indian Land Question'" (1998) 119 BC Studies 27.

Boast, R.P. "*In Re the Ninety-Mile Beach* Revisited" (1993) 23 Victoria University of Wellington Law Review 145.

Boldt, M. *Surviving as Indians: The Challenge of Self-Government* (Toronto: University of Toronto Press, 1993).

Boldt, Menno, and J. Anthony Long. "Tribal Traditions and European-Western Political Ideologies: The Dilemma of Canada's Native Indians." In Menno Boldt and J. Anthony Long, eds., *The Quest for Justice: Aboriginal Peoples and Aboriginal Rights* (Toronto: University of Toronto Press, 1985).

Boldt, Menno, Anthony Long, and Leroy Little Bear, eds. *Pathways to Self-Determination: Native Indian Leaders' Perspectives on Self-Government* (Toronto: University of Toronto Press, 1984).

–, eds. *Quest for Justice: Aboriginal Rights in Canada* (Toronto: University of Toronto Press, 1985).

Bombay, Harry, and John MacTavish. *Co-Management and Other Forms of Agreement in the Forest Sector* (Ottawa: National Aboriginal Forestry Association, 1997).

Borrows, John J. "Constitutional Law from a First Nation Perspective: Self-Government and the Royal Proclamation" (1994) 28 UBC Law Review 1.

–. "Creating an Indigenous Legal Community" (2005) 50 McGill Law Journal 153.

–. "Fourword: Issues, Individuals, Institutions and Ideas" (2002) 1 Indigenous Law Journal 7.

–. "Frozen Rights in Canada: Constitutional Interpretation and the Trickster" (1997-98) 22 American Indian Law Review 37.

–. "Ground Rules: Indigenous Treaties in Canada and New Zealand" (2006) 22(2) New Zealand Universities Law Review 188.

–. "Indigenous Legal Traditions in Canada" Washington Journal of Law and Policy [forthcoming].

–. "Measuring a Work in Progress: Canada, Constitutionalism, Citizenship and Aboriginal Peoples." In Ardith Walkem and Halie Bruce, eds., *Box of Treasures or Empty Box: Twenty Years of Section 35* (Penticton, BC: Theytus Books, 2003).

–. *Recovering Canada: The Resurgence of Indigenous Law* (Toronto: University of Toronto Press, 2002).

–. "Sovereignty's Alchemy: An Analysis of *Delgamuukw v. British Columbia*" (1999) 37 Osgoode Hall Law Journal 537.

–. "Stewardship and the First Nations Governance Act" (2003) 29 Queen's Law Journal 103.

–. "Tracking Trajectories: Aboriginal Governance as an Aboriginal Right" (2005) 38 UBC Law Review 295.

–. "The Trickster: Integral to a Distinctive Culture" (1997) Constitutional Forum 29.

–. "Uncertain Citizens: Aboriginal Peoples and the Supreme Court" (2001) 80 Canadian Bar Review 15.

–. "Wampum at Niagara: First Nations Self-Government and the Royal Proclamation." In Michael Asch, ed. *Aboriginal and Treaty Rights in Canada: Essays on Law, Equality and Respect for Difference* (Vancouver: UBC Press, 1997).

–. "With or Without You: First Nations Law (in Canada)" (1996) 41 McGill Law Journal 629.

Borrows, John, and Leonard Rotman. *Aboriginal Legal Issues: Cases, Materials and Commentary* (Toronto: Butterworths, 1998).

–. "The *Sui Generis* Nature of Aboriginal Rights: Does It Make a Difference?" (1997) 36 Alberta Law Review 9.

Bourdon, Donald J. *The Boom Years: G.G. Nye's Photographs of North Vancouver, 1905-1909* (North Vancouver: Hancock House, 1981).

Bowering, J. "Certainty and Finality in the Nisga'a Agreement" (2002) 11 Dalhousie Journal of Legal Studies 1.

Bowsfield, Hartwell, ed. *Fort Victoria Letters, 1846-1851* (Winnipeg: Hudson's Bay Record Society, 1979).

Brennan, Sean, Larissa Behrendt, Lisa Strelein, and George Williams. *Treaty* (Sydney: Federation Press, 2005).

Brigham, Clarence S., ed. *British Royal Proclamations Relating to America* (Worcester, MA: American Antiquarian Society, 1911).

Brody, Hugh. *Maps and Dreams: Indians and the British Columbia Frontier* (Vancouver: Douglas and McIntyre, 1981).

Brookfield, F.M. "The New Zealand Constitution: The Search for Legitimacy." In I.H. Kawharu, ed., *Waitangi: Maori and Pakeha* (Auckland: Oxford University Press, 1989).

–. "The Waitangi Tribunal and the Whanganui River-Bed" (2000) New Zealand Law Review 1.

Bryan, B. "Property as Ontology: On Aboriginal and English Understandings of Ownership" (2000) 13 Canadian Journal of Law and Jurisprudence 3.

Burke, B.J. "Left Out in the Cold: The Problem with Aboriginal Title under Section 35(1) of the *Constitution Act, 1982* for Historically Nomadic Aboriginal Peoples" (2000) 38 Osgoode Hall Law Journal 1.

–. "Property as Ontology: On Aboriginal and English Understandings of Ownership" (2000) 13 Canadian Journal of Law and Jurisprudence 3.

Cail, Robert E. *Land, Man and the Law: The Disposal of Crown Lands in British Columbia* (Vancouver: UBC Press, 1974).

Cairns, Alan C. *Disruptions: Constitutional Struggles, from the Charter to Meech Lake* (Toronto: McClelland and Stewart, 1991).

–. *First Nations and the Canadian State: In Search of Coexistence* (Kingston: Institute of Intergovernmental Relations, 2005).

–. "Ritual, Taboo, and Bias in Constitutional Controversies in Canada, or Constitutional Talk Canadian Style." In Alan C. Cairns, *Disruptions: Constitutional Struggles, from the Charter to Meech Lake* (Toronto: McClelland and Stewart, 1991).

Calloway, Colin G. *New Worlds for All: Indians, Europeans, and the Remaking of Early America* (Baltimore, MD: John Hopkins University Press, 1997).

Cameron, Kirk, and Graham White. *Northern Governments in Transition: Political and Constitutional Development in the Yukon, Nunavut and the Western Northwest Territories* (Montreal: Institute for Research on Public Policy, 1995).

Canby, Jr., William C. *American Indian Law* (St. Paul: West Publishing, 1981).

Cardinal, Harold. *The Unjust Society: The Tragedy of Canada's Indians* (Edmonton: Hurtig, 1969).

–. *The Rebirth of Canada's Indians* (Edmonton: Hurtig, 1977).

Cardinal, Harold, and Walter Hildebrandt, eds. *Treaty Elders of Saskatchewan: Our Dream Is That Our Peoples Will One Day Be Clearly Recognized as Nations* (Calgary: University of Calgary Press, 2000).

Carlson, Kirsten Matoy. "Does Constitutional Change Matter? Canada's Recognition of Aboriginal Title" (2005) 22 Arizona Journal of International and Comparative Law 455.

Carstens, Peter. *The Queen's People: A Study of Hegemony, Coercion, and Accommodation among the Okanagan of Canada* (Toronto: University of Toronto Press, 1991).

Carter, Sarah. *Aboriginal People and Colonizers of Western Canada to 1900* (Toronto: University of Toronto Press, 1999).

Cassidy, Frank, ed. *Aboriginal Title in British Columbia: Delgamuukw v. The Queen* (Montreal: Institute for Research on Public Policy, 1992).

Cassidy, F., and R.L. Bish. *Indian Government: Its Meaning in Practice* (Lantzville: Oolichan Books, 1989).

Charlesworth, Hector, ed. *A Cyclopaedia of Canadian Biography* (Toronto: Hunter-Rose Company, 1919).

Chartrand, Paul. *Manitoba's Métis Settlement Scheme of 1870* (Saskatoon: Native Law Centre, University of Saskatchewan, 1991).

–. *Who Are Canada's Aboriginal Peoples? Recognition, Definition and Jurisdiction* (Saskatoon, SK: Purich, 2002).

Chartrand, Paul, and Albert Peeling. "Sovereignty, Liberty, and the Legal Order of the Freemen (Otipahemsu'uk): Towards a Constitutional Theory of Metis Self-Government" (2004) 67 Saskatchewan Law Review 339.

Christie, Gordon. "A Colonial Reading of Recent Jurisprudence: *Sparrow, Delgamuukw* and *Haida Nation*" (2005) 23 Windsor Yearbook of Access to Justice 18.

–. "*Delgamuukw* and the Protection of Aboriginal Land Interests" (2001) 32 Ottawa Law Review 85.

–. "Judicial Justification of Recent Development in Aboriginal Law" (2002) 17 Canadian Journal of Law and Society 41.

–. "Justifying Principles of Treaty Interpretation" (2000) 26 Queen's Law Journal 143.

–. "Law, Theory and Aboriginal Peoples" (2003) 2 Indigenous Law Journal 67.

Chute, Janet E. *The Legacy of Shingwaukonse: A Century of Native Leadership* (Toronto: University of Toronto Press, 1998).

Ciaccia, John. *The Oka Crisis: A Mirror of the Soul* (Dorval, QC: Maren Publications, 2000).

Clark, Bruce. *Native Liberty, Crown Sovereignty: The Existing Aboriginal Right of Self-Government in Canada* (Montreal and Kingston: McGill-Queen's University Press, 1990).

Clement, W.H.P. *The Law of the Canadian Constitution*, 3rd edition (Toronto: Carswell, 1916).

Clemont, Eric. "La Trilogie *Van Der Peet, Gladstone, Smokehouse* et la Droit Autochone" (1997) 28 Revue générale de droit 89.

Clinton, Robert N. "The Rights of Indigenous Peoples as Collective Group Rights" (1990) 32 Arizona Law Review 739.

Clode, Walter. *The Law and Practice of Petition of Right* (London: William Clowes and Sons, 1887).

Coates, Ken S. *Best Left as Indians: Native-White Relations in the Yukon Territory, 1840-1973* (Montreal and Kingston: McGill-Queen's University Press, 1991).

–, ed. *Aboriginal Land Claims in Canada: A Regional Perspective* (Toronto: Copp Clark Pitman, 1992).

Cohen, Felix S. *Handbook of Federal Indian Law*, (Albuquerque, NM: University of New Mexico Press, 1945) and reprint (Washington, DC: US Department of Interior, 1945).

–. "Original Indian Title" (1947) 32 Minnesota Law Review 28.

Cohen, Morris R. "Property and Sovereignty" (1927-28) 13 Cornell Law Quarterly 8.

Cohn, Steven M. "Competing Claims, Uncertain Sovereignties: Resource Conflict and Evolving Tripartite Federalism in Yukon Territory, Canada" (PhD diss., University of California, Berkeley, 2001).

Corntassel, Jeff J., and T.H. Primeau. "'Indigenous Sovereignty' and International Law: Revised Strategies for Pursuing 'Self-Determination'" (1995) 17 Human Rights Quarterly 343.

Coyle, Michael. "Loyalty and Distinctiveness: A New Approach to the Crown's Fiduciary Duty toward Aboriginal People" (2002-3) 40 Alberta Law Review 841.

Craig, Donna. "Recognising Indigenous Rights through Co-Management Regimes: Canadian and Australian Experiences" (2002) 6 New Zealand Journal of Environmental Law 211.

Culhane, Dara. *The Pleasure of the Crown: Anthropology, Law and First Nations* (Burnaby, BC: Talonbooks, 1998).

Cumming, Peter A. "Native Land Rights and Northern Development" (1974) 12 Alberta Law Review 57.

Cumming, Peter A., and Neil H. Mickenberg, eds. *Native Rights in Canada*, 2nd edition (Toronto: Indian-Eskimo Association of Canada and General Publishing, 1972).

Curran, Deborah, and Michael M'Gonigle. "Aboriginal Forestry: Community Management as Opportunity and Imperative" (1999) 37 Osgoode Hall Law Journal 731.

Cutler, A. Claire. *Private Power and Global Authority: Transnational Merchant Law in the Global Political Economy* (Cambridge: Cambridge University Press, 2003).

Dallaire, François. *Oka: La hache de guerre* (Sainte-Foy, QC: Editions la Liberté, 1991).

Daly, Richard. *Our Box Was Full: An Ethnography for the Delgamuukw Plaintiffs* (Vancouver: UBC Press, 2005).

Daniels, Harry W. *The Forgotten People: Métis and Non-Status Indian Land Claims* (Ottawa: Native Council of Canada, 1979).

Daugherty, W. *Maritime Indian Treaties in Historical Perspective* (Ottawa: Treaties and Historical Research Centre, Department of Indian and Northern Affairs Canada, 1983).

Delâge, Denys. *Le pays renversé: Amérindiens et Européens en Amérique du Nord-Est, 1600-1664* (Montreal: Boréal Express, 1985), translated by Jane Brierley as *Bitter Feast: Amerindians and Europeans in Northeastern North America, 1600-64* (Vancouver: UBC Press, 1993).

Delgamuukw: The Supreme Court of Canada Decision on Aboriginal Title, introduction by Stan Persky (Vancouver: Greystone Books, 1998).

de Vattel, Emerich. *The Laws of Nations* (London, 1760), facsimile version, Carnegie Institute, Washington, 1916.

Devlin, Richard, ed. *Introduction to Jurisprudence* (Toronto: Emond Montgomery, 1990).

Dicey, A.V. *Introduction to the Study of the Law of the Constitution*, 10th edition (London: Macmillan, 1959).

Dickason, Olive. *Canada's First Nations: A History of Founding Peoples from Earliest Times*, 2nd edition (Toronto: Oxford University Press, 1997).

Dickason, Olive, with Leslie Green. *The Law of Nations and the New World* (Edmonton: University of Alberta Press, 1993).

Dickson, Timothy. "Self-Government by Side Agreement?" (2004) 49 McGill Law Journal 419.

Dippie, Brian W. *The Vanishing Indian: White Attitudes and U.S. Indian Policy* (Lawrence: University Press of Kansas, 1982).

Donovan, B. "The Evolution and Present Status of Common Law Aboriginal Title in Canada: The Law's Crooked Path and the Hollow Promise of *Delgamuukw*" (2002) 35 UBC Law Review 43.

Doyle-Bedwell, Patricia E. "The Evolution of the Legal Test of Extinguishment: From *Sparrow* to *Gitskan*" (1993) 6 Canadian Journal of Women and the Law 193.

Driver, Harold Edson. *Indians of North America*, 2nd edition (Chicago: University of Chicago Press, 1969).

Drucker, Philip. *The Native Brotherhoods: Modern Inter-tribal Organizations on the Northwest Coast*, Bureau of American Ethnology Bulletin No. 168 (Washington, DC: Smithsonian Institution, 1958).

–. *Cultures of the North Pacific Coast* (New York: Harper and Row, 1965).

Duff, Wilson. "The Fort Victoria Treaties" (1969) 1 BC Studies 3.

–. *The Indian History of British Columbia*. Vol. 1: *The Impact of the White Man* (Victoria: British Columbia Provincial Museum, 1965).

–, ed. *Histories, Territories and Laws of the Kitwancool* (Victoria: British Columbia Provincial Museum, 1959).

Dufraimont, L. "Continuity and Modification of Aboriginal Rights in the Nisga'a Treaty" (2002) 35 UBC Law Review 455.

Durie, E. "Constitutionalising Maori." In G. Huscroft and P. Rishworth, eds., *Litigating Rights: Perspectives from Domestic and International Law* (Oxford: Hart, 2002).

Durie, M. *Te Mana, Te Kawanatanga: The Politics of Maori Self-Determination* (Auckland: Oxford University Press, 1998).

"Economic Development and Indian Land Rights in Modern Alaska: The 1947 Tongass Timber Act" (1990) Western Historical Quarterly 21.

Elkins, David J. *Beyond Sovereignty: Territory and Political Economy in the Twenty-First Century* (Toronto: University of Toronto Press, 1995).

Elliot, D.W., ed. *Law and Aboriginal Peoples of Canada*, 3rd edition (North York, ON: Captus Press, 1997).

Elliott, Sr., Dave, and Janet Poth. *Saltwater People*, 2nd edition (Saanichton, BC: School District No. 63, 1990).

Engelstad, D., and J. Bird, eds. *Nation to Nation: Aboriginal Sovereignty and the Future of Canada* (Concord, ON: Anansi Press, 1992).

Enright, Michael. *Whose Country Is It? Law, Politics and Indian Rights* (Ottawa: Bowdens Media Monitoring, 1999).

Evans, Julie et al. *Equal Subjects, Unequal Rights: Indigenous Peoples in British Settler Colonies, 1830-1910* (New York: Manchester University Press, 2003).

Fisher, Robin. *Contact and Conflict: Indian-European Relations in British Columbia, 1774-1890*, 2nd edition (Vancouver: UBC Press, 1992).

Flanagan, Thomas. *Métis Lands in Manitoba* (Calgary: University of Calgary Press, 1991).

Fleras, A., and J.E. Elliot. *The Nations Within: Aboriginal-State Relations in Canada, the United States and New Zealand* (Toronto: Oxford University Press, 1992).

Ford, Harold A.J. *Unincorporated Non-Profit Associations: Their Property and Their Liability* (Oxford: Clarendon Press, 1959).

Foster, Hamar. "Aboriginal Title and the Provincial Obligation to Respect It: Is *Delgamuukw v. British Columbia* 'Invented Law'?" (1998) 56 The Advocate 221.

–. "Canadian Indians, Time and the Law" (1994) 7 Western Legal History 69.

–. "Honouring the Queen's Flag: A Legal and Historical Perspective on the Nisga'a Treaty" (1998-99) 120 BC Studies 9.

–. "Indigenous Peoples and the Law: The Colonial Legacy in Australia, Canada, New Zealand and the United States." In D. Johnston and G. Ferguson, eds., *Asia Pacific Legal Development* (Vancouver: UBC Press 1998).

–. "It Goes without Saying: Precedent and the Doctrine of Extinguishment by Implication in *Delgamuukw v. The Queen.*" In Frank Cassidy, ed., *Aboriginal Title in British Columbia: Delgamuukw v. The Queen* (Montreal: Institute for Research and Public Policy, 1992).

–. "Letting Go the Bone: The Idea of Indian Title in British Columbia, 1849-1927." In Hamar Foster and John McLaren, eds., *Essays in the History of Canadian Law*. Vol. 6: *British Columbia and the Yukon* (Toronto: Osgoode Society, 1995).

–. "A Romance of the Lost: The Role of Tom MacInnes in the History of the British Columbia Indian Land Question." In G. Blaine Baker and Jim Phillips, eds., *Essays in the History of Canadian Law*. Vol. 8: *In Honour of RCB Risk* (Toronto: Osgoode Society 1999).

–. "The Saanichton Bay Marina Case: Imperial Law, Colonial History, and Competing Theories of Aboriginal Title" (1989) 23 UBC Law Review 629.

Foster, Hamar, and Alan Grove. "Looking behind the Masks: A Land Claims Discussion Paper for Researchers, Lawyers and Their Employers" (1993) 27 UBC Law Review 213.

–. "'Trespassers on the Soil': *United States v. Tom* and a New Perspective on the Short History of Treaty Making in Nineteenth-Century British Columbia" (2003) 138-39 BC Studies 51.

Foster, Hamar, and John McLaren, eds. *Essays in the History of Canadian Law*, Volume 6: *British Columbia and the Yukon* (Toronto: Osgoode Society, 1995).

Frame, A. *Salmond: Southern Jurist* (Wellington: Victoria University Press, 1995).

–. *Grey and Iwikau: A Journey into Custom* (Wellington: Victoria University Press, 2002).

Fumoleau, René. *As Long As This Land Shall Last: A History of Treaty 8 and Treaty 11, 1870-1939* (Toronto: McClelland and Stewart, 1973).

Galois, Robert. "The Indian Rights Association, Native Protest Activity and the 'Land Question' in British Columbia, 1903-1916" (1992) 8(2) Native Studies Review 1.

–. "The History of the Upper Skeena Region, 1850 to 1927" (1993-94) 9 Native Studies Review 113.

Getty, Ian A.L., and Antoine S. Lussier, eds. *As Long As the Sun Shines and the Water Flows* (Vancouver: UBC Press, 1983).

Getty, Ian, and Robert J. Surtees. "Indian Land Cessions in Ontario, 1763-1862: The Evolution of a System" (PhD diss., Carleton University, 1983).

Gibney, M., and S. Frankowski, eds. *Judicial Protection of Human Rights: Myth or Reality?* (Westport, CT: Praeger, 1999).

Gibson, James R. *Otter Skins, Boston Ships and China Goods: The Maritime Fur Trade of the Northwest Coast, 1785-1841* (Montreal and Kingston: McGill-Queen's University Press, 1992).

Gilbert, Larry. *Entitlement to Indian Status and Membership Codes in Canada* (Scarborough, ON: Carswell, 1996).

Gillese, Eileen E. *Property Law: Cases, Text and Materials*, 2nd edition (Toronto: Emond Montgomery, 1990).

Gosnell, Joseph. "Speech to the British Columbia Legislature, December 2, 1998" (1998-99) 120 BC Studies 5.

Grammond, Sébastien. *Les Traités entre l'Etat Canadien et les Peuples Autochtones* (Cowansville, QC: Editions Yvon Blais, 1994).

Green, R.G. *Justice in Aboriginal Communities: Sentencing Alternatives* (Saskatoon, SK: Purich, 1998).

Groves, Robert. *Re-fashioning the Dialogue: Urban Aboriginal Governance in Canada* (Ottawa: National Association of Friendship Centres, 1999).

Haig-Brown, Celia, and David A. Nock, eds. *With Good Intentions: Euro-Canadian and Aboriginal Relations in Colonial Canada* (Vancouver: UBC Press, 2006).

Haig-Brown, Mary. "Arthur Eugene O'Meara: Servant, Advocate, Seeker of Justice." In Celia Haig-Brown and David A. Nock, eds., *With Good Intentions: Euro-Canadian and Aboriginal Relations in Colonial Canada* (Vancouver: UBC Press, 2006).

Harris, A. *Hikoi: Forty Years of Maori Protest* (Wellington: Huia, 2004).

Harris, Cole. *Making Native Space: Colonialism, Resistance, and Reserves in British Columbia* (Vancouver: UBC Press, 2002).

Harris, Douglas C. *Fish, Law, and Colonialism: The Legal Capture of Salmon in British Columbia* (Toronto: University of Toronto Press, 2001).

Harris, Richard C., and Jean Barman, eds. *Native Peoples and Colonialism* (Vancouver: UBC Press, 1997).

Haughey, E.J. "Maori Claims to Lakes, River Beds and the Foreshore" (1966) 2 New Zealand Universities Law Review 29.

Havard, Gilles. *Empire et métissages: Indiens et Français dans le Pays d'en Haut, 1660-1715* (Sillery, QC: Septentrion, 2003).

–. *La Grande Paix de Montréal de 1701: Les voies de la diplomatie franco-amérindienne* (Montreal: Recherches amérindiennes au Québec, 1992), translated by Phyllis Aronoff and Howard Scott as *The Great Peace of Montreal of 1701: French-Native Diplomacy in the Seventeenth Century* (Montreal and Kingston: McGill-Queen's University Press, 2001).

Havemann, Paul, ed. *Indigenous Peoples' Rights in Australia, Canada, and New Zealand* (Melbourne: Oxford University Press, 1999).

–, ed. *New Frontiers? First Nations' Rights in the Settler Dominions: Australia, Canada and New Zealand/Aotearoa 1975-1995* (Auckland: Oxford University Press, 1999).

Hawkes, David C. *Aboriginal Peoples and Constitutional Reform: What Have We Learned?* (Kingston: Institute of Intergovernmental Relations, 1989).

–. *Negotiating Aboriginal Self-Government: Developments Surrounding the 1985 First Ministers' Conference* (Kingston: Institute of Intergovernmental Relations, 1985).

–, ed. *Aboriginal Peoples and Government Responsibility: Exploring Federal and Provincial Roles* (Ottawa: Carleton University Press, 1989).

Haycox, Stephen. *Alaska: An American Colony* (Seattle: University of Washington Press, 2002).

Henderson, James (Sákéj) Youngblood. "Ayukpachi: Empowering Aboriginal Thought." In Marie Battise, ed., *Reclaiming Indigenous Voice and Vision* (Vancouver: UBC Press, 2000).

–. "Empowering Treaty Federalism" (1994) 58 Saskatchewan L. Review 241.

–. "Interpreting *Sui Generis* Treaties" (1997) 36 Alberta Law Review 46.

–. "Postcolonial Indigenous Legal Consciousness" (2002) 1 Indigenous Law Journal 1.

Henderson, James (Sákéj) Youngblood, Marjorie L. Benson, and Isobel M. Findlay. *Aboriginal Tenure in the Constitution of Canada* (Toronto: Carswell, 2000).

Hendrickson, James E. *The Aboriginal Land Policy of Governor James Douglas, 1849-1864* (Burnaby, BC: Simon Fraser University, 1988).

Hesketh, Bob, and Chris Hackett, eds. *Canada: Confederation to Present* (Edmonton: Chinook Multimedia, 2001), http://www.chinookmultimedia.com.

Heuston, R.F.V. *Lives of the Lord Chancellors, 1885-1940* (Oxford: Clarendon Press, 1964).

Hodgins, Bruce W., and Jamie Benidickson. *The Temagami Experience: Recreation, Resources and Aboriginal Rights in the Northern Ontario Wilderness* (Toronto: University of Toronto Press, 1989).

Hodgins, Bruce, Ute Lischke, and David McNab. *Blockades and Resistance: Studies in Actions of Peace and the Temagami Blockades of 1988-89* (Waterloo, ON: Wilfrid Laurier University Press, 2002).

Hogg, Peter W. *Constitutional Law of Canada*, 3rd edition (Scarborough, ON: Carswell, 1992).

–. *Constitutional Law of Canada: 2005 Student Edition* (Scarborough, ON: Thomson Carswell 2005).

Hogg, Peter W., and Patrick J. Monahan. *Liability of the Crown*, 3rd edition (Toronto: Carswell, 2000).

Hohepa, P., and D.V. Williams. *The Taking into Account of Te Ao Maori in Relation to the Reform of the Law of Succession* (Wellington: New Zealand Law Commission, 1996).

Hohfeld, Wesley Newcomb. *Fundamental Legal Conceptions*, edited by Walter Wheeler Cook (New Haven, CT: Yale University Press, 1919).

Home, Henry. *Historical Law Tracts*, 2nd edition (Edinburgh: A. Kincaid, King's Printer, 1761).

Hudson, Douglas R. "The Okanagan Indians of British Columbia." In Jean Webber and the En'owkin Centre, eds., *Okanagan Sources* (Penticton: Theytus Books, 1990).

Hughes, C. "The Fiduciary Obligations of the Crown to Aborigines: Lessons from the United States and Canada" (1993) 16(1) University of New South Wales Law Journal 71.

Hurley, Mary C. *The Crown's Fiduciary Relationship with Aboriginal Peoples* (Ottawa: Parliamentary Research Branch, 2000).

Huscroft, G., and P. Rishworth, eds. *Litigating Rights: Perspectives from Domestic and International Law* (Oxford: Hart, 2002).

Hutchins, Peter W., and Anjali Choksi, "From *Calder* to *Mitchell*: Should the Courts Control Cultural Borders?" (2002) 16 Supreme Court Law Review (2d) 241.

Huyer, Timothy. "Honour of the Crown: The New Approach to Crown-Aboriginal Reconciliation" (2006) 21 Windsor Review of Legal and Social Issues 34.

Imai, Shin. *Aboriginal Law Handbook* (Scarborough, ON: Carswell, 1993).

–. *The 1997 Annotated Indian Act* (Toronto: Carswell Thomson, 1996).

Imai, Shin, Katharine Logan, and Gary Stein. *Aboriginal Law Handbook* (Scarborough, ON: Carswell Thomson, 1993).

Indian-Eskimo Association of Canada. *Native Rights in Canada* (Toronto: n.p, 1970).

Indigenous Research Institute, *Te Takutai Moana: Economics, Politics and Colonisation*, volume 5, 2nd edition (Auckland: Indigenous Research Institute, 2003).

Isaac, Thomas F. *Aboriginal Law: Cases, Materials, and Commentary* (Saskatoon: Purich, 1995).

Isaac, Thomas, and A. Knox. "The Crown's Duty to Consult Aboriginal People" (2003–4) 41 Alberta Law Review 49.

Ivison, Duncan, Paul Patton, and Will Sanders, eds. *Political Theory and the Rights of Indigenous Peoples* (Cambridge: Cambridge University Press, 2000).

Jenness, Diamond. *The Indians of Canada*, 7th edition (Toronto: University of Toronto Press, 1977).

Joffe, P., and M.E. Turpel, *Extinguishment of the Rights of Aboriginal People: Problems and Alternatives*, 3 volumes, June 1995, on CD-ROM: *For Seven Generations: An Information*

Legacy of the Royal Commission on Aboriginal Peoples (Ottawa: Royal Commission on Aboriginal Peoples, 1997).

Johnson, Ralph W. "Fragile Gains: Two Centuries of Canadian and United States Policy toward Indians" (1991) 66 Washington Law Review 643.

Johnston, Basil. *Ojibway Heritage* (Toronto: McClelland and Stewart, 1976).

Johnston, Darlene M. "Native Rights as Collective Rights: A Question of Group Self-Preservation" (1989) 2 Canadian Journal of Law and Jurisprudence 19.

–. "The Quest of the Six Nations Confederacy for Self-Determination" (1986) 44 University of Toronto Faculty Law Review 1.

–. *The Taking of Indian Lands in Canada: Consent or Coercion?* (Saskatoon: Native Law Centre, University of Saskatchewan, 1989).

Johnston, D., and G. Ferguson, eds. *Asia Pacific Legal Development* (Vancouver: UBC Press, 1998).

Kades, Eric. "History and Interpretation of the Great Case of *Johnson v. M'Intosh*" (2001) 19 Law and History Review 67.

Kanakos, Jeannie L. "The Negotiations to Relocate the Songhees Indians, 1843-1911" (MA thesis, Simon Fraser University, 1974).

Kawharu, I.H., ed. *Waitangi* (Auckland: Oxford University Press, 1989).

Kennedy, Dawnis. "Reconciliation without Respect? Section 35 and Indigenous Legal Orders" (paper presented to "Law's Empire: the Annual Conference of the Canadian Law and Society Association," Harrison Hot Springs, 25-29 June 2005).

Keon-Cohen, Bryan, ed. *Native Title in the New Millennium* (Canberra: Aboriginal Studies Press, 2001).

King, M. *Penguin History of New Zealand* (Wellington: Penguin, 2003).

Klippenstein, Norman. "The Haida Struggle for Autonomy on the Haida Gwaii, 1966-1990" (PhD diss., University of Manitoba, 1991; reproduced Ann Arbor, MI: UMI Dissertation Services, 1995).

Knafla, Louis A., ed. *Law and Justice in a New Land: Essays in Western Canadian Legal History* (Toronto: Carswell, 1986).

Knight, Rolf. *Indians at Work: An Informal History of Native Labour in British Columbia 1858-1930*, 2nd edition (Vancouver: New Star Books, 1996).

La Forest, Gérard V. *Natural Resources and Public Property under the Canadian Constitution* (Toronto: University of Toronto Press, 1969).

Ladner, Kiera L. "Governing within an Ecological Context: Creating an AlterNative Understanding of Blackfoot Governance" (2003) 70 Studies in Political Economy 125.

–. "Treaty Federalism: An Indigenous Vision of Canadian Federalisms." In F. Rocher and M. Smith, eds., *New Trends in Canadian Federalism*, 2nd edition (Peterborough, ON: Broadview, 2003).

Ladner, Kiera, and Michael Orsini. "The Persistence of Paradigm Paralysis: The *First Nations Governance Act* as the Continuation of Colonial Policy." In Michael Murphy, ed., *Canada: The State of the Federation: Reconfiguring Aboriginal-State Relations* (Montreal and Kingston: Institute of Intergovernmental Relations, 2003).

Lamarche, Jacques. *L'été des Mohawks: Bilan des 78 jours* (Montreal: Stanké, 1990).

Lambert, Douglas. "*Van Der Peet* and *Delgamuukw*: Ten Unresolved Issues" (1998) 32 UBC Law Review 249.

Langton, Marcia, and Lisa Palmer. "Modern Agreement Making and Indigenous People in Australia: Issues and Trends" (2003) 8(1) Australian Indigenous Law Reporter 1.

Langton, Marcia, Maureen Tehan, Lisa Palmer, and Kathryn Shain, eds. *Honour among Nations? Treaties and Agreements with Indigenous People* (Carlton: Melbourne University Press, 2004).

LaRocque, Emma D. "Violence in Aboriginal Communities." In Royal Commission on Aboriginal Peoples, ed., *The Path to Healing: Report of the Round Table on Aboriginal Health and Social Issues* (Ottawa: Minister of Supply and Services, 1993).

LaViolette, F.E. *The Struggle for Survival: Indian Cultures and the Protestant Ethic in British Columbia* (Toronto: University of Toronto Press, 1973).

Leonard, Frank. *A Thousand Blunders: The Grand Trunk Pacific Railway and Northern British Columbia* (Vancouver: UBC Press, 1996).

Lippert, Owen, ed. *Beyond the Nass Valley: National Implications of the Supreme Court's Delgamuukw Decision* (Vancouver: Fraser Institute, 2000).

Little Bear, Leroy. "Dispute Settlement among the Naidanac." In Richard Devlin, ed., *Introduction to Jurisprudence* (Toronto: Emond Montgomery, 1990).

Llewellyn, Karl, and E. Adamson Hoebel. *The Cheyenne Way: Conflict and Case Law in Primitive Jurisprudence* (Norman: University of Oklahoma Press, 1941).

Lloyd, Dennis. *The Law Relating to Unincorporated Associations* (London: Sweet and Maxwell, 1938).

Locke, John. *Two Treatises of Government*, 4th edition (London, 1713).

McFarlane, Peter. *Brotherhood to Nationhood: George Manuel and the Making of the Modern Indian Movement* (Toronto: Between the Lines, 1993).

McFeat, Tom. *Indians of the North Pacific Coast* (Ottawa: Carleton University Press, 1987).

MacGregor, Roy. *Chief: The Fearless Vision of Billy Diamond* (Markham, ON: Viking, 1989).

McHugh, P.G. *Aboriginal Societies and the Common Law: A History of Sovereignty, Status and Self-determination* (Oxford: Oxford University Press, 2004).

–. "Aboriginal Title in New Zealand Courts" (1984) 2 Canterbury Law Review 235.

–. "The Legal Status of Maori Fishing Rights in Tidal Waters" (1984) 14 Victoria University of Wellington Law Review 247.

–. "Maori Fishing Rights and the North American Indian" (1985) 6 Otago Law Review 62.

–. *The Maori Magna Carta: New Zealand Law and the Treaty of Waitangi* (Auckland: Oxford University Press, 1991).

–. "Tales of Constitutional Origin and Crown Sovereignty in New Zealand," (2002) 52 University of Toronto Law Journal 69.

McIntyre, G. "Fiduciary Obligations of Governments towards Indigenous Minorities." In Bryan Keon-Cohen, ed., *Native Title in the New Millennium* (Canberra: Aboriginal Studies Press, 2001).

McIvor, Sharon. "The *Indian Act* as Patriarchal Control Of Women" (1994) 1 Aboriginal Women's Law Journal 41.

McKay, Bert. *"Ayuukhl Nisga'a."* In A. Rose, ed., *Nisga'a: People of the Nass River* (Vancouver: Douglas and McIntyre, 1993).

McKee, Christopher. *Treaty Talks in British Columbia: Negotiating a Mutually Beneficial Future*, 2nd edition (Vancouver: UBC Press, 2000).

Mackie, Richard. *Trading beyond the Mountains: The British Fur Trade on the Pacific, 1793-1843* (Vancouver: UBC Press, 1997).

Macklem, Patrick. "Distributing Sovereignty: Indian Nations and Equality of Peoples" (1993) 45 Stanford Law Review 1311.

–. "First Nations Self-Government and the Borders of the Canadian Legal Imagination" (1990–91) 36 McGill Law Journal 382.

–. *Indigenous Difference and the Constitution of Canada* (Toronto: University of Toronto Press, 2001).

–. "What's Law Got to Do with It? The Protection of Aboriginal Title in Canada" (1997) 35 Osgoode Hall Law Journal 125.

Macklem, P., and R. Townshend. "Resorting to Court: Can the Judiciary Deliver Justice for First Nations?" In D. Engelstad and J. Bird, eds., *Nation to Nation: Aboriginal Sovereignty and the Future of Canada* (Concord: Anansi Press, 1992).

MacLaine, C., M. Baxendale, and R. Galbraith. *This Land Is Our Land: The Mohawk Revolt at Oka* (Montreal: Optimum, 1990).

McLaren, John, Hamar Foster and Chet Orloff, eds. *Law for the Elephant, Law for the Beaver: Essays in the Legal History of the North American West* (Regina, SK: Canadian Plains Research Center, 1992).

McNeil, Kent. "Aboriginal Rights in Canada: From Title to Land to Territorial Sovereignty" (1998) 5 Tulsa Journal of Comparative and International Law 253, reprinted in Kent McNeil, ed., *Emerging Justice? Essays on Indigenous Rights in Canada and Australia* (Saskatoon: Native Law Centre, University of Saskatchewan, 2001), 58.

–. "Aboriginal Title and Aboriginal Rights: What's the Connection?" (1997) 36 Alberta Law Review 759.

–. "Aboriginal Title as a Constitutionally Protected Aboriginal Right." In Owen Lippert, ed., *Beyond the Nass Valley: National Implications of the Supreme Court's Delgamuukw Decision* (Vancouver: Fraser Institute, 2000).

–. "Aboriginal Title and the Division of Powers: Rethinking Federal and Provincial Jurisdiction" (1998) 61 Saskatchewan Law Review 431.

–. "Aboriginal Title and Section 88 of the Indian Act" (2001) 34 UBC Law Review 159-194.

–. "Aboriginal Title and the Supreme Court: What's Happening?" (2006) 69 Saskatchewan Law Review 282.

–. *Common Law Aboriginal Title* (Oxford: Clarendon Press, 1989).

–. "The Decolonization of Canada: Moving toward Recognition of Aboriginal Governments" (1994) 7 Western Legal History 113, reprinted in Kent McNeil, ed., *Emerging Justice: Essays on Indigenous Rights in Canada and Australia* (Saskatoon: University of Saskatchewan Native Law Centre, 2001), 161.

–. *Defining Aboriginal Title in the 90's: Has the Supreme Court Finally Got It Right?* (Toronto: York University, Robarts Centre for Canadian Studies, 1998).

–. *Emerging Justice: Essays on Indigenous Rights in Canada and Australia* (Saskatoon: University of Saskatchewan Native Law Centre, 2001).

–. "Envisaging Constitutional Space for Aboriginal Governments" (1993) 19 Queen's Law Journal 95, reprinted in Kent McNeil, ed., *Emerging Justice: Essays on Indigenous Rights in Canada and Australia* (Saskatoon: University of Saskatchewan Native Law Centre, 2001).

–. "Extinguishment of Aboriginal Title in Canada: Treaties, Legislation, and Judicial Discretion" (2001) 33 Ottawa Law Review 301.

–. "Extinguishment of Native Title: The High Court and American Law" (1997) 2 Australian Indigenous Law Reporter 366, reprinted in Kent McNeil, ed., *Emerging Justice: Essays on Indigenous Rights in Canada and Australia* (Saskatoon: University of Saskatchewan Native Law Centre, 2001), 409.

–. "Racial Discrimination and Unilateral Extinguishment of Native Title" (1996) 1 Australian Indigenous Law Reporter 181, reprinted in Kent McNeil, ed., *Emerging Justice: Essays on Indigenous Rights in Canada and Australia* (Saskatoon: University of Saskatchewan Native Law Centre, 2001).

–. "The Post-*Delgamuukw* Nature and Content of Aboriginal Title." In Kent McNeil, *Emerging Justice: Essays on Indigenous Rights in Canada and Australia* (Saskatoon: University of Saskatchewan Native Law Centre, 2001).

–. "Reconciliation and the Supreme Court: The Opposing Views of Chief Justices Lamer and McLachlin" (2003) 2 Indigenous Law Journal 1.

–. "Self-Government and the Inalienability of Aboriginal Title" (2002) 47 McGill Law Journal 473.

–. "The Vulnerability of Indigenous Land Rights in Australia and Canada" (2004) 42 Osgoode Hall Law Journal 271.

McRae, H., G. Nettheim, L. Beacroft, and L. McNamara. *Indigenous Legal Issues: Commentary and Materials*, 3rd edition (Sydney: Lawbook Company, 2003).

McRoberts, K., and P.J. Monahan, eds. *The Charlottetown Accord, the Referendum, and the Future of Canada* (Toronto: University of Toronto Press, 1993).

Madill, Dennis. *British Columbia Indian Treaties in Historical Perspective* (Ottawa: Indian and Northern Affairs Canada, 1981).

Mainville, Robert. *An Overview of Aboriginal and Treaty Rights and Compensation for Their Breach* (Saskatoon, SK: Purich Publishing, 2001).

Mansfield, Emily. "Balance and Harmony: Peacemaking in Coast Salish Tribes of the Pacific Northwest" (1993) 10 Mediation Quarterly 339.

Manuel, George, and Michael Posluns. *The Fourth World: An Indian Reality* (Don Mills: Collier-Macmillan, 1974).

Many Fingers, W., and G. Dacks. "Aboriginal Peoples and the Constitution: Comment" (1981) 19 Alberta Law Review 428.

Marks, Greg. "Avoiding the International Spotlight: Australia, Indigenous Rights and the United Nations Treaty Bodies" (2002) 2(1) Human Rights Law Review 19.

Marshall, Ingebord. *A History and Ethnography of the Beothuk* (Montreal and Kingston: McGill-Queen's University Press, 1996).

May, Edwin Peter. "The Nishga Land Claim, 1873-1973" (MA thesis, Simon Fraser University, 1979).

Mercredi, Ovide, and Mary Ellen Turpel. *In the Rapids: Navigating the Future of First Nations* (Toronto: Penguin Books, 1994).

Metcalfe, Peter M. *An Historical and Organizational Profile: The Central Council of the Tlingit and Haida Indian Tribes of Alaska* (Juneau: Central Council of the Tlingit and Haida Indian Tribes of Alaska, 1981).

Metcs, R., and C. Devlin. "Land Entitlement under Treaty 8" (2004) 41(4) Alberta Law Review 951.

Métis Association of Alberta. *Métis Land Rights in Alberta: A Political History* (Edmonton: Métis Association of Alberta, 1981).

Miller, Bruce G. *The Problem of Justice: Tradition and Law in the Coast Salish World* (Lincoln, NB: University of Nebraska Press, 2001).

Miller, Christina, and Patricia Chuchryk, eds. *Women of the First Nations: Power, Wisdom, Strength* (Winnipeg: University of Manitoba Press, 1996).

Miller, J.R. *Skyscrapers Hide the Heavens: A History of Indian-White Relations in Canada* (Toronto: University of Toronto Press, 1991).

–, ed. *Sweet Promises: A Reader on Indian-White Relations in Canada* (Toronto: University of Toronto Press, 1991).

Mills, Antonia. *Eagle Down Is Our Law: Witsuwit'en Law, Feasts, and Land Claims* (Vancouver: UBC Press, 1994).

Mitchell, Donald Craig. *Sold American: The Story of Alaska Natives and Their Land, 1867-1959* (Hanover: University Press of New England, 1997).

–. *Take My Land, Take My Life: The Story of Congress's Historic Settlement of Alaska Native Land Claims, 1960-71* (Fairbanks: University of Alaska Press, 2001).

Molloy, John S. "The Early Indian Acts: Developmental Strategy and Constitutional Change." In J.R. Miller, ed., *Sweet Promises: A Reader on Indian-White Relations in Canada* (Toronto: University of Toronto Press, 1991).

Molloy, T. *The World Is Our Witness: The Historic Journey of the Nisga'a into Canada* (Calgary: Fifth House, 2000).

Monet, Don, and Skanu'u [Ardythe Wilson]. *Colonialism on Trial: Indigenous Land Rights and the Gitksan-Wet'suwet'en Sovereignty Case* (Philadelphia: New Society Publishers, 1992).

Monture, Patricia. "Ka-Nin-Geh-Heh-Gah-E-Sa-Nonh-Yah-Gah" (1988) 2 Canadian Journal of Women and the Law 159.

Monture-Angus, Patricia A. *Journeying Forward: Dreaming First Nations' Independence* (Halifax: Fernwood, 1999).

Monture-Okanee, Patricia. "Alternative Dispute Resolution: A Bridge to Aboriginal Experience?" In Catherine Morris and Andrew Pirie, eds., *Qualifications for Dispute Resolution: Perspectives on the Debate* (Victoria, BC: University of Victoria Institute for Dispute Resolution, 1994).

–. "The Roles and Responsibilities of Aboriginal Women: Reclaiming Justice" (1992) 56 Saskatchewan Law Review 237.

Moodie, Doug. "Thinking Outside the Twentieth-Century Box: Revisiting *Mitchell* – Some Comments on the Politics of Judicial Law-Making in the Context of Aboriginal Self-Government" (2003-4) 35 Ottawa Law Review 1.

Morantz, Toby. *The White Man's Gonna Getcha: The Colonial Challenge to the Crees in Quebec* (Montreal and Kingston: McGill-Queen's University Press, 2002).

Morley, Alan. *Roar of the Breakers: A Biography of Peter Kelly* (Toronto: Ryerson Press, 1967).

Morris, Alexander. *The Treaties of Canada with the Indians of Manitoba and the North-West Territories* (Toronto: Belfords, Clarke and Company, 1880; reprinted 1979).

Morris, Catherine, ed. *Making Peace and Sharing Power: A National Gathering on Aboriginal Peoples and Dispute Resolution, April 30-May 3, 1996, Victoria, British Columbia* (Victoria, BC: University of Victoria Institute for Dispute Resolution, 1997).

Morris, Catherine, and Andrew Pirie, eds. *Qualifications for Dispute Resolution: Perspectives on the Debate* (Victoria, BC: University of Victoria Institute for Dispute Resolution, 1994).

Morrison, A., and I. Cotler, eds. *Justice for Natives: Searching for Common Ground* (Montreal and Kingston: McGill-Queen's University Press, 1997).

Morrison, James. "The Robinson Treaties of 1850: A Case Study." In *For Seven Generations: An Information Legacy of the Royal Commission on Aboriginal Peoples,* CD-ROM (Ottawa: Canada Communications Group, 1996).

Morse, Bradford W. "Permafrost Rights: Aboriginal Self-Government and the Supreme Court in *R. v. Pamajewon*" (1997) 42 McGill Law Journal 1011.

Murphy, Michael, ed. *Canada: The State of the Federation: Reconfiguring Aboriginal-State Relations* (Montreal and Kingston: Institute of Intergovernmental Relations, 2003).

Nadasdy, Paul. *Hunters and Bureaucrats: Power, Knowledge, and Aboriginal-State Relations in the Southwest Yukon* (Vancouver: UBC Press, 2003).

Nahanee, Teressa. "Dancing with a Gorilla: Aboriginal Women, Justice and the Charter." In Royal Commission on Aboriginal Peoples, ed., *Aboriginal Peoples and the Justice System: Report of the National Round Table on Aboriginal Justice Issues* (Ottawa: Minister of Supply and Services, 1993).

–. "Indian Women, Sex Equality and the Charter." In Caroline Andrew and Sandra Rodgers, eds., *Women and the Canadian State* (Montreal and Kingston: McGill-Queen's University Press, 1997).

Napoleon, Val. "Aboriginal Self-Determination: Individual Self and Collective Selves" (2005) 29(2) Atlantis 31.

–. "*Delgamuukw:* A Legal Straightjacket for Oral Histories?" (2005) 20 Canadian Journal of Law and Society 123.

–. "Who Gets to Say What Happened? Reconciliation Issues for the Gitxsan." In Catherine Bell and David Kahane, eds., *Intercultural Dispute Resolution in Aboriginal Contexts* (Vancouver: UBC Press, 2004).

National Indian Brotherhood. *Constitutional Strategies for Entrenchment of Treaty and Aboriginal Rights: Transcript* (Ottawa: Assembly of First Nations Constitutional Conference, 1980).

Nedelsky, Jennifer. "Reconceiving Rights as Relationship" (1993) 1 Review of Constitutional Studies 1.

Nettheim, Garth. "Constitutional Comparisons: Canadian Dimensions on Australia's Experience with Native Title" (2003) 21(1) Australian Canadian Studies 101.

–. "The Practical Relevance of International Law, CERD and the UN Draft Declaration on the Rights of Indigenous Peoples." In Bryan Keon-Cohen, ed., *Native Title in the New Millennium* (Canberra: Aboriginal Studies Press, 2001).

–. "'Retreat from Injustice': The High Court of Australia and Native Title." In M. Gibney and S. Frankowski, eds., *Judicial Protection of Human Rights: Myth or Reality?* (Westport, CT: Praeger, 1999).

–. "The Search for Certainty and the *Native Title Amendment Act 1998* (Cth.)," (1999) 22 University of New South Wales Law Journal 564.

Nettheim, Garth, Gary D. Meyers, and Donna Craig. *Indigenous Peoples and Governance Structure: A Comparative Analysis of Land and Resource Management Rights* (Canberra: Aboriginal Studies Press, 2002).

Newell, Dianne. *Tangled Webs of History: Indians and the Law in Canada's Pacific Coast Fisheries* (Toronto: University of Toronto Press, 1993).

Oguamanam, Chidi. "Indigenous Peoples and International Law: The Making of a Regime" (2004–5) 30 Queen's Law Journal 353.

Olynyk, John M. "Approaches to Sorting Out Jurisdiction in a Self-Government Context" (1995) 53 University of Toronto Faculty Law Review 235.

Opekokew, Delia. *The First Nations: Indian Government and the Canadian Federation* (Saskatoon: Federation of Saskatchewan Indians, 1980).

Orange, C. *The Treaty of Waitangi* (Wellington: Allen and Unwin/Port Nicholson Press, 1987).

Orkin, Andrew J. "When the Law Breaks Down: Aboriginal Peoples in Canada and Governmental Defiance of the Rule of Law" (2003) 41 Osgoode Hall Law Journal 445.

Pagden, Anthony. *European Encounters with the New World: From Renaissance to Romanticism* (London: Yale University Press, 1993).

Palmer, Robin. *Land and Racial Domination in Rhodesia* (London: Heinemann, 1977).

Parry, Clive, ed. *The Consolidated Treaty Series*. Vol. 100 (Dobbs Ferry: Oceana Publications, 1969).

Pastore, Ralph T. "Archaeology, History and the Beothuks" (1993) Newfoundland Studies 260.

Patterson, E. Palmer II. "Andrew Paull (1892-1959): Finding a Voice for the 'New Indian'" (1976) 6 Western Canadian Journal of Anthropology 63.

–. "Arthur E. O'Meara, Friend of the Indians" (1967) 58 Pacific Northwest Quarterly 90.

–. "A Decade of Change: Origins of the Nisga'a and Tsimshian Land Protests in the 1880's" (1983) 18 Journal of Canadian Studies 40.

Paul, Daniel N. *We Were Not the Savages: A Micmac Perspective on the Collision of European and Aboriginal Civilizations* (Halifax: Nimbus Publishing, 1993).

Paul, Stewart C., and Ronald E. Gaffney. *As Long As the Sun and Moon Shall Endure: A Brief History of the Maritime First Nations Treaties, 1675-1783* (Fredericton: Paul and Gaffney and Associates, 1986).

Pentney, William. "The Rights of the Aboriginal Peoples of Canada and the *Constitution Act, 1982:* Part I: The Interpretive Prism of Section 25" (1988) 22 UBC Law Review 21.

Peterson, Jacqueline, and Jennifer S.H. Brown, eds. *The New Peoples: Being and Becoming Métis in North America* (Winnipeg: University of Manitoba Press, 1985).

Peterson, Nicolas, and Marcia Langton, eds., *Aborigines, Land and Land Rights* (Canberra: Australian Institute of Aboriginal Studies, 1980)

Pinkerton, E., ed. *Co-operative Management of Local Fisheries* (Vancouver: UBC Press, 1989).

Plewes, Cathy. *First Nations, the Church, State and Image: Policy and Ideals Reflected in the Indian Act of 1876* (Ann Arbor, MI: University of Michigan, 1999).

Pommersheim, Frank. *Braid of Feathers: American Indian Law and Contemporary Indian Life* (Berkeley: University of California Press, 1995).

Poole, Ross. "Justice or Appropriation? Indigenous Claims and Liberal Theory" (2001) 101 Radical Philosophy 5.

–. "The Nation-State and Aboriginal Self-Determination." In Michel Seymour, ed., *The Fate of the Nation-State* (Montreal and Kingston: McGill-Queen's University Press, 2004).

Price, R., ed. *The Spirit of the Alberta Indian Treaties*, 3rd edition (Edmonton: University of Alberta Press, 1999).

Provart, John. "Reforming the *Indian Act:* First Nations Governance and Aboriginal Policy in Canada" (2003) 2 Indigenous Law Journal 117.

Prucha, Francis Paul. *Americanizing the American Indians: Writings by the "Friends of the Indian," 1880-1900* (Lincoln: University of Nebraska Press, 1973).

Pue, Wesley, DeLloyd J. Guth, and Christopher John Basil English, eds. *Canada's Legal Inheritances* (Winnipeg: Canadian Legal History Project, 2001).

Purich, Donald J. *Our Land: Native Rights in Canada* (Toronto: James Lorimer and Company, 1986).

Rappaport, Mark. "Bringing Meaning to First Nations Consultation in the British Columbia Salmon Aquaculture Industry" (2005) 14 Dalhousie Journal of Legal Studies 149.

Raunet, Daniel. *Without Surrender, Without Consent: A History of the Nisga'a Land Claims* (Vancouver: Douglas and McIntyre, 1996).

Ray, Arthur J. *I Have Lived Here Since the World Began: An Illustrated History of Canada's Native Peoples* (Toronto: Lester Publishing, 1996).

Ray, Arthur J., Jim Miller, and Frank Tough. *Bounty and Benevolence: A History of Saskatchewan Treaties* (Montreal and Kingston: McGill-Queen's University Press, 2000).

Reiter, Robert Alan. *The Law of Canadian Indian Treaties* (Edmonton: Juris Analytica, 1995).

–. *The Law of First Nations* (Edmonton: Juris Analytica, 1996).

Reynolds, H. *The Law of the Land* (Ringwood, Victoria: Penguin Australia, 1987).

Reynolds, James I. *A Breach of Fiduciary Duty: Fiduciary Obligations and Aboriginal Peoples* (Saskatoon: Purich, 2005).

Richardson, Boyce. *Strangers Devour the Land* (Post Mills, VT: Chelsea Green, 1991).

Roberts-Wray, K. *Commonwealth and Colonial Law* (London: Stevens, 1966).

Robinson, Mike, ed. *In the Spirit of Inistisinni: Exploratory Discussions on the Spirit and Intent of Treaty 7* (Calgary: Arctic Institute of North America, 1998).

Rocher, F., and M. Smith, eds. *New Trends in Canadian Federalism*, 2nd edition (Peterborough, ON: Broadview, 2003).

Romanow, Roy, John Whyte, and Howard Leeson. *Canada ... Notwithstanding: The Making of the Constitution 1976-1982* (Toronto: Carswell/Methuen, 1984).

Rose, Alex. *Spirit Dance at Meziadin: Chief Joseph Gosnell and the Nisga'a Treaty* (Madeira Park, BC: Harbour Publishing, 2000).

Rose, A., ed. *Nisga'a: People of the Nass River* (Vancouver: Douglas and McIntyre, 1993).

Ross, Rupert. *Returning to the Teaching: Exploring Aboriginal Justice* (New York: Penguin, 1996)..

Rotman, Leonard I. "Hunting for Answers in a Strange Kettle of Fish: Unilateralism, Paternalism and Fiduciary Rhetoric in *Badger* and *Van der Peet*" (1997) 8 Constitutional Forum 40.

–. *Parallel Paths: Fiduciary Doctrine and the Crown-Native Relationship in Canada* (Toronto: University of Toronto Press, 1996).

–. "Taking Aim at the Canons of Treaty Interpretation in Canadian Aboriginal Rights Jurisprudence" (1997) 46 University of New Brunswick Law Journal 11.

Royal, T.A. ed. *The Woven Universe: Selected Writings of Rev. Maori Marsden* (Otaki: Te Wananga-a-Raukawa, 2003).

Rudin, Jonathan. "One Step Forward, Two Steps Back: The Political and Institutional Dynamics behind the Supreme Court of Canada's Decisions in *R. v. Sparrow, R. v. Van der Peet* and *Delgamuukw v. British Columbia*" (1998) 13 Journal of Law and Social Policy 67.

Russell, Peter H. *Constitutional Odyssey: Can Canadians Become a Sovereign People?* 3rd edition (Toronto: University of Toronto Press, 2004).

–. "High Courts and the Rights of Aboriginal Peoples: The Limits of Judicial Independence" (1998) 61 Saskatchewan Law Review 247.

Rynard, P. "'Welcome In, But Check Your Rights at the Door': The James Bay and Nisga'a Agreements in Canada" (2000) 33(2) Canadian Journal of Political Science 211.

Salisbury, Richard F. *A Homeland for the Cree: Regional Development in James Bay, 1971-1981* (Montreal and Kingston: McGill-Queen's University Press, 1986).

Salmond, A. *Two Worlds: First Meetings between Maori and Europeans 1642-1772* (Auckland: Viking, 1991).

Salmond, Sir John. *Jurisprudence*, 7th edition (London: Sweet and Maxwell, 1924).

Sanders, Douglas E. "Aboriginal Peoples and the Constitution" (1981) 19 Alberta Law Review 410.

–. "The Indian Lobby." In Keith Banting and Richard Simeon, eds., *And No One Cheered: Federalism, Democracy and the Constitution Act* (Toronto: Methuen, 1983).

–. "Prior Claims: Aboriginal People in the Constitution of Canada." In S.M. Beck and I. Bernier, eds., *Canada and the New Constitution: The Unfinished Agenda*, volume 1 (Montreal: Institute for Research on Public Policy, 1983).

–. "The Renewal of Indian Special Status." In Anne F. Bayefsky and Mary Eberts, eds., *Equality Rights and the Canadian Charter of Rights and Freedoms* (Toronto: Carswell, 1985).

–. "The Rights of the Aboriginal Peoples of Canada" (1983) 61 Canadian Bar Review 314.

–. "An Uncertain Path: The Aboriginal Constitutional Conferences." In Joseph M. Weiler and Robin M. Elliot, eds., *Litigating the Values of a Nation: The Canadian Charter of Rights and Freedoms* (Toronto: Carswell, 1986).

–. "'We Intend to Live Here Forever': A Primer on the Nisga'a Treaty" (2000) 33 UBC Law Review 103.

Sarat, Austin, ed. *Law, Violence and the Possibility of Law* (Princeton: Princeton University Press, 2001).

Schwartz, Bryan. *First Principles, Second Thoughts: Aboriginal Peoples, Constitutional Reform and Canadian Statecraft* (Montreal: Institute for Research on Public Policy, 1986).

Scott, Colin H., ed. *Aboriginal Autonomy and Development in Northern Quebec and Labrador* (Vancouver: UBC Press, 2001).

Seidel, Peter, and Julian Hetyey. "Summary of the Yorta Yorta Nation Aboriginal Corporation/State of Victoria Co-operative Management Agreement" (2004) 6(4) Indigenous Law Bulletin 15.

Seymour, Michel, ed. *The Fate of the Nation-State* (Montreal and Kingston: McGill-Queen's University Press, 2004).

Shankel, George Edgar. "The Development of Indian Policy in British Columbia" (PhD diss., University of Washington, 1945).

Shawana, Perry. "Carrier Medicine Knowledge, Ethics and Legal Processes" (paper presented to "Law's Empire: The Annual Conference of the Canadian Law and Society Association," Harrison Hot Springs, 25-29 June 2005).

Simsarian, J. "The Acquisition of Legal Title to *Terra Nullius*" (1938) 53 Political Science Quarterly 111.

Singer, Joseph. "The Legal Rights Debate in Analytical Jurisprudence from Bentham to Hohfeld" (1982) Wisconsin Law Review 975.

Slattery, Brian. "Aboriginal Sovereignty and Imperial Claims" (1991) 29 Osgoode Hall Law Journal 681.

–. "First Nations and the Constitution: A Question of Trust" (1992) 71 Canadian Bar Review 261.

–. "The Hidden Constitution: Aboriginal Rights in Canada" (1984) 32 American Journal of Comparative Law 361.

–. *The Land Rights of Indigenous Canadian Peoples, As Affected by the Crown's Acquisition of Their Territories* (Saskatoon: Native Law Centre, University of Saskatchewan, 1979).

–. "The Legal Basis of Aboriginal Title." In Frank Cassidy, ed., *Aboriginal Title in British Columbia: Delgamuukw v. The Queen* (Lantzville, BC: Oolichan Books, 1992).

–. "Making Sense of Aboriginal and Treaty Rights" (2000) 79 Canadian Bar Review 196.

–. "The Metamorphosis of Aboriginal Title" (2006) 85 Canadian Bar Review 255.

–. "Understanding Aboriginal Rights" (1987) 66 Canadian Bar Review 727.

Smith, Melvin H. *The Delgamuukw Case: What Does It Mean and What Do We Do Now?* (Vancouver: Fraser Institute, 1998).

–. *Our Home or Native Land? What Governments' Aboriginal Policy Is Doing to Canada* (Victoria: Crown Western, 1995).

Spirit in the Land: Statement of the Gitksan and Wetsuweten Hereditary Chiefs in the Supreme Court of British Columbia, 1987-1990 (Gabriola Island, BC: Reflections, 1992).

Stagg, Jack. *Anglo-Indian Relations in North America to 1763 and an Analysis of the Royal Proclamation of October 7, 1763* (Ottawa: Research Branch, Indian and Northern Affairs Canada, 1981).

Stanner, W.E.H. *White Man Got No Dreaming: Essays 1938-1973* (Canberra: Australian National University Press, 1979).

Sterritt, Neil J., et al. *Tribal Boundaries in the Nass Watershed* (Vancouver: UBC Press, 1998).

Stevens, Robert. *Law and Politics: The House of Lords as a Judicial Body, 1800-1976* (Chapel Hill: University of North Carolina Press, 1978).

Stoljar, S.J. *Groups and Entities: An Enquiry into Corporate Theory* (Canberra: Australian National University Press, 1973).

Strickland, Rennard, ed. *Felix S. Cohen's Handbook of Federal Indian Law* (Charlottesville: Michie Bobbs-Merrill, 1982).

Sturtevant, William C., ed. *Handbook of North American Indians.* Vol. 4: *History of Indian-White Relations* (Washington: Smithsonian Institution, 1988).

Surtees, Robert J. "The Development of an Indian Reserve Policy in Canada" (1969) 61 Ontario History 87.

–. *Treaty Research Report: The Robinson Treaties* (Ottawa: Department of Indian Affairs and Northern Development, 1986).

Suttles, Wayne, and William C. Sturtevant, eds. *Handbook of North American Indians.* Vol. 7: *Northwest Coast* (Washington: Smithsonian Institution, 1990).

Svensson, Frances. "Liberal Democracy and Group Rights: The Legacy of Individualism and Its Impact on American Indian Tribes" (1979) 37 Political Studies 421.

Sweeney, D. "Broken Promises: The Crown's Fiduciary Duty to Aboriginal Peoples" (1995) 3(75) Aboriginal Law Bulletin 4.

Tanner, Adrian. *Bringing Home Animals: Religious Ideology and Mode of Production of the Mistassini Cree Hunters* (New York: St. Martin's Press, 1979).

Taylor, C. "On the Nisga'a Treaty" (1999) 120 BC Studies 37.

Taylor, John Leonard. *Treaty Research Report: Treaty Four (1874)* (Ottawa: Indian Affairs and Northern Development, 1987).

Taylor, John P., and Gary Paget. "Federal/Provincial Responsibility and the Sechelt." In David C. Hawkes, ed., *Aboriginal Peoples and Government Responsibility: Exploring Federal and Provincial Roles* (Ottawa: Carleton University Press, 1989).

Tennant, Paul. *Aboriginal Peoples and Politics: The Indian Land Question in British Columbia, 1849-1989* (Vancouver: UBC Press, 1990).

–. "Aboriginal Rights and the Canadian Legal System: The West Coast Anomaly." In John McLaren, Hamar Foster, and Chet Orloff, eds., *Law for the Elephant, Law for the Beaver: Essays in the Legal History of the North American West* (Regina, SK: Canadian Plains Research Centre, 1992).

Thompson, Andrew R., and Nancy A. Morgan. "Water Issues and Treaty Negotiations: Lessons from the Yukon Experience." In Robert B. Anderson and Robert M. Bone, eds., *Natural Resources and Aboriginal People in Canada* (Concord, ON: Captus, 2003).

Thompson, Ruth, ed. *The Rights of Indigenous People in International Law: Selected Essays on Self-Determination* (Saskatoon: Native Law Centre, University of Saskatchewan, 1987).

Thomson, Duane. "The Response of the Okanagan Indians to European Settlement" (1994) 101 BC Studies 96.

Titley, E. Brian. *A Narrow Vision: Duncan Campbell Scott and the Administration of Indian Affairs in Canada* (Vancouver: UBC Press, 1986).

Treaty 7 Elders and Tribal Council with Walter Hildebrandt, Dorothy First Rider, and Sarah Carter. *The True Spirit and Original Intent of Treaty 7* (Montreal and Kingston: McGill-Queen's University Press, 1996).

Trigger, Bruce. *The Cambridge History of the Native Peoples of the Americas*. Vol. 1: *North America* (New York: Cambridge University Press, 1996).

–. *The Children of Aataentsic: A History of the Huron People to 1660* (Montreal and Kingston: McGill-Queen's University Press, 1976).

–. *The Huron: Farmers of the North,* revised edition (New York: Holt, Rinehart and Winston, 1990).

–. *The Impact of Europeans on Huronia* (Toronto: Copp Clark, 1969).

–. *Natives and Newcomers: Canada's "Heroic Age" Reconsidered* (Montreal and Kingston: McGill-Queen's University Press, 1985).

Trigger, B.G., and W.E. Washburn, eds. *The Cambridge History of the Native Peoples of the Americas*. Vol. 1: *North America*, Part 1 (Cambridge: Cambridge University Press, 1996).

Trigger, Bruce G., and William R. Swagerty. "Entertaining Strangers: North America in the Sixteenth Century." In B.G. Trigger and W.E. Washburn, eds., *The Cambridge History of the Native Peoples of the Americas*. Vol. 1: *North America*, Part 1 (Cambridge: Cambridge University Press, 1996).

Tugwell, Maurice, and John Thompson. *The Legacy of Oka* (Toronto: Mackenzie Institute, 1991).

Tully, James. "Aboriginal Peoples: Negotiating Reconciliation." In J. Biderton and A.-G. Gagnon, eds., *Canadian Politics* (Toronto: Broadview Press, 1999).

–. *Strange Multiplicity: Constitutionalism in an Age of Diversity* (Cambridge: Cambridge University Press, 1995).

Turner, Dale. *This Is Not a Peace Pipe: Towards a Critical Indigenous Philosophy* (Toronto: University of Toronto Press, 2006).

Turpel, Mary Ellen. "Aboriginal Peoples and the Canadian Charter: Interpretive Monopolies, Cultural Difference" (1989-90) 6 Canadian Human Rights Yearbook 3.

–. "Home/Land" (1991) 10 Canadian Journal of Family Law 17.

–. "Indigenous People's Rights of Political Participation and Self-Determination: Recent International Legal Developments and the Continuing Struggle for Recognition" (1992) 25 Cornell International Law Journal 579.

–. "Patriarchy and Paternalism: The Legacy of the Canadian State for First Nations Women" (1993) 6 Canadian Journal of Women and the Law 174.

Upton, Leslie F.S. *Micmacs and Colonists: Indian-White Relations in the Maritimes, 1713-1867* (Vancouver: UBC Press, 1979).

Van Dyke, Vernon. "Collective Entities and Moral Rights: Problems in Liberal-Democratic Thought" (1982) 44 Journal of Politics 21.

Venne, Sharon. "Treaty-Making with the Crown." In J. Bird et al., eds., *Nation to Nation: Aboriginal Sovereignty and the Future of Canada* (Toronto: Irwin, 2002).

–. "Understanding Treaty 6: An Indigenous Perspective." In Michael Asch, ed., *Aboriginal and Treaty Rights in Canada: Essays on Law, Equality and Respect for Difference* (Vancouver: UBC Press, 1997).

Vincent, Sylvie, and Garry Bowers, eds. *Baie James et Nord Québécois: Dix Ans Après* (Montreal: Recherches amérindiennes au Québec, 1988).

von Haast, H.F., ed. *New Zealand Privy Council Cases, 1840-1932* (Wellington: Butterworth, 1938).

Waldram, James B. *As Long As the Rivers Run: Hydroelectric Development and Native Communities in Western Canada* (Winnipeg: University of Manitoba Press, 1988).

Walkem, Ardith, and Halie Bruce, eds. *Box of Treasures or Empty Box? Twenty Years of Section 35* (Penticton: Theytus Books, 2003).

Walters, Mark D. "British Imperial Constitutional Law and Aboriginal Rights: A Comment on *Delgamuukw v. British Columbia*" (1992) 17 Queen's Law Journal 350.

–. "The 'Golden Thread' of Continuity: Aboriginal Customs at Common Law and under the *Constitution Act, 1982*" (1999) 44 McGill Law Journal 711.

Ward, A. *A Show of Justice: Racial "Amalgamation" in Nineteenth-Century New Zealand*, 2nd edition (Auckland: Auckland University Press, 1995).

Weaver, John C. *The Great Land Rush and the Making of the Modern World, 1650-1900* (Montreal and Kingston: McGill-Queen's University Press, 2003).

Weaver, Sally M. "An Assessment of the Federal Self-Government Policy." In A. Morrison and I. Cotler, eds., *Justice for Natives: Searching for Common Ground* (Montreal and Kingston: McGill-Queen's University Press, 1997).

–. *Making Canadian Indian Policy: The Hidden Agenda 1968-1970* (Toronto: University of Toronto Press, 1981).

Webber, Jean, and the En'owkin Centre, eds. *Okanagan Sources* (Penticton: Theytus Books, 1990).

Webber, Jeremy. "Beyond Regret: *Mabo*'s Implications for Australian Constitutionalism." In Duncan Ivison, Paul Patton, and Will Sanders, eds., *Political Theory and the Rights of Indigenous Peoples* (Cambridge: Cambridge University Press, 2000).

–. *Reimagining Canada: Language, Culture, Community and the Canadian Constitution* (Montreal and Kingston: McGill-Queen's University Press, 1994).

–. "Relations of Force and Relations of Justice: The Emergence of Normative Community between Colonists and Aboriginal Peoples" (1995) 33 Osgoode Hall Law Journal 623.

Weiler, Joseph M., and Robin M. Elliot, eds. *Litigating the Values of a Nation: The Canadian Charter of Rights and Freedoms* (Toronto: Carswell, 1986).

White, Richard. *The Middle Ground: Indians, Empires, and Republics in the Great Lakes Region, 1650-1815* (Cambridge, UK: Cambridge University Press, 1991).

Wickwire, Wendy. "'We Shall Drink from the Stream and So Shall You': James A. Teit and Native Resistance in British Columbia, 1908-22" (1998) 79 Canadian Historical Review 199.

Wilkins, Kerry, ed. *Advancing Aboriginal Claims: Visions/Strategies/Directions* (Saskatoon: Purich, 2004).

–. "Conclusion: Judicial Aesthetics and Aboriginal Claims." In Kerry Wilkins, ed., *Advancing Aboriginal Claims: Visions/Strategies/Directions* (Saskatoon: Purich, 2004).

–. "Negative Capacity: Of Provinces and Lands Reserved for the Indians" (2002) 1 Indigenous Law Journal 57.

Wilkinson, C. *American Indians, Time and the Law* (New Haven, CT: Yale University Press, 1987).

Williams, D.V. "The Annexation of New Zealand to New South Wales in 1840: What of the Treaty of Waitangi?" (1985) 2 Australian Journal of Law and Society 41.

–. *Crown Policy Affecting Maori Knowledge Systems and Cultural Practices* (Wellington: Waitangi Tribunal, 2001).

–. *"Queen v. Symonds* Reconsidered" (1989) 19 Victoria University of Wellington Law Review 385.
–. *"Te Kooti tango whenua": The Native Land Court 1864-1909* (Wellington: Huia, 1999).
–. "Te Tiriti o Waitangi: Unique Relationship between Crown and Tangata Whenua?" In I.H. Kawharu, ed., *Waitangi* (Auckland: Oxford University Press, 1989).
Woodward, Jack. *Native Law* (Toronto: Carswell, 1989).
Woolford, Andrew. *Between Justice and Certainty: Treaty Making in British Columbia* (Vancouver: UBC Press, 2005).
York, Geoffrey, and Loreen Pindera. *People of the Pines: The Warriors and the Legacy of Oka* (Boston: Little, Brown, 1991).
Zalewski, Anna. "From *Sparrow* to *Van Der Peet:* The Evolution of a Definition of Aboriginal Rights" (1997) 55 University of Toronto Faculty Law Review 435.
Zlotkin, Norman K. "The 1983 and 1984 Constitutional Conferences: Only the Beginning" (1984) 3 Canadian Native Law Reporter 3.
–, ed. "Documents from the 1987 First Ministers' Conference on Aboriginal Matters" (1987) 3 Canadian Native Law Reporter 1.

Government Reports
Aboriginal Land Rights Commission. *Second Report* (Canberra: Australian Government Publishing Service, 1974).
British Columbia Claims Task Force. *The Report of the British Columbia Claims Task Force* (Vancouver: British Columbia Claims Task Force, 1991).
British Columbia Ministry of Aboriginal Affairs. *The Nisga'a Final Agreement in Brief: Bringing BC Together* (Victoria: British Columbia Ministry of Aboriginal Affairs, 1999).
British Columbia Treaty Commission. *What's the Deal with Treaties? A Lay Person's Guide to Treaty Making in British Columbia* (Vancouver: BC Treaty Commission, 2003).
British Columbia Treaty Commission/Canada Law Commission. *Speaking Truth to Power: A Treaty Forum* (Ottawa: Law Commission of Canada, 2001).
British Parliamentary Papers: Colonies New Zealand. Vol. 5 (Shannon: Irish University Press, 1969).
Canada. *Gathering Strength: Canada's Aboriginal Action Plan* (Ottawa: Minister of Indian Affairs and Northern Development, 1997).
Canada. *Report of the Royal Commission on Aboriginal Peoples* (Ottawa: Canada Communication Group, 1996).
Canada, Department of Indian and Northern Affairs, Treaty Guide to the Williams Treaties: http://www.ainc-inac.gc.ca/pr/trts/hti/guid/twil_e.html.
Canada, Department of Indian Affairs and Northern Development. *In All Fairness* (Ottawa: Department of Indian Affairs and Northern Development, 1981).
Canada, Department of Indian Affairs. *Indian Treaties and Surrenders from 1680 to 1890 in Two Volumes* (Ottawa: Queen's Printer, 1891, Coles reprint 1971).
Canada, Department of Indian Affairs and Northern Development. *Outstanding Business: A Native Claims Policy: Specific Claims* (Ottawa: Minister of Supply and Services Canada, 1982).
Canada, Department of Indian Affairs and Northern Development. *Statement of the Government of Canada on Indian Policy* (Ottawa: Queen's Printer, 1969).
Canada, Minister of Indian Affairs and Northern Development. *Aboriginal Self-Government* (Ottawa: Public Works and Government Services Canada, 1995).
Canada, Minister of Indian Affairs and Northern Development. *Gathering Strength: Canada's Aboriginal Action Plan* (Ottawa: Minister of Indian Affairs and Northern Development, 1997).
Canada, Task Force to Review Comprehensive Claims Policy. *Living Treaties, Lasting Agreements: Report of the Task Force to Review Comprehensive Claims Policy* (Ottawa: Department of Indian Affairs and Northern Development, 1985).
James Bay and Northern Quebec Agreement and Complementary Agreements (Sainte-Foy: Gouvernement du Québec, 1998).
MAWIW District Council and Indian and Northern Affairs Canada. *"We Should Walk in the Tract Mr. Dummer Made": A Written Joint Assessment of Historical Materials ... Relative to*

Dummer's Treaty of 1725 and All Other Related or Relevant Maritime Treaties and Treaty Nego-tiations (Ottawa: Department of Indian and Northern Affairs Canada, 1992).

National Archives of Canada, *Aboriginal Peoples and Archives: A Brief History of Aboriginal and European Relations in Canada* (Ottawa: National Archives of Canada, 1997).

New Zealand, Department of the Prime Minister and Cabinet. *The Foreshore and Seabed of New Zealand: Protecting Public Access and Customary Rights: Government Proposals for Con-sultation* (Wellington: Department of the Prime Minister and Cabinet, 2003).

New Zealand, *Facsimiles of the Declaration of Independence* [1835] *and the Treaty of Waitangi* [1840] (Wellington: Government Printer, 1976).

New Zealand Law Commission, *Maori Custom and Values in New Zealand Law*, Study Paper 9 (Wellington: New Zealand Law Commission, 2001).

Palmer, H.A., and J. Christie, eds. *The Public Acts of New Zealand (Reprint) 1908-1931*. Vol. 6 (Wellington: Government Printer, 1932).

Papers Connected with the Indian Land Question, 1850-1875 (Victoria: Queen's Printer, 1987).

Royal Commission on Aboriginal Peoples. *Aboriginal Peoples and the Justice System: Report of the National Round Table on Aboriginal Justice Issues* (Ottawa: Minister of Supply and Servi-ces, 1993).

Royal Commission on Aboriginal Peoples. *For Seven Generations: An Information Legacy of the Royal Commission on Aboriginal Peoples*, CD-ROM (Ottawa: RCAP, 1997).

Royal Commission on Aboriginal Peoples. *Partners in Confederation: Aboriginal Peoples, Self-Government, and the Constitution* (Ottawa: Minister of Supply and Services Canada, 1993).

Royal Commission on Aboriginal Peoples. *The Path to Healing: Report of the Round Table on Aboriginal Health and Social Issues* (Ottawa: Minister of Supply and Services, 1993).

Royal Commission on Aboriginal Peoples. *Report of the Royal Commission on Aboriginal Peoples* (Ottawa: Minister of Supply and Services Canada, 1996).

Royal Commission on Aboriginal Peoples. *Treaty-Making in the Spirit of Co-Existence: An Alternative to Extinguishment* (Ottawa: Minister of Supply and Services Canada, 1995).

Te Puni Kokiri/Ministry of Maori Development, *He Tirohanga o Kawa ki te Tiriti o Waitangi/ A Guide to the Principles of the Treaty of Waitangi as Expressed by the Courts and the Waitangi Tribunal* (Wellington: Te Puni Kokiri/Ministry of Maori Development, 2001).

Cases

A.G. of British Columbia v. A.G. of Canada, [1914] A.C. 153 (P.C.).

A.G. Ont. v. A.G. Can., [1912] A.C. 571 (J.C.P.C.).

Alexkor Ltd v. Richtersveld Community and Others, C.C.T. 19/03 (S. Afr. S.C.).

Amodu Tijani v. Secretary, Southern Nigeria, [1921] 2 A.C. 399.

Apsassin v. Canada (Department of Indian Affairs and Northern Development) (1993), 100 D.L.R. (4th) 504.

Attorney-General (NSW) v. Brown (1847), 1 Legge 312.

Attorney-General for Canada v. Attorney-General for Ontario, [1898] A.C. 700.

Attorney-General of Ontario v. Attorney General of Canada: Re Indian Claims, [1897] A.C. 199 (J.C.P.C.).

Attorney General for Ontario v. Hamilton Street Railway, [1903] A.C. 524 (J.C.P.C.).

Attorney-General v. Ngati Apa & Others, [2003] 3 N.Z.L.R. 643 (C.A.).

Bolton v. Forest Pest Management Institute (1985), 21 D.L.R. (4th) 242.

Bone v. Sioux Valley Indian Band No. 290 Council, [1996] 3 C.N.L.R. 54.

Breen v. Williams (1996), 186 C.L.R. 71.

Brown v. Board of Education, 347 U.S. 483 (1954).

Bryan v. Itasca County, 426 U.S. 373 (1976).

Calder et al. v. Attorney-General of British Columbia (1969), 8 D.L.R. (3d) 59 (B.C.S.C.).

Calder et al. v. Attorney General of British Columbia (1970), 74 W.W.R. 481, 13 D.L.R. (3d) 64 (B.C.C.A.).

Calder et al. v. Attorney-General of British Columbia (1973), S.C.R. 313, 34 D.L.R. (3d) 145.

Campbell v. British Columbia (Attorney General) (2000), 79 B.C.L.R. (3d) 122, [2000] 4 C.N.L.R. 1, 189 D.L.R. (4th) 333 (B.C.S.C).

Campbell v. Hall (1774), 1 Cowp. 204, 98 E.R. 1045, [1558-1774] All E.R. Rep. 252 (K.B.).

Canadian Pacific Ltd. v. Paul (1983), 2 D.L.R. (4th) 22 (N.B.C.A.).
Canadian Pacific Ltd. v. Paul, [1988] 2 S.C.R. 654.
Casimel v. Insurance Corp. of British Columbia, [1994] 2 C.N.L.R. 22 (B.C.C.A.).
Cherokee Nation v. State of Georgia, 5 Pet. 1, 30 U.S. 1 (1831).
Chief Max "One-Onti" Gros-Louis c. Société de développement de la Baie James, [1974] R.P. 38 (Sup. Ct.).
Commonwealth v. Yarmirr (2001), 208 C.L.R. 1.
Connolly v. Woolrich (1867), 17 R.J.R.Q. 75 (Que. S.C.).
Cooper v. Stuart, [1889] 14 App. Cas. 286.
Corbière v. Canada (Minister of Indian and Northern Affairs), [1999] 2 S.C.R. 203.
Corinthe v. Ecclesiastics of the Seminary of St. Sulpice, [1912] A.C. 872.
Crow v. Blood Indian Band Council, [1997] 3 C.N.L.R. 76.
Davis v. Sitka School Board, 3 Alaska 481 (1908).
Delgamuukw v. British Columbia (1991), 79 D.L.R. (4th) 185 (B.C.S.C.).
Delgamuukw v. British Columbia (1993), 104 D.L.R. (4th) 470 (B.C.C.A.).
Delgamuukw v. British Columbia, [1997] 3 S.C.R. 1010, 153 D.L.R. (4th) 193 (SCC).
Dyson v. Attorney General, [1911] 1 K.B. 410 (CA).
Eastmain Band v. James Bay and Northern Quebec Agreement (Administrator) (1992). 99 D.L.R. (4th) 16.
Fejo v. Northern Territory (1998), 195 C.L.R. 96.
Fletcher v. Peck (1810), 10 U.S. 97.
Francis v. Mohawk Council of Kanesatake, [2003] 3 C.N.L.R. 86.
Gann v. Free Fishers of Whitstable (1865), 11 H.L.C. 192.
Guerin v. The Queen, [1984] 2 S.C.R. 335, 13 D.L.R. (4th) 321 (SCC).
Haida Nation v. British Columbia (Minister of Forests), 2004 SCC 73, [2004] 3 S.C.R. 511, 245 D.L.R. (4th) 33.
Hamlet of Baker Lake v. Minister of Indian Affairs and Northern Development (1979), 107 D.L.R. (3d) 513 (F.C.T.D.).
Hayes v. Northern Territory (1997), F.C.R. 32.
Hohepa Wi Neera v. Bishop of Wellington, [1902] 21 N.Z.L.R. 655 (C.A.).
Hospital Products Ltd. v. United States Surgical Corporation (1984), 156 C.L.R. 41.
Huakina Development Trust v. Waikato Valley Authority, [1987] 2 N.Z.L.R. 188.
Hualapai Indians v. Santa Fe Railroad, 314 U.S. 339 (1941).
In re the Bed of the Wanganui River, [1962] N.Z.L.R. 600 (C.A.).
In re Southern Rhodesia (1919), A.C. 210 (P.C.).
Jensen v. Corporation of Surrey (1989), 47 M.P.L.R. 192 (B.C.S.C.).
Jock v. Canada (Minister of Indian and Northern Affairs), [1992] 1 C.N.L.R. 103.
Johnson and Graham's Lessee v. M'Intosh, 8 Wheaton 543, 21 U.S. 543 (1823).
Koowarta v. Bjelke-Petersen (1982), 153 C.L.R. 168.
Kruger and Manuel v. The Queen, [1978] 1 S.C.R. 104.
Lake Shore & M.S.R. Co. v. Kurtz (1894), 10 Ind. App., 60, 37 N.E. 303.
Mabo v. Queensland (No. 1) (1988), 166 C.L.R. 186.
Mabo v. Queensland (No. 2) (1992), 175 C.L.R. 1 (H.C. Aust.).
Manu Kapua v. Para Haimona, [1913] A.C. 761.
Mason v. Churchill, U.S. District Court for the District of Alaska, First Division, No. 2242-A (1922), Alaska State Archives.
McLeod Lake Indian Band v. Chingee, [1999] 1 C.N.L.R. 106.
Members of the Yorta Yorta Aboriginal Community v. Victoria, [1998] F.C.A. 1606.
Members of the Yorta Yorta Aboriginal Community v. Victoria (2002), 194 A.L.R. 538.
Mikisew Cree First Nation v. Canada (Minister of Canadian Heritage), 2005 SCC 69, [2005] 3 S.C.R. 388.
Milirrpum v. Nabalco Pty Ltd (1971), 17 F.L.R. 141.
Mitchell v. M.N.R., [2001] 1 S.C.R. 911, 199 D.L.R. (4th) 385 (SCC).
New South Wales v. The Commonwealth (1975), 135 C.L.R. 337.
New Zealand Maori Council v. Attorney-General, [1994] 1 N.Z.L.R. 513 (P.C.).
Nireaha Tamaki v. Baker, [1901] A.C. 561.

NZ Maori Council v. Attorney-General, [1987] 1 N.Z.L.R. 641 (C.A.).
NZ Maori Council v. Attorney-General, [1989] 2 N.Z.L.R. 142 (C.A.).
Ontario Mining Company v. Seybold, [1903] A.C. 73 (J.C.P.C.).
Osoyoos Indian Band v. Oliver (Town), [2001] 3 S.C.R. 746.
Paul v. British Columbia (Forest Appeals Commission), [2003] 2 S.C.R. 585.
Pilmer v. Duke, [2001] H.C.A. 31.
Province of Ontario v. Dominion of Canada and Province of Quebec; In re Indian Claims (1895), 25 S.C.R. 434.
The Queen v. Symonds, [1847] N.Z.P.C.C. 387 (SC).
R. v. Adams, [1996] 3 S.C.R. 101 (SCC).
R. v. Badger, [1996] 1 S.C.R. 771 (SCC).
R. v. Bartleman (1984), 55 B.C.L.R. 78, 12 D.L.R. (4th) 73 (B.C.C.A.).
R. v. Bernard, 2005 SCC 43.
R. v. Côté, [1996] 3 S.C.R. 139 (SCC).
R. v. Demers, [2004] 2 S.C.R. 489.
R. v. Gladstone, [1996] 2 S.C.R. 723 (SCC).
R. v. Marshall (No. 1), [1999] 3 S.C.R. 456 (SCC), 177 D.L.R. (4th) 513.
R. v. Marshall (No. 2), [1999] 3 S.C.R. 533 (SCC).
R. v. Marshall; R. v. Bernard, [2005] 2 S.C.R. 220 (SCC).
R. v. Morris, [2004] 2 C.N.L.R. 219 (B.C.C.A.).
R. v. Pamajewon (1994), 21 O.R. (3d) 385 (Ont. C.A.).
R. v. Pamajewon, [1996] 2 S.C.R. 821, 138 D.L.R. (4th) 204 (SCC).
R. v. Powley, 2003 SCC 43, [2003] 2 S.C.R. 207.
R. v. Rahey, [1987] 1 S.C.R. 588.
R. v. Sappier; R. v. Gray, 2006 SCC 54.
R. v. Secretary of State for Foreign and Commonwealth Affairs, ex parte Indian Association of Alberta, [1982] 2 All E.R. 118.
R. v. Sikyea (1964), 43 D.L.R. (2d) 150 (N.W.T. C.A.), aff'd. [1964] S.C.R. 642.
R. v. Sioui, [1990] 1 S.C.R. 1025, 70 D.L.R. (4th) 427 (SCC).
R. v. Sparrow (1986), 36 D.L.R. (4th) 246 (B.C.C.A.).
R. v. Sparrow, [1990] 1 S.C.R. 1075, 46 B.C.L.R. (2d) 1 (SCC), 70 D.L.R. (4th) 385.
R. v. Sundown, [1999] 1 S.C.R. 393.
R. v. Van der Peet, [1996] 2 S.C.R. 507, 137 D.L.R. (4th) 289 (SCC).
R. v. White and Bob (1964), 50 D.L.R. (2d) 613 (B.C.C.A.), aff'd. (1965), 52 D.L.R. (2d) 481 (SCC).
Randwick Corporation v. Rutledge (1959), 102 C.L.R. 54.
Re Cities Service Oil Co. and the City of Kingston (1956), 5 D.L.R. (2d) 126 (Ont. H.C.).
Re Lundon and Whitaker Claims Act 1871 (1872), 2 N.Z.C.A. 41.
Re the Ninety-Mile Beach, [1963] N.Z.L.R. 461 (C.A.).
Re Paulette (1973), 39 D.L.R. (3d) 45.
Re Southern Rhodesia, [1919] A.C. 211 (J.C.P.C.).
Reference Re Canada Assistance Plan (B.C.), [1991] 2 S.C.R. 525.
Reference Re Remuneration of Judges of the Provincial Court of Prince Edward Island, [1997] 3 S.C.R. 3.
Reference Re Secession of Quebec, [1998] 2 S.C.R. 217.
Saanichton Marina Ltd. v. Claxton (1989), 36 B.C.L.R. (2d) 79, 57 D.L.R. (4th) 161 (B.C.C.A).
Salt River First Nation 195 (Council) v. Salt River First Nation, [2003] 3 C.N.L.R. 332.
Santa Clara Pueblo v. Martinez, 436 U.S. 49 (1978).
Simon v. R., [1985] 2 S.C.R. 387, 24 D.L.R. (4th) 390.
Société de développement de la Baie James c. Kanatewat, [1975] C.A. 166.
Sparvier v. Cowessess Indian Band #73, [1994] 1 C.N.L.R. 182.
St. Ann's Island Shooting and Fishing Club Ltd. v. The King, [1950] S.C.R. 211.
St. Catherine's Milling & Lumber Co. v. R. (1887), 13 S.C.R. 577 (SCC).
St. Catherine's Milling & Lumber Co. v. R. (1888), 14 App. Cas. 46 (U.K.P.C.).
State of Alaska v. Udall, 420 F. 2d 938 (Ninth Circuit, 1969).
Tainui Maori Trust Board v. Attorney-General, [1989] 2 N.Z.L.R. 513 (C.A.).

Taku River Tlingit First Nation v. British Columbia (Project Assessment Director), 2004 SCC 74, [2004] 3 S.C.R. 550, 245 D.L.R. (4th) 193.
Tamihana Korokai v. Solicitor-General, [1912] 32 N.Z.L.R. 321 (C.A.).
Te Runanga o Muriwhenua v. Attorney-General, [1990] 2 N.Z.L.R. 641 (C.A.).
Te Runanga o Wharekauri Rekohu v. Attorney-General, [1993] 2 N.Z.L.R. 301.
Te Runanganui o Te Ika Whenua Inc. v. Attorney-General, [1994] 2 N.Z.L.R. 20.
Te Weehi v. Regional Fisheries Officer, [1986] 1 N.Z.L.R. 680.
Tee-Hit-Ton Indians v. U.S. 120 Fed. Supp. 202 (Ct. CL. 1954), 348 U.S. 294 (1955).
Texaco Canada v. Corporation of Vanier, [1981] 1 S.C.R. 254.
Tlingit and Haida Indians of Alaska v. U.S., 177 F. Supp. 452, 147 (Ct. Cls. 1959).
Tlingit and Haida Indians of Alaska et al. v. U.S., 389 Fed. 2nd 778 (Ct. Cls. 1968).
United States v. Wheeler, 435 U.S. 313 (1978).
Waipapakura v. Hempton (1914), 33 N.Z.L.R. 1065.
Waitangi Tribunal, *Kaituna River Claim Report* (Wellington: Waitangi Tribunal, 1984).
Waitangi Tribunal, *Mohaka River Report* (Wellington: Waitangi Tribunal, 1992).
Waitangi Tribunal, *Motunui Waitara Report* (Wellington: Waitangi Tribunal, 1983).
Waitangi Tribunal, *Muriwhenua Fishing Claims Report* (Wellington: Waitangi Tribunal, 1988).
Waitangi Tribunal, *Radio Frequencies Report* (Wellington: Waitangi Tribunal, 1990).
Waitangi Tribunal, *Radio Spectrum Final Report* (Wellington: Waitangi Tribunal, 1999).
Waitangi Tribunal, *Report on the Crown's Foreshore and Seabed Policy* (Wellington: Waitangi Tribunal, 2004).
Waitangi Tribunal, *Te Ika Whenua – Energy Assets Report* (Wellington: Waitangi Tribunal, 1993).
Waitangi Tribunal, *Whanganui River Report* (Wellington: Waitangi Tribunal, 1999).
Wallis v. Solicitor-General, [1903] A.C. 173.
Western Australia v. Commonwealth (1995), 183 C.L.R. 373.
Western Australia v. Ward (2002), 213 C.L.R. 1.
Wewaykum Indian Band v. Canada, [2002] 4 S.C.R. 245, 220 D.L.R. (4th) 1.
Wi Parata v. Bishop of Wellington (1877), 3 N.Z. Jur. 72 (N.S.S.C.).
Wik Peoples v. Queensland (1996), 187 C.L.R. 1.
Williams v. Attorney-General (NSW) (1913), 16 C.L.R. 404.
Wilson v. Anderson (2002), 213 C.L.R. 401.
Worcester v. State of Georgia, 6 Pet. 515, 31 U.S. 515 (1832).
Yanner v. Eaton (1999), 201 C.L.R. 351.

Contributors

Michael Asch is Professor Emeritus in Anthropology at the University of Alberta and Professor (limited term) in Anthropology at the University of Victoria. He has served as Director of the Dene/Métis Mapping Project and as Senior Research Associate for Anthropology with the Royal Commission on Aboriginal Peoples. His publications include *Home and Native Land: Aboriginal Rights and the Canadian Constitution* (1984) and *Aboriginal and Treaty Rights in Canada: Essays on Law, Equality and Respect for Difference* (1997).

John Borrows is the Law Foundation Chair of Aboriginal Justice and Governance in the Faculty of Law at the University of Victoria, a Fellow of the Trudeau Foundation, and a member of the Chippewas of the Nawash from the Anishinabek First Nation. He writes and teaches in the area of indigenous laws, indigenous rights, and comparative constitutionalism.

Hamar Foster is a Professor of Law at the University of Victoria who has been teaching and writing about law and legal history for over thirty years. A primary focus has been how law has affected relations between Aboriginal and non-Aboriginal peoples, notably with respect to what used to be known as the BC Indian land question.

Christina Godlewska is a graduate of the Faculty of Law at the University of Victoria and is completing her articles at the BC Civil Liberties Association. Her research interests include the law of torture, democratic accountability, and the policing of marginalized communities.

Stephanie Hanna is a graduate of the Faculty of Law at the University of Victoria and is currently pursuing graduate studies at the University of Western Ontario.

Stephen Haycox is an American cultural historian. His graduate degrees are from the University of Oregon. He has published widely on Alaska Native history. His two most recent books are *Frigid Embrace: Politics, Economics and Environment in*

Alaska (2002) and *Alaska: An American Colony* (2002). He is the recipient of an Alaska Governor's Humanities Award and the University of Alaska Edith R. Bullock Prize for Excellence and was named Alaskan Historian of the Year in 2003. He teaches Alaska history, history of the American West, and American environmental history.

Gérard La Forest, a former judge of the Supreme Court of Canada, is currently Counsel with the law firm of Stewart McKelvey and Distinguished Legal Scholar in Residence in the Faculty of Law at the University of New Brunswick. He has been involved in Aboriginal issues from the early 1960s, first as an academic and then as a senior public servant, consultant, and judge.

Kent McNeil is a professor at Osgoode Hall Law School in Toronto, where he has taught since 1987. He is the author of numerous works on the rights of indigenous peoples, including two books: *Common Law Aboriginal Title* (1989) and *Emerging Justice? Essays on Indigenous Rights in Canada and Australia* (2001). His work has been relied upon in leading court decisions on indigenous rights in Australia, Canada, and South Africa.

Garth Nettheim is Professor Emeritus in the Faculty of Law at the University of New South Wales. He has written extensively on human rights and indigenous legal issues.

Heather Raven is a member of the Brokenhead Ojibway First Nation and is a senior lecturer in the Faculty of Law at the University of Victoria, where she teaches courses in employment law, contracts, secured transactions, legal mooting, and indigenous law.

Brian Slattery is Professor of Law at Osgoode Hall Law School in Toronto, where he writes and teaches in the areas of indigenous rights, constitutional law, and legal theory. He is a fellow of the Royal Society of Canada.

Jeremy Webber is Canada Research Chair in Law and Society in the Faculty of Law at the University of Victoria, Director of the Consortium on Democratic Constitutionalism, and Visiting Professor of Law at the University of New South Wales. He has written extensively on constitutional theory and indigenous rights.

David V. Williams is a Professor of Law at the University of Auckland in New Zealand and currently is the Deputy Dean of Law. The main areas of his research and writing concern colonial legal history, legal pluralism, and the rights of Maori – the indigenous peoples of Aotearoa New Zealand.

Index